PRACTICAL ADVOCACY IN THE SHERIFF COURT

AUSTRALIA
Law Book Co.
Sydney

CANADA and USA
Carswell
Toronto

HONG KONG
Sweet & Maxwell Asia

NEW ZEALAND
Brookers
Wellington

SINGAPORE and MALAYSIA
Sweet & Maxwell Asia
Singapore and Kuala Lumpur

PRACTICAL ADVOCACY
IN THE SHERIFF COURT

By

Charles Hennessy, LL.B.
Solicitor Advocate

Published in 2006 by
W. Green & Son Ltd
21 Alva Street
Edinburgh EH2 4PS

www.wgreen.thomson.com

Typeset by LBJ Typesetting Ltd, Kingsclere
Printed and bound in Great Britain by MPG Books, Bodmin, Cornwall

No natural forests were destroyed to make this product;
only farmed timber was used and replanted

A CIP catalogue record for this book is available from
the British Library.

ISBN-10 0-414-01503-7
ISBN-13 978-0-414-01503-6

PREFACE

This book started as a labour of love some time ago. On the way, the "love" factor has diminished somewhat. Recording all of the nuances and subtleties of advocacy skills, in the broad sense in which it is used in this book, was no easy task. Rules and practice kept changing, and I kept noticing new quirks as I conducted my own cases and taught various courses. I have attempted to state the law, practice, and my experience, up to January 1, 2006, and, where possible, I have included material after that date.

Revealing my innermost thoughts, tactics and strategy was at times a liberating, and at times a disturbing, experience. (Is that what I actually do? Does it just prove that I am hopeless/lucky/psychologically disturbed/ insufferably pompous or arrogant?). From this turmoil, there emerged what you now have, namely the best book on advocacy for sheriff court lawyers—otherwise known as the *only* book on advocacy for sheriff court lawyers. Use it wisely.

I would like to thank those who helped and encouraged me in this project. In no order of importance, I should thank Sally McKenzie (I told you I would give you a mention!) whose interest and enthusiasm was representative of so many of the trainees who have attended the PCC courses I have given. Secondly, the "usual suspects", being friends and colleagues who have looked at drafts, tolerated my liberty taking and will not mind (indeed, will expect) that I cannot name them and have forgotten what exactly they did for me. Thirdly, my own "wee sheriff", Sheriff J. Irvine Smith, who has often assisted me in advocacy courses in the last few years and whose love of the subject shines through in all of his quasi judicial pronouncements and advice from his mock bench. He also read some of the chapters for me and is responsible, amongst other things, for tempering my childish humour. Fourthly, I am most grateful to Sheriff Principal Sir Stephen Young for reading the chapter on Appeals and commenting on it. Thanks also to Philippa Blackham at Greens for coping with the novel stylistic issues involved in putting together this book.

Lastly, a word about the family contribution. With a wife and son in the law, and not averse to passing the odd comment, I was doubly cursed with my own in-house editorial team. Many a happy supper was spent debating the comparative merits of open and closed questions: *"How much did it cost?"* against *"That was expensive wasn't it?"* Just another normal evening in the Palais de Justice, chez Hennessy.

CONTENTS

TABLE OF CASES

TABLE OF STATUTES

TABLE OF STATUTORY INSTRUMENTS

PRACTICAL ADVOCACY IN THE SHERIFF COURT

Aims

The basic aim of this book is to provide a foundation for the handling of civil litigation in the sheriff court, and to give some guidance in the proper preparation for, and presentation of, oral advocacy. My focus is upon the practical skills involved, and the book is based on my own experience in conducting sheriff court litigation for over 25 years and in trying to teach the subject to an assortment of budding litigators over many years.

This is intended to be a "How to do it" book. It is not a book about how to do it in theory, but about how to do it in practice. It is also about how it is actually done in practice. Most readers will appreciate that there can be no single way of "doing litigation" in practice, and no guaranteed effective way of handling different kinds of case. The book provides a basic guide to the handling of civil litigation and the conduct of court hearings in an ordinary action in the sheriff court. It discusses what you might actually do in a given case, and what you might actually say in court when appearing. There is simple guidance about the skills of handling litigation and the skills and techniques of rudimentary advocacy, coupled with the practical application of these skills in realistic examples. This book is written primarily for law students, trainee solicitors, and qualified solicitors who are still gaining experience in court work, and who do not have the opportunity to watch, learn or study the topic closely before they are first let loose on the courts and unsuspecting clients. There is material which may be of assistance for more experienced lawyers dealing with hearings in court with which they are not familiar. Older hands may also find it of interest and some benefit and might want to compare and contrast their own approach.[1]

You cannot learn about advocacy by reading a book. However, enough people have encouraged me to write these things down, for me to think that there is a need for something which will, at least, provide a broad foundation from which to learn, or to develop, advocacy skills. There is, of course, no substitute for experience. You cannot learn experience. You can watch and listen to experienced practitioners conducting cases, but it must be said that the opportunities for such a luxury seem to have diminished in our busy professional world. In this book, I have tried to understand, formulate, and analyse what experience

---

[1] But old hands might be surprised to know that they have an "approach": in Scotland we do not like to talk about, or analyse, the skills we have acquired.

has taught me. It is based upon my experience in doing cases and trying to teach basic advocacy skills to students and young lawyers. It is also based upon many years of listening to good and not so good litigators and trying to understand what works and does not work in a variety of civil hearings. I have a slight concern, which is healthy enough, that some people might read all of this and wonder what kind of strange world of litigation I have inhabited for the past several years. I am prepared to concede that there have been times[2] when my incompetence and inability have been exposed. All I can say is that it has not happened too often, and the approaches I discuss here seem to have worked for me without too many embarrassing humiliations. If you follow the guidelines and advice given here then I am reasonably confident that this should provide you with a basic introduction to the skills of conducting an ordinary action effectively within our sheriff courts.

Courts and clients

Clients consult litigation lawyers about disputes which will require resolution. Many disputes can be resolved without resort to the courts. If disputes cannot be resolved by negotiation and agreement, then one means of resolving them is by litigation. The court will decide the dispute and make an appropriate order, or the parties will, in the course of the litigation, find some means of agreeing their dispute before the court intervenes by deciding it.

Court actions are expensive, unpredictable and fraught with all kinds of danger, as any experienced litigator will tell you. Court actions are rarely straightforward. The facts and the law can be problematic. Funding the litigation can lead to inequality of arms, or inability to investigate and prepare as well as you would like. Different courts have different practices, different sheriffs have different views, and different opponents contest the case in different ways. Clients come in all shapes, sizes and psychological profiles. However, if the dispute does "go to court", the solicitor must do their best for their client, represent him or her effectively at every stage of proceedings, utilise the court rules and procedures to their client's advantage, and generally act to the best of his ability in persuading the court that their client is in the right. It is easy to see that with all of these variables there could never be one rigid way of dealing with a case at any stage. It is necessary to remain flexible, and parts of what is suggested here may be effective while other parts might not work. Ultimately you will have to make the choices which best suit the client, the case, and you.

Advocacy

The book deals with advocacy in a much broader sense than simply the art of presenting a case in court. Solicitors in the sheriff court who handle their own cases from the initial contact with the client have to do much more than just presenting evidence or arguments in court. As for court advocacy, my approach is pragmatic rather than idealistic. I

---

[2] And, I am afraid, there still are.

acknowledge that you do not have to be the finest living orator of our generation to make a motion for the sist of an action for legal aid, but you may well need quite highly developed oral and presentational skills to persuade a reluctant sheriff to do something which he or she really does not want to do.

It is worth explaining the structure of this book so that the reader can understand the overall approach taken to the subject.

Pre-litigation

What happens pre-litigation can be extremely important for the litigation itself. The way in which a client is treated, and the way in which a case is handled and prepared at that stage, can make the oral and written presentation of the case in a subsequent litigation considerably easier. Accordingly, I am going to open with discussion about the handling of disputes pre-litigation. Consideration is given to fact finding, problem solving, tactics, letter writing and pre-litigation strategy.

Investigation

Proper investigation of any case will be necessary, and in sheriff court litigation you normally do not have the luxury of having someone else carry out that investigation.[3] Accurate precognitions should provide the raw material on which your action is based. The importance of proper and timely preparation of cases both pre-litigation and post litigation cannot be overemphasised. The strength of your argument, the quality of your pleadings, the direction you want the litigation to take, and your appreciation of the prospects of success[4] are dependent upon the breadth, suitability and accuracy of your precognitions. I have often seen cases lost almost entirely as a result of inaccurate, inadequate or just plain poor precognitions, taken at the outset of a dispute. At the very least, a basic failure to carry out proper investigation can make the case much harder to handle and much harder to win.

Written pleadings

While the emphasis in our system on written pleadings may now be altering,[5] there is no doubt that this is an area of advocacy which causes many litigators considerable anxiety. The prospect of losing a perfectly stateable case as a result of your own inadequacy to express it acceptably in writing is a constant worry. Failing to plead the case fully and properly and facing dismissal of your action on relevancy or lack of specification is your worst nightmare. This can mean pleading everything or "wishful" pleading of the worst kind[6] and this can cause as many problems as lack of proper detail in pleadings. Inexperience in this area is difficult to

---

[3] I would always choose to do my own investigation, if possible. Apart from anything else, you will know the case so much better if you do—but, of course, you have no one else to blame if you slip up.

[4] And advice to the client.

[5] In personal injury litigation, it may soon be disappearing entirely for all but the most complex of cases.

[6] You just say anything you have to say in the hope it will do.

overcome, but this book tries to give practical illustrations of some of the more obvious problems and solutions to pleadings issues.

Oral advocacy skills

The specific skills of oral advocacy are considered in detail. There are books which provide guidance on the general theories of advocacy, but this book will concentrate on the practical application of advocacy skills within the context of a "typical"[7] sheriff court action. The advocacy scenarios involve motions, debates, proofs, examination and cross-examination, submissions after proof and appeals. We will look at how these could be presented in the two sample cases. The actions which we will use as examples are outlined in the case studies at the end of this introduction. One is a contract action and the other is a reparation action

Learning advocacy

Learning advocacy by seeing it done, listening to it being done, and doing it yourself, is the perfect approach. Reading about it is not ideal, but I have tried to include virtually the full text of what would actually be said in various hearings. With a bit of imagination you should be able to visualise the scene and hear the words. The sample cases are real cases, and the particular examples I am going to use are realistic examples of what did happen, or, at least, what could have happened in court. I have attempted some analysis of how the advocacy element might be prepared and planned. An important feature is the identification of a structure for presenting arguments which, I hope, can be adapted to deal with a wide variety of situations.[8] I hasten to say that neither the suggested approach nor the precise words used is clearly the best by any stretch of the imagination. Nor are they the only way to act in conducting these hearings. I do not claim to know what is best and can often find myself adopting an approach which commends itself to no one, least of all the sheriff. I do not subscribe to the view that there is a "correct" or universal advocacy approach which practitioners in the sheriff court must follow to be effective representatives of their clients. Different things work for different lawyers in different hearings before different sheriffs.

Sods law

There are many occasions when what should work in theory does not work in practice, when what you thought you could assume or anticipate does not materialise, and when your carefully planned and structured approach is greeted with apathy or ridicule from some ignorant bruiser on the bench.[9] There are even, thankfully, occasions when an ineffective presentation will be received with warmth and understanding and will actually be good enough. That is all part of life's rich tapestry and one of

---

[7] There is no such thing.
[8] It is very important to appreciate how you can transfer the structure to other hearings and develop the habit of following a structure in every case.
[9] I mean that in a humble and respectful way.

the joys—and terrors—of appearing in court. Court lawyers do strive to be good and effective advocates for their clients at all times, but sometimes cases will be decided by matters over which they have little control, no matter how hard they try. The ultimate aim is to get the sheriff's nod. One early tip for you is that you should accept the credit even when it might not exactly be due. There are bound to be times when it will go the other way.

Acquiring the skills and applying them

It is extremely difficult to be an advocate in the courts—anyone who suggests otherwise is either extremely brilliant or exceptionally stupid. Standing up in court with everyone looking at you, and a sheriff (not to mention the clerk, your client, and your witness) listening critically to every word you say, is daunting enough. Add to this the task of trying to make sense of complex facts or law, and explaining them in some sensible way when your brain has temporarily left your skull and your thought processes have jumped out of gear so that you have no idea what sounds are coming out of your mouth, if any, nor whether they make the slightest sense to anyone (or are even expressed in English), is an experience to which any honest court lawyer will admit. Rest assured, the only people who did not feel these emotions acutely for at least the first 10 years of their court lives were in the early stages of brain death.[10] The book is intended to give some guidance which might reduce the frequency or duration of those traumatic moments. You can only improve by understanding, thinking about, and applying it in practice.

Practical case based study

It is helpful to set this all in a practical context, and to enable the reader to appreciate the practical significance of some of the advice. To this end, I have prepared an outline of two realistic cases—based on real court actions—and I will be referring to these at appropriate stages throughout the book. One is an action for payment for the design and supply of a kitchen. The other is a public liability reparation action. The reader is asked to refer back to the outline facts of these cases and use a little imagination to see how the issues considered could well arise in real life, and might therefore suggest solutions, techniques or approaches to handling cases of their own in the future. The only way in which these cases might be regarded as unrealistic or unrepresentative of a lawyer's case load is that it is well known that many actions proceed as undefended, and in many cases the claim itself, or the defence to it, can be fairly spurious. A significant number of cases which are "contested" do not really reflect a genuine dispute. Dilatory defences and unjustifiable actions exist frequently, and although it is part of advocacy skills to expose these and have them dismissed, it is not something I will deal with specifically.[11] For present purposes, I am only going to look at cases in which, rightly or wrongly, there are genuine and conflicting views on

---

[10] And are now on the bench. (This is a joke.)
[11] Although the chapter on motions will provide a generic structure for procedural motions which can be utilised in such cases.

the merits and where the other side thinks it has a winnable argument of some kind.

Perils of litigation

It may seem ironic to say so here, but no one in their right mind would advise a client to enter into litigation if it could possibly be avoided. The cost of litigation, the risks associated with it, and the disruption to the life of the client should never be underestimated. It is easy to become blasé about a process with which lawyers are familiar, and fail to realise the impact it may have on clients for whom this is likely to be an unpleasant and traumatic experience. Try to remember this.

Common problems any client might have are:

- First, they may not really understand what is happening in the court action and why, unless they happen to be serial litigants.
- Secondly, they may well assume that all court cases inevitably take forever and they are not supposed to ask their lawyer about progress.
- Thirdly, they may think that it is probably going to cost them every time they want to speak to their lawyer.
- Fourthly, it all seems terribly complicated and unfair.
- Fifthly, it may all end with a compromise at which you tell the client that the case you thought was a good one might not be as good as all that and there are real risks of losing because the courts are ultimately unpredictable. (So why did you take the case—and spend their money—in the first place?)

What are the questions they will ask at the initial interview? They are not interested in whether the Inner House of the Court of Session has expressed the view that a certain area of law is in need of revisiting. They may listen patiently while you explain the difficulties you can foresee and the problems you may encounter. But what do they really want to know? Put briefly, they usually want to know if they will win and what it will cost. While it is vital to appreciate and learn the skills of presenting the case properly, you must not forget your client's concerns, vulnerabilities, and interests. Your client is not too worried about how you did it[12] as long as they get a result. Of course, the two should, but do not always, go hand in hand.[13]

Conclusion

After all is said and done, a dispute which cannot be resolved by agreement will be resolved by the courts. If the client's court case is prepared and presented well, then their chances of winning it will improve—it is as simple as that. It is easy to be misled, however, into

---

[12] Although if a client sees and hears you in action in court and is impressed you have a friend for life—which may not necessarily be a good thing. Do not ask what the implications are if he thinks you are rubbish.

[13] Which would you (and the client) prefer: "We won Mr Hennessy, you are a star." Or "How come we lost Mr Hennessy even though you presented my case impeccably?"

thinking that a successful judgment in your case means that you are indeed a brilliant lawyer and were right all along—at least until the appeal is marked. That same rationale can be applied to an unsuccessful judgment which can, in darker moments be interpreted as meaning that the other side were right, you were wrong, you are hopeless and you ought to have stuck to conveyancing.[14]

But if you are reading this book, you did not stick to conveyancing and probably do not want to do so. There is hope for you yet.

Now go on and read the two cases which form the practical background to the book.

---

[14] It is also perfectly legitimate and understandable to have doubts about the sheriff's sanity and fitness for judicial office around this time.

CASE STUDIES

Case 1: Contractual Dispute

Parker Kitchen Design v John and Ellen Gray

John and Ellen Gray bought a new kitchen from Parker Kitchen Design in the spring of 2004. It was going to cost them about £11,500, although there is perhaps something of a question mark over the exact price agreed.

The kitchen was to be designed and then fitted by September 2004, but there were delays in completion and, after they made a fuss, Parkers arranged for the fitting to be done on November 10 to 12, 2004. There have been problems with it ever since.

The Grays paid a deposit of £5,000 when the order was placed and the balance due was invoiced to them in late December 2004. They are querying a number of items on the invoice and have a number of complaints. These can be summarised as follows:

1. The original price was to be £10,500 plus VAT (total £12,337.50). Parkers offered a discount of 10 per cent if the order was placed before the end of May 2004. The discount is not shown on the invoice.
2. The wood of the doors of the units was not as agreed on the original order. By the time the work was done Parkers had stopped using this wood, but they had provided a substitute. The Grays were told about it, were unhappy about this but allowed the fitting to go ahead. They do not think it looks as good as it should.
3. There is a larder cabinet unit which simply does not work properly. It is supposed to pull out smoothly but it has always stuck and it seems that it is the wrong size for the unit into which it fits. It will need to be altered or replaced, or the carcase of the unit into which it fits will need to be removed and a new one manufactured.
4. The standard of workmanship is very poor. There are a number of scratches on doors and handles. There are holes in some of the drawers where they were badly and incorrectly fitted in the first place. There is a gap where some of the units meet the floor.
5. A joiner friend of the Grays has had a look at the kitchen. He reckons that most of the workmanship defects can be tidied up. He has quoted a cost of £1,200 plus VAT to do so, but he thinks the larder unit cannot really be repaired and will have to be replaced. Parkers are the only people who can do that but it will involve removing the adjacent units and the worktop, and realigning other units.

Parkers have been told of the complaints. Its simple response is:

1. There was no discount on the price. In any event, the deposit was not actually received until June 2, 2004.

2. The Grays agreed to the different wood before fitting took place and it is fine.
3. The reason the larder unit is not working is that it has been overloaded to the extent that the runners have been buckled and the base unit has been distorted. It can possibly be remedied without being replaced. The cost of replacement of the unit and the cabinet would be £925 plus VAT.
4. The kitchen has been in use for six months. It is by no means clear that these scratches, etc. were present at the time of the completion of the work. In fact, the Grays never mentioned this until it started chasing them for the balance of the invoice.

Parkers doubts that the Grays have any genuine complaint about the units at all and is highly sceptical of the estimate from their joiner "friend". It wants to press ahead and recover what it is owed. If it takes the raising of court proceedings to recover their bill then so be it.

Case 2: Reparation Action

George Hamilton v Argyll Properties Plc

George Hamilton, 35 years of age, was walking in the Argyll Street Shopping Centre, Glasgow, one Saturday afternoon. It was July 23, 2004 about 14.15. He was with his friend, John Wallace, and they had been for a couple of pints before they went to the centre. They were meeting up with their wives later that afternoon.

Men had been carrying out building work at the centre in the weeks before. He knew this, because he had seen them on previous days and it was a bit of a mess in places. He is not sure what they were doing. He is fairly sure there would not have been any work going on at the time of his accident. He does not remember seeing any building workers around after the accident. He caught his foot in a hole in the surface of the walkway and he tripped and fell.

He was taken into one of the shops nearby and received initial first aid. His ankle hurt. He did not want to make a fuss. He declined to have an ambulance summoned. He hobbled home with the assistance of a taxi. The next day, he had to go to the Western Infirmary. He was found to have a fractured ankle. He could not attend his work for about nine months as a result of his injuries. He works as an electrical engineer for a company on the south side of Glasgow. It paid him basic wages for the first three months after the accident but he was only getting sick pay after that. He had to go back as quickly as he could because he needed the money but he does not feel he is fully fit and he still has some continuing discomfort and restriction in function.

He went to see lawyers some time after the accident and just before he went back to work. A claim was intimated to the owners of the centre. Their insurers declined the claim and repudiated liability. They said there was no proof of the accident actually happening. It was not reported to anyone at the time. Their insured had done nothing wrong. They had employed workmen to refurbish the centre. The contractor which did some of the work was MD Construction, and it was unaware of any accident or any defect which might have caused an accident. It had completed the work satisfactorily, and left the place in good condition. Mr Hamilton obviously was not keeping a proper look out, and no one else fell in this busy place during the time of the contract.

Mr Hamilton is unhappy with the repudiation. He wants to pursue a claim through the courts if that is what is necessary to recoup his damages. He lost earnings while off work and he is still struggling in coping with his work. He has a slight concern that he might not be able to stay in the job in the future because he might be required to work at heights from time to time and he cannot negotiate ladders very easily.

Chapter 1

PRE-LITIGATION

"Thank you very much, Mr Hennessy. I did not think that I had a problem until I met you." (A client)

This book is primarily concerned with litigation. Before you can have **1–01** litigation you need a client and a dispute. Even with those necessary ingredients, remarkably few disputes progress to litigation. Those readers who have spent any time in a law office may find this opening chapter to be no more than a series of similar statements of the obvious. For those who have not, it may contain a series of revelations, the likes of which they could never have imagined. Welcome to the joys of the practice of Law!

In practice, the cost of lawyers and the cost of litigation is an extremely significant factor in anything that you can or must do. The unpredictability of any form of dispute resolution, including litigation, is another factor which only experience can equip you to take into account fully. Cases do not present themselves to lawyers in neat packages tied up in pink ribbon. They do not come accompanied by a label indicating what questions of law are going to be important. Most clients would rather not be in their lawyers' office.[1] They do not want to make legal history, nor spend the next three years wondering and worrying about how it will all turn out. Much as you might welcome the opportunity to tackle their interesting problems, if truth be told, they really just want you to make this go away. With experience, you will realise that this is quite an acceptable objective for you too.[2] There are skills involved in handling disputes and clients prior to litigation and I am going to consider some of these briefly here. Acting in certain ways can avoid litigation—which should probably be the most acceptable objective of all—and, if it cannot be avoided, certain strategies can make the client and the litigation easier to handle.

Costs of litigation

It is beyond the scope of this book to cover in any detail the costs and **1–02** funding implications which affect the handling of cases prior to and during litigation. It will have to suffice to say that, in the real world, this is often the most important consideration. The action which you can take for a client, and the action the client may instruct you to take, will be largely influenced by what your firm will charge for your time, how

---

[1] A revelation indeed.
[2] Indeed, if it all starts to go wrong, it may be your only objective.

the charges will be met, and whether and what the client is prepared to pay. Cases in which the client has, or wishes, legal aid or legal advice and assistance complicate the picture further. Often what you (and the client) would like to do simply cannot be done because the client cannot afford to do it. Some clients will be very anxious about costs and want to restrict or control them closely. Some clients will not. Few clients want to spend as much money as it might take to handle a dispute fully and properly. Few of them are prepared to sign a blank cheque or pay legal fees by monthly instalment without question. This can make it all the more important to find ways of dealing with disputes simply, quickly, and cheaply, and should normally encourage both sides to stay out of court if at all possible. If a client's dispute cannot be resolved easily prior to litigation, the client's eyes[3] will have to be wide open on the potential costs of proceeding to litigation. That in itself is a powerful incentive to settlement pre-litigation, and a fundamental factor in the advice given and decisions that must be taken in the client's interests.

Most members of the public think that lawyers and court actions cost a fortune. Unfortunately they are often right, and never more so than in litigation. The unsuccessful party at the end of a sheriff court action in which there was a two-day proof could easily have to pay judicial expenses to the other side of no less than £5,000. Add to that, the costs of that party's solicitors amounting to no less than that, and you can well see that even in a straightforward case the total costs of a fully contested court action would be over £10,000. Even the successful party in a litigation is unlikely to be able to recover all of the costs from the opponent.[4] These simple realities affect various important strategic decisions which have to be made about handling the dispute.

Can the client afford to instruct lawyers in the dispute at all? Can the client afford to pay for the time and work involved pre-litigation which might be necessary to put together a good case?[5] Can the client afford to be involved in litigation, if it cannot be resolved pre-litigation? In practice, a balance has to be struck between what the lawyer must do, what the lawyer might do, and what the lawyer can do. The likely cost to the client, and the client's ability and willingness to pay those costs controls that balance, and dictate what "ideal" strategies can or cannot be followed. A failure to deal with this could leave you, and, more importantly, the client in a litigation from which you cannot find an acceptable escape. You must advise the client fully and accurately at the outset about costs and the cost implications of every prospective course of action.

Unpredictability

1–03   This is the joker in the pack. At its most extreme, it makes the remainder of this chapter pointless. Life is unpredictable. Disputes and

---

[3] And the client's wallet.

[4] "Why is it that I won my case and yet it cost me £2,000?" is not an unusual question from the client at the end of a litigation.

[5] e.g. Mr and Mrs Gray might be well advised to instruct an "expert" at an early stage—he might cost £500 for a report—can they afford to spend that? Can they afford not to? Could they delay it?

litigation are unpredictable too. There is no doubt that, after a few years of experience, you can see certain disputes going down a well-trodden path towards outcomes you could anticipate or could recognise. You may have acquired that knowledge through experience of how people react to certain things you might do, or how certain lawyers will deal with particular disputes when they are against you. You may have a particular insight into the way the courts will view certain behaviour or respond to certain pieces of evidence. In all of these ways, you may convince yourself that you can minimise the risk of the unforeseeable. But "minimise" is the appropriate word, and sometimes it is simply the best you can do, because, deep down, the resolution of disputes and the outcome of litigation can often be depressingly uncontrollable. You must tell clients about the potential frustration, disruption and personal trauma of being involved in a dispute, and in litigation.[6]

For example, halfway through your dispute/action on behalf of the Grays, Parker Kitchen Design could go bust. The Grays might decide to move house and lose interest in the state of the kitchen if they get a good price for the house. Your "expert" joiner witness could turn out to have no qualifications at all, or have moved to Canada without telling anyone. Documents which should be available might not be traced or might say the wrong things. If the dispute were to proceed to proof, a witness might not be prepared to turn up at court to support your client or indeed your opponent. Witnesses on either side who seemed confident and clear might be completely hopeless and tongue-tied when giving evidence. All of these have happened in my experience and have changed a good case into a bad one, and vice versa. This works both ways, so do not feel obliged to tell the client at the outset, or at any later stage, that they have a good case, or a bad case, if you do not know or are not sure. Can you ever be sure?

That does not mean to say that you should be unduly pessimistic about the prospects of success for any client involved in a dispute. The only sensible answer to the client's question "Will I win?" is usually "It depends". Lest that be thought of as a typical lawyer's answer, you must then go on to elaborate. "It depends" is always the appropriate answer, provided you tell the client what it "depends" on, and why. For example, "If the court believes you/your expert"; "If we do not get Sheriff X"; "If the proper way to interpret this letter is . . ."; "If the court takes the view this was a material breach"; "If we can find a witness to confirm x, y, or z", etc. This is professional detachment and actually assists you to focus on the essence of the dispute and the crux of the arguments. Sometimes the outcome of cases cannot be analysed with precision, and it is essential to make an allowance for the indefinable and unpredictable. You must advise the client of the "risks of litigation", which means that there is always a risk of losing (and winning) over which the client and you may have little control.

Clients are people

The outline of the dispute in Case Study 1 omits what are probably the **1–04** most important features of the case on a practical level: the personalities

---

[6] If the client says that, "There is no way I could stand up in court and give evidence", then this limits your options and you ought to know about this earlier than two days before the proof.

and expectations of the parties. You must understand these and take them into account in order to handle the case more effectively. There is far more to the case than the facts on the page.

Let us start by assuming that Mr Parker of Parker Kitchen Designs is your client. He has used your firm for a number of years and has been involved in a good few disputes/litigations in his time. He is a business-man who thinks that his time would be better spent selling kitchens than having a major dispute with a dissatisfied customer. As far as he is concerned, the customers are just looking for an excuse to obtain some kind of discount on the price because they were just unhappy about the general delays and aggravations during the fitting. There is no real merit in what the customers are saying and although he might accept a small reduction in the price simply to bring this to an end, he feels that the customers are "at it" to a large extent. He would rather not pay money in lawyers' fees if he could avoid it but, in any event, he knows that if it goes to litigation you will be able to recover a fair amount of the fees from the unsuccessful defender if you win. He can afford to pay you and can afford to instruct technical reports if necessary, but would like a quick solution to this problem. He thinks that the report by the joiner "friend" of the customers is rubbish and obviously biased in their favour. On another level, he does have his firm's reputation to think about, and would not like it thought that it does not provide a good service.

Now turn things around and assume that Mr and Mrs Gray are your clients. They have just received a letter from the lawyers of the kitchen firm to say that if they do not pay the balance within seven days then they will be sued. They have experience of dealing with solicitors in connection with the purchase of houses but they have no experience of claims/disputes of this kind. They feel very aggrieved about the perfor-mance of the kitchen firm. They are indignant at the threat to sue them and worried about what this will all mean for them. They are also worried about the cost of court proceedings. Mr Gray works and has a decent salary. Mrs Gray has a part-time job. They would not qualify for legal aid and they have heard that the cost of court proceedings is prohibitive. Having said that, Mrs Gray in particular feels very strongly that the "dream" kitchen she thought she was buying has not mater-ialised. Her husband's friend, who is a joiner, has told her on a few occasions that the work is shambolic and that it could cost quite a bit to repair. He would be willing to tidy it up to some extent as a favour to the family, but she doubts if that will work and she does not want anyone suggesting that their own workmen were responsible for some of the damage. She had always tried to be pleasant to the kitchen people but she now feels that they had taken advantage of her good nature and she is determined not to give up the fight until she has satisfaction. Ideally, she wants the parts replaced and the kitchen reinstalled at no cost to her. She has brought with her a couple of handwritten pages of notes giving the whole history of the contract from beginning to end, including a record of all of the telephone conversations with details of all of the excuses made by the firm about the delay in starting and completing the work.

It should be obvious that you cannot begin to handle the case effectively without knowing all of this.[7] There are infinite variations on

---

[7] In modern speak, I think this would be described as "client-centred".

these themes and there was a time when I thought that I had seen them all. I have not, and you will not either, so all I can do is give some general guidelines about dealing with clients.

Solicitor-client relationship

I am assuming that you have never acted for the client before. You have to establish a relationship with the client. What should you be aiming for? **1–05**

You should have a professional relationship with clients. This means that you do not instantly become bosom pals. A professional distance is appropriate and can be achieved without being rude or uncaring.[8] Familiarity can imply empathy with clients, which is good,[9] but, on the other hand, keeping a distance between yourself and clients while being sympathetic, pleasant and courteous is to be preferred. You may ultimately have to give your clients advice which they will not like to hear, and you must retain a degree of objectivity. **1–06**

You have to give clients confidence in you and trust in your approach and advice. Paradoxically, this can sometimes be achieved by telling clients at the first interview that you do not know the answer to their problem. If you really are not sure[10] what the answer is and how best to deal with the problem, then tell your clients. Explain why you cannot be sure. You may need to know more information than they have given you. You may need to see other documents or find out what other potential witnesses might have to say. You may not be familiar with or even know anything about the area of law involved in their problem. Clients are likely to have more confidence in you if you come clean and explain your difficulty, than if you waffle away with an unconvincing answer and hedge your bets to the point of giving no advice at all. **1–07**

Talk to clients in terms which they can understand. Do not use legalistic words, phrases and concepts without explaining them to clients. Outline a clear plan of action. Make sure they are satisfied that you understand what the clients' story is, make sure they understand what advice you have given them, make sure they are clear about what you have decided to do, what is to happen next, what you are going to do and what else they might have to do or think about. Most clients will nod their head and agree that they do understand. Most clients do not fully understand. So repeat it all.[11] **1–08**

Make sure clients appreciate that you consider their interests to be paramount. "We must find a way of solving this for you." **1–09**

Remember, it is for solicitors to give advice. It is for clients to give solicitors instructions. You can and should give clients options based on **1–10**

---

[8] Are you best pals with your doctor?
[9] Clients are more inclined to like and trust you if you have sympathy with them and treat them well. They may also be more inclined to take your advice.
[10] And it is dangerous to be dogmatic at the first interview.
[11] They still will not fully understand. I usually repeat it three times—they still may not understand but might at least appreciate your efforts.

your understanding of their problem. Do not tell clients what you would do in their position. Especially when they ask you—as they often will.

1–11　*Try to be aware of the significance of communication.*　It is very easy to overlook this. If you are giving good advice and handling their dispute promptly and properly this may count for nothing if clients do not realise it. It is a very good idea to write to clients after the first meeting and confirm, albeit briefly, what you discussed, what generally you are going to do for them, what they have to do (if anything) and what time-scales might apply. Let them know when they might expect to hear from you again. They should not hesitate to call you (or your secretary or office) if anything happens which has a bearing on the problem or if anything important occurs to them. This should have the effect of impressing clients with your professionalism and efficiency right at the start. It should also mean they have no unreasonable or unrealistic expectations about possible outcomes[12] and likely time-scales.

1–12　*Return clients' telephone calls and reply to their letters.*　I suspect that the most common complaint by clients about lawyers is that they never return calls. We are all guilty of this and some more regularly than others. This can undermine your relationship and can mean that when you give advice (after apparently neglecting the client for weeks) you may have a credibility obstacle to overcome. If you cannot return a call within a reasonable time[13] then let clients know that you will be unable to do so and give some time-scale for coming back to them. Serial callers can be a problem and the more you ignore them, the harder it is going to be to speak to them the next time.

1–13　*Do not fear to give "hard" advice, if you consider that is appropriate.*　This is difficult especially if you are inexperienced. Problems can emerge in handling disputes because the lawyer did not want to tell clients the bad news that the issue about which they felt incredibly strongly was an argument they were bound to lose. Or that they were being unreasonable.[14] If clients are unlikely to succeed, or the costs of pursuing/defending will be prohibitive, or if you are not willing to take the case on or take it any further for some reason then tell them. Tell clients to their face, or, if you tell them in a letter, give them an opportunity to come in and see you to discuss the written advice. I find it helpful to warn clients at the initial interview that I may not consider they have a good case once I have all of the information I need to enable me to assess their chances. At the same time, I tell clients that if I do reach that view I will not hesitate to tell them. It is usually possible to get clients to agree, there and then, that they would not want it any other way, and are prepared to face up to this if it happens. Believe it or not,

---

[12] "But you told me I had a very good case."

[13] As a little tip, return an odd call well outwith normal office hours. Many clients will be impressed and feel privileged and valued, although I have to confess that one particularly perverse private client told me that she only conducted business during normal office hours.

[14] To soften the personal blow you could say that, "A court might well consider that unreasonable/unjustifiable."

that can foster as much trust and confidence from clients as telling them what they want to hear.

It may be necessary to see clients through the eyes of a sheriff. If their **1–14** dispute cannot be resolved pre-litigation then you will be acting for these clients for some time to come and may end up taking evidence from them in court and seeing them being subjected to cross-examination. You have to see your clients objectively as a witness in the case. If you cannot recognise their potential shortcomings you may be storing up a major problem for both of you in the future. This is much easier to do once you have handled a number of cases which have gone the whole way and seen how some clients are their opponents' best weapon.

Clients and their expectations

In the real world of legal practice, the most important questions for **1–15** clients when they consult you about a legal dispute are probably:

- Have I got a good case?
- Will I win?
- How long will it take?
- How much will it cost?

That is what they really want to know. Different clients will have different perceptions of what a lawyer can do and/or should do for them. In the sample cases we are going to consider, the solicitor could be taking initial instructions from Parkers which is a client with whom they are very familiar, for whom they have acted before, and for whom they have already pursued a number of defaulting customers. Alternatively, the solicitor could be instructed by Mrs Ellen Gray, the customer of Parkers, who has rarely seen a solicitor in her life and has never met this one. She may have no idea, or worse still, an inaccurate idea, of what solicitors can do and what happens when claims are contested. On the other hand, the solicitor could be instructed by George Hamilton, a man who had previously pursued a personal injury claim after a car accident 10 years ago, and just remembers that it took ages to be finalised even though it was "obviously the other driver's fault". Each one of these clients will require different handling and a slightly different approach. Many clients have unrealistic expectations or simply inaccurate[15] appreciations of what is likely to be involved in the dispute. It is helpful to think about this from the perspective of the client and identify some basics that the lawyer should provide and the client is entitled to expect. In this way you can manage those expectations at the outset—an effective and essential feature for a satisfactory relationship with the client. You should try to provide:

- Clear, accurate, and understandable advice on first consultation. If it is not possible to give this, the client is entitled to a reason for the lawyer not being able to do so, and an indication of how and when the lawyer should be able to give that advice.

---

[15] But genuinely held.

- Identification of matters of fact which will need to be established in evidence and how that might be done.
- Identification of areas of the dispute which are going to be contentious and exploration of the possible strengths and weaknesses in these areas.
- Explanation, in lay terms, of any legal issues which impact upon the problem.
- Advice regarding the costs and time-scales involved in pursuing the avenues suggested.
- Control of the dispute by deciding on a plan of action in consultation with the client and adhering to this unless circumstances change.
- A clear idea of the parameters for success.
- A strategy that avoids litigation, if at all possible.
- Communication about progress in the case in an agreed or accepted manner.
- Written advice where complexity makes this appropriate, or where the client requests it, or where it is helpful to have a record of the matters discussed and a plan of action agreed upon.[16]

Taking instructions: First interview

Listen

1–16   Just listen to what the client is telling you about the dispute. Some lawyers seem to find that hard to do. Take Mrs Gray, for example. You may find that the best way to take instructions from her would be to ask her to tell you all about it and just listen until she has finished the whole sorry tale. Do not take a note. It is quite likely that she will not describe the problem in a coherent and logical way but that does not matter at that stage. Show an interest in what she is talking about and try to understand the whole story in broad terms. Ascertain her perception of the problem. That is a start.

Precognosce

1–17   Once you have an appreciation of her full story then you can start taking some notes. You can go back over the story in a logical way and ask her to confirm information or expand on it. A question may arise at that stage as to whether you should be taking a precognition from her. Different people have different views about this. However, you have an opportunity here to obtain a full and clear record of what this case is about. If you anticipate a major contentious dispute I would certainly

---

[16] A good succinct letter of advice is very useful for a number of reasons. Apart from anything else, it is always difficult for a lay client to assimilate all of the advice you have given and to understand what you have said, no matter how clearly you express yourself. It also shows you have a professional approach to the problem and sets you off on a good footing with the client. If the client does not agree with what you say in the letter, or does not understand it, then you have an early opportunity to clarify and avoid any long-term misunderstanding.

want to have a precognition. In fact, unless the issue was crystal clear and unlikely to involve more than a couple of letters, I would insist upon doing it. This could well involve spending a considerable amount of time with the client but, if done properly, it is time well spent. You cannot begin to solve the problem if you have not identified exactly what the problem is, and what has been happening between the parties. You are "fact finding" and this involves considering and noting all of the information available regarding the dispute, all of the potential evidence, witnesses, documents, etc. There is the benefit, when you extend the precognition, of being forced to express in a coherent way all of what the client has to say. This often reveals that you do not fully understand some aspect of the case, for example, the sequence of events, who actually spoke to whom on June 5, and where, etc. In turn, this gives you the chance to fill in the gaps or correct the errors while it is fresh in your mind (and the mind of your client).

Analyse

While you are taking information from the client, you should also be **1–18** analysing the nature and extent of the problem and, tentatively or otherwise, considering solutions. Often, the process of careful fact finding with the client can itself suggest solutions or highlight difficulties. If you are experienced then you may have had something similar to deal with in the past and this might assist you in your approach.[17] If you are inexperienced, you will be thinking feverishly about what you should do. The time and discipline involved in a rigorous exploration of the facts will give you an opportunity to think about solutions as you go. There is no need to form or express a view until you have a full appreciation of the problem and the chance to analyse it. You may need more information or documents to satisfy yourself about crucial matters. What matters of fact or law[18] do the parties disagree about? Why has it come to this? What exactly are they arguing about?

Advise

You will then have to give some advice. By that I do not mean that **1–19** you have to give the full and final answer to the problem you have identified. There is merit in being guarded if you are not convinced that you have the full facts. It does not need to be full advice. It does not need to be conclusive advice. There may be a good reason for not being able to give some preliminary advice at this stage, but you ought to know exactly why you are unable to reach a view and what you will need to do to be able to do so. You will want to advise clients as far as you are able and let them know why you can advise no further at this stage.

Take instructions

You then have to take some instructions from your clients. You have **1–20** told them what you think, in whole or in part, about the problem. You

---

[17] But no two cases are ever alike.
[18] Or both.

have outlined what else you might need to find out, etc. You may have given them various options for dealing with the problem. What do they want to do? Do not forget that they do not need to make an instant decision. Do they want to go away and think about it? Do they want you to write them a brief letter explaining the position and the advice being given so that they can consider it? Sooner or later, however, you must secure their instruction—even if this is that you should do nothing.

Agree a plan of action

1–21　　You might want to identify some aims and objectives (e.g. avoid court action at all costs, get out of this for no more than £3,000, or conclude a settlement by Christmas). What are you trying to achieve? What are the parameters of success?

Implement that plan

1–22　　Actually do what you have agreed to do. This should be easy. If you are busy and have other priorities and pressures, you can find yourself slipping up on this from time to time.[19] If so, rectify the position immediately and let the client know about it if it is material to the plan of action you have agreed.

Remain flexible

1–23　　The best course of action one day can be the worst a few days later. A letter from the other side can change the whole approach to resolving the dispute which you had agreed with the client. An informal phone call can give rise to some important change in the range of options open to your client. There is strength in a single-minded and determined approach which states your position clearly and forcefully. There is weakness in it too if it simply means that you are not prepared to be open-minded and recognise circumstances which should change your approach. Be prepared to reconsider the advice, the plan, and the strategy, if there is good reason to do so.

Lawyers are people

1–24　　It is dangerous to generalise about how to handle a client or a dispute. They are all unique, and some are considerably more unique than others. Similarly, different lawyers representing clients in disputes can also adopt quite divergent approaches, even though they are all capable professionals. At one extreme, you can have the "aggressive" lawyers who apparently take it as read that all of their clients are genuine, reasonable and decent people who have a clear and valid case, and have been very hard done by. They request instant recompense, and demand instant replies to prevent them unleashing a court action which will end in shame and humiliation for those who dare to stand in their client's way. At another extreme, there are the lawyers who will take basic instructions, send off a bland letter of claim, happily write another odd

---

[19] I am being ultra realistic here.

letter, or even two (or perhaps even 53), without thinking about litigation in the hope that something will turn up. They then pass the file to the young court assistant as soon as a court action looms into view. One could be seen as looking for litigation. The other could be seen as looking for anything but litigation. It may not seem like it, but both extremes are engaged in their own form of "problem solving" for the client. No one can say which of the two approaches will lead to a more satisfactory resolution of the client's problem. In reality, lawyers can adopt any attitude between these extremes in different cases depending upon a variety of factors—the stronger the apparent case, the more positive/aggressive one might be. Experience helps you assess the strength of your position at an early stage and this might influence the manner, tone and content of your correspondence with the other party and their advisors or agents. It is a matter of personal and professional judgment as to which approach to take, but it is worth noting that different clients, cases and opponents might require different approaches if the best interests of your client are to be served. A co-operative and light-handed approach may be the best way of resolving the dispute, although it may be seen as a sign of weakness. A firm and formal approach might encourage an opponent or their adviser to deal with the dispute promptly or, on the other hand, might discourage them from exploring the possibility of a compromise. You may develop your own "style" but remember that, at this stage, your primary objective should be to resolve the dispute in the best interests of your client. You should also be thinking about what might happen if you do not resolve it. Can you use the communications with the other lawyer as a means of identifying some of the matters which are going to be crucial if the case proceeded to court? Can you draw out those issues which are not disputed? Can you obtain an idea of the evidence available or not available to either side if the dispute were to be litigated? Can you determine more accurately the strength of your claim or defence?

Settlement of the dispute

All clients want to settle their disputes. Every solicitor wants to do so **1–25** too. Clients should be encouraged to settle their disputes. There is no harm in asking clients at an early stage what they want you to achieve for them. How would they want the dispute to be resolved? This gives you something to work towards, and anchors clients to something tangible and not just to a sense of grievance which might always be with them. It may not be achievable, but it gives you a goal of some kind. It is not a sign of weakness to try extremely hard to settle a dispute before litigation. Indeed, it might be easier to settle some cases at this stage before the parties become entrenched in their positions and have incurred legal fees of some consequence, which might provide an obstacle to settlement.

The plan of action following upon the initial interview with the client will usually involve some practical step being taken on the part of the solicitor. In most cases you would envisage writing a letter of some sort to the opponent. You would not normally start the process of representing the client in an action of payment or a personal injury claim by drawing up a writ and serving it on a defender without any prior warning.[20] You may well threaten court proceedings in the opening correspondence or declare the irrevocable intention of defending any such proceedings in response to an intimation of claim,[21] but that would rarely be regarded as an indication that some negotiation and settlement of the dispute would be excluded.

For present purposes, I will assume that a letter of claim or a letter demanding payment has been sent and a solicitor has been instructed on the other side of the dispute. The correspondence might set out the parties' respective positions and should give some indication of whether some settlement is likely. On the other hand, the correspondence can often involve firm declarations of the many areas of conflict between the parties. These could sometimes be seen as setting out no more than a negotiating position for discussions, formal and informal, between the parties in due course. The correspondence might discourage any such discussions, might narrow down the areas of dispute, or might hold out the hope that some agreement on how to resolve the issue might be possible.

1–26   In the contract dispute previously outlined, we could envisage an initial letter of claim going from the solicitors acting for Parker Kitchen Design to Mr and Mrs Gray, and being taken by them to their solicitor for advice. We could then envisage a course of correspondence between the respective solicitors with widely divergent aims and interests, but aimed at bringing the dispute to some resolution in due course. The way in which legal disputes are handled by lawyers pre-litigation will often have an effect on whether the dispute ends up in the courts and, in certain cases, may have some influence on whether one or other party will win. One of the best pieces of advice I remember receiving was that you should not assume that other lawyers will adopt the same approach as you to situations their clients were in. I know what I would do, or what I would think, if I received these instructions, or if I received a letter in those terms from another solicitor, but that does not necessarily mean that the opposing solicitor will react in the same way when they receive such a letter from you. It does not necessarily mean that they will give the client the advice you would have given if you had been in their position.

I will confine the rest of these observations to the action for payment we are considering. Correspondence, discussions and negotiations pre-litigation in personal injury claims are quite unique and reference should be made to specialist works.[22] There is no accepted standard form of letter of intimation of claim and no accepted or normal form of response. There is no need to set out the details of your claim or the details of your defence to a claim in such a letter, although you might give the other side the broadest indication of what is in dispute and why. In practice, and in the course of correspondence, most solicitors will

---

[20] Although, of course, there may be cases, e.g. interdict, where that is exactly what you would have to do. A failure to give a warning of impending litigation might result in a problem with expenses if the defender was always willing to pay but had never really been asked to do so.

[21] Well, you would, wouldn't you?

[22] R. Conway, *Personal Injury Practice in the Sheriff Court* (2nd edn, W. Green, Edinburgh, 2003).

eventually write and say in detail what their argument is, and justify their position. This could be to persuade the other side to back off by demonstrating that there is no strength in their argument, that the facts do not support their claim, or that there are documents which are fatal to the case. On the one side, the line of correspondence says, "Pay up or we will sue you". On the other side, "If you sue us you will lose". The solicitors on each side will correspond in such a way as to try to demonstrate that their argument will succeed. On the other hand, they might not want to reveal all of their evidence until later. They might want to flush out the nature and strength of the counter-argument, so that they can advise their own client. It may be necessary to know what the other side have to say about some thing particular in the case, before they can give their own client advice about whether they might win or not. The nature, content, and tone of the correspondence between solicitors at this stage can reasonably be expected to influence where the dispute goes.

Consideration should then be given to what such correspondence is trying to achieve. If it degenerates to a process of scoring points off the other side or consists of emotive and argumentative propositions which are calculated to demonstrate how tough your clients are and how preposterous any defence must be, then it will serve no purpose at all, although you can always send copies of your macho letters to your clients to let them know how uncompromising you are, and that you are well worth the fees.

It is hoped that pre-litigation correspondence can be seen as an **1–27** opportunity to become better informed about the nature of the dispute and obtain sufficient information, either directly or by inference, to enable you to give even better advice to the client about the nature of the problem and the means of solving it. That may lead you to conclude that you had better settle it because you would struggle if it was litigated. On the other hand, it may mean that you can see quickly that litigation is the only way to solve it. That is a benefit in itself.

If involved in conducting such correspondence, you might want to ask yourself: What are the aims and objectives of correspondence with the other side? Why is that particular letter being written? What kind of reply are you hoping to receive? What information would you like to find out from the other side, which might help you assess the prospects of success for you or the strength/weakness of their case? What matters of fact are not in dispute? Is there any basic factual misunderstanding which could explain the dispute? Why do they think their client is in the right? Is there any dispute about the underlying legal principles involved in the dispute?

The good and prudent solicitors will be mentally drafting their writ or their defence after taking instructions, and the position they adopt in any pre-litigation correspondence, action or advice should be dependent on their perception of the strength of their client's case if proceedings were to follow.[23] There may be features of the claim[24] which can be established

---

[23] This means obtaining clear and accurate information early and assessing the legal rights and wrongs accurately as soon as the facts are known.

[24] Crucial facts, documents, patent truths, etc.

clearly, or are not likely to be in dispute. These may be apparent at initial interview. If not, it may be possible to use correspondence to identify them and give better advice once that has been done. If the solicitor has not properly ascertained the facts[25] and given the legal principles[26] full consideration, they run the risk of giving inappropriate advice and pursuing unhelpful lines of approach in correspondence pre-litigation. There is considerable benefit in putting the time and effort into a thorough assessment of the merits of the dispute at the very start of it. That applies equally to the opening interview with the client and the initial correspondence with the other side about the merits of the claim. You do not want to do that exercise properly for the first time when you have reached the conclusion of the appeal,[27] by which time a great deal of money, anguish and time may have been expended on an ill-founded claim.

Without prejudice letters

1–28   This seems an appropriate place to provide some explanation about the use of "without prejudice" on legal letters and the effect that such a docquet on a letter might have upon the admissibility in evidence at a subsequent proof of letters written in this way. It is quite important to understand exactly what this means.

Many letters sent by lawyers in relation to disputes both before and during litigation will be sent with the docquet, "without prejudice".[28] In general terms this means that the lawyer does not intend any part of the letter to be produced later in court, and relied upon by the opponent as signifying a concession or admission which could be interpreted against their client's interests. Letters are sent routinely on that basis, even when the content of the letter could not possibly be interpreted in that way and would not require any such protection. It is worth elaborating on what the phrase means and the limits of the protection which it might afford. In its true meaning, the phrase has limited efficacy, and many lawyers do not appreciate this.

The docquet "without prejudice" is a shortened form of something like, "This letter is written without prejudice to our client's rights and pleas and is not to be founded upon in any subsequent proceedings". It could also be a shortened form of something like "Without prejudice to any questions of liability for [the payment]" or some such. The shortened form is used more often than not, although there is a suggestion that a more specific reference to the particular "rights and pleas" which are not being conceded would be desirable. Indeed, in light of the decisions on the effect of the phrase, you could justify extending it even further and adding, "and it is not to be treated as any concession or admission of fact or law nor can it be relied upon as such in any court proceedings whatsoever", but that may just be taking things a bit far. Conventionally, most lawyers will treat the shortened form as intending to convey the

---

[25] Which is not easy to do after just one interview.
[26] Such as, what the law is in this situation, what evidence is required, what about onus, presumptions, etc.
[27] See Ch.12.
[28] i.e. these words are written somewhere on the letter, usually as the last paragraph.

meaning of the slightly longer form, and treat it as such; but this particular point has never really been tested.

It has been said that the privilege attached to a letter with that docquet **1–29** on it is justified as a matter of public interest. It is in the public interest that lawyers[29] should be assisted to settle disputes, and to do so by negotiation rather than by litigation. Being able to write and make offers or concessions as a means of trying to compromise a claim without having those letters thrown back at you will encourage you to explore a compromise without giving up your arguments. I will sometimes add at the start of the phrase, "This letter is written with a view to exploring a compromise of the claim", but, again, that may be unnecessary. On the other hand, it could be seen as conveying the true meaning, intention, and effect of the qualification.

The letter itself may contain concessions or admissions of fact and/or law as well as proposals inviting negotiation or settlement. It may contain a specific offer of settlement, or an offer to reduce or restrict the claim. This may simply be proposed as a means of trying to reach a settlement and avoid a litigation. The intention of the docquet is to make it clear that, if the proposal is not acceptable, the terms of the letter may not be relied upon in any way as proving or admitting essential parts of the opponent's claim or defence. In practical terms, a letter of that type could not be lodged as a production, nor used as evidence against the client of the writer of the letter.

However, it is not quite as clear and simple as that. It has been stated authoritatively that:

> "'Without prejudice' formulae are perhaps a useful and effective shorthand in various situations, to make plain what might perhaps be better expressed somewhat more fully — for example, in the course of negotiation, that a party reserves the right, if negotiations fail, to depart entirely from positions adopted or suggested for the purposes of negotiation. And no doubt, where there is a problem between two parties, involving questions both as to liability and as to the quantum of damages in the event of liability, it may be desirable in the course of discussing the latter to make it plain that discussion of quantification is entirely hypothetical, with the issue of liability being held over or perhaps left to others . . . But . . . it appears to me that each situation must be judged upon its own facts."[30]

And approval was given to the opinion that: **1–30**

> "'Without prejudice' in my view means, without prejudice to the whole rights and pleas of the person making the statement. If, however, someone makes a clear and unequivocal admission or statement of fact, it is difficult to see what rights or pleas could be attached to such a statement or admission other perhaps than to

---

[29] And individuals.
[30] *Richardson v Quercus Ltd*, 1999 S.L.T. 596.

deny the truth of the admission which was made. I see no objection in principle to a clear admission being used in subsequent proceedings, even though the communication in which it appears is stated to be without prejudice."[31]

It would therefore appear that the standard shortened form of docquet is not an absolute guarantee that the letter cannot be produced and referred to in some, albeit limited, way. For example, if, in the course of correspondence pre-litigation, the defender concedes that delivery of goods for which payment is being withheld was, in fact, made, then, even if that letter was written with the docquet without prejudice it could probably be relied upon[32] if the defender ultimately denied delivery in a subsequent court action. The meaning and effect of the phrase was considered authoritatively in the House of Lords this year in the case of *Bradford & Bingley Plc v Rashid*[33] which obviously merits detailed consideration.

---

[31] *Daks Simpson Group Plc v Kuiper*, 1994 S.L.T. 689, *per* Lord Sutherland.
[32] And would be admissible as evidence.
[33] [2006] UKHL 37. In particular, the speech by Lord Hope is essential reading.

CHAPTER 2

PRECOGNITIONS

"A precognition is a statement taken from a person . . . for the purpose of discovering what the foremost evidence is to be in a legal action. . . . [In a precognition] . . . you cannot be sure that you are getting what a potential witness has to say in a pure and undefiled form. It is filtered through the mind of another whose job it is to put what he thinks the witness means into a form suitable for use in judicial proceedings."[1]

Is precognition taking important? It is not easy for law students and **2–01** newly-qualified solicitors to appreciate fully the significance of taking good precognitions and the skills involved in doing so. After all, you are just asking someone to tell you their story and then writing it down. What is so difficult about that? It is possible to overstate the case and say that good precognitions are utterly vital to the success of a litigation. How can that be so, when they have no status themselves and are simply a private aide-memoire to the lawyer conducting the case? In reality, an experienced, lucky or foolhardy lawyer may be able to get away with handling a litigation with poor precognitions. In the normal course, however, failing to take accurate precognitions and express them clearly can be a recipe for disaster. Many precognitions of witnesses will be taken by newly-qualified lawyers[2] but there is often little guidance as to what to do. Many law offices will have their own office "style" or approach to this exercise. However, it is apparent from the wide variety of precognitions produced in law offices, that there is quite a divergence of approach. Experience shows that the standard of precognition taking, and the depth, accuracy and content of precognitions is extremely variable. There is no "perfect" precognition and no "correct" style of precognition but in this chapter we are going to consider what precognitions are, the ways in which they can be taken and the ways of realising their full value in a litigation.

In civil cases, a precognition can be described simply as a document which comprises any written statement compiled from information taken from a party or a potential witness in the case by someone who has an interest to do so. Rather confusingly, the word "precognition" can also be used to describe the whole process of taking such a statement.[3] This

---

[1] *Dorona Ltd v Caldwell*, 1981 S.L.T. 91, *per* Lord Ross, quoting *Kerr v HM Advocate*, 1958 S.L.T. 82.
[2] Whose youth, energy, and unquestioning obedience will make them prime candidates for the midnight precognition of Mr Bloggs in his cottage in Patna.
[3] The difference between the "abstract" meaning of the word (the process) and the "concrete" meaning of it (the product) was explained in *F v Kennedy*, 1992 S.C.L.R. 750, *per* L.J.C. Ross.

would include making arrangements to speak to the witness, asking questions, obtaining answers, clarifying or expanding upon those answers, recording all that the witness says at that interview verbatim, or in the precognoscer's own words, or a combination of both, and finally, "extending" the written precognition. "Extending" means putting into a written document what the precognoscer understands the witness will actually say in court about anything the precognoscer has asked the witness.[4] Precognoscing can sometimes be regarded as a more formal process than taking a statement, and a precognition can be seen as a more formal document than a "witness statement", but it is not. A "statement" has no special status just because it is called a "precognition".[5] It is one of the most important products of the fact-finding process and, to be worthwhile, it must be an accurate record of the witness's evidence.[6] I will discuss its evidential status and value more fully later.[7]

Good precognitions are worth their weight in gold—regrettably, many people do not appreciate this until they have lost a case in which the evidence did not match the precognitions. There is a real skill involved in taking a precognition properly and accurately. Information has to be extracted, understood and recorded clearly. Often a witness can be reluctant, monosyllabic, inarticulate, or just confused, so it is necessary to be very careful in putting down in writing what you think the witness actually means to say. Putting down in writing what the witness actually does say, i.e. putting this in their own words, can be a very effective way of recording their expected evidence. On the other hand, the words of the witness themselves may not be easy to understand or follow, so some explanation or interpretation of those words may be needed. That is the area in which criticism of the contents of a precognition can legitimately be made. "Polishing up" or "tidying up" a statement made at precognition can, quite unintentionally, distort the statement.

2–02   In the previous chapter we discussed the strategy of handling a litigation, and a significant part of that strategy is fact finding. Finding out what the witness has to say is more than simply asking them to tell you their story and listening to what they say. Satisfying yourself that what the witness tells you at an interview in your office[8] is what they are likely to say when they are giving evidence in court, is really the only product of the whole process of fact finding which is of any true significance for the lawyer who conducts litigation. If you do not know what the witness will say in court when pressed on a point, or cannot rely upon the witness speaking to that fact or those facts which are crucial to your case, this undoubtedly influences your decisions about the case and

---

[4] "[P]recognoscers as a whole appear to be gifted with a measure of optimism which no amount of disillusionment can damp": *Kerr v HM Advocate*, 1958 S.L.T. 82, *per* L.J.C. Thomson, explaining why a reliable and accurate precognition may be regarded as a contradiction in terms.

[5] Precognitions in criminal cases can have special status, e.g. precognition on oath, but there is no such thing in civil cases.

[6] Despite judicial scepticism which is justified, most decisions about a case will be taken by a party on the basis that their precognitions are accurate and reliable.

[7] See para. 2–24.

[8] Or on the phone, or in their front room, or standing chatting on the factory floor.

your appreciation of the prospects of success. Remember that, in litigation, a "fact" is only a fact when someone gives evidence on oath about it, and is accepted by the court as credible and reliable. Whether you, or the precognoscer, believe the witness or not is unimportant. Whether that witness's evidence, as you understand it from the precognition, is likely to entitle a sheriff to hold that fact or those facts proved is the crucial point.

For the purposes of advocacy, in its wider sense, the reliability of the fact-finding process and the accuracy of the fact recording method is vital. It is important to appreciate and practise the skill involved in taking a good precognition. You might get away with something less than a brilliant precognition in many cases, but if you learn the habit of taking good precognitions in all cases you will reap the benefits in your conduct of any litigation. You will see particular benefits when conducting a proof and examining or cross-examining a witness who has been well precognosced.

What functions do precognitions perform?

Precognitions can be taken at any time and for any reason.[9] This is a **2–03** matter of practice and personal preference. Some solicitors may not want to take a precognition too early. Some may want to extend a precognition as soon as the client or witness is seen. Each side would normally take its own precognitions of the relevant witnesses. They are not normally exchanged between the parties,[10] although this could be done. I would only exhibit my precognition of a witness to my opponent in very few circumstances,[11] although I would not have a problem in telling my opponent what I understood the witness was likely to say.[12] Precognitions can perform various functions during the handling of a dispute.

> 1. Precognitions can be a part of the initial investigation process of any case. At that stage they might be brief and simply provide a basic, clear record of what a witness (or client) has to say which is expected to be relevant to the case. It might even confirm that the witness has little or nothing to say which is relevant to the case. In practice, if it appears that the case on which you have been consulted by an individual is going to lead to a significant dispute and/or probable litigation, there is ample justification for taking full statements/precognitions at the first interview. They will often constitute a useful and comprehensive aide-memoire for future reference. The exercise of assimilating all of the information given to you by a client

---

[9] Some of the older cases may suggest that a statement is not a precognition until a certain time has been reached: see *Moffat v Hunter*, 1974 S.L.T. (Sh. Ct) 42. The difference is truly academic.

[10] Although they can be—I do not advise it. It is difficult to imagine your opponent sending you anything other than a precognition favourable to them.

[11] It could be used for cross-examination.

[12] But my precognition is only for my benefit, and the benefit of anyone else handling the case on my behalf.

and/or witness, and having to write out a coherent version of events, can, if properly done, act as a pointer to you in understanding the important issues in a case, or in realising that you have not fully understood the facts of some aspect of the case.

2. Witness statements, either individually or collectively, can, and often will, be used as the principal basis for making a decision on whether, what and how to litigate. They will influence the advice given by the solicitor as to what the prospects of success on some or all aspects of the case might be; whether to advise a settlement or not; what further detailed enquiries might be needed in a case; or whether to emphasise or abandon one line of approach or another. Many of these decisions will be made on the assumption that the precognition is "true" and that it reflects what the witnesses will undoubtedly say. The basic facts uncovered in the investigation process can then be considered along with the legal principles applicable to the dispute to enable sensible and informed decisions to be made about cases prior to litigation. The ability of any solicitor to give good advice and act effectively in the client's interests is heavily dependent upon the range, content, quality and accuracy of the witness statements available at that time.

2–04
3. On another level, the precognition can be taken to be a clear and accurate reflection of what the witness is undoubtedly going to say in court when asked questions about the case. This might be a more detailed precognition[13] and record not just what the witness has to say, but how they would respond to specific questions, why they are sure or not sure about certain matters, how far they could be persuaded to stray from their basic view and any other matters bearing upon the way in which their evidence might emerge at the proof. This will usually mean that the statement should address all of the issues which are likely to arise in any actual or subsequent court action. The statement could/should also give some indication of the strength or otherwise of the witness's evidence, and impressions[14] about their character, credibility, and reliability. Ideally, a person who was going to conduct a proof would be looking for a precognition which would provide a clear and firm basis for examination and cross-examination of a witness in court. On this level, the solicitor would expect the precognition to test[15] the basic assertions of the witness, the accuracy of their recollection, and their response to contrary assertions. However, as a matter of common sense, a precognition of that detail is not always required. It is a matter of judgment depending upon a variety of factors, including the value of the case, as to what level of witness statement might be sufficient in any one case and/or at different stages of any case.

---

[13] Although there is no reason why it could not, or should not, be a detailed precognition at the start.

[14] In the form of a note at the end of the precognition.

[15] And not simply to record.

4. They can be used as a means of refreshing memory. It is perfectly legitimate to send out to a witness a precognition which you took from them and ask them if that is accurate and will be their evidence in court. This is not the same as telling them what to say[16] and it would almost certainly lead to a reprecognition of some kind, with the witness qualifying or adding to what has been said. This would be especially so, if the precognition had been taken from the witness some time before. Reprecognoscing might be prudent in certain circumstances,[17] and may be necessary for good reason,[18] but this usually involves a degree of duplication and expense which could be avoided if a good, accurate and reliable precognition is taken at the outset. In real life, however, witnesses do change their minds and change their perceptions of events. Sometimes they simply do not give matters the fullest of attention until the court hearing looms large. There is often an element of mutual reassurance involved in reprecognoscing a witness later in a litigation. This may indeed be prudent, no matter how well the original statement might have been taken.

What skills are required?

A good precognition can help lawyers to give good advice and make **2–05** sensible decisions in the interests of their clients. A "bad" precognition can cause untold problems. Sometimes, there is nothing you can do about it and no way you could have approached it any better. Some witnesses simply tell lies or half-truths for various reasons. Some cannot be bothered thinking too hard about the questions, and some do not care too much about the precise accuracy of their answers at what may seem to them to be an informal (and inconvenient) interview. You can avoid this to some extent by considering the skills which you ought to be using and the following points for guidance.

Good precognitions require:

1. Ability to understand the detailed factual and legal issues involved or anticipated in the case.
2. Ability to understand the significance of the witness's evidence in the case.
3. Ability to question openly, accurately and clearly.
4. Ability to listen and to record.
5. Ability to probe and explore the facts meticulously and sympathetically.
6. Ability to express in writing what a person means to say, and will say—using their words and making sense of their expected evidence.

---

[16] In this context, it is recommended that you read Lord Hardie's opinion in the case of *Watson v Student Loans Co Ltd* [2005] CSOH 134.

[17] If the original precognition was taken a long time ago, it is sensible to confirm that the witness still adheres to their position at a later stage.

[18] e.g. if there has been a material change in some aspect of the case since the first precognition or a shift in emphasis about the matters in dispute about which the witness may not have been asked in sufficient detail.

Points for guidance

2–06   Circumstances[19] will dictate the extent to which you can or should follow any of these suggestions. I am conscious of the fact that this may appear to be a counsel of perfection. Time and resources may militate against this and make the adherence to these guidelines somewhat unrealistic. I have seen many cases flounder during proof as a result of bad preparation, and, particularly, poor precognition. I would suggest that you ignore or scoff at these pointers at your peril.

Taking precognitions from a reluctant/hostile witness

2–07   Many witnesses will be reluctant to speak to a lawyer about a case. This is perfectly understandable and allowance should be made for this. Indeed, it should be expected and anticipated. If you witnessed an accident or knew something about the circumstances of a dispute in which you were not directly involved, then you might well be unwilling to spend half an hour of your time when you could be watching football on TV or should be carrying on your own work. There will of course be degrees of reluctance and differences in the way this is expressed.[20] You have to be alive to this. A simple courtesy of thanking the witness and saying that you do not want to take up too much of their valuable time never goes amiss. Letting them know that you appreciate their help[21] would also be appropriate. If they are reluctant and irritated you will not get a good precognition from them.

　　　　If the witness is positively "hostile", for example, "I will tell you right now, you do not want a statement from me because I don't like your client and there is no way I am coming to court", then you have to find some way of breaking that down without getting their back up further. You could say that you are obliged to carry out enquiries and it would be helpful if they assisted you. You could say pleasantly that you appreciate they might not be well disposed but would they mind if you phoned them back or called to see them at a more convenient time or place. My experience is that if you address that issue affably and courteously the witness is more likely to succumb after their first salvo. The bottom line, of course, is that if you think you need them and they will not give you a statement, then you will just cite them as a witness in court and they will be arrested if they do not turn up.[22]

Time

2–08   Allow sufficient time for the taking of a precognition, and allow sufficient time for the preparation for taking a precognition. If you are still trying to remember what the case is about, and are still trying to remember what clever questions had occurred to you when you first saw the papers, then you are not properly prepared, and the precognition will suffer. This means you should spend some time in advance of the

---

[19] Not to mention time and money.
[20] Or not expressed out loud.
[21] Even if they have not been helpful or are giving you evidence you do not want to hear.
[22] Save this to the very end, but if you really need their statement you may have to use it— politely, of course.

appointment and have some written or mental plan of what you are proposing to ask. If you are in a hurry to take the precognition, then the witness will gain that impression and will not be too concerned about giving you a careful expression of their views. I would normally want to approach the witness's evidence on a crucial matter from at least two different standpoints in order to test that particular part of the statement and that requires a more expansive approach, which in turn requires a little more time than usual. The more time you take, the more information you are likely to obtain even if it is only to confirm the clear first impression which the witness gave.

Environment

While this may not be entirely within your control, it is important that **2–09** the taking of the precognition is done at a time and in a place where the witness is going to be required to give you their full attention, and concentrate for at least a short period of time on what they are being asked. Without putting the witness off, it might be useful to make it something of a formal exercise. Otherwise there is a chance the witness will simply treat it as a casual, informal, unimportant and superficial chat, which is a waste of everyone's time.

Precognitions are often taken over the telephone. On many occasions that is the sensible and practical thing to do. Most solicitors would say, however, that it is never as satisfactory as a face-to-face precognition. There is nothing inherently wrong with a telephone precognition. It is better than nothing, when it is difficult to contact someone or the witness is reluctant to become involved. It is less satisfactory because you may have problems in having the witness focus upon the issue. You may have less time to take it. You will not be able to form a full impression about the witness and test or explore their evidence fully.

If you do precognosce over the telephone, however, you can try to make it more satisfactory by:

(a) Telling the witness firmly and clearly that you want to spend a little time talking about it. Not just "a couple of quick questions".
(b) Do not rush—be a little ponderous. Force the witness to take their time and to think about their answers. It is not just a chat on the telephone.
(c) Tell the witness that you have to note the information down, that you are noting it down, and ask them to repeat and clarify anything of significance.
(d) Suggest that you will extend their statement and send it out to the witness for checking. You might want to do this anyway for a face-to-face precognition.
(e) Make it clear to the witness that this is not an ideal way of proceeding, and that if matters go further then you may well need to see them person to person.

Relationship

Statement taking must be a "one-to-one" arrangement. The presence **2–10** of another person, whether he or she is vocal or not, can and does influence what a witness might say. It is difficult to take an accurate and reliable statement from a person with another person or witness present. More importantly, you do run the risk of contributing to the idea that the witnesses may have put their heads together and come up with an agreed story. Even if this is not indicative of dishonesty or uncertainty, it would reflect badly on reliability. It should be avoided at all costs.

It can be helpful to make it clear to the witness where they fit in. Why is it thought that their evidence is significant?[23] Ask them to help you, understand what is supposed to have happened, encourage them to "get involved" in the claim. If they want to draw a picture or a diagram, encourage them to do it (and keep it, no matter how rough). If they want to check their diary or other paperwork before responding, then let them (and take a copy of that document for your reference).[24]

A witness who is reluctant to give you a precognition will cause particular problems. You have to understand their reluctance and conduct yourself in such a way as to empathise with them. You need their co-operation. You do not necessarily need their agreement or sympathy. If they are saying something contrary to your interest then you had better know it. You should thank them anyway and you want to be sure if their evidence is actually against you or whether there are some features of it which assist. Often witnesses think that if they say what you do not want to hear you will not trouble them further. Many witnesses will tell you they saw nothing, and then tell you exactly what they did see. No one wants to be a witness in a case, and many people have the intelligence to figure out that you may not call them as a witness if they are against you or can say nothing. That is not always the case. Polite insistence on asking your questions and getting your answers without annoying the potentially hostile witness is a particular skill.

You should let a witness know why you are making the enquiry at that stage. They should be advised that you may want to follow up the exercise with some further questions later. Perhaps you might say that one of your colleagues may follow this up. You can let them know the basis on which the case is being pursued/defended at that particular time, but advise them that this might change or that others may alter their stories, so it might be necessary to see them again for that reason. The witness really also ought to know who you are by name,[25] and be invited to contact you if any additional information occurs to them or if they want to clarify any matters later. You should have their home address and home telephone number. You should let them know who you actually represent.[26] It is amazing how many people do not grasp such a simple fact, and you should not take it for granted that if you say it once, that will suffice.

---

[23] This may be counter-productive if their evidence is against your interest—but it is better to know this.

[24] You could attach it to the precognition by stapling it to the back. If you are likely to use it as evidence in the case, keep it yourself and give them a copy.

[25] It is particularly humiliating to spend an hour-and-a-half taking a statement from a witness who then phones your office three months later and does not remember who came to see them. How much attention were they paying? How reliable are they going to be? How unmemorable are you as a person?

[26] There is no professional or other obligation on you to do so, but it makes sense.

Priorities/Issues?

There will be various background matters which might be interesting **2–11** but may not be contentious or important issues in themselves. To make the exercise manageable these can in certain circumstances be glossed over. On the other hand, if the individual giving the statement is being expected to make some particular comment from their own knowledge or experience, and if this is all considered to be significant, then that knowledge and experience should be fully explored. Realistically, you will have to have in mind certain pieces of information which you would regard as priorities, and which you think will have a bearing upon the issues which will arise in the case. There can be a difficulty that, when you are first carrying out investigations, the real issues may not have been clarified.

Curiosity

You clearly have a distinct interest and purpose in seeing the witness, **2–12** but what you really have to find out is what is this witness going to say (whether you like it or not). An open mind in the precognition-taking process is helpful. A curious mind is also helpful. One of the best questions to deploy when taking statements is, "Why?". It may be self-evident to the witness that a particular state of affairs existed. They may think it will be obvious to you. At the risk of convincing them that lawyers are not very clever, there is no harm in inviting the witness to treat you as an idiot and explain to you things which they take for granted. This will inevitably aid your understanding of what the witness is saying and why they can say it, and can also assist in assessing the strength and admissibility of their evidence generally. For example, if they were asked to give some detailed quasi-technical explanation at the proof would they be capable of making it understandable to the court? Or should you look to someone else for that?

Clarity

Many witnesses are unable to give their statements clearly. This can be **2–13** for a variety of reasons. There is no benefit in converting an incoherent jumble of impressions into a clear piece of logical prose in the precognition. This will not give the true impression of the witness's evidence. Ideally the precognition should show clearly what the witness will say. If they are unsure about any particular feature or indeed if they are unsure about all of the witness's evidence, then that should be demonstrated within the statement. For example:

> "I think the car was going at slightly over the speed limit. I am asked why I think that. It has been suggested to me that the car was doing no more than twenty-five miles per hour. I am not sure if I could disagree with that. I do not drive myself but I think I have a reasonably good picture of the normal speed of the traffic which uses that road and I would say that this car was going a little greater than the normal speed. It is just an impression but maybe I could be wrong. If someone said to me the car was going at over thirty-five miles per hour, then that might be right as well. I would not have said it was doing more than forty

miles per hour. Maybe it was round about the speed limit. I think I saw it briefly just before the impact. I am asked what I mean by 'briefly'. I would say that when I first saw it the car was beginning to skid so it must have travelled about three or four car lengths while I was watching it."

This witness is not going to be very clear about speed. They could be persuaded to say a variety of things, but a witness statement taken along the above lines would provide all kinds of clues as to the strength or otherwise of the evidence and the approaches to examination and cross-examination of the witness in court which might assist when leading evidence. A precognition which simply said, "I am not sure what speed he was doing but I think it was just over the speed limit", is an accurate statement of the gist of this same evidence, but it is clearly a poor reflection of what that witness might, or might not, be prepared to say. The difference might not be crucial depending upon the context, but anyone looking at the first precognition would have a much clearer picture of what to expect. Ask yourself what is this witness actually going to say when they are standing in the witness box being examined, and cross-examined, in detail on oath.

Chronology

2–14   While it is true to say that the best witness statements should be in the words of the witness as far as possible, I think that the chronology of the witness statement should be tidied up so that events are put in sequence. If there is a question about the sequence of events which might become relevant, then great care should be taken to confirm that the chronology is accurate. A comment in an accompanying note that the witness is hopeless on times, dates, meetings, etc. without the benefit of notes, diaries, etc. is very helpful indeed in enabling you and others to assess the value of the oral evidence of the witness and how it may have to be supplemented by documents (which may have to be lodged as productions if the case went to proof). There may be perfectly good reasons for the witness being confused or uncertain about certain details, and this will enable you to address the issue of whether documentary evidence would be helpful or necessary to support the oral evidence of a vague but honest witness.

> *"I am not very good at dates . . . I cannot remember exactly which came first . . . I am unable to say when . . . I have had an opportunity to refresh my memory/check my file/notes/letters and I can see that, contrary to what I thought, this happened a week before . . .".*

Leading/Non-leading questions

2–15   While this, of course, has particular importance in the leading of evidence in court, its significance at the stage of taking precognitions should not be minimised. It is very important not to lead a witness on any material issue when you are taking a precognition from him or her. Questioning the wife, who is a witness for the defender, by saying, for example, "I believe the kitchen company only came out to look at the job once, is that right?" which produces an affirmative response, "Yes, I think so", might well be the wrong approach and might transpose itself to a sentence in a precognition which confirms that this particular witness will positively say, "They only came out once." You are effectively suggesting to the witness what she can say. Most people, without any bad faith or attempt to mislead, will happily go along with a leading question unless it is blatantly inaccurate. This is especially so in the more informal context of taking a statement and it can seriously affect the whole flavour of the precognition. It is necessary to ask leading questions sometimes, just to move the process along, but you should take great care about this. In an area where the evidence might be doubtful and in which there are known to be conflicts, it is particularly important not to ask a witness a leading question. Ask the witness to explain and clarify issues in their own words, in preference to giving them an explanation for what you believe happened, to see if they agree with it.

Understanding

If a witness says something which you do not understand (and **2–16** remember you have already asked them to treat you as an idiot) then you should persevere with the point until you do understand it. If it does not make sense to you, then ask them to help you make sense of it. Frame the precognition so that the next person to read it will understand it too. Your written description of events and evidence should be capable of standing on its own, and being understood on its own. If it does not make sense to you, then you will not be able to make it make sense to anyone else. If you do not do this, then you might be tempted to be a little more creative than is suitable and substitute your own evidence for the evidence of the witness.

Illustration

I have already mentioned that you can ask a witness to draw a diagram **2–17** or a sketch to supplement their evidence. I do not think this should be regarded as replacing the witness's evidence, but it can often be extremely helpful. You should be able to understand the witness's statement by virtue of the spoken word alone and the illustration should, in a sense, confirm that. Sometimes there is an advantage in keeping the rough sketch by the witness and attaching it to the precognition. Reference to photographs in a precognition can also be helpful. Make sure you identify in the body of the precognition the actual photograph/document/plan which the witness is speaking about. Do not forget to be clear about who took them; and when; and even why. If you show a witness a document or a photograph when taking a statement from them, then their response to questions about the photograph or diagram should be incorporated in the body of the statement, because it serves as useful confirmation of what they intend to say. It should also confirm your understanding of what they have to say and whether their evidence requires supplementing by documents.

Obtaining documents

If, in the course of giving the statement, the witness makes reference **2–18** to documents which might be relevant or it seems to you that there are documents which will be relevant, then you ought to take steps to obtain these documents straight away. If you cannot get originals, then copies should be taken. The whereabouts of the originals should be confirmed if you cannot obtain them at the time. You should incorporate in the precognition the witness's reference to the documents and their explanation of what the documents show, or do not show, together with an explanation of what the documents actually are. Remember to be curious, and remember that if you do not understand why, for example, a telephone complaints book is completed in a particular way, then you should ask the witness. Incorporate their explanation in the statement so that everyone who reads the statement, and has no knowledge of the type of document/record under consideration, will understand the position.

Testing of evidence

2–19   While taking the precognition from the witness you should, in a sense, be cross-examining them as well. Obviously you cannot do this overtly, and there is a positive disadvantage in doing it aggressively, but you should listen to their answers and decide whether there is an inherent consistency or inconsistency in them. Can you make the witness change their evidence broadly or in detail? In this way, you can determine how much reliance can be placed upon it. This testing process can be incorporated in the precognition itself, but you could also do a note at the end of the precognition or on a separate sheet at the back of the precognition[27] with some observations upon the witness's credibility and reliability in whole or in part. If you identify a crucial issue in the case and you have observations to make upon the witness's statement regarding that crucial issue, then it is important to make a note regarding this. It is only your opinion, but it is useful to have a record of your impressions of the witness.

Relationship with other evidence

2–20   If you are seeing a witness as part of a fact-finding process in which you have already taken other statements, there is no harm, and often real benefit, in putting to the witness what some other witnesses might have said. You would not do this before obtaining their own story however. To do so would really be leading the witness and asking them merely to agree or disagree with what has been said by others. However, once you have clear in your mind what they have to say, then it is useful to pass on to them what other witnesses might have to say and to obtain their comments upon that. If you are trying to clarify their evidence by asking for their comment, then it would be helpful to record that in their witness statement by starting with:

> "*I am asked if I have any comment to make about Mr Parker's assertion that he was never told that the doors were all scratched until March 2002. That is not true. I remember quite distinctly that my wife*

---

[27] Be careful only to let this be seen by those who ought to see it. If it is critical or quizzical about the witness's statement, do not let them see this note.

telephoned him at his place of business. I was working at home that day and she came off the phone to tell me what he had said about our complaints. And that he did not accept any of them."[28]

Recording of precognition

Recording what the witness says verbatim and in longhand is time-consuming and unnecessary. I have seen it done[29] and it is a laborious process which has its own dangers. I am not sure that it is any more accurate than a well-taken precognition compiled by handwritten notes followed by a dictated document. I doubt if it is helpful in more complex cases where the witness has a lot to say. It will lead to brief, simple statements which can obscure the intricacies and nuances of the witness's evidence. In many cases, a short, sharp statement might suffice but it is just as good noting this down in whatever shorthand you can use and then transposing it as quickly as possible after that. If you have asked sensible questions, have noted things down properly and accurately, then you are likely to give a much better flavour of the witness and of the statement if you can dictate it subsequently and have it typed.[30] **2–21**

Extending the witness statement

If you are able to record the statement as above, then the extending of **2–22** the statement simply involves converting the notes into a coherent body of testimony. It should be done soon after the statement is taken. If you cannot type or dictate the statement shortly after (and that is undoubtedly best) then you can quickly try to check and edit your notes of the precognition so that it makes sense. Coming back to extend the precognition a few days, or even weeks, later increases the scope for fiction as you struggle to remember what the witness actually said. It should be in the witness's words so far as possible. If the witness has any particular pet phrases or sayings, or curious or unusual phrases or sayings which might be regarded as compelling and credible, then these should certainly be in the witness statement verbatim. In order to understand the witness statement, it might be necessary to put the words of explanation which I have suggested above where, for example, the witness is being asked specifically to explain something, or to justify something. In that way, the extended statement will reflect the fact that the point was very specifically put, may have been closely explored and cross-examined, and presumably can be relied upon with more than passing confidence.

Checking the precognition

You do not have to do it, but I think it is sensible to send the **2–23** precognition to the witness to check over and to confirm that it is

---

[28] *N.B.* He is going to be able to confirm that a call was made. Can he confirm what was actually said? The precognition would have to go on and deal with that, e.g. "He had said that these were just minor points and he could send us out touch-up paint if we settled the bill now." That is the kind of thing which could be regarded as having the legendary "ring of truth".

[29] I have had it done to me.

[30] *N.B.* Keep your handwritten notes. Apart from anything else, the witness might die and these notes might be evidence.

accurate. This can be an embarrassing process. The witness can often say that they did not say that, or they did not mean that, or this has all been made up, etc. The mere thought of a witness phoning you up to berate you about getting the statement wrong can often be enough to assure very high quality control in extending the statement, and prevents you from using any literary excesses which you might be tempted to throw in. When you are faced with complicated or technical information[31] you may be unclear about what was said, and what you recorded. What you may initially have thought was simple and obvious may not appear to be so when you are trying to remember what the witness actually said, describe it coherently in writing, and in such a way as others will be able to understand. If you find that problem arises, it is no admission of incompetence to go back to the witness before finalising the precognition and to ask them further questions. You can achieve the same end by sending your precognition (in draft), containing your version of what you think is a good description, but ask them to check it over because you may not have done them justice. Flattery does you no harm. It might make the witness feel important and make them even more determined to see that it is accurate. Signing the precognition is not necessary. It can put some witnesses off. "I am signing nothing until I see my lawyer. Why do you need me to sign it?" If it is signed[32] then that might just affect its evidential status. However, in normal practice in Scotland I think that most precognitions are unsigned, and there is rarely any pressing need to have them signed.

Evidential status of precognitions

2–24   In this chapter, I have used "precognition" and "statement" inter-changeably. The distinction between a precognition and a statement may be a little clearer in criminal proceedings.[33] In the case of statements made to the police by potential witnesses while the police are investigating a crime, the courts are less inclined to regard these as "precognitions", but the question still depends upon the precise circumstances in which they were taken and the nature of the statement in question.[34] A statement which appears to have "filtered through the mind of another person" might be regarded as precognition, and one which appears to be "pure and undefiled" might not.[35]

The distinction is not so easy to make in civil cases, and even more difficult to make in the light of recent developments in civil law. The

---

[31] e.g. what were all of those kitchen units called again? What exactly went wrong with the sliding larder unit?

[32] And especially if it is altered by the witness and then signed.

[33] See, e.g. *Kerr v HM Advocate*, 1958 S.L.T. 82; *Low v HM Advocate*, 1988 S.L.T. 97; *Hall v HM Advocate*, 1968 S.L.T. 275. "In my opinion, one should, in general, be very slow to confer on statements made to the police by potential witnesses the confidential status which attaches to precognitions in the proper sense of that word".

[34] "Broadly speaking, I think that there is an important distinction between statements made to the police in the course of their investigations before apprehension and statements taken after apprehension on the authority of the procurator-fiscal for the purposes of a trial. The latter are prima facie of the nature of precognitions, but that does not mean that the former may not also be precognitions. Whether they are or not seems to me to depend very much on the circumstances and on the nature of the particular statement."

[35] *Kerr v HM Advocate*, above; *Low v HM Advocate*, above.

principles are similar, but in civil cases the types of "statement" which have been considered by the courts are more varied than in criminal cases. The suggestion[36] that "everyone could recognise a precognition when they saw one" might have been a little optimistic. There are older civil cases which give some basic guidance in what is a precognition and what is not.[37]

It seems fairly clear that a "precognition", i.e. the written document called a precognition,[38] still has no evidential status. However, documents which might be regarded in some ways as similar to precognitions may have some evidential status. Statements made by a witness during the course of a precognition exercise may have some evidential status. The best way to try and explain the present position is to give an outline of the recent civil cases which have a bearing upon this. This section is intended to be no more than a summary and reference should be made to the cases themselves for further details.

The starting point for considering the issues which arise is the Civil **2–25** Evidence (Scotland) Act 1988.[39] Reading this shortly and paraphrasing it somewhat, the Act provides: (a) that a statement made prior to the proof is admissible as evidence of any matter contained in the statement[40]; (b) that a statement made prior to proof by a witness is admissible in so far as it reflects on the witnesses credibility[41]; and (c) that a "statement" referred to above includes any representation (however made) of fact or opinion, but does not include a "statement in a precognition".[42] It should be noted that ss.2 and 3 of the Act are distinct.

In essence, therefore, a prior statement by a party or a witness can itself be evidence in the case. Separately, a prior statement by a party or a witness can be used to support or attack the credibility of a witness. However, a "statement in a precognition"[43] cannot be used for either of these purposes—or can it? The cases which have considered these sections are as follows:

Highland Venison MKT Ltd v Allwild GmbH, 1992 S.C.L.R. 415

A solicitor interviewed a witness (who was deceased by the time of the **2–26** proof). The solicitor took notes and prepared a draft precognition for revisal by the witness. The witness sent back the revised precognition, which had been retyped to incorporate the revisals and had been signed by him. This document was lodged as a production and the solicitor's notes were also lodged as a production. The party led evidence about both of them. Objection was taken to both.

Lord Cullen was able to decide the case without reference to these matters, but he said obiter: (1) the evidence of the solicitor about what

---

[36] *McAvoy v City of Glasgow DC*, 1993 S.C.L.R. 393

[37] The most comprehensive summary can be found in *Moffat v Hunter*, 1974 S.L.T. (Sh. Ct) 42, but I think it is clear that the distinction has become fudged somewhat.

[38] The "extended" precognition, if you like.

[39] c.32.

[40] s.2(1)(b).

[41] s.3.

[42] s.9.

[43] In this context, I mean a statement in a document called a precognition.

she was "told" (supplemented and assisted by her notes) was admissible and it was for the court to decide what weight to attach to it; and (2) the document lodged would probably not have been regarded as a "precognition". The witness had altered and signed the original precognition and had, in effect, made it his own document and not someone else's record of what his evidence was.[44]

William Anderson v James B. Fraser & Co Ltd, 1992 S.C.L.R. 417

2–27   This was an accident claim in which, among other things, it was disputed that any accident had taken place at all. A witness for the pursuer corroborated him and it was alleged that this witness had told his employer, an insurance representative, and the defender's solicitor that he had not witnessed any accident. Evidence seems to have been heard from the employer and the insurers regarding what was said to them by the witness, but objection was taken to the evidence of the solicitor for the defender on the grounds, inter alia, that the solicitor had been taking a precognition at the time when he spoke to the witness.

Lord Morton said that the only reason to exclude a precognition as hearsay evidence in any case is that the precognition might be supposed to be an edited version of the witness's statement. His Lordship took the view that the actual document should be excluded, but that the oral evidence of what the witness actually said to the precognoscer should not be excluded. In other words, his Lordship interpreted a "statement in a precognition" as being the document comprising the precognition. His Lordship took the view that the solicitor's evidence of what was actually said, "for what it is worth", was admissible.

JF v Kennedy, 1992 S.C.L.R. 750

2–28   Objection was taken to the evidence of social workers regarding allegations of abuse made to them by children regarding a third party. The social workers had obtained certain information as a result of interviewing children as part of an investigation process to decide if the children required compulsory care. There was an argument that the statements given by the children to the social workers ought to be regarded as precognitions.

The Inner House of the Court of Session took the view that there was no adversarial litigation in existence at the time when the statements were taken and the purpose of the interviews was to determine whether grounds existed for concluding that the children were in need of compulsory measures of care. There was no reason to think that any document was ever prepared by a "precognoscer" containing what the precognoscer thought the child, or children, would say in evidence. The evidence of the statements of the children on interview was admissible.

---

[44] Similar reasoning can be found in *Rodger v C & J Contracts* [2005] CSOH 47, in which the court allowed evidence of a statement given by a witness to an insurance representative who had interviewed the witness some months after the accident. It was sent to the witness for checking and signature. The witness did not alter it at all and signed it on each page. The court considered it to be a "writing under his own hand" and admissible.

McAvoy v City of Glasgow District Council, 1993 S.C.L.R. 393

Attempts were made to lead evidence about what a deceased witness **2–29** had said about an accident. The evidence took two forms. First, there was the evidence of the solicitor who had interviewed the witness on three separate occasions in connection with the litigation. Secondly, the precognitions which were prepared on each of these occasions were lodged as productions. The solicitor gave evidence to the effect that he had used the witnesses own words so far as possible in the precognitions, and on at least one occasion he had dictated the precognition in the presence of the witness. Objection was taken, but it appears from the report that the objection was only taken to the precognitions themselves and not to the evidence of the solicitor speaking to what had been said at interview for the purposes of precognition.

His Lordship said that he formed the view that the solicitor had, in many instances distilled and translated the witness's own words. He was not being critical of the solicitor, but he regarded the precognition as "an account of what the witness said" and not what the witness actually did say. In that sense, they could truly be regarded as precognitions and the documents themselves were therefore inadmissible. They had not been "converted" into something other than a precognition.

Cavanagh v BP Chemicals Ltd, 1995 S.L.T. 1287

The evidence of a witness was challenged on cross-examination on the **2–30** basis that he had said something different at an interview with a solicitor, who was taking a precognition for one of the defenders. Objection was taken to that line of questioning but then, counsel having considered the four previous cases mentioned above, the objection was departed from. It does not appear that any attempt was made to lodge the precognition document, but that is not absolutely clear from the report.

Lord Clyde said that he did not require to rule on the question of the competency of the solicitor's evidence. In other words, it was conceded that it was admissible to put this to the witness and admissible to lead evidence from the solicitor about what was actually said in the course of the precognition exercise. His Lordship said that he only had to assess what weight to put on the evidence of the solicitor about what was said. His Lordship expressed some misgivings about that and said that without a precise record of what was asked and what was answered, whatever the witness said in conversation with the solicitor was of little weight compared with what he said on oath in the witness box.

Davies v McGuire, 1995 S.L.T. 755

This was an action for damages for the death of a boy who had been **2–31** run down and killed by a car driven by the defender. The defender attempted to lead evidence from a police officer about statements made to him by witnesses to the accident during the police officer's investigations. After the proof it was held, without reference to the statements made to the police officer, that the accident had been solely the fault of the boy.

Two distinct matters were considered. First, whether it was possible to lead evidence from the police officer to contradict evidence of witnesses, in advance of the witnesses actually giving their evidence. It was held that the witness must first give evidence in the case before proof of his previous statement becomes admissible. Secondly, how the court should treat the evidence of the witnesses contained in the police statement[45] as compared to the evidence given by the witnesses in the proof. It was considered that the court should proceed with extreme caution in applying the provisions of the 1988 Act in these circumstances. The court reached the view that the statements really had no impact upon the assessment of the credibility and reliability of the witnesses, nor on the facts of the case. They added nothing to the evidence given in court.[46]

Stevenson v Chief Constable of Strathclyde, 1998 Rep. L.R. 136

2–32   Witnesses were cross-examined about what was said at a precognition interview, and evidence was led from the precognoscers regarding this. The interview had been arranged with the witnesses specifically for the purpose of providing a precognition, but the precognition had been taken by two precognoscers. In this case, the issue of real significance on the evidence was not a matter of detail or a matter of interpretation, but it was whether the pursuer had been involved in an assault and robbery of which the two witnesses had already been convicted but the pursuer had been acquitted. This had significance in relation to the pursuer's credibility because he had denied categorically at the proof that he had been involved in the crime, and indeed he had been acquitted of it in criminal proceedings. The witnesses volunteered at the precognition exercise that the pursuer had taken part but they denied this rather diffidently at the proof. The precognoscers had written out in advance the precise wording of the questions they were going to ask at precognition and, so far as possible, they wrote down the answers verbatim. They were careful to record this accurately. Objection was taken to this evidence.

The sheriff understood the law to be that,

> "what a person said to a precognoscer at interview is admissible, provided that what is recorded at the interview proves to be an accurate and precise record of what was asked and what was answered. The Court is looking for an as near as may be verbatim account of what the person interviewed actually said at the time not a distillation or approximation of the words used".

In this case, he had already formed the view from the outset that both witnesses were unreliable and not prepared to tell the whole truth, so the point was not fully considered. However, he considered the documents

---

[45] Which was considered not to be a precognition because of the circumstances in which it was given.

[46] This can be compared and contrasted with the courts view of the police statement taken immediately after the accident in *Currie v Clamp's Exrs*, 2002 S.L.T. 196, whose evidential status was not discussed nor challenged. The court had no reason at all to suppose that what the police officer noted in his notebook, and spoke to at the proof, was inaccurate. Indeed, it was never suggested that the note was anything other than an accurate account of what the witness had told the police officer.

which had been lodged in process which were the "transcripts" of the interview (not precognitions as such) were sufficiently verbatim to be allowed in evidence.

Ellison v Inspirations East Ltd, 2003 S.L.T. 291

In an action of damages for injuries sustained in a coach crash in **2–33** Turkey, the defenders led evidence at proof from a solicitor who had taken a statement from the coach driver. The coach driver could not be traced and the solicitor had taken a statement from the bus driver shortly after the accident. She had subsequently interviewed him in Turkey where she used the services of an interpreter. The pursuer disputed the admissibility of the solicitor's evidence as her notes were not a "statement" for the purposes of the 1988 Act, and that she had required to work through an interpreter. It was, however, conceded by the pursuer that the solicitor's notes were not a precognition "in the traditional form".

The objection was repelled on the assumption that the witness was speaking to an interview and her notes reflected the answers to questions which she was putting to the witness. The court could see no justifiable reason for excluding the evidence on the basis that it was anything other than a statement made by the driver to the solicitor for the insurers. The evidence was admissible, but the court said that the real issue was the weight to be attached to the evidence contained in the notes. The court clearly derived little assistance from it and placed little weight upon it.

The court also took the view that to exclude the statement because the services of an interpreter were employed would be contrary to public policy and would discriminate against people whose first language was not English.

Rodger v C & J Contracts [2005] CSOH 47

A statement taken by an insurance representative within months of an **2–34** accident had been prepared and sent to the witness, who signed it on each page and returned it to the insurers. The judge considered that it was admissible as evidence even though it had not been lodged as a production at the required time.[47] His Lordship thought that it could legitimately be used to test the credibility of the witness by virtue of s.3 of the 1988 Act, and he also thought that it would constitute admissible hearsay by virtue of s.2. His Lordship did not consider that there was any legal basis on which he was obliged to leave it out of account.

Conclusions

1. It would be dangerous to encourage the use of statements/ **2–35** precognitions as a means of catching out witnesses or setting up witnesses—the courts would most certainly discourage this, and anything which suggested there had been any unfairness, deception or persuasion would be frowned upon.
2. The precise circumstances in which the "statement" was given would have to be considered—and evidence led about this

---

[47] It appears to have been lodged well into the proof.

before consideration would be given to whether the evidence
about the content of the statement was admissible or not.

3. A written record of what was actually said would not be
   considered to be a "statement in a precognition" and therefore
   would be admissible.

4. The actual notes of the person conducting the interview might
   well be admissible if they are simply an aide-memoir to remind
   the person of what was said. Whether the words in the notes
   were the words of the witness or the words of the precognoscer
   is a moot point. One way to cover this might be for the person
   taking the statement/precognition to put the verbatim account
   (words, or phrases) of the witness in inverted commas when
   note-taking.

5. Even where a statement might be admissible, the important
   question is what weight should be attached to it. The cases
   suggest that, only in the most particular circumstances would
   the court attach significance to the details of what was contained in such a statement.

6. In civil cases, statements made by a witness to the police soon
   after an accident or incident will not be regarded as precognitions. They will usually be regarded as admissible. It may well
   be assumed that the written notes of the statement are accurate
   and reliable. They can, however, be challenged on both
   admissibility and content in appropriate circumstances.

Now look at the precognitions in Appendices 1 and 2. They both say
basically the same thing. One is very short, and one is very long. It might
be said that the detail is not required when you are first considering the
case on initial instructions. The position of the witness is clear enough. It
might also be said that the time involved in taking the longer one is not
justified unless and until there is actually going to be a proof and you
need to know the detail of the evidence of this witness. Which one would
you rather have to enable you to understand the strengths and weaknesses of the case and advise on the prospects of a good claim/defence?
Which one would enable you to prepare fully for a proof? Do not forget,
however, that, in the final analysis, neither of them would be of any
benefit, and could be positively detrimental, if they are not an accurate
representation of what this witness is going to say when examined in
court.

CHAPTER 3

WRITTEN PLEADINGS

"It is believed and averred further that, separatim, esto the aforesaid obligations which are held to be repeated herein brevitatis causa were owed by the defender as hereinbefore condescended upon (which is denied) the defender duly complied with said obligations as condescended upon by the defenders in Answer 4 which are adopted and repeated herein mutatis mutandis, insofar as consistent herewith."

After taking instructions from a client and investigating the circum- **3–01** stances of his case, you will usually try to resolve the dispute and settle the case. If you cannot do so, and the only reasonable option is to proceed to litigation, you will have to start thinking about drafting your written pleadings. In fact, most litigators will already have given considerable thought to the pleadings long before the time comes to draft them. Having a clear idea of the essential facts of your case, the precise legal basis of your claim or defence, and the areas of contention between you and the opponent are crucial to a proper understanding of the nature of the dispute. Formulating these ideas in writing can often help to focus your mind on the strengths and weaknesses of your position. The exercise itself can help in your understanding of your own case and highlight fundamental problems which you may not have fully appreciated. It would be foolish indeed if your first thought about the content of your written pleadings occurred just when you proceeded to draft them.

The terms of your pleadings are an extremely important part of your presentation of the case to the court, and this "written advocacy" is the cornerstone of our civil procedures.[1] The pleadings often reflect the quality of your advocacy. If you have set out the essentials of your case clearly, logically, and simply in your pleadings, it is likely that you have investigated it well, analysed it intelligently and carefully, and have given it sufficient thought to enable you to present it well at any hearing. Having a succinct written document which summarises the essence of the case and the defence is helpful to all concerned in any litigation. When you are starting off in litigation, the "record" can be a strange and challenging document. Once you have a little experience, it is the first thing you would look for, and rely upon, in trying to understand the real essence of the dispute.

The role of written pleadings in our civil litigation system has been undergoing revision in recent years. Problems have arisen because of an

---

[1] Despite recent developments which have restricted its significance in some ways, about which I will be saying more later in the chapter.

overemphasis on the form of the pleadings and an undue concentration on the technicality of "rules" of written pleadings. This can lead to a considerable amount of time and effort—not to mention expense— apparently being spent on "getting the words right", rather than on ensuring that each party to a litigation has a reasonable idea of their opponent's position on facts and law before any hearing of the case takes place. There are two broad bodies of opinion about written pleadings among lawyers. At one extreme there are those who will regard the precise wording and form of pleadings as absolutely critical, and at the other, those who regard them as technical obstacles to be largely ignored. Some lawyers would be salivating at the prospect of analysing and criticising the quotation at the start of this chapter. Some would simply scoff at the legal gobbledygook. In practice, it is necessary to keep a balanced view, and not be misled by the extremists.

    (a) From the pursuer's perspective, your pleadings should give the court and your opponent reasonable notice of the facts which justify your case and upon which you would be proposing to lead evidence at proof, together with an outline of the legal propositions which justify the remedy which you are seeking from the court.

    (b) From the defender's perspective, the pleadings should respond by detailing what facts are in dispute, what additional facts are of importance to the defenders, whether the legal propositions are disputed, and whether there are any other legal propositions which do not justify the remedy sought.

It is not too difficult to explain the requirements in this way. It is the practical application of these principles which causes all of the problems.

3–02   The pleadings should comprise a summary of the case. This is not as easy as it sounds. There are considerable skills involved in doing this. If you can plead a case concisely and logically you can influence the course of the proceedings and the outcome of the action. Pleading a case clearly and accurately, anticipating any possible defences and making the formulation of the case fit your view of its merits and of the evidence available to you, might persuade a defender of the strength of your argument and the weakness of their position before the litigation has gone very far. Making a dog's dinner of pleading your case, might be a powerful factor in persuading your opponent to adhere to a claim or a defence, even one of doubtful merit. One look at your pleadings might suggest to your opponent that you plainly have no idea what you have to do to establish your case or your defence. Your opponent might be encouraged to maintain a position which might have been exposed as largely untenable, if the pleadings had been well prepared. Many cases in the sheriff court go to proof or, at least, do not settle until very close to the proof, because one side simply has not grasped and expressed in writing what the case is really about, and the other side does not fully understand it and/or feel that they might just win by default.

    Bad pleading makes good advocacy much more difficult. In the sheriff court, the standard of written pleadings is extremely variable. Frankly, in many cases it does not matter very much, but in some instances the failure to understand and observe some very fundamental rules can lead to unnecessary problems in advancing the case to a hearing, or in ensuring that the hearing can cover all of the relevant issues between the parties. When understood and applied properly, the basic rules of written pleadings should make it easier for you and the court to reach a decision about your case or the way in which it should be dealt with by the court. In that sense, pleadings can be a direct and powerful element of good advocacy.

This chapter will try to look at written pleadings in practice and give some basic guidance on the process of drafting them. I shall not explore the technical issues or "rules" too closely. I shall explore the process of drafting pleadings, and I intend to provide a more strategic view of the function of pleadings. For the more precise details and the authorities on some of the "pleadings points" reference should be made to books on written pleadings and styles of written pleadings.[2] In my opinion, the chapter on written pleadings in Macphail contains the most comprehensive and helpful analysis of the technical rules of pleading you could possibly want. There is no benefit in repeating them in a shortened version here.[3] Pleadings perform a very significant function in many litigations and a failure to plead a case properly often demonstrates an underlying failure to appreciate the important facts and legal principles involved.[4] The problem is that, over the years, pleadings have been regarded as an art form in themselves, and have assumed a significance in the minds of some litigators which they do not necessarily merit.

An overview

The starting point for any sensible and practical guidance about written pleadings can be taken from two recent sources. **3–03**

In *ERDC Construction Ltd v HM Love & Co*,[5] Lord Prosser said:

> "Whatever machinery is used for the resolution of a dispute, there is likely to be some place for both written and oral material. A requirement that each party should formulate its position in writing at the outset has fundamental advantages, not only as a means of giving fair notice to the other side and helping to focus and cut down the issues in dispute, but also, and fundamentally, as an encouragement to each party to analyse the substance of the case, before trying to give it expression in writing. In my opinion, if a high quality of written formulation can be achieved at the outset, much expensive and time consuming oral procedure can often be avoided. I would not therefore wish to say anything which might be interpreted as denying the importance of written formulation, or encouraging recourse to oral evidence or submissions without such a written foundation. . . . That said, I am quite satisfied that pleadings of the type currently used in ordinary court procedure are fre-

---

[2] I.D. Macphail, *Sheriff Court Practice* (3rd edn, W. Green/Scottish Universities Law Institute, 2006). See also *Greens Litigation Styles*.

[3] Some of the more common "pleading" issues are dealt with briefly in Charles Hennessy, *Civil Procedure and Practice* (2nd edn, W. Green, Edinburgh, 2005), Ch.3.

[4] For further discussion of this see Hennessy, above, Ch.3.

[5] 1997 S.L.T. 175.

quently, and indeed normally, ill suited to their true function, failing to put essentials in sharp focus, and often putting in sharp focus inessential matters of detail, which then become the subject of pointless procedural scrutiny."

3–04 In the Report of the Working Group under the Chairmanship of Lord Coulsfield on personal injury cases,[6] the group noted:

"The object of a written pleading system is to require each party to set out his case clearly in such a way as to enable the other side to have a fair chance to meet it. The advantages claimed for the system are that it should enable evidence to be concentrated on the points which are truly in issue and should also enable the court and the parties to avoid the expense of making enquiries into, and leading evidence about, matters which either have no connection with the real issue or which, even if established, cannot lead to any legal consequence. That statement of the advantages, however, also highlights the problems to which undue reliance on elaborate written pleading may give rise ... A glance at the historical background enables one to identify some of the ways in which the difficulty has been created or increased and, in particular, why written pleadings have demonstrated a tendency to expand, whatever the general rules are supposed to be. Four factors can be identified.

(1) The demand for 'fair notice' has a tendency, which it is difficult to control, to expand the averments thought necessary beyond the facts to be proved, so as to bring in evidence used to prove them.

(2) There is a corresponding anxiety on the part of the pleader not to risk being excluded from leading essential evidence.

(3) The risk remains that a judge looking at the pleadings may be disposed to take a view about matters of probability which will influence his decision, even if that is not made blatant as it was in some of the earlier cases.

(4) In any case, written pleading is part of the pleading in the case, and a set of pleadings which look comprehensive and convincing may play a part in influencing the views of the judge or the conduct of the opposing party. Such well drawn pleading can be extremely valuable when the court has to discuss, for example, procedural matters."

Whenever one looks at detailed criticism of the terms of written pleadings in any case, these passages should be borne in mind, and the higher objective of the whole system of written pleadings in Scotland should be emphasised. For example, a complaint by a defender that an injured employee has not specified in his pleadings the type of ladder he was climbing at the time of his accident, may be justified if there were numerous different types of ladder available and the defender had no

---

[6] Available at *www.scotcourts.gov.uk/session/injuries/index.asp*.

way of knowing which one it was, but not if the defender is said to have issued him with it. A failure to aver the date of the acceptance of an offer by a defender might be of real importance in a case if there is an argument that the claim is time-barred, but might be purely incidental and quite unimportant (and may be within the knowledge of the other party) otherwise. As most people will appreciate, commercial causes in the Court of Session and the sheriff court, and personal injury actions in the Court of Session, have made some inroads into the requirement for precisely detailed and technically formal pleadings. There is a considerable paradox in the field of personal injury litigation between an action in the Court of Session which must only have extremely abbreviated pleadings, and the same action in the sheriff court whose pleadings will have to be formal and technical and may well be subjected to minute criticism.[7] It is not unlikely, in my opinion, that the formalities will relax to some extent in future years. I am not making this assumption in this chapter, but an appreciation of these likely developments will assist in reminding you, your opponent, and the court of the true purpose of our system of written pleadings. The system is admirable and invaluable if it is fairly, properly and sensibly operated on both sides of a dispute.

Basic requirements for pleadings

The writ and defences will be in a standard format as provided by the **3–05** Rules of Court. The Rules actually prescribe relatively little as to what the pleadings must say in individual cases.[8]

Putting it crudely, pleadings of a pursuer should be sufficient if they:

1. State all of the important facts.
2. Give sufficient information to allow the opponent to carry out enquiries (if they want) to see if the facts are true.
3. Give an outline of the legal principles which provide you with a remedy in your case.
4. (In claims for money) tell them how much you want, why you are entitled to claim this, and broadly how you calculate it.

Pleadings of a defender should be sufficient if they:

1. State the defender's response to all of the important facts which are within their knowledge.
2. Indicate what facts are in dispute.
3. State whether the legal principles in support of the claim are disputed and/or whether there are any other legal issues which might amount to a defence to the claim.
4. (In claims for money) make it clear what is accepted as a legitimate claim and what is disputed—and why any such claim is disputed.

---

[7] In this context, it should be noted that Glasgow Sheriff Court has recently introduced a pilot scheme for personal injury cases which is likely to adopt the more relaxed approach of the Court of Session.

[8] For detail, see *Hennessy*, above, Ch.3.

3–06 The system depends upon parties abiding by some fundamental rules of practice. Abuses of the system often involve breaches of these rules.

1. You should only plead facts where you have evidence to support those facts.
2. You should act with candour and honesty in drafting your pleadings, even if this will be against your interest.
3. You cannot, and should not, draft pleadings just because this will help your case, if you do not know or do not honestly believe that you have evidence to support what you are going to say.
4. It is always open to a party to put an opponent to proof of what they aver, but if the party knows that certain facts averred by the opponent are indeed true then they must admit them.
5. If they *suspect* that they are true but do not know it, then they do not need to admit them.

Some people are not very good at pleading. Some are excellent. Experience is obviously of considerable help, and, regrettably, some of the best experience comes from being on the wrong side of a pleading argument at a proof or debate, when the case appears to be going down the toilet and your whole legal career is following closely behind. I find that many new litigators can be hamstrung by the worry that drafting pleadings is a very mysterious skill which requires special knowledge, language and expertise. The more experienced you are, the more you appreciate that simple everyday words, short and simple sentences, and simple legal propositions work best. In the infuriating words of many exponents and teachers, you just have to tell a story. Unfortunately, the skills of doing so are not really taught very well before you are first unleashed on a real action. Let us introduce matters gently with an example.

Initial writ: An example

3–07   *"On March 23, 2003, a woman drank a bottle of ginger beer in which were the partially decomposed remains of a snail.*

She now seeks damages from the manufacturer of the ginger beer who ought to have known about its contents and ought to have appreciated she would have been upset by the experience.

She has been terribly unwell since. A medical report from her doctor is attached."

If you saw a sheriff court initial writ consisting of one single page which just said those words, what would be wrong with it? You might be surprised at how little. Of course, it would not comply with the basic requirements for a writ as set out in the Ordinary Cause Rules 1993, but if you actually look at the rules and Form G1, you will find that the basic requirements are very basic indeed.

1. You have to say what court you are raising the action in—"the heading".
2. You have to give the name and address of the woman and the name and address of the manufacturer—"the instance".

3. You are required to state the specific decree sought, i.e. what damages she is seeking—"the crave".
4. You have to say why the court has jurisdiction to deal with the case—"the grounds of jurisdiction".

Once you have complied with these requirements, all you need to do is insert the "condescendence". What is the condescendence? It is simply the written expression of your particular case.[9] The requirement is that it should be set out in numbered paragraphs and should contain the facts which form the grounds of action. No further direction is given. You can put as many numbered paragraphs into the writ, or as few, as you like. It can be as short, or as long, as you want.

Finally, you are required to state your "pleas in law". What are these? They are the expressions of the legal basis or bases for the claim.[10] They should be stated in numbered sentences. Normally each distinct legal proposition applicable to the facts averred should have its own sentence.[11]

Once you have done all of this, you will have converted the story into a writ. Indeed, the condescendence and pleas in law could competently be expressed thus:

"Condescendence

1. On March 23, 2003, the pursuer drank ginger beer in which were the **3–08**
partially decomposed remains of a snail.

2. The defenders, who are the manufacturers of the ginger beer, ought to have known about its contents and ought to have appreciated she would have been upset by the experience.

3. The pursuer has been terribly unwell since. A medical report from her doctor [named] is attached.

Pleas in law

1. The pursuer's injury has been caused by the fault of the defenders." **3–09**

On one view, that would be perfectly acceptable and sufficient to meet the requirements of the rules, but a writ would never be expressed as briefly as that. Some might say that it should be, but this simple approach has its own drawbacks. Not least of these might be the fundamental issue that, for example, the defenders may manufacture the ginger beer in their factory in Perth, but it is bottled by contractors in Edinburgh. Alternatively, that she had actually poured the ginger beer from the bottle into a glass in her own home, etc. The simplicity of the expression of the case might then be seen as obscuring major and

---

[9] The "condescendence" is the general name given to your statement of claim. Strictly speaking, the numbered paragraphs are "articles of the condescendence" but are often just called "condescendences".

[10] An excellent and recent explanation of the function of pleas in law can be found in *A Kelly Ltd v Capital Bank Plc*, 2004 S.L.T. 483.

[11] With one or two minor exceptions, you are not obliged by the rules to put anything else in your writ.

fundamental problems with the claim. Worries about missing out essential features of a case, which, in turn, means you may not be able to lead evidence about them if the case goes to proof, sometimes encourage litigators to say far more than is absolutely necessary to express the essentials. The length and complexity of a writ can then obscure the real issues just as badly as its brevity and simplicity might have done. Theory and principle are important for understanding the proper drafting of pleadings, but I am going to concentrate now on the practicalities of doing so.

Drafting a writ

Preliminaries

3–10   Let us take this a little further, now, by considering the drafting of a writ for Parker Kitchen Designs against Mr and Mrs Gray. Assume that you have been given a statement from the owner of Parker Kitchen Designs which explains briefly the problem with the Grays. You have also been given the sales invoice and original quotation, along with other contract documents. You have also been given copies of the correspondence which sets out some of the reasons why the Grays are not willing to pay. You have been asked to raise proceedings. What could/should you think about?

You are required to raise proceedings as quickly as you reasonably can. You have not been requested to submit an entry for the Nobel Prize for Literature. Under no circumstances would I suggest that the precise terms of the writ are unimportant. You should take your time and take care to apply your mind fully to them. Realistically, however, this is not going to be the beginning of a long journey into the dark underbelly of the kitchen design business.

A style writ requiring little more than filling in the blanks might well suffice to obtain a warrant and effect service of the proceedings on the defenders, but it will be appreciated that there is little point in dwelling on this kind of written pleading here. You may find that your firm has a style of writ for this very thing. It is an action of payment. It is a fairly standard set of circumstances. Even if there is no style as such within the office, it should not be too difficult to find one in the books.[12] There is a danger in relying too heavily on styles however. If you do not try to understand why the style says a particular thing, or is set out in a particular way, you will never be able to appreciate the skills involved in doing this properly. You will have difficulty in transferring any skill that copying a style might give you to the drafting of a writ in which the circumstances are more complex or unique.

It is important to have a framework or skeleton idea in your mind of how the writ would be set out. You can take this confidently from a style, even if you can take little else. Your framework will have:

1. a heading;
2. an instance;

---

[12] See, e.g. *Greens Litigation Styles*.

3. a crave for payment of a sum of money;
4. articles of condescendence, including grounds of jurisdiction; and
5. a plea(s) in law.

The articles of condescendence will probably comprise: **3–11**

> Article 1—Parties, designations, and jurisdiction.
> Article 2—The agreement to supply and fit the kitchen; the price; the implementation of the contract by the pursuers; the partial payment by the defenders; the legal obligation on the defenders to pay for the job in full; the balance remaining due.
> Article 3—The request for payment and the delay/refusal to make payment.

The pleas in law will probably be something like:

> *"1. The pursuers, having supplied goods and services to the defender as contracted for, are entitled to payment for them.*
> *2. The sum sued for being the remaining balance of the contract price, decree therefor should be granted as craved."*

I am not suggesting that you write this type of skeleton out in each case, or indeed in any case, although in complex actions it will undoubtedly assist you to do so.[13] It would be sufficient if you simply thought out in advance the type of things that you need to say and the structure in which you intend to place them. It may be unnecessary in a simple action in which you could quite profitably copy a standard style almost to the exact words. Be aware, however, that if you get into the habit of copying a style without thinking why the style works, you may not be able to recognise the cases in which some real independent thought is necessary. Many people find that the easiest way to approach drafting of written pleadings is to do a rough draft and then edit it until it is satisfactory. Others might prefer to do all of the editing before committing anything to paper. It is a matter of personal preference. In more complex writs it is highly desirable to do a written draft and edit it. Draft it on the basis that you expect that you are going to have to edit it critically. Try to think of the writ (and the pleadings generally) as the only document that anyone will ever see about the case so that it alone contains the essence of the case. Try to make yourself forget what you know about the background of the case and read your draft objectively to see if it (and it alone) says what you want it to say.

First draft

Without further ado, let us look at a draft of pleadings for this action **3–12** and concentrate on the averments in Article 2 of condescendence, which has been outlined above.

---

[13] Sometimes it is quite helpful to start by thinking what your pleas in law are going to say. This gives a focus for the rest of the writ—even though they come last in the writ itself.

"On or about April 3, 2004, the pursuer provided the defenders with a quote for the design, supply and fitting of a fitted kitchen at the defenders' house at the address stated in the instance. The pursuers are specialists in the supply and fitting of continental manufactured kitchens. It is averred that they had never dealt with the defenders before. The pursuer's employee Mrs Anna Stewart had attended at the defenders said house to carry out the design and had agreed the design with them both before submitting a price to them in writing as hereinbefore condescended upon. The quotation was for the sum of £10,500 plus VAT, making a total of £12,337.50, and a copy of the said quotation which the said pursuers provided to the said defenders will be lodged. The specification of the finish of the kitchen had to be altered because the manufacturers had stopped doing this particular type of kitchen and the said Mrs Anna Stewart advised the said Mrs Gray by telephone on or about the end of May 2004 that she could supply a similar type of finish to that which she had quoted originally, following which she sent out a sample of the finish to her and Mrs Gray indicated that she was satisfied with it. On or about May 30, 2004 the defenders wrote to the pursuer having considered the said quotation and accepted said quotation thus indicating that they were agreeable to the alteration and to the price remaining as before. Said letter will be produced in the process to follow hereon. Although it was just signed by Mr Gray it is believed that it was done so on behalf of both of them. On June 6, 2004 the defenders paid a deposit of £5,000 by cheque. The pursuer sometimes sub contracts the fitting of kitchens to other contractors but, in this case, they had the work carried out and supervised by their own staff. It is averred that the kitchen was fitted by employees of the pursuer between November 10 and 12, 2004. The pursuer invoiced the defenders for the balance of the price. The defenders have not paid same."

Editing thoughts

3–13   To what extent do you think that this has:

1. stated your position simply and clearly;
2. put you in a position in which you can lead particular evidence from particular witnesses;
3. influenced the reader, the judge and the opponent;
4. focused the issues;
5. drawn in the opponent to the process by saying things to which the opponent (according to the "rules") has to reply; and
6. given "fair notice" of the matters on which you are proposing to rely at any proof?

More editing thoughts

3–14   1. Read it on its own, discarding your knowledge of the background. If you had nothing else to go on but the writ, does it make sense?
   2. Read it as if you were writing it for a reasonably intelligent 12-year-old whose only knowledge of the case will be the writ. Would he or she understand basically what all the fuss was

about and would he or she be able to explain it to someone else?

3. Remember, it is a summary, not a novel. Do not have too many articles of condescendence. Most styles and examples of pleadings will have relatively few articles of condescendence. There is no limit to the number of articles but fewer articles usually suggest a more focused writ.[14]

4. Paradoxically, if there is background information which you feel you must state in order to make the nature of the dispute intelligible, you might want to do a separate article(s) of condescendence dealing solely with this. You may be able to draft that article in such a way that it contains a succession of simple, explanatory facts which may well be admitted by the defender. That may enable you to go on to your averments of the accident or the critical events without diversionary descriptions. It is just another way of using the structure of the writ to focus the issues.

5. You should try to put your factual averments in strict chronological order. It will be so much easier to understand the "story" if you do.

6. You have an idea of what the defence is likely to be. Do you want to anticipate this by emphasising some facts of the case and making your pleadings particularly clear on them? Alternatively, do you want to leave it for the defender to explain their position before you say anything specific in your writ? That is a matter of judgment. The answer may vary with the circumstances of each individual case. In this case, there is a whole long sentence regarding the "variation" of the contract. You might want to ascertain if the defender thinks that this alters the contractual position materially, so you put in an averment about it, which will, hopefully, draw out the defender's response.

7. Use simple sentences.

8. Use short sentences.

9. Do not plead evidence.

10. You should only plead facts that are relevant. Sometimes it helps to aver background facts by way of explanation, simply to allow the pleadings to be "read" more easily. That is a matter of judgement but you can overdo the explanations if you are not careful.

11. Try to ensure that each article of condescendence contains a distinct chapter of information and/or a distinct legal basis for the claim.

12. Use plain English. Sometimes Latin phrases are the best way of expressing certain ideas in the pleadings, but most of them have English equivalents and you ought to try and use those.[15]

13. Do not repeat things.

---

[14] In my experience, excessive numbers of articles of condescendence in a writ usually suggest a party litigant.

[15] This is the point at which the traditionalists will start calling for my head.

14. Do not say "the said" unless absolutely necessary to understand the proper meaning of the words.
15. Do not say "It is averred that". These are your "averments". Therefore all of your pleadings are by definition "averred".
16. Try to use precise language where it is justified. Sometimes you have to be circumspect,[16] but get into the habit of precision unless there is a good reason for being vague
17. When referring to documents and wanting to have the words of the documents read as part of your pleadings, the most satisfactory way is to quote the particular passage of the document which is important, provided it is relatively short, and to refer to the whole document for the sake of brevity. The precise formula for this is mentioned in various cases,[17] but it is difficult to justify ignoring a document which has been lodged because the magic words of the formula have not been used.

Final version

3–15   Let us now go back and do some alterations:

> *"On April 3, 2004, the pursuer provided the defenders with a quote for the design, supply and fitting of a fitted kitchen at the defenders' house. The quotation was for the sum of £10,500 plus VAT, making a total of £12,337.50. A copy of the quotation is referred to for its terms, will be lodged in the process to follow hereon, and is to be treated as repeated herein for the sake of brevity. By letter of May 30, 2004 the defenders accepted the quotation. Said letter will be produced in the process to follow hereon. On June 6, 2004 the defenders paid a deposit of £5,000 by cheque. The parties subsequently agreed an alteration to the specification for the kitchen units, at the same contract price. The kitchen was fitted by employees of the pursuer between November 10 and 12, 2004. The pursuer invoiced the defenders for the balance of the price. The defenders have not paid same."*

It can be suggested that there was absolutely nothing wrong with the first version, in the sense that it would undoubtedly have been sufficient for you to obtain a warrant on the writ. Indeed, the original pleadings could never be said to have been "wrong". You will find that the editing has simplified the writ quite considerably. Indeed it could be argued that the final version is no more than a simple, standard, action for payment which could easily have been drafted off the top of your head. However, you should reflect upon the thought process which took you to the final version. Decisions have been made about leaving things in, taking things out, simplifying the wording, re-organising the order, etc. In some cases, these features might not be critical. In a more complex set of circumstances, they could be. In a sense, you have made the case "simple",

---

[16] e.g. when the evidence of a particular matter is not very clear.
[17] See *Eadie Cairns v Programmed Maintenance Painting*, 1987 S.L.T. 777, *Steelmek Marine and General Engineers' Trust v Shetland Sea Farms Ltd*, 1999 S.L.T. (Sh. Ct) 30 and *Royal Bank of Scotland Plc v Holmes*, 1999 S.L.T. 563.

whereas the earlier version introduced some unnecessary complexities which might have meant the written pleadings would have developed in a different way. You have also taken a strategic decision[18] which will influence the way in which the pleadings are likely to develop. You know that the defenders are going to say something about price and about workmanship. You can leave this to their defences. During the adjustment period you will respond to the defences at the end of your article of condescendence, if necessary, but, in doing so you will still be left with the beautiful simplicity of the basic case, namely:

> *"We had a contract. We had a price. You paid a deposit. We agreed a small variation in the contract. We did the work. You owe us the balance."*

The first thing that the sheriff will read in the pleadings will be that. It is clear and concise. You have set the agenda, and it is the defender who is going to complicate matters by saying other things in their defences. Now this might not seem particularly earth-shattering in the context of this particular action, but the principles which I am trying to illustrate are of universal application and will undoubtedly produce a benefit when pleading more complex disputes.

Defences

Assume now that you have been instructed by the defenders in this **3–16** case and you have the final version of the writ and instructions to lodge defences to it, along the lines previously discussed. How should you go about this?

If you do not have clear instructions,[19] or if you do not have time, or if you do not know exactly what you want to do, you could always lodge skeleton defences. I will not give any guidance as to how these should be drafted. Experience demonstrates that an expertise in doing so can be acquired rather easily. Skeleton defences do expose you to the possibility of a motion for summary decree,[20] but it is fair to say that if your choice is between lodging no defences, for the reasons given above, and lodging skeleton defences, the latter is to be preferred. I think it is appropriate and reasonable to intimate such defences with a letter explaining that you will be expanding on these "shortly" and perhaps even explaining why you are unable to lodge detailed defences. In this case, we shall assume that you have sufficient instructions to enable you to lodge full defences (if, indeed, you choose to do so).

Drafting defences

You might find it useful to do a rough draft of the defences and edit **3–17** it. In fact, it is particularly helpful to work in this way, because it is sometimes necessary to "juggle" the form of your defences to make them coherent and logical. The best approach is:

---

[18] Although you may not have noticed it.
[19] See Ch.1.
[20] Although this does not happen as often as it should.

1. Read the writ sentence by sentence, and note your response to the content of each individual sentence.
2. Admit the facts in the sentences that you want or need to admit, based on your instructions. Remember that if there are averments about matters which are or should be within your (client's) knowledge you should be admitting or denying them. If you do not deny such averments, then you will be deemed to have admitted them.[21]
3. If there are averments about which you have no knowledge or information then you would respond to this by saying "Not known and not admitted that".
4. If you have no knowledge of a fact averred but it does not seem to you to be particularly material, you can say "Believed to be true that" although that formula should be used cautiously and is not recommended.
5. Finally, note what sentences are denied.
6. Once you have done this exercise, go back and group together all of the admissions, then all of the "not known and not admitted" and then all of the denials. Rearrange your answers so that they fit into that order, i.e. all of the admissions first, and so on.
7. You will find that, once you have the admissions, and the "not known and not admitted" out of the way, everything else is, inevitably denied, and it is normal then just to say "*Quoad ultra*[22] denied", which covers you if you have missed out something.
8. A formula which is also used in relation to denials is "*Quoad ultra* denied, except in so far as consistent or coinciding herewith*", which means usually that there are some averments which are ambiguous or unclear, and you are about to give your "explanation" or substantive defence which may demonstrate that some of these averments or, at least, some parts of them, are not really denied.
9. Then go on to insert your own substantive averments, in other words, your "story". You would start this by saying, "It is explained that" and then making your own averments.
10. Some people have a practice of making admissions of facts and then qualifying those admissions by adding "under explanation that". I do not recommend that. Apart from anything else it breaks up the structure of your defences and it can cause some confusion.

3–18 What does this mean for the defences to the final writ mentioned above? Here is how you might have started:

> "*Admitted that the pursuer provided the defenders with a quote for a fitted kitchen on April 3, 2004. Admitted the quote was for a total price, including VAT of £12,337.50. Admitted that the defenders*

---

[21] Ordinary Cause Rules 1993, r.9.7.
[22] "As for the rest of the averments".

*accepted that quote by letter of May 30, 2004. Admitted that they paid
the pursuer £5,000 by cheque on June 6, 2004. Admitted that the
pursuer advised the defenders of an alteration to the specification of
the units. Admitted that the kitchen was fitted from November 10 to
12, 2004. Admitted that the pursuer invoiced the defenders. Admitted
that the defenders have not paid that invoice.* Quoad ultra *denied. It is
explained that".*

- In this case, most, if not all of the material facts are known to
  the defenders. That is not unusual in a contract dispute.
  Accordingly, there is no "Not known and not admitted".
- Technically, it could be suggested that the admissions ought to
  repeat the exact words of the averments, but they admit the
  critical parts of them and that would suffice in these circumstances to indicate that the sentence is not disputed. Contrast
  this with the admission, "Admitted the pursuer invoiced the
  defenders." That omits to admit the part of the averment which
  says the invoice was for the "balance of the price". Of course,
  that is one of the points at issue in the case as the defences will
  go on to demonstrate.
- Could it be argued that the admission about the invoice could
  be read as an admission about the true balance of the price?
  This is an example of the "technical" approach to pleadings
  which can cause some people concern. The defences will go on
  to make it absolutely clear that the contract price is in dispute.
  The original dealings (quotation and acceptance) are not. The
  pleadings do not require to be subjected to the minute scrutiny
  of a conveyancing document. If you look at the defences as a
  whole is there going to be any doubt about what is or is not at
  issue?
- There might have been a temptation to say, "Admitted the
  pursuer invoiced the defenders *under explanation that this was
  not for the agreed contract price*" but there is no need to do so.
  The point about the contract price will emerge in a coherent
  way in the explanation in the defences and there is no benefit in
  introducing an explanation, or partial explanation, here.
- You may have noted that the fact that the writ is drafted in
  short, clear sentences has meant that the defences[23] are obliged
  to follow them. This dictates, to some extent, the development
  of the pleadings.
- Imagine that the writ had simply been left in its first draft form.
  Look at its terms. Imagine you had to do defences, following
  the same approach mentioned above. There are some averments which would have been difficult to answer with clarity.
  Your defences would have been longer and perhaps more
  obscure. You might have been well advised to deny certain
  things because of the uncertainty of the terminology used. This
  might all have led to the defences being unfocused too, and this

---

[23] If properly drafted.

will give you some insight into the problems that poor pleadings can cause. A rambling writ, with long and ambiguous defences, followed by mutually irrelevant adjustments might well produce the type of record which has everyone scratching their heads trying to find what is really in dispute and why.

3–19 Let us now go on to look at the rest of the defences. We are coming to the part of the pleadings where the defenders are telling their "story". The same rules and practices are recommended for that. Short, simple sentences, explaining their side of the argument in a logical sequence would be the best way of proceeding.

> "*It is explained that on or about the May 15, 2004, Mrs Anne Stewart, an employee of the pursuer, telephoned the second defender. She advised that the pursuer was willing to offer a discount of 10 per cent on the price quoted, on condition that the quote was accepted by the end of the month. The defenders agreed to this and wrote to the pursuer to accept the amended quotation on May 30, 2004. The quote provided that the kitchen units and doors were to be of 'Nobilia Vienna', light beech wood. The pursuer subsequently advised the defenders that this line had been discontinued and offered a replacement. The replacement offered was 'Nobilia Graz' light beech reproduction. The defenders agreed to this on the understanding that the colour and quality was similar. This was not so. The work was to be carried out and completed by September 2004. This was not done until November 2004. In carrying out the work, the pursuer's employees damaged some of the units. Two end panels of the run of units were scratched. The cutlery drawers were left with holes in them where the pursuer's employees had failed to fit them properly. The base plates for the units are too small and do not reach the floor. The larder unit which was located in the centre of the main run of units would not slide freely. The defenders complained to the pursuer and asked the pursuer to attend to these defects. The pursuer refused to do so. The defenders will have to replace the end panels, the cutlery drawers, the base plates and the larder unit. The larder cabinet runners were wrongly located or fitted and the unit in which it was housed has distorted. It will have to be replaced and the defenders may have to replace the whole run of units or at the very least those which are adjacent to the larder unit. The cost of carrying out all of the remedial work is reasonably estimated at £4,210 plus VAT.*"

3–20 I do not want to dwell on the details of these averments, or on the merits (or otherwise) of the defence, but it is worth pointing out some features of the pleadings.

- As you can see, there are three points made by the defenders. First, the price was amended. Secondly, the replacement units were not satisfactory. Thirdly, the workmanship was poor. These defences are expressed briefly and succinctly. Each one stands on its own. It should be easy for the reader to understand this.

- There are averments about the time when the job was to be done, which are probably irrelevant because time was not of the essence of the contract from what I can see.[24] I have heard this type of averment being described as "good prejudicial stuff", i.e. even if it is not strictly relevant, it might reflect badly on the opponent. I suggest that you resist the temptation to draft pleadings on that basis. A good opponent could take you to debate to have them excluded from any proof and you may just waste time and money by doing this.
- It might be supposed that the defenders have a report from an expert of some sort which would be the basis for the averments about the defective workmanship and the estimate of the cost of rectification. It is not necessary to refer to that report in the pleadings provided that the terms of the pleadings accurately summarise the critical defects upon which the defenders are proposing to rely. That is not to say that it is unnecessary or unhelpful to refer to the report in the pleadings, but if you have understood and summarised the report properly, that would suffice. Many people would prefer to make an averment that "Reference is made to the report by Mr X dated March 12, 2006 for its terms which are adopted and held to be repeated herein for the sake of brevity" or words to that effect. This does cover you if there are some essential features of the report which you have omitted to mention in your pleadings[25] but it is a good discipline and good practice for you to assimilate the terms of any such report to the extent that you can state succinctly the parts of it which are material to the case.

We cannot leave the defences, however, without considering the pleas in law which the defenders will have to insert. The defenders should start with the legal propositions which are the opposite of the pursuer's pleas in law, then go on to state the legal propositions which express the basis for the defence. Pleas in law do cause problems for new litigators, but it is beyond the scope of this book to discuss all of the intricate legal principles which might arise in different cases and influence the nature and content of pleas in law. A suggested set of pleas in law for this case might be: **3–21**

> "1. *The pursuer's averments being irrelevant and lacking in specification, the action should be dismissed with expenses.*
>
> 2. *The pursuer's averments, in so far as material, being unfounded in fact, the defender should be assoilzied with expenses.*
>
> 3. *The pursuer not having supplied goods and services to the defenders as contracted for, the defenders should be assoilzied with expenses.*

---

[24] And since I have made it up, I should know.

[25] Theoretically, you would not be able to lead evidence about them if they were not mentioned in the pleadings, although, in practice, if the report had been lodged, you would probably get away with it. If the report had not been lodged, then you would have a problem.

> *4. The pursuer being in material breach of the contract with the defenders, the defenders are entitled to damages from the pursuer therefor.*
>
> *5. Esto the pursuer is entitled to any payment from the defenders (which is denied) the defenders are entitled to set off against any such payment, the amount due to them by way of damages for the breach of contract by the pursuer.*
>
> *6. In any event, the sum sued for being excessive, decree therfor should not be granted as craved."*

For the avoidance of doubt, this is not necessarily intended as the perfect set of pleas in law which would be appropriate for the facts of this case, but as an illustration of what pleas in law might say and how they would come into play in such a dispute. It is critical that you understand their role in pleadings because they are the legal justification for the case, or the defence, and if you do not state them properly there is a real risk that you will miss the point of the whole litigation. You need to spend a great deal more time considering them than you might think. There are "standard" pleas in law which are well known and can be trotted out in routine cases. Again there is a danger that if you only draft pleas in law from a style, and routinely repeat the standard pleas in every case, you may not properly understand their significance generally, and their particular significance in the circumstances of your case.

I will look briefly at the individual pleas:

3–22   **Plea 1**   This could be described as the standard plea to the relevancy which features in many defences. It is arguably inappropriate here because, if the pursuer's averments are proved, the claim is plainly relevant, and the terms of the contract are set out clearly and sufficiently. It can probably be justified, however, on the basis that, if one takes a snap shot of the pleadings at the date of lodging of defences, the defenders are now saying many things to which the pursuers have not replied and may also raise questions of relevancy until, at least, the pursuers pleadings have "caught up" with the defences.

Plea 2   This is also a standard plea for defenders. It simply argues the proposition that the pursuer will not be able to prove their case.

Plea 3   This is simply the contradictor of the pursuer's own plea in law number 1. It is common and probably necessary for the defender to have a plea, or pleas, which are the opposite of the pursuer's pleas for reasons which should be obvious.

Plea 4   One part of the defence is that the contract was conditional on the replacement materials being of a certain type. It is argued that they were not. This would be a breach of contract. Furthermore, another part of the defence is that the pursuer's operatives did not do the job properly. It would have been an implied term of their contract that the work would have been done in a workmanlike fashion. You can claim damages if it was not. You would have to prove these points, of course, but if you did, the legal consequence would be that you would have an entitlement to damages from the pursuer.

Plea 5 Set off is tricky, but your position is that: (a) you agreed a reduced price for the contract; (b) you imposed a condition regarding the materials which has not been met; and (c) it is going to cost you money to fix the problems with the units. Even if[26] you are wrong about (a) and (b), if you are right about (c) you can reduce any payment your client might have to make by the amount you may prove that it will cost you to fix them.

Plea 6 This again is a fairly standard plea which is usually taken by defenders in most cases.

Assuming that you have now completed your defences, you will **3–23** intimate them and then both parties will have an opportunity to adjust. It is possible that the defences, while not skeletal, may not cover matters which you want to cover because of lack of information, or indeed for many other good reasons. You do not need to wait for the pursuer to respond to the defences before doing your own adjustments to them, and the order in which the adjustments might be done is entirely down to the parties. It can be awkward and frustrating when the other side send you adjustments shortly before you had just finished your own adjustments and were about to intimate them. You can, of course, adjust as often as you want. In complex cases it is not too difficult to become confused about the current state of the pleadings during extensive adjustment, and that can sometimes account for pleadings going off the rails. The possibilities for development of the pleadings in our mock action from now on are endless, but before I leave our detailed consideration of pleadings practice I can make some general observations about the adjustment process

Adjustments

When the pursuer is responding to detailed defences like those **3–24** drafted above, the simplest approach is to adjust Article 2 of condescendence by adding, at the end, "With reference to the defenders' averments in answer, it is admitted that. . .". In this way, the pleadings necessitated by the defences will stand out as being a response to what the defenders say. This helps the pleadings to develop in a relatively structured way which should be easier to follow. The pursuer would deal with the substantive averments by the defender in the same way as the defender should have dealt with the pursuer's writ, i.e. admissions, not knowns, and so on. It is a mistake to depart from this kind of structure. You may get away with it in a simple case, but it can make the pleadings very difficult to analyse and follow in most cases. If you have to make additional factual averments to answer the defences, add these at the end of your adjustments so that you have a supplementary "story" about the defences in your pleadings.

An alternative might be to take some of the defenders' averments and then go back into the terms of the original pleadings and adapt or expand on them. Sometimes it is necessary to do that but it should be

---

[26] That is what *"Esto"* means.

avoided if possible. Altering the original pleadings might necessitate the altering of the original defences and can involve far more adjustment than is strictly necessary.

On the defenders' side, further adjustments by the pursuer should ideally be answered by following the structure (if you had one) of the original defences, so as not to destroy the clear distinction between your answers to the pursuer's averments and your own substantive averments. This preserves the logic and "readability" of your averments. However, it may be unhelpful to generalise too much about this.

Sometimes, the only sensible course might be to take all, or part, of the original pleadings out and start afresh. Obviously, if you follow a completely different structure in doing so, this necessitates extensive adjustment on the other side. Indeed, they may be well advised to scrap their own pleadings up to there and start again. Thankfully, this does not happen too often.

You can use the adjustment period to "tidy up" errors in pleadings and it is perfectly sensible to do so. Sometimes the terms of the defences help to emphasise a shortcoming in the original pleadings, which can be sharpened up. The opponent has to watch out for "tidying up" adjustments which do not do exactly what they say on the tin, and make subtle—or unsubtle—changes to the critical averments.

3–25　　It is easy for the pleadings to become confused and confusing during the adjustment period, especially if you do not follow the structures suggested here. It is important that you keep track of the current state of the pleadings. Undoubtedly, the best way of doing this is by using the "track changes" function available in many computer software packages, and intimating the adjustments in this way. Traditionally, adjustments are done by a "First/ Second/Third, etc. Note of Adjustments" intimated to the other side which will say things like:

> "1. In Article 2 of condescendence, line 15, delete the word 'Smith' and substitute therefore 'Jones'.
> 2. In Article 3 of condescendence, add at the end the following 'With reference to the defender's averments . . .'".

It is easy to see how the track changes function would simplify this. For it to work properly in relation to the pleadings as a whole it is necessary to email pleadings to each other, but that should not cause too many problems nowadays.[27]

It is also easy to miss the significance of apparently innocuous adjustments hidden away[28] in the remote corners of a lengthy note of adjustments. Watch out for pursuers adding new articles of condescendence which have to be answered even if they contain little new substantive averment.

Regrettably, many adjustments are done on or close to the last date for adjustment, so that the other side cannot answer them in the time allowed. There may be good reasons for this, but this should be avoided.

---

[27] Indeed, there are moves to make this practice universal, if not obligatory, in the sheriff court.
[28] Deliberately or otherwise

Sometimes people treat this as part of the pleadings "game", the object of which is to bat the ball to the other side of the net a split second before the game is over. It is another example of the use of the "technical" rules, and one to be deprecated where its main purpose seems to be to frustrate the proper resolution of the issues between the parties. If you do adjust very late, and the adjustments contain averments of some significance, it would be professionally courteous to indicate to the other side that you would have no objection to adjustments from them after the close of the adjustment period.[29] Alternatively, you could indicate that you have no objection to the options hearing being continued to enable the other side to answer the adjustments. These would, in my opinion, be reasonable and sensible concessions which any litigator in a genuine dispute should be willing to make.

Drafting strategies and skills in personal injury actions

Many litigators in the sheriff court have particular difficulty in **3–26** understanding how to draft personal injury actions. Part of the reason for this may be that, historically, these claims often gave rise to debates about the precise terms of pleadings. Indeed, to read some of the older cases, you could be forgiven for thinking that the pleadings were far more interesting to the courts than the poor unfortunate man who lost a leg but could not aver satisfactorily who did it or why. Defenders enjoyed considerable success in having actions dismissed at debate or in restricting the scope of any claim by having various averments deleted from the pleadings. This produced considerable anxiety amongst those who pursued personal injury cases, that their pleadings would be examined critically by the courts and the opponents—and found wanting. In Scotland, there are few firms who pursue personal injury claims exclusively and even fewer who do so in the sheriff court. There are usually well-organised and experienced defender firms on the other side. Personal injury work is a specialised area in some respects, and there is an appearance of an uneven playing field when pursuers and defenders compete in this particular pleadings "game".

This is something of an illusion nowadays. The rules have changed. The requirements for detailed pleadings in personal injury actions have been significantly relaxed in the Court of Session. Sheriff court actions should only be sent to debate for substantial reasons.[30] Personal injury actions should only be dismissed at debate in rare and exceptional cases. However, old habits die hard and old fears run deep. A combination of inexperience, lack of expertise and uncertainty does produce some strange sets of pleadings in what might be regarded as relatively simple actions. These are picked over by defenders in the sheriff court sometimes justifiably, sometimes not. I thought it would be helpful to give some general guidance about pleading a personal injury case in the

---

[29] In the sheriff court, the court usually has no knowledge of what goes on during the adjustment period and is only interested in the pleadings put before it for the options hearing. This often permits a period of "unofficial" adjustment after the date for adjustment has ended.

[30] i.e. not to allow the defenders to whinge at the precise way in which the claim has been pled. I am paraphrasing r.9.12(3)(c) of the OCR.

sheriff court. Remember the rules and procedures and practices of pleadings are just the same as for any civil case, and the process of doing pleadings will be the same as outlined in this chapter already. I am going to concentrate on the words of the pleadings themselves and see if I can suggest a sensible way to approach the exercise. There will be some duplication of the advice already given, which is hardly surprising and should be helpful. Read and digest it carefully and think about how some of the comments might apply to different situations.

A reparation action: The writ

3–27   Let us look at a writ which has been drafted in the reparation action for Mr Hamilton. Assume that liability has been repudiated entirely. According to the correspondence pre-litigation, the defenders are unaware of any problem with tiles, they did not know of any accident, they think the pursuer was under the influence of alcohol, and they suggest that the work was being carried out in an area which was usually closed off to the public when work was being done. We will look at the averments of the facts of the accident first (Article 2 of condescendence), and then look at the averments of fault (Article 3).

Article 2

3–28   *"2. On or about July 23, 2004 at or about 14.15, the pursuer, who was with his friend, Mr John Wallace, 34 Jarvie Street, Airdrie, was shopping in Glasgow city centre. It is averred that they were walking in the Argyll Street Centre there and were intending to go to the shops contained within the centre. It is further averred that as they passed the entrance to the shops on the first floor of the centre, the pursuer suddenly caught his foot in a hole or opening in the flooring which was caused by a broken or missing tile which he could not see because of the inadequacy of the lighting in the vicinity. It is believed and averred that the tile had been missing for a considerable period of time and the defenders knew or ought to have known about this and taken steps to prevent it happening. Esto, they ought to have kept the public, such as the pursuer, away from the particular area while work was ongoing there. He tried to keep his balance but lost his footing and fell to the ground. He hurt his ankle in doing so and was taken to a shop nearby which is owned by the Fine Gowns group and in which he received first aid from the manager of the shop, Mrs Deirdre Gordon. She suggested that he contact an ambulance to take him to hospital but he did not want to do so because he thought his ankle was not too bad and was just sprained. He required to be taken home in a taxi by his friend and attended the Western Infirmary in Glasgow the next day. He was found to have sustained a broken ankle and was unable to go back to his work for a period of about nine months, as a result of which he has suffered loss, injury and damage all as more specifically condescended upon hereinafter."*

Editing

3–29   I am going to look at these pleadings sentence by sentence and analyse the words and the approach taken.

"On or about July 23, 2004, at or about 14.15, the pursuer, who was with his friend, Mr John Wallace, 34 Jarvie Street, Airdrie, was shopping in Glasgow city centre."

Is there any reason to be imprecise about the date or is that just what everyone else does? If you know the date, why not say so? Do we need to know that the pursuer was with his friend? Do we need to know his friend's address? There is no harm in putting this in as a matter of background, but there is no obligation to do so. Do we need to know that he was shopping in Glasgow city centre? Again, there is nothing wrong with saying that but it is background, it is not essential, and there would be no harm in leaving it out.

"It is averred that they were walking in the Argyle Street Centre there and were intending to go to the shops contained within the centre."

The use of the words, "It is averred that", is an irritating matter of style. There is nothing wrong with saying so. Some people might think that they have to say so and express things in this way because it is a legal writ. There is no need to do so and the writ will be a lot neater and tidier if you do not. An even more extravagant use of the phrase starts the next sentence in the writ. Neither of them is necessary and, for the avoidance of doubt, neither of them is obligatory.

Do we need to know that the pursuer was walking in the Argyle Street Centre and intending to go to shops in the centre? The answer is, Yes. It is an essential part of his story. It will be relevant where he was going from and to and it is a useful part of the narrative. In this sense, it is of course a matter of degree and judgement whether that kind of information is essential or not. There are no rules about this and, of course, there is nothing to stop you having pages of irrelevant and immaterial averments.[31]

"It is further averred that as they passed the entrance to the shops on **3–30** *the first floor of the centre, the pursuer suddenly caught his foot in a hole or opening in the flooring which was caused by a broken or missing tile which he could not see because of the inadequacy of the lighting in the vicinity."*

This sentence may be unrealistically long, although I have seen many pleadings with sentences considerably longer than that. There is no merit in having long sentences. In fact, there is merit in keeping them short. This sentence actually incorporates crucial information about where the pursuer was, what happened to him, the nature of the defect which caused his accident, and the lighting. Four crucial points in the one sentence. This is not a good idea.

Look at the sentence a little more closely, if you did not know where his accident happened, would you be able to go to the Argyle Street Centre and point out the location? The answer is that you would not. In

---

[31] Until some sheriff goes ballistic at your efforts.

some cases, the precise location of an accident is not material but, in this case, the precise location is going to be material in at least three respects. First, the defenders are disputing whether an accident of this kind happened at all. Secondly, they are going to say that the pursuer should not have been there. Thirdly, there are going to be questions about restriction of access to the public and lighting. If you do not establish where the accident happened then how are you going to deal with these other vital issues? That is not to say that you have to be absolutely precise and provide a plotting of the accident location which could be traced by a good map-reader.

This is where we start to enter into the area of "fair notice". You might want to anticipate the defenders' argument that they do not have fair notice of where the pursuer says the accident happened. Questions which a nit-picking defender might ask would include: What entrance to the shops on the first floor? There are three. What do you mean by "as they passed"? Were they at the entrance, past the entrance, or 40 yards away? Did the pursuer catch his foot in a hole or in an opening? Does the use of the word "opening" imply that something had not been completed and had been left off or does it imply some hole had opened up? Was the tile broken or was it missing? Is the pursuer saying there was absolutely nothing there, which he might have been expected to notice, or is he saying that there were the remnants of a broken tile? This might be relevant in relation to the question of whether the defenders could ever have discovered this in advance. What is all of this about "inadequacy of the lighting"? No one has mentioned problems with lighting pre-litigation. What lighting was there? Was it on? Where was the nearest light? What does the pursuer mean by "inadequate"? Were all the lights not working, or was one light out? These may all be legitimate questions the defenders could ask because your pleadings have left so many features of the accident inadequately explained. Whether that should prevent you securing a proof before answer may be another question, but hopefully you can see how the pleadings can be subjected to criticism.

3–31 Let us just pause there and look at what the pursuer might have said in the writ. I would emphasise the "might" because this is not the right answer but only a suggestion.

> "2. On July 23, 2004 the pursuer entered the Argyle Street Centre by the Queen Street entrance on the ground floor. He was intending to go to a shop on the first floor. He went up the escalator and turned to his right. On the section of walkway leading from there to 'Fine Gowns' the flooring was made up of tiles. That section of walkway was in darkness. None of the lighting at that part of the centre was working. The pursuer lost his balance when his foot came into contact with a tile which was broken and part of which was missing."

Now, of course, on the face of it, this really just says the same thing. Perhaps it is a little neater and a little clearer but then again, perhaps not. The first version might be good enough to get you a proof before answer if the defenders do not take issue with the description of events. However, it is suggested that is not the way to look at matters. By putting it in this alternative way, you can focus on the essential facts which have to be proved. You do not use any imprecise language. You are clear in your mind as to what your description of the accident should be.

You should, of course, realise that you can only be clear about this if you have clarified the matter with your client. In other words, when he told you that he tripped on a broken tile, you cannot really plead this properly and fully (especially if there is going to be a dispute about the existence of a broken tile) without asking him a lot more about it. If you ask him a lot more about it you can plead it better.[32] If you plead it better and more accurately you will know, and the defenders will know, what your case is. You will be able to focus on that point and you will be able to ask your client questions during examination in chief based on your proper understanding of precisely what it was that caused them to fall. At this stage I would pause only to say that it would be unrealistic not to acknowledge that there are some cases where the clients are so vague and uncertain about what happened and what caused an accident that no amount of precognoscing, questioning or encouraging, will obtain a clear and articulate description. That is difficult to deal with and there is some considerable skill involved in pleading a case properly and adequately when there is some uncertainty or inconsistency in your client's version of events.

Let us now go back to the individual sentences of the writ: **3–32**

> *"It is believed and averred that the tile had been missing for a considerable period of time and the defenders knew or ought to have known about this and taken steps to prevent it happening."*

The use of "believed and averred" is commonly misunderstood.[33] An averment of belief which is not supported by other averments from which the belief may be inferred is irrelevant. What are the facts upon which the "belief" is based? It is reasonable to say that a pursuer in this position cannot be expected to know how long the tile had been missing. However, how does he know that it had not just fragmented half an hour beforehand, and how does he know that the defenders ought to have realised that this was the case? Once again, one can ask, what are the facts upon which that belief is based or is it just wishful thinking? Furthermore, on what basis can it be said that the defenders "knew" about this? What are the facts upon which the pursuer says the defenders had the knowledge? On what basis can it be said that the defenders ought to have known about this? It might be easier to say that they ought to have known about it if it had been broken for a considerable period of time, but that rather begs the question.

Does the pursuer say anything about how long it had been broken? Yes, he does. Is a "considerable period of time" specific enough? What is he actually going to say at proof? Are there witnesses who can speak to this? What are they going to say? If they have something specific to say then maybe you should be averring that. For example, "It had been

---

[32] One of the main reasons for taking a good precognition from him. See Ch.2.
[33] For the cases, see Macphail, *Sheriff Court Practice*, above, para.9.54; Hennessy, above, pp.55–56.

missing for at least two weeks". What do your precognitions actually say?

3–33   If you dwell upon this for a while it may then lead you to a consideration of what the obligations of the defenders would have been in these particular circumstances. The defenders are the owners and landlords of the Argyle Street Centre. Does a landlord have any duty to do anything about a defect like this? Maybe the shop owners who are the tenants of the centre have a responsibility rather than the landlords. How is it being suggested that the defenders ought to have taken steps to prevent "it" happening? In other words, to prevent the tile breaking or, in other words, to prevent the accident happening? What steps could they have taken?

In this simple sentence, the whole essence of the legal basis of this claim has been rather fudged and obscured. Why does the pursuer think the defenders are liable as a matter of law, and what obligation to him have they breached? Additionally, this is an averment dealing with the legal basis of the claim and it is not good pleading practice to insert in the "factual" averments of Article 2 of condescendence legal propositions which explain the basis of the claim. There is no obligation to put the pleadings in a particular form. There is no reason why you cannot jumble up facts and law and even the quantification of the claim all in one condescendence (as happens here to a certain extent). However, there is no doubt that if the case is pled and set out in writing in a clear structure it will be considerably easier to understand. The conventional approach, and the recommended approach, would be to put the factual averments in one or more distinct articles of condescendence and to put the averments containing legal propositions about fault into another article, or other articles. Apart from anything else, you are more likely to give some detailed thought to both the factual and legal basis of your claim. This will not turn a losing case into a winning case, and the court could find in your favour if all of the words of the pleadings are in there somewhere no matter how they are arranged, but it is obvious that a logical and structured arrangement of your pleadings is preferable.

3–34   *"Esto they ought to have kept the public, such as the pursuer, away from the particular area whilst work was ongoing there."*

What does *"Esto"* mean? Is there any obligation to shove in a Latin word because it will make the pleadings look more like legal pleadings? This is a common fault. There are times when Latin words and phrases are appropriate and are the best way of expressing something clearly because they have acquired a well-known and accepted meaning within the legal profession. However, I would be reluctant to use Latin, and prefer plain language. Do not use Latin without knowing what it means. In this case, the word means nothing in the context, no matter how "legal" it sounds.

The sentence itself canvasses the obligations on the defender which are said to have been breached, which again ought to be in a different condescendence. The last part of the sentence says that, "work was ongoing there". What does that mean? Does it mean that people were actually working there at the time of the accident? Does it mean that the public should not have been allowed access to the shops at all? The difficulty here might be that this purported obligation on the defenders may have come from the fertile imagination of the person pleading the case. If you are going to have work carried out which might cause breakages of tiles then you should not let the public anywhere near it. Should you close the centre? Should you cordon the area off? How should, or could, that have been done?

There may well be something in the general idea that the public should not be exposed to dangers caused by contractors who might inevitably damage the walkway. This is not the best place in the pleadings in which to raise it, and this rather tentative sentence is not really the way to do it either. That is not to say, that the pursuer could not argue that the sentence is a plausible statement of the legal duty incumbent upon the defenders and obtain a proof before answer. It may beg a number of other issues about the relationship of the defenders to the contractors and the occupiers of the shops in the centre. Perhaps that is something that a carefully drafted writ would have thrown up at an early stage.

> *"He tried to keep his balance but lost his footing and fell to the* **3–35** *ground. He hurt his ankle in doing so and was taken to a shop nearby which is owned by the Fine Gowns Group".*

There is nothing wrong with this as a narrative. Some people might say it is unnecessary to talk about what happened after the accident, and the fact that he received first aid from an individual. It is unnecessary to name the individual. It is probably irrelevant but it is not "wrong" to do so. It would be perfectly reasonable to say, "He hurt his ankle in doing so and received first aid in a nearby shop." On the other hand, there is perhaps a hint in the position adopted by the defenders that they think the pursuer was under the influence of alcohol at the time. They are not convinced that he had his accident in the way he said he did and indeed they are not even convinced that the pursuer had an accident of this type at all. The individual concerned and mentioned in the averments might be able to say something about that so there may be some benefit in naming her. It could amount to a subtle demonstration that you have no qualms about giving her details to the court and the other side (because you know she is going to back up your client on his state of sobriety). It still is not necessary to plead evidence, but you could perhaps make out a tactical case for going into this detail at this stage, because of the line which you anticipate the defenders will take.

> *"She suggested that he contact an ambulance to take him to hospital* **3–36** *but he did not want to do so because he thought his ankle was not too bad and was just strained. He required to be taken home in a taxi by his friend and attended the Western Infirmary in Glasgow the next day."*

There is nothing strictly wrong with any of this, but most of it is relatively immaterial. As previously suggested, the defenders might raise an issue about the pursuer's state of sobriety and the reason why he did not go and obtain hospital assistance straight away. This could be regarded as anticipating any such issue. You do not really need to say it. Would you be prevented from leading evidence about all of this if you did not say it? The answer is, No, because you have given the defender fair notice of your claim. If they want to raise an issue in their defences you may want to respond to it. For example, if they say that the pursuer did not receive treatment until the next day there may be no harm in pleading this as a response to the defences. Do you anticipate this or do you wait until the defenders take the point? It is a matter of opinion. I would wait until the point was taken formally in the case itself, but others might differ.

Consider again how the latter part of Article 2 of condescendence could be modified:

> "He tried to keep his balance but lost his footing and fell to the ground. He fractured his right ankle. He went home in a taxi and attended the Western Infirmary, Glasgow the next day. He has suffered the loss, injury and damage detailed in Article 5 of condescendence."

This is short, and perhaps unnecessarily so. For the time being, however, all we really need to know is that he suffered some kind of injury and some kind of loss. You would be well advised to keep your detailed averments about injury and loss of earnings to the article, or articles, of condescendence which deal solely and specifically with these. There is nothing wrong with doing it in this way and, as already pointed out, you could actually put the whole detailed averments about injury into the same condescendence as the averments of fact. That is not a very good idea. It is preferable to have minimal duplication in the averments. If necessary, you could have a simple cross-reference between these averments.

Article 3

3–37   Let us now look at what might be said in Article 3 of condescendence. Traditionally, one would expect the averments about the legal basis of the claim to appear here. So far as possible, the facts justifying the claim against these particular defenders in these particular circumstances should already have been set out in the earlier condescendence. There is no obligation to do so but again it just makes logical sense. Let us again take the averments sentence by sentence.

> "3. Said accident was caused by the fault and negligence et separatim breach of statutory duty of the defenders. They are the owners of the centre and responsible for its maintenance. They had a duty to take reasonable care for members of the public using the centre and to ensure the safety of members of the public such as the pursuer who were using the centre at the material time. They owed duties under the Occupiers Liability Act 1961, s.2(1) to take care as was necessary to prevent individuals such as the pursuer from sustaining accidents such as the accident hereinbefore condescended upon. They knew or ought to have known that persons such as the pursuer would be walking in the centre and would be likely to have an accident if the tiles on the floor were broken and likely to cause people to trip. They failed in the duties incumbent upon them and thus caused the accident."

"Said accident was caused by the fault and negligence et separatim breach of statutory duty of the defenders."

What this means is that the pursuer is going to argue both a breach of common law duty and a breach of statutory duty. In other words, there will be at least two separate legal bases of claim against the defenders. In general terms, it is simply not a good idea to put more than one legal basis for your claim into one article of condescendence. If there was also a breach of statutory duty then you should save this for another condescendence, and set it out in full there. If there was more than one breach of statutory duty then you ought to put each individual breach into individual articles of condescendence. I have seen cases where breaches of Regulations have been argued with four separate regulations pled in one condescendence. It is perfectly understandable why that should be done. It saves time and space, but it does make the condescendence very lengthy. It can make it rather over complicated. It may be difficult to focus upon what is being argued in relation to each regulation. It is not wrong, and it can be justified in some circumstances. However, if there are distinct legal bases for the claim it is usually preferable to have them set out in different articles of condescendence.

"They are the owners of the centre and responsible for its **3–38** *maintenance."*

Has the pursuer already said that the defenders are the "owners of the centre". The answer is that they have not. Until the pursuer says something about the defenders which links them to the accident in some way, it can be argued that the claim is completely irrelevant. It may not be disputed that they are owners but there is a more important issue in this simple sentence.

When the pursuer says that the defenders are "responsible for its maintenance" what does that mean? That innocent phrase covers a multitude of possible meanings. What does "maintenance" mean? What do they actually do in connection with the maintenance of the centre? A cursory examination of the available textbooks[34] will tell you that there is no liability upon an owner of premises simply by virtue of the fact that they happen to have a legal title to the premises. Liability in these circumstances depends upon "possession and control". If the defenders leased out the whole of the centre as shop premises, and if the owners of the shop premises were responsible for maintenance of the common walkways then would the defenders have any responsibility for this accident? To say that the defenders were responsible for maintenance could mean that they simply had security staff constantly on patrol at night to prevent vandalism. Where does that leave the defenders? What are their precise obligations to people such as the pursuer, and what entitles the pursuer to say that the defenders do owe certain specific duties to the public, such as him?

---

[34] See, e.g. Walker, *The Law of Delict in Scotland* (2nd edn, W.Green/Scottish Universities Law Institute, 1981).

These are all very pertinent questions which are not answered by the sentence quoted. Maybe the defenders will not dispute that they have certain responsibilities for "maintenance", and, in fact, maybe "maintenance" has nothing to do with this accident. The problem is that by using what is, on the face of it, a perfectly innocuous phrase with some legal connotation, the pursuer has by-passed a detailed consideration of the obligations on the defenders. This needs to be done to determine whether they owe any duties at all to the pursuer. The pursuer must think about this. He must think about the relationship between the defenders and the owners of the shop premises who occupy the centre. He has to think about the basis upon which a "landlord" (which is what the defenders seem to be) has responsibility for the state of his premises. Of course, the situation may be different if the owner/landlord had instructed the contractors to carry out work within the centre. Does the pursuer say anything about this? If not, should he do so? Otherwise, his pleadings might be irrelevant because there is no factual justification for arguing that the defenders have any responsibility for the state of the walkway on the day in question. If the defenders had instructed contractors to work there, does that impose some obligations on the defenders in relation to the actings of these contractors? Does that mean that the defenders can be said to have taken over some possession and control of the walkway for the purpose of having the works carried out? What did the defenders actually do (if anything) in relation to the care and maintenance of the centre? What did they actually *do* in relation to the repair contract which they presumably instructed? What does that contract say? If they actually did certain things, or had the right to do certain things, which would have a bearing upon the state of the walkway and the safety of the walkway while work was being carried out, then that takes us considerably closer to imposing legal liability on them. The difficulty, however, is that at the moment there are no *factual averments* about these matters. The issue is one of whether there is a legal duty, but the pleadings argument would be that there are no factual averments from which that legal duty could be said to arise.

3–39   *"They had a duty to take reasonable care for members of the public using the centre and to ensure the safety of members of the public, such as the pursuer, who were using the centre at the material time."*

Everyone has a duty to take reasonable care for any person who they can reasonably foresee would be likely to be injured by their acts or omissions. That is basic and fundamental. In any common law case, that general duty should be pled. However, does that duty extend to "ensuring" the safety of members of the public? The answer is, No. If one read the pleadings strictly, then they are saying that the defenders have an obligation to *make sure* that no one has an accident rather than to take reasonable care. These are just sloppy pleadings. The court might be persuaded to overlook the strict technical reading of the words and proceed on the basis that everyone knows that there can only be a common law duty to take reasonable care. However, there is more to the sentence than that. If you aver that the defenders have a duty to take "reasonable care to ensure" certain things, you still have to aver facts and circumstances from which that duty of reasonable care can arise and which demonstrate that breach of that duty. Did they (the defenders or their employees) know that there was a defect there at the time? If you cannot say that, should they have known about it? How could they have acquired that knowledge? Should they have been arranging for frequent patrols? Should they have had someone stationed permanently at the work site to observe and deal with any dangers caused by the work? Was this broken tile caused by the work? You will not find any of these issues considered and set out in the pleadings as they are presently framed.

> *"They owe duties under the Occupiers Liability Act 1961, s.2 to take* **3–40** *care as was necessary to prevent individuals such as the pursuer from sustaining accidents such as the accident hereinbefore condescended upon."*

At first glance, this sounds kind of legal, and the type of thing you might expect to find in a personal injury action. There are so many things wrong with this sentence that it is difficult to know where to begin. First, there is not an Occupiers Liability Act 1961. It is the Occupiers Liability (Scotland) Act 1960. Secondly, there is no s.2 as such. Section 2 runs to three sub-sections—which one would you like the defender to choose? Thirdly, the sentence does not actually say what s.2(1) of the Act says. Fourthly, the use of "hereinbefore condescended upon" gives the sentence that air of legal language which may be regarded by the pleader as giving the sentence the final seal of legality. The whole approach is misconceived.

The claim under the Act should probably be in a distinct article of condescendence.[35] Undoubtedly the best practice in pleading a statutory basis for the claim is to do it something like this:

> *"The accident was caused by the breach of statutory duty of the* **3–41** *defenders. Section 2(1) of the Occupiers Liability (Scotland) Act 1960 provides that:[quote section at length]. The defenders were the occupiers of the centre in terms of that section. The Argyle Street Centre was 'premises' to which the Act applies. The pursuer was a person to whom the defenders owed the duties imposed by the section. The defenders had duties to . . . The defenders were in breach of their statutory duty. They failed to . . .".*

Start by setting out exactly what the section says by quoting it. Relate the circumstances of the case to the particular terms of the section. Then state why the section applies to the defenders and applies in favour of the pursuer. You emphasise the facts which mean that these obligations were incumbent upon the defenders. You point out that the defender was in breach of the statute by failing to do various things. It is rather simple and straightforward if you simply follow this formula. It applies in relation to every statutory case. It should be followed in every statutory case. It should inevitably stimulate a clear answer from the defenders

---

[35] Although there is an ongoing debate as to whether this statute should be regarded as "separate" from the common law obligations—over which, I shall gladly pass for present purposes.

which makes it clear if they are taking issue with the proposition that the statute applies in the circumstances, that it does impose duties on the defenders, and that it does benefit the pursuer. Apart from anything else, you will find it very handy when it comes to a debate by the defenders arguing that the averments do not make it clear why the Act applies to the case.

3–42   *"They knew or ought to have known that persons such as the pursuer would be walking in the centre and would be likely to have an accident if the tiles on the floor were broken and likely to cause people to trip."*

My first reaction to this is—is that all? What should the defenders have done? Did they break the tile? Did they know that a tile was broken? Should they have known it was broken? How should they have known it was broken? Yes, they can accept that a broken tile might be likely to cause people to trip. Did the defenders break it? Did they allow others to break it knowingly? Did they know this was present? Should they have realised it was going to be present because of the work they were asking to have carried out? Should they have imposed obligations on the contractor to shut off the area? In simple terms, what is it that the pursuer is saying the defenders did wrong. What legal duty, in general terms, did they breach and what, as a matter of fact, did they actually do or did they omit to do which would have prevented the accident happening? These are the important issues to be considered. Again, they run the risk of being obscured by these pleadings.

A better draft

3–43   On a more positive note, let us finally consider an alternative draft which takes into account some of the observations made above. This might illustrate the way that different pleadings might have addressed and focused some of the issues we have identified. Indeed, it could be assumed that the exercise of doing the first draft may well have alerted the pleader to the lack of evidence on some of the crucial issues, and perhaps even caused him to reprecognosce witnesses or make further enquiries into the merits. There is doubt about the status of the defenders and the nature of their obligations for the state of the premises. There may also be some difficulty in describing exactly where the accident occurred. We should remind ourselves that the defenders dispute whether the accident happened in the way the pursuer said. On the other hand, it is not too clear if the defenders are disputing that there was a broken/missing tile at the location on the day in question.

In order to bring this out, the pleader has decided to start the factual averments with what could be regarded as an additional, and slightly unusual, article of condescendence. It is important to understand the reasoning behind this. It may give some insight into how pleadings can be used positively by a pursuer to focus issues and make a case easier to prove and/or harder to defend. The suggested Article 2 of condescendence makes simple factual averments about matters which are or should be within the knowledge of the defenders. It is reasonable to expect admissions or denials to these individual averments. If the defenders dispute any of these matters of fact, that dispute will be brought out into the open. Contrast this with a general denial by the defenders to the original Article 3 of condescendence which might well be justified because of the way it was framed. This would obscure the defenders' position on what might turn out to be a critical matter of fact. By approaching it differently, and by keeping the pleadings short and concise, you should be able to force the defenders to disclose their position.[36] In this way, you can shorten and simplify the proof and reduce the number of contentious matters which you may have to prove. It does not guarantee that you will win, but it could certainly make life considerably easier for a hard-pressed litigator. Do not expect this to apply to all such cases,[37] but perhaps you can see how a considered use of pleadings might actually achieve some of the objectives of the system outlined in the passages quoted at the beginning of the chapter.

Pleadings

3–44
   "2. *The defenders are the owners and occupiers of the Argyle Street Centre. They have possession and control of the common parts of it. They employ staff to maintain the common parts of the centre. They employ staff to attend to the security of the centre. Their staff patrol the common parts, including walkways, of the centre daily, at regular intervals. The centre consists of a basement, a ground floor, and a first floor of shops and offices. The public can access the centre from Queen Street. There are escalators within the centre. Members of the public use these to gain access to shops or offices on the first floor. The walkways at the first floor level are surfaced in tiles. The tiles are approximately 300 millimetres square. Persons entering the centre from the Queen Street entrance and going to the first floor have to use the escalator. At the top of the escalator there is a walkway which is about 5 metres wide and 15 metres long. This extends alongside the frontage of a shop named 'Fine Gowns'. On July 23, 2004, there was a broken tile in about the middle of that section. All or part of it was missing. The tile had been in this condition for a considerable period of time prior to the pursuer's accident.*

   3. *On July 23, 2004 the pursuer entered the Argyle Street Centre at about 14.30. He entered by the Queen Street entrance. He took the escalator to the first floor. He walked along the section of walkway mentioned above. He caught his foot on the broken tile. He lost his balance. He fell heavily and injured his right ankle. He received first aid in a shop and then went home. He had to attend the Western Infirmary, Glasgow, the next day and was found to have sustained a broken ankle. He suffered the loss, injury and damage specified in condescendence X.*

   4. *The accident to the pursuer was caused by the fault and negligence of the defenders. They were the owners and occupiers of the walkway on which the pursuer sustained his accident. They were responsible for maintaining the walkway. They had a duty to take*

---

[36] If they do not do so, you can attack their pleadings as being irrelevant or lacking in specification by failing to give you "fair notice" of matters in your pleadings which ought to be within their knowledge.
[37] Do not use it in every writ from now on.

reasonable care to avoid acts or omissions which they could reasonably foresee would be likely to cause injury to persons such as the pursuer who were likely to use the walkway. They had a duty to take reasonable care to devise, institute and maintain a system of inspection mainte- nance and repair of the public areas of the centre including the walkways. They had a duty to have their employees inspect the walkway at least twice a day. They had a duty to instruct their employees to note any part of the walkway which was likely to cause a danger to persons walking on it. They had a duty to instruct their employees to take immediate steps to guard same temporarily and to arrange for a prompt and permanent repair to be carried out. They knew or ought to have known that tiles were likely to break from time to time as a result of wear and tear and normal usage of the centre. They knew or ought to have known that if tiles broke they were likely to constitute a danger to pedestrians using the centre. They knew or ought to have known that the tile was broken and defective prior to the date of the pursuer's accident. . . .

5. Further, the accident was caused by the fault and negligence of employees of the defenders, for whose acts and omissions in the course of their employment with them, the defenders are vicariously liable. The defenders employed persons to patrol the walkways of the centre. They were required to inspect the walkways and note any defects which might cause a danger to members of the public.

6. The accident was also caused by the breach of statutory duty of the defenders [Occupiers Liability (Scotland) Act 1960] . . .

7. The accident was also caused by . . .

8. As a result of the defenders fault and negligence and breach of statutory duty, the pursuer has suffered loss, injury and damage. He sustained a . . .

9. The pursuer has applied to the defenders for reparation . . .

PLEAS IN LAW

1.   . . .
2.   . . .
Etc.   . . ."

CHAPTER 4

ADVOCACY SKILLS

"A litigation is a dispute between two parties to decide which one has the better lawyer".

In this chapter we will discuss the basic personal skills required to enable **4–01** you to be effective advocates in the sheriff court. These do not come easily. You will not have been born with too many of them. You will have to acquire them or develop them somehow. The popular impression of advocates, or court lawyers, portrays them as independent, confident, articulate and fearless.[1] Many of them have maverick tendencies and curiously flawed personal lives and habits. These are not obligatory. Competence, efficiency, courtesy and clarity of thought and word would be perfectly acceptable to most civil advocates. These characteristics might make poor drama but it is a mistake to base your perception of what might be required on the popular misconceptions touted in the media and elsewhere. At least, save the court room fireworks until after you have learned where they keep the matches.

Once again, there is no substitute for experience. The more you practise advocacy the better you should become.[2] There are some books on advocacy skills and the principles of good advocacy,[3] but you cannot learn to be a good advocate by reading about it. Doing it yourself, and watching and listening to others doing it, and doing it well, is probably the most helpful training. Thinking about what works, and what does not work, and why you do something a particular way, or not, is also useful. In fact, it is essential to think in advance of such things. The best ad-libs are the ones you had prepared earlier because you knew the point would come up. I will try not to say this too often, but preparation is undoubtedly the key. However, you need a little knowledge and experience before you can appreciate what you should be preparing for, and how you should be doing it most effectively.

On the other hand, you do already have your personal abilities and natural talents. You do know something about the law. You have read books. You have passed exams. Someone gave you a job and thought

---

[1] Not to mention duplicitous, amoral and opportunistic—but we will not mention that here.

[2] Although the opportunities to "practise" advocacy are limited and you may end up "practising"—and practising—in real cases which is not ideal.

[3] I would highly recommend J. Munkman, *The Techniques of Advocacy* (4th edn, LexisNexis Butterworths, London, 2003), which is short, incisive and practical. The National Institute for Trial Advocacy (NITA) book on *Modern Trial Advocacy* by Steven Lubet is an American book. It is much longer and contains extremely useful material which can be adapted and used in our system.

that you were capable of appearing in court.[4] Your personality, style of speech, command of language, mental agility, knowledge of law, ability to prepare, thoroughness, alertness, logic, etc. should be known to you by now. When you start you are unlikely to be brilliant,[5] but do not worry about this. No one was brilliant to start with, and few have acquired brilliance since. This should not be a cause for dismay. How many people are stars as advocates? Not that many. But then, you do not need to be a star to do an effective job for your client in court. If you take your own abilities and are prepared to work at developing them, then you have a chance of achieving that aim.

Advocacy has been described as the art of persuasion. How do you make the court see things the way you want it to see them and how do you make the court do what you want it to do? In all court hearings you will have the sheriff—the "decision-maker"—to persuade and, as in real life, some people are more easily persuadable than others. Each sheriff is an individual with individual characteristics.[6] One of the interesting features of sheriff court advocacy is the fact that the decision-maker is an individual whose knowledge, views and likes may be quite different from other decision-makers. He or she will, of course, be bound by the same procedural rules as every sheriff,[7] and will be applying the same law to each case, but there are large areas of discretion and many decisions where the sheriff can properly jump one of several different ways. It is in these areas particularly that an attractive argument, or a compelling submission, can win the day. This is so among sheriffs in the same sheriffdom, and even more so of sheriffs in different sheriffdoms. Accordingly, it can be appreciated that if we are going to talk about the skills involved in persuading decision-makers with many diverse characteristics, it is unrealistic to discuss specific approaches which will always work and always persuade. The only person whose views and opinions ultimately count is the sheriff before who you are appearing. If he or she can be persuaded then you will win. Your job as an advocate is to persuade him or her.

The incredibly basics

4–02   At the risk of insulting your intelligence, I am going to start with some brief practical points which many might take as read. I can assure you that I have been asked to explain all of these to students and trainees in the past, and I see no harm in repeating them here. Anyone who has not experienced at least some of these problems is being economic with the truth.

- Make sure you know the court in which you are appearing.[8] Do you know how to get there? The Scottish Courts website will give you the location of the court house.[9]

---

[4] This passage has been inserted as an aid to positive thinking.
[5] A degree of realism is important too.
[6] At least, so far as I am aware.
[7] Although many sheriffdoms apply the rules differently—more or less strictly.
[8] I am fairly sure everyone has gone to the wrong sheriff court at least once. Indeed, I recently had a case in which the part-time sheriff went to the wrong court. Not his fault, I believe.
[9] See *www.scotcourts.gov.uk/locations*.

- Do you know the specific court room in which your case is being heard, or the specific sheriff hearing it? Find out by telephoning the day before and asking the civil clerk, or by turning up early.
- When is the case due to call in court? Are you sure about this? For courts in which you do not normally practise, telephone the clerk or your local agent and check if you have the slightest doubt. Often they cannot be precise, so assume the earliest possible time. Turn up comfortably early anyway.[10] With experience you may be able to work out just how late you can leave it. At the beginning of your career do not even think about cutting it fine. It is not worth it. If you are going to be late—for some good reason I assume—then telephone the clerk, or have your office telephone the clerk, with an explanation before you even arrive.[11] All the more so in smaller courts where there may be fewer cases calling at any one time.
- Who are you appearing for? I have heard countless agents advise the sheriff that they are appearing for the "wrong" side. It is embarrassing to say the least.
- Why are you going there? As you travel to court it is helpful to run over this in your mind just in case you are still not sure.[12]
- What are you looking for? What result would justify your appearance? Again, just remind yourself in general terms what you will be wanting the court to do and what will give you a satisfied glow on the journey back to the office.
- Do you have your gown,[13] your file, your authorities?
- When you arrive in a strange[14] court, go to the main desk and speak to the court attendant or go to the sheriff clerk's civil office and speak to someone there. Confirm that the case is on, when it is on, who is hearing it, and what court it will be heard in.[15]
- Then ask for the agent's room.[16] Go there and put on your gown, then go to the toilet.[17] Speak to the local agents. Own up to your inexperience and the fact that this is your first time there. Rest assured they will know already. They will normally be helpful.[18]
- Go to the courtroom as early as you like—you can soak up the atmosphere.
- Speak to the clerk in the court, give the clerk your name and tell the clerk the name of your case just to be absolutely sure that it is indeed in this court.

---

[10] Apart from anything else it will be helpful to observe how the earlier business is conducted to give you an idea of what is expected of you.

[11] Having to do this more than once is a concession of incompetence.

[12] I am serious about this. I have seen and heard submissions which failed to provide the answer to that simple question.

[13] Yes, I have seen that one too. I have done it.

[14] I use this term to mean one in which you do not normally practise, of course.

[15] Do not be surprised if the answers are slightly equivocal.

[16] I am assuming that you are not rushing in five seconds before lift off, which, of course, you should not be doing.

[17] Or perhaps the other way round, if you prefer.

[18] It is pleasing to record that most agents, in that situation, are incredibly helpful and supportive if you just ask. Your opponent might, justifiably, be the exception to that rule.

- Stand up when the sheriff comes on to the Bench, and when the sheriff comes off the Bench.
- Do not talk in court when waiting for your case.[19]
- If you leave the court or come in when the sheriff is on the Bench, bow to the sheriff. Make a point of doing this. By definition, the sheriff has earned the respect.
- When the time comes for your case to be heard, come forward to the table at the front of the Bench, if you are not already there.[20]
- In a busy court you might have to "muscle" your way forward to the table[21] and stand where you can. Otherwise, pursuers will normally take up position on the right of the sheriff as they face the sheriff. Defenders will be on the left.[22]
- Now open your mouth and hope that something comes out along the lines set out below.

Basics

Form of address

4–03   The sheriff is "My Lord/Lady" or "Your Lordship/Ladyship". For the first few months this might sound a little weird to you. Then it will become second nature.[23] Like so many of the formal aspects of court appearance, it soon becomes a habit.[24] Do not say "Your Honour" which signifies demotion for him/her and bad news for you. Do not say "You", as in, "I am moving you to". It should be, "I am moving your Lordship to".

Who are you?

4–04   In many sheriff courts, especially those in which you have not appeared frequently,[25] it is unlikely that the sheriff will know who you are. The clerk might have given the sheriff your name in advance, but not necessarily. It makes sense therefore to introduce yourself. Nothing too flowery of course. "My name is Hennessy. I appear for the pursuer", should be sufficient. Say this clearly—it may be the last thing you do well. It rather spoils the effect if the sheriff cannot hear you. If your name is unusual, or the spelling is unusual, spell it for the sheriff.

Legal language

4–05   There are words and phrases used in court which, again, will become second nature but have to be ingrained in your language at an early

---

[19] Most people do it, without a problem. Some sheriffs do not like it, and they are quite right, because it can be distracting and is disrespectful. If you must talk, keep it short and very quiet. Otherwise go outside the court and do it.

[20] Different courts have slightly different layouts, but most, if not all, will have a bench with a table or desk for the clerk and agents at right angles in front of the Bench.

[21] I am not entirely joking here.

[22] No doubt someone will say "not in X sheriff court you don't", but this is my experience—certainly for proofs, debates, and lengthy contentious motions.

[23] I heard of an advocate who had reached the stage of familiarity with the form of address to a male sheriff being faced with a female sheriff for the first time. The advocate was so anxious not to say "My Lord" but to say "My Lady" that she contrived to call her "My Dear".

[24] Leave "M'lud" or "M'lid" until you are older and do not care.

[25] I am assuming this will apply to many readers of this chapter.

stage. "In my submission", as opposed to, "What I am saying is". "My motion is", as opposed to, "I would like your Lordship to". "It respectfully seems to me that my friend's argument is unsound", as opposed to, "He is talking rubbish". There is no great benefit in giving further examples because there are so many ways in which your words or turn of phrase may have to be amended from your normal speech. Watch, listen, recall and copy. I suppose that the desired aims are clarity, courtesy and restraint. This can be learned and is a style worth cultivating.

Legal terminology

I can often tell if someone has not been appearing in court for long by **4–06** their use of inappropriate legal terminology. "I crave your Lordship to grant my motion", confuses craves and motions. Do you know what a crave is? "My motion, in terms of crave 2 of the initial writ", would, however, be appropriate. Do you know why? "As it says in the summons, my Lord", is not right because in the sheriff court we have writs or initial writs and not summonses—except in summary causes of course, in which that would be perfectly correct. Again these may be statements of the obvious, but I believe that they are by no means obvious to new litigators. How do you deal with this? You can learn again by listening and also by thinking much more clearly about what exactly you are saying. I mean, About-Every-Single-Word-That-You-Are-Saying. Do you want the sheriff to "repel" a preliminary plea or "reserve" it? Do you know the difference? The words sound alike but their meaning and effect is worlds apart.

Latin language

Some of the more perceptive of you may have noticed that there is **4–07** quite a bit of Latin cropping up in court cases, from time to time. Sometime, sooner or later, you are going to have to speak it—or at least words and phrases of it—out loud. For those who have not had a classical education this might be a problem. For those who have had a classical education, the problem might be that the sheriff had a different classical education and his or her pronunciation and yours might be several declensions apart. I know that some people do worry about this, and the solution is to pay attention to how the standard Latin words and phrases are pronounced in court to see if there is a conventional way of doing it. If in doubt at all, ask someone else how they would say it. The alternative is to make it up, and there is always the worry that this will lead to embarrassment. Try this one out: *Ex turpis causa non oritur action*. Finally, do you know what that Latin word or phrase means? If not, look it up.[26]

Precision of language

This takes me on to one of the most significant features of generic **4–08** advocacy skills. When appearing in court you must use precise language,

---

[26] See, e.g. Trayner, *Latin Maxims* (W. Green, Edinburgh).

and be prepared for the court and your opponent to scrutinise minutely what you say. It is not a conversation with your pals in the pub. The casual, offhand, ill-prepared remark in the course of your submissions can often come back to haunt you mercilessly. "My client is largely concerned about", may be met by the sheriff asking immediately, "So you are not opposing the other parts of this motion then?" "The real reason why I would wish to", could attract the (perfectly justifiable) response, "So all of the other reasons you have given so far were not real reasons?" Perhaps this sounds farfetched. It is not. I have heard much worse. With experience, these problems can be avoided; but the important point to appreciate is that it is fundamentally essential to sharpen up your thinking and your language for the purpose of advocacy. You simply will not be used to every word you say being analysed. The perfectly acceptable casualness of thought and language which suffices for most social and working environments, including most legal work, simply will not do. Be prepared for this, and make a deliberate effort to move up several gears when you are on your feet until your experience[27] kicks in automatically.

Know the Rules

4–09   You might think that you know them. When you start appearing in court you will find that you do not know them well enough. This does not mean that you must study them intimately until you can memorise them and repeat them verbatim on demand. What to do is to concentrate on the rule, or rules, which you know or suspect will come into play in your hearing. Read them properly. For example, do they give the court a discretion or is the rule mandatory? If it is important, look for authorities on the interpretation of the rule, or rules. Understand what they provide. Have a copy of the Rules with you in court at all times.[28] Over time you will become familiar with the rules which are of real significance and of the way in which a particular court or sheriff is likely to interpret them. In this way you will acquire the necessary detailed knowledge. Remember also that if you are addressing the sheriff on one of the more obscure rules the sheriff might be quite unfamiliar with them too. By the same token, the sheriff will require little guidance on the application of rules which feature frequently. Make sure you know how they are likely to be applied.

Know the facts of your case and have full instructions

4–10   A word of explanation is required here. If it is your case, i.e. you have had it since day one, there is no excuse for not knowing every nuance of it. If there are important facts which the sheriff needs to know then you should be able to tell the sheriff, or it may be assumed that you have not investigated it properly or kept on top of it. That is unforgivable. It is your fault, and the remedy is down to you. Similarly, you should know what you want to happen procedurally or otherwise with your own case, so you should be able to react and respond to whatever the sheriff might

---

[27] Usually, but not always
[28] You know this makes sense and it is a small book which fits easily into your case.

decide at the hearing.[29] Sometimes,[30] however, you will be appearing in cases which you have not handled personally from day one. You may have taken the case over from a colleague, or simply been asked to attend court for a specific hearing on behalf of a colleague. You might have been asked to appear for another firm because you happen to be going to court that day anyway. This type of appearance gives invaluable experience,[31] but it also exposes you to the possibilities of a legal "hospital pass". You may not know as much about the case as you should, and you may find that it has all kinds of complications in its subject-matter or its history of which you were blissfully unaware. The real problem for you is that, if you are appearing in court in that case and on that day, it is your case. In other words, you must know all of the relevant material about it that the principal solicitor would know. If you do not, there is no excuse, and it is quite unacceptable to say to the court as you are being slowly roasted on a spit by the sheriff, "It is not my case". Yes, it is.

If you are asked to appear in these circumstances, then you must ensure that you obtain full instructions which means you want to know everything you could reasonably need to know to handle that hearing. If your work colleague or your boss hands you the case 10 minutes before it is due to call, then you should ask questions about it until you are satisfied you have all of the (up-to-date) information you might need to answer any of the awkward questions the sheriff might come up with.[32] Check that you know what your position is to be if the sheriff does not do what you will be asking him to do, and what your position will be if the sheriff does something you certainly do not want him to do. Too often, you could be landed with a dodgy hearing where your client's position is weak and unacceptable to the court. You are the person appearing. It is entirely your responsibility. If someone else asks you to appear you should conduct the same exercise, with the added option that if you are unhappy about the position you can decline the instructions. It is actually a compliment that people might hesitate to try and foist poor instructions on you because they know that you will put them through the mill before accepting the instructions. There are experienced practitioners who can take a one line instruction in an unknown case and convert it into a learned and sympathetic submission, which would convince all and sundry that they had spent all day studying the pleadings and analysing the previous procedure. That is a true skill, but even they will be reluctant to act on hopeless and illusory instructions.

Reputation and respect

You will not acquire a good reputation over night. You have to work **4–11** at it and prove yourself. You can acquire a bad reputation instantly. If you are ill-prepared, poorly instructed, and, worst of all, considered to be not entirely reliable by the court, then you are in big trouble. Every time

---

[29] In some circumstances, you may well have taken specific instructions from the client as to what you should be doing if this or that happens at the hearing.

[30] Perhaps often.

[31] It is one way in which you can "practise" advocacy.

[32] And the sheriff will.

that you appear you will have a credibility hurdle to overcome. It should not need saying but, of course, you must be entirely truthful with the court. The information you give to the court should be accurate. You do not need to vouch for everything. "I am advised by my client, the pursuer, that", makes it clear that this is based upon what your client has told you. "I can advise your Lordship that", would suggest that you have satisfied yourself that this is true. There is an important difference between the two. You are an officer of the court, and you have duties to the court which you must not neglect nor play down.[33] Show respect and you will receive it in most cases. It is disrespectful to be badly prepared, have totally inadequate instructions, be unaware of the Rules, or of the basic substantive law underlying your case or your motion. Need I say more? Most sheriffs will appreciate that you are just starting off[34] and will not be too harsh nor expect too much from a novice. On the other hand, some might just be tempted to give you a taste of your inadequacies as an incentive to do it better next time. There is no point in, and indeed no justification for, complaining about it. Deal with it like a grown-up professional person. Apologise, if appropriate; do not do it again[35]; and do it better next time. Think about it as a lesson learned— the hard way—and make sure that when you next appear in similar circumstances, or before the same sheriff, you can demonstrate that you have improved.[36] The court will respect you for that.

Presentation skills

4–12   I hesitate to describe this in this way because I have nightmare visions of flip charts, computer software package presentations, and other devices beloved of those who are selling something or just themselves. What we are looking at here is the presentation of persuasive argument, or the presentation of evidence followed by persuasive argument, to a sheriff. I am sure that I had no conception of this idea when I started. I simply copied what everyone else was doing and figured that it seemed to work for them so it would do for me. I do not recall dwelling too long on the shock of hearing what my voice sounded like, or the horror of noticing that what I was saying in court was not exactly what my brain was thinking at the time. I did not think about making life easy for the "decision-maker" nor about painting a story nor about constructing a road map. I wish I had, as I do not subscribe to the view that things were better in the old days when you just got on with it, and it either worked or it did not. Without being too theoretical there are a number of things you can think about which might enhance your presentation of cases and evidence in court, and I am going to list them here. Some of them will be developed more fully in context in later chapters.

Preparation

4–13   Sorry to mention this again. We all know what it means, and that it is crucial, but it might be worth elaborating a little. Telling people to

---

[33] Have a look again at *Watson v Student Loans Co Ltd* [2005] CSOH 134.
[34] I am sorry, it is usually obvious; but do not worry about it.
[35] It is said that a professional only makes the same mistake once.
[36] This is the legendary "deep end" teaching. It was done to me. It is not pleasant, and can put some people off for life.

prepare properly does not really tell you much if it does not indicate what kind of things you should be doing or thinking about. I will deal with preparations for debates and proofs in later chapters. To prepare for contentious hearings,[37] you might want to think about, and, in appropriate circumstances, write down:

- How much time can you afford to spend on the preparation?
- What do you want from the court?
- What rule says the court can give it to you?
- What case or cases have dealt with the same or a similar issue and how were they decided? Note them.
- Anticipate the counter-arguments—there are always counter-arguments—and think about your answer to them. Note these.
- What would defeat your argument entirely, and how would you deal with that? Note it.
- What if the sheriff asks you the one question—or more than one question—which you really do not want to hear him ask? Think hard about this and note it. (Are there any authorities on the point?)
- Do you think it is going to be a long submission or a short one?
- If it is long, should you provide an outline for the sheriff before you launch into it?
- Similarly, do you want to work on the structure of the submission: What would you say first/last?
- How do you make notes to enable you to present the argument more effectively: Read them? Headings only? Write out verbatim?
- Do you have a fall-back position?
- How do you pull all of this together and make your papers and notes accessible and easy to manage when you are standing up in court?
- How will you finish?

Your speech

I mean by this the way in which you are going to say what you have **4–14** prepared. Teaching inexperienced court lawyers has highlighted a number of common problems which can be solved.

The sheriff has to hear what you are going to say. Do you speak **4–15** loudly enough and clearly enough? When you start appearing in court, you probably do not, so without any scientific evidence, I am going to tell you to speak up already. Now speak even louder. In fact speaking clearly is probably preferable to speaking loudly, and not always the same thing. Think about that. Now speak even louder again.

Speak 'up', by which I mean do not address the sheriff while **4–16** hunched over your notes. This makes you talk at the desk in front of you and does not make it easy for the sheriff to hear you. Hold your notes up

---

[37] I am using a loose term deliberately.

in front of your face—but not between you and the sheriff's ears—or use the notes for reference and refreshing of your memory before speaking to the sheriff without looking at them.

4–17   **Lack of confidence in yourself is understandable when you start off.**   Anxiety makes you mumble. Lack of confidence in your material can also make you mumble quietly.[38] You can alleviate this to some extent by preparing top-class material which you know is good. You can alleviate the anxious mumble by—well, you know—speaking up. You can do it.

4–18   **Look at the sheriff while addressing him.**   Is the sheriff noting what you are saying and looking at you? Is the sheriff following/hearing what you are saying? Tune in to this. Is the sheriff nodding/looking quizzical/ filling a fountain pen? You are supposed to be persuading him. Does the sheriff look like he is being persuaded?

4–19   **Do not talk too quickly.**   The sheriff might tell you to slow down but one way to check your speed is to watch if the sheriff is noting what you are saying. Is the sheriff writing it down at about the same speed that you are saying it? Someone said to me that speaking quickly is not a problem as long as you pause for a while between sentences. That might be true. Start slowly—especially when you are just beginning your submissions and it is all new to the sheriff. Keep going slowly. The sheriff can think about what you are saying while writing it down if you go slowly. It is rare indeed that a sheriff asks an agent to hurry up, so you should be safe if you go slowly.

4–20   **Take your time generally.**   If you are referring the sheriff to parts of the record or documents, wait until he has it in front of him and has read it and digested it. Watch the sheriff. Once the sheriff has it and appears to have absorbed it move on, but not before. The same goes for referring the sheriff to authorities, which is dealt with specifically later.[39]

4–21   **Be precise, accurate and truthful about details and dates that are important.**   For example, in a motion for decree by default for a failure to lodge defences on time, an explanation that,

> *"We received very basic instructions a couple of weeks ago and have been unable to speak to the defender yet, although we are hoping she will attend for an appointment soon",*

is likely to attract judicial cross-examination and sounds as though you do not know/care about this. Contrast,

> *"We received a file of papers from the insurers on October 14 but there was no detail of the defender's response to the claim on the file. I am*

---

[38] Maybe the sheriff will not hear this properly and interpret it favourably.
[39] See Ch.6.

advised that the reason for this is that there was some doubt about the insurance cover applicable at the time. Fortunately, that issue had been resolved by the insurers shortly before we were instructed. We wrote/ telephoned her on October 15 and were advised by her daughter that she and her husband had departed on holiday on October 14. They are returning to this country on October 28 and an appointment has been made for the defender to attend at our offices on October 29 to give a detailed statement. We would be proposing to lodge full and detailed defences immediately thereafter and accordingly".

If you are not able to do this, the sheriff might smell a rat—you.

Try to modulate your voice. This makes your submission easier and **4–22** more pleasant to listen to. The sheriff will be more inclined to give you what you are after if your submission is made in an orderly way, and expressed in an interesting voice. Do you know if your voice is boring? Does anyone know? It is impossible to be objective about this, but try to be aware that if you speak loud and clear, pause for emphasis, raise your voice and lower it, speak higher and lower from time to time, change your tone of presentation, etc. this is likely to sound more attractive than a monotonous[40] booming speech. Decision-makers prefer the former.

Give an outline for certain submissions. If your submission is going **4–23** to be long—and you should know—and involves more than one simple proposition of law or a complex factual background, I would suggest that you advise the sheriff that you have detailed submissions to make and that you give him an outline/structure/road map of what you are going to be saying before you launch into the speech in detail. This makes it easier to follow.

Interpersonal relationships

I will now go on to look at some general advocacy issues arising out of **4–24** the relationship with others in court.

Who speaks first? The party who is moving the motion will normally speak first. If the basis for the motion is self-evident, but the motion is opposed, then you may have to say very little, and the sheriff may invite the other side to start. If the case is calling for further procedure of some kind, then either agent may start. Do you want to make the running? Get your oar in first? Set the agenda for the submissions? Or would you prefer to hear what the other side have to say—and how the sheriff deals with that—before you state your position? It is difficult to explain the subtleties in the abstract, but there are ways in which you can influence matters by going first or by going second.

Do not interrupt the other side. When your opponent is on his or **4–25** her feet and talking, your position is on your seat with your mouth shut. If your opponent says something to which you take exception in relation

---

[40] Which as well as meaning "unvarying" also means "dull and tedious".

to the merits or history or otherwise, you will have your chance to comment upon this when you make your submissions, and you should wait your turn. It would be acceptable to interrupt your opponent's submission only if you are doing so to assist him or her and the court by, for example, advising that X or Y is not being disputed, or is agreed.

4–26 **Do not interrupt the sheriff.** When the sheriff's mouth is open, yours should instantly be closed.[41] When the sheriff talks, you listen, and wait until he has finished.

4–27 **Answer the sheriff's questions directly.** There is no place in court for a politician's answer to a direct question. It is another example of the obvious difference between casual discussion and court advocacy. Any exchange will be designed to focus issues and sheriffs are good at doing this—and properly taking you to task if you are trying to obscure them.

4–28 **When to stop.** You should pay attention to how the sheriff is responding to what you are saying. Is the sheriff listening, interested, etc.? In a longer submission, you may gain the clear impression that the sheriff has heard all he wants, or needs, to hear from you. It is entirely up to you how, and how detailed, you want to make your submissions and you will not be stopped by the sheriff if you want to say more. However, it is desirable to watch for the signs and quit, especially if it appears to you that you are ahead at the time.

4–29 **When to concede.** You may be presenting submissions in which you may not have the greatest confidence,[42] or in which you can clearly see the sheriff is not with you. It is for you to consider whether you concede the point or not. You are perfectly entitled to say that those are your submissions,[43] and leave it to the sheriff to rule on the point or, alternatively, you could say that you are no longer insisting in your position. Remember, however, that the court interlocutor is likely to reflect that fact. If you are in court to oppose a motion, but the interlocutor records that it was granted "of consent" would that cause any problem with your boss or with your client? Watch and listen to the sheriff to see how the land lies.

4–30 **What to concede.** Conceding something may not be the same as conceding the whole argument. A prudent and judicious concession may even strengthen your argument. Adhering to a weak position on some part of your case might affect your credibility, and the receipt of your arguments on other parts. Again, you must think about how this all appears, and sounds, to the sheriff.

4–31 **Etiquette.** Try to look alert and respectful in court. Do not carry on conversations, make loud noises, laugh, chat to clients, eat,[44] etc. Some

---

[41] Leaving aside the unlikely scenario that the sheriff is yawning.
[42] Although you should be wary of presenting them in such a way as to make it clear that is what you think.
[43] Whether you agree with them or not.
[44] I saw that once.

sheriffs can tolerate a degree of informality in a busy court. Others can hear a pin drop two courts away and would be distracted and irritated by it. When you are starting off, you must avoid drawing attention to yourself for the wrong reasons. Carry on your conversations with solicitors or client outside the court. And make sure to bow on the way out and into the court when the sheriff is on the Bench.[45]

Dress. Dress properly for court.[46] **4–32**

Courtesy. Do not get personal with your opponent. You are agents **4–33** for clients whose respective interests you represent. These will inevitably conflict. You do not need, and should not want, to adopt their personal antagonism towards each other. Indeed, one of the benefits to the court in having lawyers representing parties is that they expect the dispute to be confined to issues and not personalities. You can, among other things, provide a line of communication between the parties which is always preferable to naked and outright hostility from all concerned. Treat your opponent the way you would like to be treated by others. Do not take advantage of your opponent's inexperience—someone could do that to you. Do not sulk. Do not snort, roll your eyes, throw pens, or jump up and down banging the desk while your opponent is addressing the sheriff. That is not to say that there might not be room for a little bit of gamesmanship,[47] but I do not recommend it.

Preparation: A practical illustration

Let me conclude this chapter with a practical illustration of the **4–34** preparation and thought process you might be advised to follow for a relatively routine, but by no means straightforward, motion. Assume that you have been instructed to attend on behalf of the pursuer and ask for the time for the amendment to be (further) prorogated. You are not dealing with the case personally. What might you want to know to enable you to make the motion effectively? What will you want to think about (and prepare for) in advance?

- What is the case about?
- When was it last on?
- What happened then?
- When should the amendment have been in?
- Why exactly was it not lodged on time?[48]
- What are you proposing to do?
- Is it being opposed?
- What are the grounds of opposition?

---

[45] An elementary courtesy which, I can assure you, will not go unnoticed by the sheriff. The precise angle of the bow may be found in the Practice Notes for the particular sheriffdom.

[46] At the risk of confirming the huge generational gap between myself and the reader, can I just borrow from Monty Python here and hope you understand, "Say no more".

[47] I am being realistic here. I am told I do something with my eyebrows but, of course, I have never seen it myself.

[48] "Difficulty in obtaining instructions" might sound lame and unacceptable.

- What do the rules say about this?
- Does the sheriff have a discretion?
- Can the sheriff do this?
- Have there been any cases about it recently, and is there a relevant rule?
- What exactly am I going to say?
- Am I going to be confident/apologetic/business-like, etc.?
- What if the sheriff asks me about X?
- What is to happen next if it is granted/refused?
- What about expenses?

Of course, you realise that, having gone through this whole process the hearing itself may just amount to:

> "*I appear on behalf of the pursuer, my Lord. My motion is to extend the time allowed for lodging the minute of amendment by a further seven days.*"
> "*No objection to my friend's motion, my Lord.*"
> "*So be it.*"

Illustrating, additionally, the essential truth that, if you prepare fully and properly, it will be easy. On the other hand, if you do not prepare that is when it can go wrong.[49] In the realistic world of the sheriff court lawyer, you cannot prepare for absolutely everything but you have to identify those hearings which may cause problems and put the appropriate work in to them. Experience will tell you when to do this, and you will probably pitch it right about 90 per cent of the time. Until you reach that stage, and until you can trust yourself to respond appropriately to any situation which the case, your opponent, or the court can throw at you, then do the preparation. It is worth it, and your advocacy skills should flourish.

---

[49] You do not want to see the script for the ill-prepared solicitor presenting this motion to an inquisitive sheriff—it is scary.

CHAPTER 5

MOTIONS

"I appear on behalf of the defender. My friend, Ms Thomson, appears on behalf of the pursuer. This is the defender's motion to sist the cause for investigation. This is an action for damages for. . .".

Short version

"Defender, my Lord . . . sist for investigation . . . Obliged."

General

In simple terms, a motion is a request by a party in the litigation for the **5–01** court to do something or allow something to be done. The sheriff will usually only make an order if one or other, or both, of the parties ask him to do so.[1] Many motions are unopposed, and granted without a hearing. If a motion is opposed, or if the sheriff wants a hearing of a motion, then it will be necessary for the party who makes the motion to make submissions in support of it. Basic advocacy skills are required in the presentation of such motions to the court. Formerly,[2] all motions would call in court, notwithstanding a lack of opposition. It was necessary for the person moving the motion to say something about it and, if required by the sheriff, to justify the granting of the motion. This gave young lawyers practice at simply standing up and speaking in court. These opportunities are less frequent now, but there is a benefit in examining and dissecting the presentation of even the simplest motions, as a means of highlighting some of the basic tools and techniques required as a foundation for successful advocacy.

Procedure

In the sheriff court, motions may be made "orally with leave of the **5–02** court during any hearing of a cause or . . . by lodging a written motion in Form G6".[3] In this section, we shall look briefly at the procedure in written motions.[4] The motion has to be intimated to the opponent. The opponent can: (1) positively consent to the motion; (2) not oppose the motion; or (3) mark opposition to it by lodging and intimating a notice of

---

[1] If the sheriff makes an order of his or her own volition, this is termed *"ex proprio motu"*.
[2] Before the Ordinary Cause Rules 1993 (hereafter "OCR").
[3] OCR, r.15.1.
[4] For fuller details of the procedural rules, see OCR, Ch.15; I.D. Macphail, *Sheriff Court Practice* (2nd edn, W. Green/Scottish Universities Law Institute, Edinburgh, 1998), Vol. 1, paras 5.44–5.55; Charles Hennessy, *Civil Procedure and Practice* (2nd edn, W. Green, Edinburgh, 2005), para.15–03.

opposition.[5] If the motion is opposed or if the sheriff, for some reason, requires to hear a party on a motion which is not opposed, the sheriff clerk will fix a hearing.

In the first instance, the maker of the motion will have to ensure that the procedural requirements of intimation are complied with, otherwise the motion cannot be heard.[6] The principal motion has to be lodged with the sheriff clerk within five days after intimation.[7] The court must have the principal motion before it for the hearing.

Written motion

5–03   The precise wording of the written motion is not absolutely crucial,[8] but inadequate wording can cause a problem and there may be an advantage in giving more than just the bare words of what is sought. For example, a written motion "to discharge the proof fixed for April 10, 2002" might lead to a sheriff fixing a hearing of the motion even if not opposed, whereas a motion "to discharge the proof fixed for April 10, 2002 in respect that the defender is scheduled to undergo surgery on April 7 and will not be able to attend the proof" might avoid the need for a hearing.[9] By the same token, there may be an advantage in setting out in the motion, the rule which is being relied upon to justify the motion, especially in some of the more obscure or contentious motions. For example, a motion "to remit to James Anderson, architect, as a man of skill, . . . the question of whether . . . , in terms of Rule 29.2(1) of the Ordinary Cause Rules 1993", might be preferable to a motion which simply asks for a remit to a named man of skill.

The majority of motions nowadays are decided without a hearing. With continued pressures on court time and the administrative aim that cases should only call in court when necessary, it is quite possible that, in years to come, there will be more emphasis placed upon the terms of a written motion. Ultimately, the motion itself may require to contain additional material to justify the order sought, possibly even including legal argument.[10] For the time being however, when a motion is heard, the solicitor will normally present all of their submissions and arguments orally.

Motions at the Bar

5–04   If the court is actually hearing some aspect of a case,[11] it is always possible to make a separate motion at the Bar during the course of that hearing. This can be used as a device to speed up procedure and avoid

---

[5] OCR, Form G9.

[6] A common problem arises in a motion and specification of documents for recovery of hospital records where no intimation has been made on the Lord Advocate.

[7] Where the other party is legally represented intimate by fax. The principal motion can be sent off to the sheriff clerk at the same time, along with the certificate of intimation, and this saves any worry about complying with the this time-limit.

[8] For styles of motion, see *Greens Litigation Styles*.

[9] Then again, this might not suffice—although in practice, if it was not opposed by the pursuer, the sheriff would almost certainly grant it.

[10] The form of motion in the Court of Session has a section asking the party to state the reason for the motion "if reason required".

[11] e.g. an options hearing.

unnecessary formality (and expense). It would be wise to advise the opponent in advance that this was intended, although sometimes the need for it will not emerge until the court has made some other order at the hearing itself.[12] There may be occasions when the opposing agent may properly say that they would need instructions before responding to it. If so, then the motion probably would not be heard. Accordingly, if it were possible to make some informal intimation in advance[13] that would be sensible.[14] If the opponent were to be advised as soon as reasonably possible that this is going to be done then the court could hear the motion on grounds of expediency and the interests of justice, notwithstanding the lack of a formal motion and intimation. The general moral is that most things can be done by way of verbal motion at the Bar, provided there is no real prejudice to the other side and provided that some reasonable notification of the intention has been given.[15] It is unlikely, however, that a sheriff would hear a motion at the Bar which would have the effect of deciding the merits of the case, in whole or in part.[16]

Advocacy in simple motions

Let us look again at the words of the submissions made in support of **5–05** the motion at the start of this chapter. Experience shows that the alternative version might actually suffice in certain circumstances, before certain sheriffs, and with certain agents. However, for the avoidance of doubt, it is not good enough. Many simple procedural motions[17] will in fact go through "on the nod" and it would be foolish not to acknowledge this. This usually only happens to agents who know what they are doing anyway, so this probably will not assist the reader.[18]

In the first version, we are looking at the opening remarks of the defender's agent[19] who has made a written motion which has been opposed by the pursuer, or in which the sheriff wants to hear submissions though unopposed. A realistic scenario could assume that the motion has been made after the options hearing at which the court has fixed a date for a debate on the relevancy of skeletal defences lodged by the defender. One could anticipate strong opposition from a pursuer in these circumstances.[20] In any event, we shall assume that the defender has to make all the running. The defender might say something along these lines:

---

[12] e.g. refusal of a written motion by you to discharge a proof because of the unavailability of a witness might prompt a motion at the Bar to take evidence on commission.

[13] e.g by flagging it up in a letter to the opponent.

[14] Say, e.g. a case was calling for proof on February 12, and there was a r.18.3 hearing fixed for February 10 to finalise an amendment procedure, it may well be possible to make other motions at the bar in connection with the forthcoming proof (e.g. to discharge it because of serious problems with witnesses).

[15] An interesting illustration and commentary on this point can be found in *Richardson v Rivers*, Sheriff Principal Macphail, August 23, 2004, unreported.

[16] In that case, a sheriff might suggest that a formal written motion should be made.

[17] And even some potentially complex motions.

[18] This is down to "experience", "sod's law" or just plain "unfairness", but that is the way it is.

[19] The agent for Mr and Mrs Gray in the kitchen case.

[20] If the pursuer did not oppose the motion, the sheriff could still order a hearing if the sheriff felt the motion was coming too late and the sheriff wanted to keep control of the litigation regardless of any consensus between the parties.

> "*My Lord, my name is Mr Carter. I appear on behalf of the defender in this case. This is the defender's motion to sist for investigation.*
> *[The motion is unopposed but I understand from your Lordship's clerk that your Lordship wishes to hear me on the reasons for it]* or *[My friend, Ms Thomson, appears on behalf of the pursuer. The motion is opposed.]*
>   *As your Lordship will appreciate,*[21] *this is an action of payment for kitchen furniture and fittings supplied by the pursuer to the defender. The pursuer has recently produced a report from an expert on the condition of the furniture . . . The report has not yet been lodged by the pursuer but I have a copy with me if your Lordship wishes to see it . . . The defenders require to consider this and the implications of it, which might well include instructing an expert of their own . . .*
>   *I may also say that the report has given rise to further informal discussions between the parties and there is at least some prospect of matters being resolved by agreement rather than incurring the expense of continued court action . . . .*
>   *In these circumstances, I would move your Lordship to grant the motion . . .".*

In this apparently simple submission we can find most of the basic ingredients for a properly presented motion. What should you look for?

5–06   *Who are you? Who are you appearing for? Who is your opponent?*   The start is standard. Develop the habit of saying this. Eventually you will do so automatically. It is not as simple as it might look. I have often heard young (and not so young) agents start by appearing for the "wrong" party or not being absolutely sure who they do appear for.

5–07   *Why are you there?*   Tell the sheriff why we are all congregated before him and not safely ensconced in the Bar common room drinking coffee.[22] "This is the pursuer's motion to" or "This is the motion of the second defender to".

   By the time you are appearing, you should know the basis of your opponent's opposition and been unable to resolve it by agreement. You may be able to say that "the motion is opposed in part" or "in one particular respect" which will help to set the scene for the detail you are going to give next. Alternatively, if the sheriff has asked for the hearing, you should have checked with the clerk, as a matter of prudence, what is bothering him.

5–08   *Give the sheriff time.*   This will be a recurrent theme and an important aspect of advocacy skills. You should be watching the sheriff as you make your submissions. Is the sheriff ready to hear what you have to say? Is the sheriff writing things down? Is the sheriff paying attention to you? Your case may be news to him or, at least, the motion may be news to him. It is

---

[21] And if his Lordship does not appreciate that, then you must give him time to understand what it is about. See Ch.4.

[22] A particular advocacy skill which seems to come naturally to beginners and requires no intensive training.

vital to give the sheriff time to listen and digest what you are saying. A pause after the formalities of the introduction to your submissions makes sense and will remind you about pacing the submissions.[23]

Explain briefly what the case is about. Do not take it for granted that **5–09** the sheriff will know. If the sheriff has a record in front of him he could read it, but it will be lengthy and he probably wants an overview of the case before he hears what the point of an opposed motion is. If the sheriff has no record, then it will be even more helpful if you advise him generally what the case is about and what points are at issue. The more complex, difficult or contentious the motion might be, the more you ought to explain to the sheriff about the case as an introduction. You may want to go on to look at the detailed pleadings, but if you dive straight into a detailed exposition of the whole case at this stage of your submissions you are running the risk of obscuring what is relevant.

What is the reason for your motion? Give the sheriff a clear and **5–10** succinct reason for the motion. In this case, you feel that a report is necessary for you to defend the case properly. There may not be enough time for you to obtain a report before a significant procedural event in the case (the debate on your skeletal pleadings). Your client will be prejudiced if the case continues. There is a genuine defence albeit that this has not been pled—you might want to say what that defence is, or is likely to be, and explain why you have not or cannot elaborate on it at the moment and in what way the report is necessary.

Acknowledge the reason for the opposition and deal with it. If you know **5–11** why the motion is being opposed then it is useful to address this as you continue with your submissions. You may know generally that it is opposed without having precise detailed reasons, and in that case it might be prudent to await the detailed opposition before dealing with this yourself. It is a matter of judgment whether it would be more effective trying to anticipate the opposition or not.[24] If you are not clear what the other side are likely to say then there is no benefit in trying to speculate about their precise reasons. In a case where the motion has been fixed on the sheriff's request then you should know why he is concerned beforehand and indicate that you understand why there might have been a concern on his part—this can be good advocacy provided you do not grovel your way into sycophancy.[25]

Where does this all fit within the action as a whole and what effect will it **5–12** *have on it.* The action has been raised to secure the resolution of a dispute between two parties, by settlement or by court order. Any motion should somehow fit into that overall scheme. Will the objective be frustrated by granting the motion? This could be a powerful factor in

---

[23] This is one of the most common problems—speaking too quickly.
[24] That is an advocacy skill and only you can judge how to play it—but you should be aware of it.
[25] There can often be a fine dividing line between the two. Crossing the line is a major error.

granting or not. The court must have regard to the "interests of justice" and motions will often be decided by the sheriff's perception of what is in the interests of justice. There is legitimate scope for a wide range of interpretations of that term. The sheriff frequently has a discretion to decide motions one way or another. On the one hand, your client may have a good defence which cannot be put because of the time constraints. On the other hand, the pursuer is entitled to expect the action to follow the timetable provided in the rules.[26] Questions of fairness will arise and matters of detail can then be considered. Such as:

- How long did it take for the pursuer to raise the action in the first place?
- When did the defender know the pursuer had an independent report?
- Should the defender have obtained such a report earlier anyway?
- Should such a motion have been made earlier?
- When is the debate to take place?[27]

The impact of these issues may have to be addressed when the motion is made and this would mean going into some detail about dates, procedure, time-scales, etc. Some sheriffs might look for such information and some may be more relaxed. It may not be necessary to provide this in the opening submissions, but if you are aware that these are going to be matters of concern then precise and accurate information along these lines could form part of the submissions. If this is done well, it could leave very little for the opponent to say, and could go a long way to persuading the sheriff to decide in favour of the defender before the pursuer has even had a chance to say anything.[28]

5–13   *Use of language.*   Take as an example, "There is at least some prospect of matters being resolved by agreement". This holds out the possibility that, if the case was sisted for this purpose, the action as a whole might be settled. A sheriff might consider this to be a desirable end and preferable to the delay and expense of a full-blown court action taken to its conclusion. But the solicitor is careful not to say it will settle. One aspect of advocacy skills is to persuade the sheriff that this possibility (which might only be a theoretical possibility) is worth taking into account. In a sense, the words can be taken to mean whatever you want them to mean. You are not telling lies, or misleading the court, but there is no guarantee of settlement and no commitment on your side.[29] Consider the different nuances of meaning in these phrases: "There are good prospects of settlement", "There are some prospects of settlement", "There is at least some prospect of certain matters being agreed". These are the kind of

---

[26] And proceed "expeditiously".

[27] If it is eight weeks away, why not just leave that date as fixed? The defender would have time to instruct a report, and if the defender obtains a report in the intervening time then there may be no real prejudice to them if the case continued as timetabled.

[28] You should be looking for a reaction from the sheriff as you make your submissions: Is the sheriff with you or not? Are you persuading the sheriff this sounds reasonable?

[29] The sheriff might ask you how realistic that possibility is, and you should be ready to respond to such an interjection.

subtle differences which you will learn and use when practising advocacy. There are many words and phrases like this which can be inserted in your submissions to make them more effective.

Do not forget the "what if".   "What if" the sheriff asks you why the **5–14** motion is being made at this stage, or how long the investigation might take, or whether you have identified or instructed an expert already. The number and variety of questions an inquisitive[30] sheriff might ask are endless. When starting to appear in court, it would be as well for you to know the answer to all of these questions and more. You have to be prepared, and the sheriff will expect you to be instructed. The sheriff is perfectly entitled to expect you to have full instructions for even the simplest motion. You are appearing in court. You are the representative of the party. Even if it is not your case[31] it is your responsibility when standing up in court to know everything about the case and about the Motion.

Conclusion.   It is important to draw your submissions to a close by **5–15** repeating and confirming what it is that you want the court to do.[32] If nothing else, it gives you something to aim at when making your submissions and enables you to finish on a clear and professional note.

Accordingly, you can appreciate that, even in a relatively straightforward procedural motion, you still ought to present the motion in a logical and coherent way. You have to justify the motion and you have to be aware of the possible concerns from your opponent and/or from the sheriff. You have to be aware of the implications of the motion being granted or refused for the future of the action itself. There is a risk of making this sound a highly complex process even in the most simple of motions[33] but that would be the wrong impression. Countless motions are heard and decided on a daily basis in the sheriff court without any detailed or structured submission. The point is that you should start with the good habit of having a mental checklist and a structure to your submissions which will apply in every case. You can discard it or shorten it once you have a feel for what is required in different situations. You will be able to appreciate this with experience, but when you are starting off it does make sense to think about all of the matters which I have mentioned and to anticipate any difficulties which could arise, even in the simplest of motions.

Go back to the outline of the words of the submissions made earlier[34] and compare them with this:

"My Lord, I am appearing on behalf of the defender. The defender requires an expert's report on the kitchen furniture which is the subject of

---

[30] Some might say difficult. Others might say incisive or conscientious.
[31] Which can happen quite often. But remember, you are standing there, therefore, it is your case.
[32] All the more so if you have been addressing him for a little time.
[33] The agent doing a dozen motions a day might even find it preposterous to go into such detail.
[34] See para.5–05.

dispute in this case and it might take quite a while for this to be done. The pursuer has its own expert's report and our clients need one too. Would your Lordship sist the case for this purpose?"

5–16 The submission is obviously shorter and simpler. It might be sufficient in the circumstances. The sheriff might have had a quick look at the papers and seen what the case was about. The sheriff might have seen that the pursuers have lodged an expert report as a production. The sheriff might look at the pursuer's agent when the motion is being presented or after the motion has been made and he may have reached an early view that he would grant the motion unless the pursuer started jumping up and down and complaining about it vociferously. Indeed, the sheriff may take the view that unless the pursuer makes any vociferous opposition he is not too concerned about the precise merits or otherwise of the motion.

Look at it another way, however. The sheriff has not really been told very much about the motion and the number of questions he is likely to ask is indeed countless. If the sheriff has to "extract" information from you in support of the motion, or senses that you do not have information which he thinks is relevant, then the sheriff will be much less inclined to grant the motion.

With experience, you will be able to "read" the likely attitude of the sheriff in advance. You will be able to work out how much or how little you might have to say. You will be able to tell when you are presenting your motion if the sheriff is inclined to grant it, and whether he is looking for more information or not, without him having to ask you. However, when you are starting off, you do not have these benefits. Of course, you will be embarrassed and self-conscious initially simply to be standing on your feet and speaking in court. You will want to say as little as possible and sit down again as quickly as possible. However, you have to resist that temptation. You may well want to write out in advance what you are going to say, even in the simplest of motions to be sure that it sounds right. How are you going to describe and summarise the nature of the action itself? It actually takes some skill to describe the content of a detailed writ and defences sufficiently clearly and accurately in one sentence, and you may want to think about how you would do this. You could just have said that it is "an action of payment". You could just have said that the defender disputes payment. That might be sufficient in certain circumstances but it is much more preferable to have in mind that you ought to define the action and the defence in more detail. The idea is to find a structured approach which works for presenting motions of every type and in every circumstance. If you do develop that habit then you will find this very helpful. It will be particularly helpful, if not absolutely essential, when presenting more complex motions in contentious cases and that is what we shall consider next.

Advocacy in more complex motions

5–17 I am going to use the term "complex" to describe motions in which both parties are likely to have to address the sheriff in detail on the facts of the case, or the law surrounding the motion, or the rules of procedure surrounding the motion.[35] First, you have to be able to identify it as such.[36] You are going to have to explain the circumstances of the case in more detail, you may have to make reference to procedural rules and/or the law, and you are going to have to present the argument in a structured way in order to make it attractive and understandable to the sheriff.

We are going to take, as an example, a motion for summary decree by the pursuer in the kitchen furniture case. Let us assume that the defenders lodged defences which are relatively brief. In the course of their defences, they have admitted that there was a contract to supply and fit the kitchen furniture. They have admitted that they paid a deposit of £5,000. They have said, in general terms that, "some of the work was unsatisfactory". They have not gone into any detail. They have not adjusted their defences, and six weeks have passed since the defences were lodged.[37] The pursuer has decided to lodge a motion for summary decree. The rules about this are contained in Chapter 17 of the Ordinary Cause Rules 1993, and such a motion will be prepared and intimated in precisely the same way as any other motion.[38]

The same basic structure mentioned above will apply here except that, since it is a more lengthy motion, it may be much more helpful to the sheriff[39] if you give him an outline of what you are going to be saying in advance of your detailed submissions. In other words,[40] it would be helpful to provide a "road map" for the sheriff. Here is an extract of what might be said by the pursuer making this motion:

"My Lord, my name is Ms Thomson. I appear on behalf of the pursuer **5–18** *in this case. My friend,[41] Mr Black, appears on behalf of the defenders. This is the pursuer's motion for a summary decree and it is opposed by my friend.*

My Lord, this is an action for payment for the supply and fitting of kitchen furniture. These proceedings were served on the defenders on January 17, 2005 and the defenders lodged fairly skeletal defences on February 20, 2005. It is now six weeks since those defences were lodged and there has been no further adjustment by the defenders. It is the pursuer's position that there is no valid defence to this action and the pursuer is entitled to summary decree. **[Pause.]**

I propose to address your Lordship, first, on the rules regarding the grant of summary decree, secondly, on the principles which the court should follow when applying these rules, and thirdly, on the facts of this particular case. I will be submitting that, in the present circumstances, your Lordship would be entitled, in the exercise of his discretion, to grant

---

[35] We are assuming the motion is opposed, but there can be complexities in unopposed motions too.

[36] There is nothing worse than giving the impression you had no idea this was going to be complex.

[37] Needless to say, this approach to defences is not recommended.

[38] Given the potential benefits of a motion for summary decree and the frequent lack of detail in defences, it is very surprising that such motions are not used more often, especially in actions for payment where there is a suspicion of a dilatory defence.

[39] Who has to note and understand your argument.

[40] A touch of jargon coming up.

[41] A legal term of endearment meaning "my enemy".

my motion. I will be proposing to move your Lordship for summary decree in the sum of £X. **[Pause again, is he still with you?]**

The rules regarding applications for summary decree are contained within the Ordinary Cause Rules 1993, Chapter 17. Rule 17.2(1) provides that, 'a pursuer may, at any time after a defender has lodged defences, apply by motion for summary decree against that defender on the ground that there is no defence to the action or part of it disclosed in the defences.' **[Take your time when reading this.]**

5–19   Rule 17.2(4) provides that, when considering such a motion, the sheriff may, '(a) if satisfied that there is no defence to the action or to any part of it to which the motion relates, grant the motion for summary decree in whole or in part'. **[Is the sheriff following you? Look.]**

Accordingly, as your Lordship will appreciate, your Lordship has a discretion whether to grant the motion or not and in order to grant the motion, your Lordship has to be satisfied that there is no defence to the action.

The terms of this rule are considered by Macphail in Sheriff Court Practice, Third Edition at page 510, paragraphs 14.71 to 14.74. My Lord, I have a copy of the relevant pages for your Lordship's convenience. **[Or otherwise.]** . . .

As Macphail says in paragraph 14.74, 'a court must consider the defence presented as at the date of the motion and should concentrate on the substance and authenticity of the defence, rather than just on the manner which it is expressed in the defences'. His authority for that proposition is the case of Frimokar which is referred to in the footnote, and your Lordship will also find reference in the footnote to the case of Whiteway Laidlaw Bank Ltd v Green, 1993 S.C.L.R. 968. This case is actually reported in 1994 Scots Law Times under the name of Whiteaway Laidlaw Bank Ltd v Green which is in 1994 S.L.T. (Sh. Ct) 18, and I have a copy of this case for your Lordship. **[Pause.]**

This case is a decision by Sheriff Principal Risk. It is not binding on your Lordship but, in my submission, it is highly persuasive and it contains guidance on the principles which should be applied when considering such a motion. The case also contains a useful summary of the prior decisions on the question of summary decree. So far as my researches are concerned, it is the last reported case on summary decree in the sheriff court in an action of payment and may be of assistance to your Lordship in considering the present motion.

5–20   In the Whiteaway case, the Bank raised an action of payment against three guarantors of a company. Defences were lodged and then the Bank made a motion for summary decree which was granted. One of the guarantors appealed to the sheriff principal. I should say that, at the time this case was being considered, the rule which was applicable was rule 59A of the old Ordinary Cause Rules. I have a copy of that rule for your Lordship and as your Lordship will see, the relevant parts of rule 59A are simply repeated in rule 17.2 of the Ordinary Cause Rules 1993 so I would submit that the decision in Whiteaway is equally pertinent to the present circumstances and the present rules.

In Whiteaway, the sheriff principal took the view that the sheriff had misdirected himself in granting the motion for summary decree and considered the whole question de novo.[42] The sheriff principal consid-

---

[42] "Of new".

ered that guidance could be obtained from an equivalent rule in the Court of Session and, at page 19, paragraph X, he comments that he was referred to a number of cases in which the Court of Session rule was considered. He then goes on to quote the relevant parts of what was said in these cases about the proper approach to considering a motion for summary decree and concludes by saying at page X, paragraph X, the following: 'I respectfully agree with the Opinions which I have cited above and consider that they should be applied mutatis mutandis in the application of Rule 59A of the Ordinary Cause Rules . . . (at this stage I would say, of course, that I am submitting that they should also apply to the current Rule 17.2 of the OCR 1993). . . . The purpose of the Rule is to enable the Sheriff to penetrate the form and examine the substance of the dispute between the parties. To that end he is entitled to take account not only of the pleadings but also of any productions which are placed before him and of information given to him in the course of the respective submissions . . . Summary Decree will not pass against a defender who appears to have the basis of a statable defence but who has expressed it badly . . . there will be some cases in which a defender is justified in stating a bald denial . . . but such cases do not include those in which the pursuer's pleadings and productions indicate that there is a prima facie case calling for an answer . . . where the defence stated is manifestly irrelevant and not capable of rectification by adjustment or amendment it would be appropriate to grant Summary Decree . . . whether or not there is a statable defence is a matter to be tested at the time when the Sheriff is hearing the Motion.'

Now, my Lord, what I take from that is that, in considering such a motion, your Lordship has to examine the substance of the dispute between the parties. He has to consider the pleadings and productions and what is said today by the parties. There is a prima facie case calling for an answer here and the facts are entirely within the defenders' knowledge. Your Lordship is entitled to look at the case on the basis of where the pleadings stand at the moment.

Turning now to the facts of this case, as I have already indicated, the **5–21** writ was served on January 17, 2005. The reason that proceedings were taken in this case is that the defenders had given no indication, prior to the raising of proceedings, that they had any specific complaints about the kitchen furniture supplied, apart from a query regarding the price of the furniture. At the same time that the writ was served, the pursuers lodged an inventory of productions and intimated this to the defenders. That inventory of productions is number 5/1 of process. As your Lordship will see, the first item on that inventory is a copy of the order form provided by the pursuer to the defenders and your Lordship will also see that this is accepted by the defender. On the face of it, this is the signature of the defender and the price given is the price for which the pursuer is now suing.

As I have said, it appeared that, prior to the raising of proceedings, the only issue the defenders were taking with the pursuer was that the price was overstated. It would appear that, once they had the opportunity to see the defenders had agreed to the price, as per the documentation to which I have referred, defences were then lodged which contained a very broad and general complaint that the kitchen furniture was not satisfactory. The defenders have not specified in what way it was

*unsatisfactory. They have not said whether it was the wrong colour,
whether it was the wrong specification, whether it was fitted wrongly,
whether it does not work or whatever. The defenders have had adequate
opportunity to expand upon the basic defences but they have not done so
and indeed they have not done so even following upon the intimation of
this motion. It is difficult to resist the conclusion that the only basis
upon which the defenders were really in dispute with the pursuer, prior to
litigation, was in relation to the actual cost and it was only when they
realised that they had no argument on cost that they introduced this
defence on the 'unsatisfactory' nature of the service. It is again difficult
to resist the conclusion that this is purely a dilatory defence which has
no substance and cannot be regarded as 'authentic' as described in
Macphail. In my submission, your Lordship can go beyond the bare and
skeletal nature of the defences lodged on behalf of the defenders and
your Lordship can be satisfied that there is no defence to this action as
matters presently stand.*

*Accordingly, I would move your Lordship to grant the pursuers'
motion and to grant summary decree in favour of the pursuer for the
sum of £X which is the full sum sued for. If your Lordship is with me on
this, then I would also move your Lordship to make an award of
expenses in favour of the pursuer."*

Structure of submissions

5–22   As you can see, the presentation of this motion is substantially different
and more complex than the presentation of the earlier motion.[43] However,
the framework in which the motion is presented is the same. The structure
of the submissions can be outlined as follows:

- Who you are, who you represent, and what your motion is.
- In simple terms, what the case is about, or, at least confirming
  that the sheriff knows, in simple terms, what the case is about
  from his or her own reading of the writ.
- An outline (road map) of what you are about to say so that the
  sheriff can see you are going to follow a certain structure and you
  are going to deal with things in a certain order. In this way, you
  can prevent the sheriff jumping forward in the argument and it
  also means that if you are taken off the point somewhat, you
  have a framework to come back to.
- What is the rule (or legal principle) upon which you are relying
  which makes it competent for the sheriff to grant your motion? It
  cannot be taken for granted that your motion is competent[44] or
  that the sheriff will think that your motion is competent. It
  cannot be taken for granted that the sheriff is familiar with the
  terms of the rule or its application.
- It is useful to give the sheriff some illustration of the application
  of the rule in practice. It would be very helpful if you had an

---

[43] Without significant interruption it might take 20–30 minutes to present. There are no
bonus points for presenting it too quickly.
[44] Although the competency of many familiar motions may be taken as read—but how do
you know?

authoritative and binding case but, in the absence of this, then you would want to present the sheriff with something which he would regard as highly persuasive and which illustrated the way in which the rule applies, and the way in which he should address the matter. By doing this, you are making it easier for the sheriff. By making it easier for the sheriff to consider the complexities of the case you are helping to persuade him. This is good advocacy.

- Because you are going off into a long discussion about legal principles, the framework which we have discussed earlier becomes even more helpful. The sheriff can still see that what you are saying fits into a context and is not just a ramble. You have explained to the sheriff beforehand, why you are referring him to this case.
- You are then going to come back and, having established the basic legal principles which the sheriff has to bear in mind, discuss the way in which they can be applied to this case. This means addressing the sheriff on all of the relevant facts of this case and tying them back (if possible) to your earlier submissions about what the sheriff can or cannot do, or should or should not do.
- In doing this, you are also anticipating what your opponent might say. You are cutting off avenues of escape. You are indicating to the sheriff that there is legitimate cause for concern about the authenticity of the defences so that, by the time the defender is standing up and speaking, they have a lot of work to do.
- You are concluding at the end by repeating what you are asking the sheriff to do and making it clear what your motion is.

Presentation of submissions

When making your submissions, you should be thinking about the way **5–23** in which you are presenting the argument to the sheriff.

1. You are trying to persuade the sheriff to decide in your favour. The easier you make it for the sheriff by providing chapter and verse and addressing all of the relevant considerations, the more likely the sheriff is to decide in your favour.
2. The sheriff probably has not seen the papers in this case until you are standing up appearing before him. You will have to take your time. Some sheriffs will tune into your motion very quickly. They will be ahead of you and they will appreciate where you are likely to be going. Some sheriffs will like to have a think about this as you are going along and take time to consider all that you have to say. It is better to go too slowly than too quickly. If you are going too slowly, and if there are points which the sheriff really does not need explained, then he will probably tell you. It may not seem that way at the time, but it might be a good sign if the sheriff hurries you up in this way, and it would be appropriate to thank him for allowing you to skip over part of your submissions. If you do have a clear and structured framework, such a (helpful) intervention from the sheriff will not put you off your stride or affect the presentation of the argument.

3. At the risk of being controversial, it is important to remember that the sheriff will probably know something about the law surrounding the motion that you are making to him but that the sheriff will not necessarily have an intimate and detailed knowledge and understanding of it. At least, the sheriff may well not have this at his fingertips. It may have been some time since the sheriff last had to consider the point. The sheriff is unlikely to have the precise wording of the rule indelibly imprinted in his mind. There is no disadvantage, and there are indeed several benefits, in taking him slowly through the rules and legal principles.

4. It is vitally important for you to have the pace of your submissions right. As already mentioned, some sheriffs will want to hear the arguments at a different pace. You have to try and tune into this. You have to give the sheriff time to listen to what you are saying, note down what he wants to note, understand your argument, digest it, and see how it applies to the motion before him. The sheriff can do all of this in a split second in some circumstances, but you should not take it for granted. Watch to see if the sheriff is writing/listening and respond accordingly.[45]

5. You should be pausing at appropriate points to ensure that the sheriff understands what you are saying, that he is following your argument, and that he is noting what is important. This also gives the sheriff an opportunity to query any significant things you are saying as and when they arise. If the sheriff has serious doubts about some aspects of what you are saying then it might be as well to deal with it there and then.

6. When presenting the arguments you should be looking at the sheriff and watching what he is doing. Satisfy yourself that the sheriff is focusing on the points that you are making. If the sheriff looks quizzical or uncertain then you may want to address that as well.

7. You should deal with any questions the sheriff might ask and not avoid them. However, you do not want to lose the thread or structure of your submissions. This means that you can say to the sheriff that you will be coming on to deal with that point at the later part of your arguments. ("But if your Lordship wishes me to deal with it now then I will do so."[46]) If you do deal with the sheriff's questions there and then, you must always remember to go back to the point that you left. It is, of course, easy to do this if you prepared your submissions following a particular structure.

8. In a case like this, you may not want to write out the full details of your submissions in advance, but you would certainly want to have some good notes containing the outline of your submissions and the sequence you will follow.[47] If you try to make it up as you are going along you will not present it as effectively and indeed you may present it very poorly.

---

[45] Do not listen to what you are saying—listen to what the sheriff is listening to. Put yourself in the sheriff's earholes.

[46] That often works.

[47] I still do that—even if it is just headings.

9. You would also hope to have put the defenders on the spot in a very particular way by highlighting the areas of weakness they are bound to have and by indicating that if they had said or done different things then your position might have been different. When the defender stands up, they are going to have quite a bit of work to do.

Responding to motions

As you might appreciate, the defender may have some difficulties in **5–24** responding to this argument because of the assumed facts of the case. The question then is what slant can be put upon those facts. The implication is that there is no real defence and that the defender is simply trying to delay the fateful day and avoid their clear obligations. Let us look at how the defender might respond:

"My Lord, I can well understand my friend's concern and your Lordship's concern that this may appear to be a case in which the defenders have no real defence and the defences are purely dilatory. I appreciate that is the way it may seem, but I can advise your Lordship that this is not so and I will expand upon this shortly.

First of all, I should say that I agree with what my friend says regarding the terms of rule 17.2 and that your Lordship has a discretion whether to grant this motion or not. I accept what is said in Macphail regarding the circumstances in which summary decree can be granted and I accept that the comments by Sheriff Principal Risk in the Whiteaway *case accurately reflect what was said in earlier Court of Session actions and can be used as a basis for considering the present case. I propose, however, to go on and emphasise precisely what Sheriff Principal Risk said about the way in which your Lordship has to consider the defenders' position in such a motion*

I do accept, of course, that the pleadings are relatively skeletal. I would say, however, that they are not irrelevant, in the sense that although I concede there is a lack of specification as to the way in which the defences have been expressed, when that specification is provided, it will be a relevant defence to say that the work was not satisfactory. What has happened here is that the defenders have never been satisfied about the work done by the pursuer in supplying and fitting their kitchen. They were both concerned about the contractual price because they had agreed with one of the pursuer's salespeople that there would be a discount on the price and that was something which was agreed at the time when the invoice was being signed. The fact that the invoice was signed by the defenders does not prove conclusively that this was the price.

There are problems with the furniture itself and when I was first **5–25** *consulted in this matter, I suggested that the clients obtain a report on the kitchen furniture. My clients were concerned about the costs of obtaining such a report and indeed about the costs of this litigation generally but they have come to realise that a report will be necessary and they are going to obtain this. I have details of the complaints regarding the furniture which my clients have given me. I did not consider it appropriate to make specific averments about those com-*

plaints until such time as we had a report. Putting the matter simply, the furniture is not working properly. Various cupboards and doors will not open and close properly. Some of the furniture is marked and will have to be repainted or even replaced. I am waiting for full information on these particular points and it is my intention to lodge adjustments as soon as I have that information. I will also be obtaining a report which I would be proposing to lodge as a production in the case. The adjustment period still has two weeks to go, and in my submissions the defenders have a genuine defence to this case and it would be inappropriate to grant the pursuer's motion.

*[**Pause and refer to book again.**] In the passage read by my friend on page X 'Summary Decree will not pass against a Defender who appears to have the basis of a statable defence but who has expressed it badly'. Your Lordship is entitled to take into account 'information given to him in the course of the respective submissions'. This is not a case in which there is a bald denial by the defender. The defender has stated his position in very general terms but the defence is 'capable of rectification by adjustment'—or more properly—'amplification' by adjustment. That is precisely what the defenders are proposing to do. In my submission, there is a statable defence and the motion should be refused."*

You might want to contrast this response with the following:

5–26   *"My Lord, this action is still in the adjustment period. It is open to the defenders to lodge adjustment to the defences which are rather skeletal at the moment and that is what the defenders will be doing. It is premature for the court to grant any motion while the case is capable of being adjusted and in my submission it would be inappropriate for your Lordship to do so.*

I am waiting for further information and further instructions from the defenders which might well enable me to expand upon the defences as they presently stand. My clients have a genuine defence to this case and that will be made clear in the fullness of time."

If you look at this carefully, you will see that this submission actually says the same as the earlier response by the defender in the sense that it covers the same issues although obviously in vastly different ways. It would be wrong to say that this response might not be sufficient, but it is asking for trouble.[48] Of course, it is quite possible that the sheriff may already have given an indication in the course of the pursuer's submissions that he is very reluctant to grant this motion while the defender can adjust. The defender could well tune into this and capitalise on any such reluctance or note any comment, qualification or reservation expressed by the sheriff on listening to the pursuer's submissions. Again, that is all part of advocacy skill. You will appreciate, however, that if the pursuer has done his job properly[49] the sheriff may have reached the stage when he comes to hear from the defender that he is going to need a great deal of persuading not to exercise his discretion in favour of the pursuer.

---

[48] Especially if the sheriff seems sympathetic to the pursuer's argument.
[49] And anticipated the possible excuses from the defender.

Of course, it can be appreciated that the transcripts above are not **5–27** entirely realistic in the sense that they do not include any interventions from the Bench. The sheriff may, and often does, make his views known quite clearly about the whole case or some aspect of the submissions, while he is listening to you or your opponent. You might want to think about this in advance.[50] In fact you really ought to have considered this in advance by asking yourself the "what if" questions. You might have appreciated that there was a good chance the sheriff would not entertain this argument and you could have thought of why the sheriff might take that view and whether you could head that off in some way. If you are receiving discouraging signals it is up to you to decide whether to keep going.[51] You will have to prepare in such a way that you remain flexible in your approach. You may have to ditch some or all of what you were planning to say. If you have a structure and have planned it thoroughly then this is easier to do. It is a matter of judgment how to deal with this, but it is considerably easier to handle if you understand the line your argument is following. What if the sheriff tells you, the pursuer's agent, that he refused a similar motion last week and he cannot remember ever granting one.[52] You might be able to respond by saying that it is, of course, a discretionary matter for the court, it is competent to grant such a motion in appropriate circumstances and you would hope to persuade him that the circumstances in this case[53] would justify a decision in your favour. It would, nevertheless, be realistic to assume that the sheriff would need a large amount of persuading. And to tailor your submissions accordingly.[54]

Where are you left after these competing submissions? The pursuer will usually have a chance to come back and reply to any points made by the defender. The explanation given may be the first time that this has been said during the case.[55] You may have information to contradict some of the more significant assertions made by your opponent.[56] It is sensible to note the "main" points made and to deal with the ones which have appeared to the sheriff to be significant or important. Repeating the original submissions is inappropriate and unwise. You should concentrate on the strengths and weaknesses, as you perceive them, disclosed in the reply. You are now into the uncharted waters in which the advocacy skills of thinking on your feet, remaining flexible, being aware and mentally agile, will come into play. You are looking for a way of "persuading" the court to support you. Weigh everything up and see if you can find a way. If you can find a way that makes it easy for the court to decide in your favour then that always helps. The variations of what might happen now are endless. However, just to follow this through to its conclusion,[57] let us look at a couple of scenarios and fall back positions for the pursuer in the event that you see the motion being refused.

---

[50] From the perspective of both sides.
[51] This applies to both sides.
[52] Maybe the sheriff should not really say this, but it does happen.
[53] Which the sheriff has not heard yet.
[54] "Okay, well I'll not bother then", would not be an appropriate response.
[55] That, in itself, might be worthy of comment.
[56] It is hoped that you would have anticipated these somehow by thinking in advance about the things they could say which would cause you a problem
[57] Because the court will, in most cases, have to do so.

5–28   If the sheriff was unimpressed by the defender's conduct and not entirely happy about the explanation given, you could always ask the court to continue the motion for, say, two weeks. Indeed, this might be a good move, if, in the course of the defender's submissions, the agent had said that they were just about to lodge detailed adjustments which would blow your socks off. If there was cause for scepticism of this, and some doubt about the good faith and genuine nature of the defence, this might be a helpful option. It keeps the matter before the court, it avoids the sheriff having to make a final decision, and it puts pressure on the defender to do what they have said they will do[58] or to come back for a further dose of the same treatment and a much less sympathetic hearing. If there remains the risk that the motion might be granted, that might be an incentive to settle and it puts a time-scale on the defender's further deliberations.

Another option for the pursuer might have occurred to someone who had read the rules fully and properly. Rule 17.2(4)(b) of the Ordinary Cause Rules 1993 entitles the sheriff, among other things, to order the defender to lodge an affidavit in support of their position.[59] This is rarely[60] done as far as I am aware, but it would be open to the pursuer to ask the sheriff to have the motion continued for the defender to lodge an affidavit from Mr and/or Mrs Gray in relation to any explanation given at the hearing. In these circumstances, it might not commend itself to the sheriff but, if you have prepared properly, you might have anticipated a problem with the motion and you might have lined this up as one potential fallback if you did not succeed in the first instance. Of course, the circumstances of the hearing might make you think this would not be worth pursuing but at least you have considered it.

Another option, if the motion is refused, is to appeal the decision. Is the decision appealable by either party? Do you need leave? Presumably you have looked at that during your preparations as well. If not, you might want to read Chapter 12 to find out.

---

[58] i.e. lodge those compelling adjustments.
[59] Read the rule for the precise terms.
[60] If ever?

CHAPTER 6

DEBATES

"As long as the ingredients of some form of a relevant claim can be discerned from a close inspection of all of the pleadings, it appears that the court is urged not to dally in the field of debate but to push the case on to inquiry as quickly as possible."[1]

For a new lawyer, the prospect of conducting a debate can be particularly **6–01** disconcerting and the last field in which he would care to dally is the one marked "debate". It is often regarded as a mysterious form of procedure for which diploma training and office practice gives no real guidance. There is also the notion that you have to be a particularly clever and accomplished lawyer to conduct a debate properly. It is undeniably true that if you do not know what you are doing or talking about in a debate you can be painfully exposed.[2] Furthermore, you will probably never be able to understand fully the significance and implications of a debate until you have the experience of taking a few actions all the way through to a concluded proof and seen how the form and the content of the pleadings has impacted upon the way in which you, or your opponent, could conduct the proof and lead evidence.[3] At its most extreme, a debate can result in an action or defences being dismissed and the case lost or won forever.[4] Beyond that, the subtle ways in which effective criticism or defence of the pleadings might affect the conduct of the action can be extremely difficult to measure or anticipate. An effective argument at debate, while not "killing" the action, or the defence, can lead to it being irreparably damaged or, on the other hand, significantly improved. Then you might begin to realise what you should have done (or what had been done to you) at the debate. It is entirely forgivable for any newly-qualified lawyer to be mystified about what they or their opponent is trying to do at a debate and what may, or may not, be achievable.[5] For some people it takes much more than just a few cases to reach any level of real understanding of what a debate is all about. Before we look at the specifics of advocacy and the presentation of debates it is vital to try and reach some general understanding of what debates are about.

What are debates about?

Putting it very loosely at this stage, a debate in an ordinary action **6–02** involves one party analysing the written pleadings in the record and

---

[1] *MacFarlane v Falkirk Council*, 2000 S.L.T. (Sh. Ct) 29.
[2] And I mean painfully.
[3] This should not concern you—nobody understands it until they have done so.
[4] Although if the action is dismissed it can be raised again. If decree of absolvitor is granted then you could not reraise the action. Fortunately, decree of absolvitor will not be granted following a debate.
[5] Often there can be justifiable wonderment about what on earth the opponent is on about.

arguing that the pleadings are inadequate in some sense. The pleadings must be read as if the words used are true. The inadequacy of the pleadings[6] is flagged up by the opponent taking a preliminary plea. You will only be allowed a debate if you have a preliminary plea in your pleadings, and you have lodged a rule 22.1 note in support of that plea at least three days before the options hearing.[7] The note must justify, explain or support the reason for taking the preliminary plea. The court may allow a debate after hearing argument at the options hearing as to whether debate is appropriate. The argument or arguments at debate are usually confined to those stated in the note.[8]

These particular features of sheriff court procedure are relatively new.[9] Formerly, you could have a debate if you had a preliminary plea and it was not necessary to say why a debate was sought nor to justify that procedure in any way. You could insist on the case going to debate, and no one could stop you. Debates in the sheriff court were regarded as a procedural obstacle which had to be overcome in almost every case. Hours would be spent in court arguing the subtle nuances of written pleadings. Lengthy and costly amendment procedures following a debate happened frequently. This was especially so in personal injury cases in which every detail of the pursuer's averments would be analysed for some theoretical ambiguity, uncertainty, inadequacy or irrelevancy. Debates were virtually obligatory for one or other party to put their pleadings in order, and awards of expenses against the unsuccessful party made this all a worthwhile exercise.[10] The tide has begun to change, however, and the courts are beginning to take a different view about debates, aided and abetted by new rules and judicial decisions. This is not to say that debates are worthless, pointless, and a thing of the past, which never serve any useful purpose. If this procedure is properly understood and responsibly utilised, debates can be used in particular cases to good effect and can give rise to "real" legal arguments, of the type law students thought lawyers engaged in every day.

It should also be noted that a wide variety of judicial attitudes to debates still exist within the sheriff courts in Scotland. As with all other aspects of advocacy,[11] you will have to know your sheriff and his attitude to debates before you can prepare an effective presentation.

Although most of this chapter has been written on the assumption that a debate is being sought by a defender because of some problem with the pursuer's pleadings, it would be quite wrong to assume that only defenders want debates or take cases to debate. There are many cases in which it can be argued that the defences are irrelevant, the most obvious being cases in which there are skeletal defences.[12] Pleas to the relevancy

---

[6] In whole or in part.
[7] Ordinary Cause Rules 1993 (hereafter "OCR"), r.22.1, a truly significant rule with which most people (but not all) have come to terms.
[8] Although the court can allow "on cause shown" other matters to be raised: OCR, r.22.1(4).
[9] Starting with the OCR 1993.
[10] If a defender could rack up awards of expenses against a pursuer for debates, amendments, etc. before the action reached a proof, one practical effect would be that this would reduce the cost of a settlement because the expenses could be set off against the opponent's principal sum and expenses.
[11] And perhaps even more so.
[12] *Castleton Homes Ltd v Eastern Motor Co Ltd*, 1998 S.L.T. (Sh. Ct) 51; *EFT Finance Ltd v Hawkins*, 1994 S.L.T. 902; *Gray v Boyd*, 1996 S.L.T. 60.

and lack of specification of pursuer's pleadings are not just limited to this however, and the guidance which follows relates *mutatis mutandis* to debates sought by defenders against pursuers.[13]

When is a debate appropriate?

Many experienced sheriff court practitioners would find the statement **6–03** about debates at the start of this chapter to be unduly cavalier, if not downright controversial. It is, however, taken from one of the more recent decisions about the role of debates in sheriff court procedure,[14] and you should immediately take a copy of it, read it, and understand its significance.[15] It is worth considering what the sheriff principal said:

> "Prior to 1993 it was common for debates to take place in virtually every personal injury case, during which metaphysical speculation and semantic hair splitting were given serious consideration and often as a result led to unfairness and significant and unnecessary delays in the progress of claims. The rules now appear to recognise that, because of the increasing complexity of modern life, other pressures on advocates, or a decline in the standards of pleading generally, the simple, orderly and lucid expression of a claim which avoids repetition, incoherence and irrelevant detail is a thing of the past."

While this was a personal injury case[16] and the arguments made to try and justify a debate were specific to that type of action, these comments simply reflected what had been said already in other cases.[17] It would be wrong to assume, on the one hand, that you can get away with anything in your pleadings now or, on the other hand, you should not bother seeking a debate even though your opponent's pleadings are hopeless.

Can I suggest two rather different practical ways of expressing the **6–04** "test" for when a debate would be appropriate[18]:

Relevancy The case, or some significant part of it,[19] is plainly irrelevant on a sympathetic and charitable reading of one party's pleadings. In other words, "the snowball's chance in hell" argument.[20]

Specification The pleadings are so confused, lacking in detail, or unintelligible that the opponent can reasonably say[21] that there are

---

[13] Other examples can be seen in *Edwards v Butlins Ltd*, 1998 S.L.T. 500; *Lutea Trustees Ltd v Orbis Trustees Guernsey Ltd*, 1998 S.L.T. 471.

[14] *Macfarlane v Falkirk Council*, 2000 S.L.T. (Sh. Ct) 29.

[15] It actually gave rise to a change in the wording of the OCR.

[16] *Letford v Glasgow CC*, 2002 Rep. L.R. 107 is another personal injury case worth looking at in this connection.

[17] *Gracey v Sykes*, 1994 S.C.L.R. 909; *Blair & Bryden v Adair*, 1995 S.C.L.R. 358, both of which pre-dated the change in the wording of the rule.

[18] These are derived largely from personal injury cases but the expressions are still, I think, of general application.

[19] It is important to appreciate this qualification. How would a problem with a "part of the case" justify debate? For example, if the plea was sustained in relation to that part, it might reduce significantly the amount of evidence required and/or the length of the proof.

[20] As I heard one of our most eminent judges describe it pithily one day.

[21] And perhaps require to demonstrate exactly how.

enquiries which they cannot carry out to enable them to prepare for the proof, or some significant part of it, because of the party's inability to give proper notice of the facts on which they are going to rely to prove their case.[22]

Further support for these expressions of approach can be derived from, inter alia, many decisions in personal injury actions in the Court of Session at procedure roll hearings, the comments about pleadings in the Coulsfield Report,[23] and the developments in pleading practice which may follow on from the new rules in personal injury actions in the Court of Session.

6–05   In my experience, there is more scope for arguing for outright dismissal of an action at debate on grounds of relevancy[24] and/or lack of specification in other types of action. This is especially so where the precise legal basis for the claim may not have been understood or identified by the pursuer, or conversely where the defender has a skeletal or obscure defence. Skeletal defences in such cases may well justify the pursuer taking the defender to debate but remember that, in personal injury actions[25] and in other forms of action,[26] it is always for the pursuer to prove their case, and while skeletal defences are frowned upon they are not per se irrelevant,[27] and will not automatically be dismissed at debate.

For any inexperienced lawyer who wants to understand how this procedure works and whether debates are "justified" or not, I would strongly recommend that you copy, read and keep *Gracey v Sykes*,[28] *Blair & Bryden v Adair*,[29] *Macfarlane v Falkirk Council*,[30] *Letford v Glasgow City Council*,[31] *Cyma Petroleum (UK) Ltd v Total Logistic Concepts Ltd*[32] and *IST Marine Ltd v Dillon*.[33]

What general preparation can you do?

6–06   Follow these general tips if you are doing or likely to be doing debates:

> 1. Read Macphail[34] about written pleadings generally and preliminary pleas. Do you understand the procedural framework?
> 2. Look at some recent cases in which actions were or were not dismissed at debate, or at a procedure roll hearing.[35] What

---

[22] In other words, that they are "prejudiced by the lack of fair notice".
[23] Which can be downloaded from the Scottish Courts website: *www.scotcourts.gov.uk*.
[24] If you know what that means—and are you sure that you do?
[25] *Keppie v Marshall Food Group*, 1997 S.L.T. 305.
[26] *Castleton Homes Ltd v Eastern Motor Co*, 1998 S.L.T. (Sh. Ct) 51.
[27] See the notorious case of *Gray v Boyd*, 1996 S.L.T. 60.
[28] 1994 S.C.L.R. 909.
[29] 1995 S.C.L.R. 358.
[30] 2000 S.L.T. (Sh. Ct) 29.
[31] 2002 Rep. L.R. 107.
[32] 2004 S.L.T. (Sh. Ct) 112.
[33] Sheriff Principal Kerr, September 16, 2005, unreported.
[34] *Sheriff Court Practice* (3rd edn, W. Green/Scottish Universities Institute, Edinburgh, 2006), Ch.9; see also Charles Hennessy, *Civil Procedure and Practice* (2nd edn, W. Green, Edinburgh, 2005), Ch.3.
[35] Which is the Court of Session equivalent.

happened in those cases? What arguments were advanced?[36] What was the procedural consequence of the decision the court reached? Try to understand the reason why a party won or lost or why there was a partial victory. Do not concern yourself too closely with the precise facts and law in such cases, but satisfy yourself that you have a good overview of what happened and why.[37] Do you understand what procedural order the court made following a successful or unsuccessful argument at debate and why it was made?

3. Go and watch a debate, or a number of debates. Try to watch a case where the agents/counsel are good.[38] Even watching a debate done poorly might help.

4. Think about compiling a list of cases that could come in handy for dealing with some of the general issues which arise frequently at debate. You will come to know them from experience, but keeping a copy of them in a handy place can save great time and effort and is extremely useful. As you gain experience, the list of cases will undoubtedly expand, and if you locate cases which deal with general principles of pleading or points which seem to arise time and time again,[39] keep a copy of them. The random list which follows is not exhaustive, or even representative, but can be treated as a starting point for your collection. You will also find reference in these cases to other authorities on and around the point, and you might want to copy some of those too. I have added a brief comment on, or quote from, each.[40] Do remember, however, that you have to look at the cases and the quotes in the context of the facts of each case.

Some debate authorities of general application

Jamieson v Jamieson, 1952 S.L.T. 257

For the purposes of argument at debate, the opponent's averments **6–07** must be read as if they are true. "The true proposition is that an action will not be dismissed as irrelevant unless it must necessarily fail even if all the pursuer's averments are proved. The onus is on the defender who moves to have the action dismissed, and there is no onus on the pursuer to show that if he proves his averments he is bound to succeed."

Jamieson v Allan McNeil & Son W.S., 1974 S.L.T. (Notes) 9

"[O]ur system of pleading still requires in actions for damages for **6–08** negligence first, that the essential facts relied on should be set out

---

[36] The judgments will usually summarise the arguments presented by advocates on behalf of both parties briefly and logically, so you can learn from that.

[37] *Cosar Ltd v UPS Ltd*, 1999 S.L.T. 259; *Hand v North of Scotland Water Authority*, 2002 S.L.T. 798; *Green v Moran*, 2002 S.L.T. 17; *Smiths Gore v Reilly*, 2003 S.L.T. (Sh. Ct) 15; *Bennet v J. Lamont & Sons*, 2002 S.L.T. 17; *Tartan American Machinery Corporation v Swan & Co*, 2003 S.L.T. 1246; *Royal Bank of Scotland v Bannerman Johnstone McLay*, 2003 S.L.T. 181; *Duncan v Beattie*, 2003 S.L.T. 1243.

[38] Admittedly, impossible to know.

[39] *Hughes v Lord Advocate*, 1963 S.L.T. 150 (foreseeability of accident to a child).

[40] It goes without saying that the whole case has to be read to understand its true meaning or significance (or not).

with reasonable clarity; second, that the duties alleged to have been breached should be plainly stated and should be duties which the court can be satisfied at least might have been incumbent upon the defenders in law in the circumstances averred; third, that it should be reasonably apparent how any alleged loss is claimed to be attributable to any one or more alleged breaches of duty; and, fourth, that in so far as the nature of any head of patrimonial loss permits, at least some notice should be given of the amount claimed under that head and, in any event, of the basis of quantification proposed to be relied upon."

Miller v South of Scotland Electricity Board, 1958 S.L.T. 229

6–09   "It is only in rare and exceptional cases that an action of damages for personal injury should be dismissed at Debate."

This case explains why a proof before answer should be fixed where there is a dispute on the facts or the precise facts are unclear. It may not be possible to argue at a debate whether a duty in law exists, because the existence of that duty may well depend upon the precise facts of the case which can only be determined finally at proof. Once the precise facts have been determined, then you can renew the argument about the applicable law and, in this case, whether a duty did indeed exist.

Strathmore Group v Credit Lyonnais, 1994 S.L.T. 1023 and *Partnership of Ocean Quest v Finning Ltd*, 2000 S.L.T. (Sh. Ct) 157

6–10   The correct usage of "believed and averred".

Bryce v Allied Ironfounders Ltd, 1969 S.L.T. (Notes) 29

6–11   Proper specification of complaints.

McMenemy v James Dougal & Sons Ltd, 1960 S.L.T. (Notes) 84

6–12   "[A] record should not be subjected to the careful and meticulous scrutiny devoted to a conveyancing deed. The matter must be looked at broadly with a view to ascertaining whether the defenders have been given fair notice of the case which the pursuer intends to prove."

Lockhart v National Coal Board, 1981 S.L.T. 161

6–13   (A criminal case): "[E]ach case has to be considered on its own particular circumstances to see whether the absence of further specification has resulted in a lack of fair notice *to a degree that material prejudice has been suffered*."[41]

Boulting v Elias, 1990 S.L.T. 596

6–14   In contrast to the above, an example of lack of notice causing prejudice.

---

[41] Emphasis added.

Macdonald v Glasgow Western Hospitals, 1954 S.L.T. 226

The plea of lack of specification finds its proper application in a case **6–15** where a defender does not know the case to be made against him and objects to be taken by surprise at the proof (i.e. the defender should not be insisting on you providing specification of something of which they obviously should have knowledge).

Rowallan Creamery Ltd v Henry Dawes & Sons, 1988 S.L.T. 95

Sufficient notice. **6–16**

ERDC Construction Ltd v HM Love & Co, 1997 S.L.T. 177

On what function written pleadings should serve (and what they do **6–17** not need to do).[42]

Steelmek Marine and General Engineers' Trustee v Shetland Sea Farms Ltd, 1999 S.L.T. (Sh. Ct) 30

"[T]here is no rule ... which prevents the court looking at **6–18** documents at the stage of debate, provided the terms of the documents have been properly incorporated as part of the pleadings of the party who seeks to rely on them."

As you will appreciate, these cases are necessarily limited in number and scope, but you should be able to see that some of them will have general application to a wide variety of cases.

DEBATE: THE SPECIFICS

So, what are they really about?

A debate would be appropriate where there is a preliminary plea for **6–19** any party and the sheriff is persuaded at the options hearing or a continuation of same,[43] that there is a preliminary matter of law which justifies a debate.

I would suggest that this can be understood as a substantial argument which, if successful, would lead to decree in favour of the pursuer or defender or would limit the method or extent of proof to a considerable degree, or where the pleadings are such that one or other side would be materially prejudiced in its ability to prepare for and present any proof. The essential features required are:

- a preliminary plea;
- persuasion of the sheriff at the options hearing (requiring a rule 22.1 note and submissions to support or amplify it);
- a substantial argument;

---

[42] See Lord Prosser, p.180. Well worth reading.
[43] Or at a procedural hearing

- possible decree in favour of pursuer/defender;
- considerable limitation of method/scope of proof;
- material prejudice in ability to prepare or present the subsequent proof.

Preliminary pleas

6–20   It is beyond the scope of this book to discuss and analyse the different varieties of preliminary plea. For a learned discussion of these, see Macphail.[44] The most common pleas are taken to relevancy and lack of specification, either together or separately. The plea counts for nothing, however, if it is not supported by a rule 22.1 note[45] and, indeed, it will be repelled automatically if there is no rule 22.1 note lodged in accordance with the Rules.[46] It must be lodged and intimated not later than three days before the options hearing.[47] One rule which can be lost sight of is the requirement that, if a preliminary plea has been added in the course of amendment procedure, the note of the basis of that preliminary plea should be lodged at the same time as the amendment or answers which contain it.[48] A failure to comply with this will lead to the additional plea being repelled. Accordingly, although the plea is essential for a debate, it is equally essential for there to be a note.[49]

Rule 22.1 note

6–21   There is no guidance given anywhere as to what a rule 22.1 note should say. The Rules simply state that it should be a note "of the basis for the plea".[50] The sheriff has to be persuaded by the note and by anything said at the options hearing in support or supplement of it, to allow a debate. It makes sense, therefore, for the note to contain a coherent explanation and argument which can be understood by the sheriff in the absence of additional oral submissions. The sheriff will have the time and opportunity to consider the record and the note before the options hearing and it is obvious that the sheriff can be influenced, and the options hearing made easier, if the note does outline the substantial arguments of the type mentioned above. Normally, only matters raised in the note itself can be argued at the debate,[51] so the note should be comprehensive A brief outline may well suffice, however, if the point is made clearly enough.

I have seen two line notes and four page notes. I have seen notes with reference to legal authorities and quotes from the judgments in decided cases. I have seen notes which merely restate the words of the plea

---

[44] *Sheriff Court Practice*, above, paras 9.116 *et seq.*
[45] It is possible that a plea to the competency does not require a r.22.1 note: see *Hill v Law Society of Scotland*, Sheriff Morrison, July 14, 2005.
[46] OCR, r.22.1(3).
[47] It might be as well to remind you at this stage that a record has to be lodged not later than two days before the options hearing: OCR, r.9.11(2). See *DTZ Debenham Thorpe v I. Henderson Transport Services*, 1995 S.L.T. 553; *Mills v Chief Constable*, Sheriff Principal Stewart, April 25, 2005, unreported; *O'Callaghan v Simpson*, 2004 G.W.D. 33–669.
[48] OCR, r.18.8.
[49] An interesting recent case with a detailed discussion regarding preliminary pleas which is well worth reading is *Humphrey v Royal and Sun Alliance Plc*, 2005 S.L.T. (Sh. Ct) 31.
[50] OCR, r.22.1(1)(a).
[51] Although other matters can be raised "on cause shown".

without any indication of the "basis" for it. There is no universally accepted style. However, I offer for consideration the following:

1. In a case where a debate is sought— **6–22**

> "[1] The defender has one preliminary plea namely plea in law number one which is to the effect that the pursuer's pleadings are irrelevant and lacking in specification. The defender intends to insist upon that plea.
> [2] This is an action of payment raised by the pursuers who designed, supplied and installed kitchen furniture for the defenders. It is averred by the pursuer in condescendence 2 that . . .[52] and that . . . The pursuer has not averred . . .
> [3] In these circumstances, the defenders are unclear as to what the pursuer is averring regarding the . . . The defenders do not have notice of the pursuer's position in relation to . . . The defenders are prejudiced in their preparation for any proof in this action in the absence of specific averments about . . . If they knew what the pursuer was intending to prove about X then they would be able to obtain and call their own witnesses on this specific point.
> [4] . . .
> [5] In these circumstances, the defenders intend to insist upon their preliminary plea and seek a diet of debate.
> IN RESPECT WHEREOF".

2. In a case where the party wants to reserve the plea (and agree a **6–23**
proof before answer)—

> "[1] The defender has one preliminary plea namely plea in law number one to the effect that the pursuer's pleadings are irrelevant and lacking in specification. The defender intends to maintain that plea but is content to reserve consideration of the plea until after proof.
> [2] In this case the pursuer is claiming payment for kitchen furniture which it supplied, designed and installed in the defenders' home. The pursuer avers that . . . It also avers that . . .
> [3] The defenders' position on their pleadings is that. . . There is a clear factual dispute between the parties in relation to this matter.
> [4] . . .
> [5] It is submitted that the legal question of [whether the terms of the written contract can be adjusted by the parties by way of a verbal agreement] cannot be decided until such time as all of the evidence regarding the circumstances of the agreement has been led. It is a mixed question of fact and law. The defenders are content to

---

[52] You may want to summarise the appropriate part of the pleadings but make sure your summary is accurate and fair. Alternatively you could quote a pertinent short part of the pleadings.

reserve their plea and argue the question of law after
proof.

[6] In these circumstances, the defenders wish to reserve
their preliminary plea and seek a diet of proof before
answer.

IN RESPECT WHEREOF".

It should be noted that even though you do not want a debate in this
second note, you still have to lodge the note to support the preliminary
plea. Explaining why a preliminary plea should be reserved can be a
difficult task. It does involve knowing the difference between a proof and
a proof before answer.[53]

6–24   The numbering of the note is not essential but does give it some
structure. Parts of these notes are, in a sense, superfluous because when
the sheriff is preparing for the options hearing, he will no doubt read the
record to see what the plea is and will read the averments as well.
However, a good summary of what it is all about in one relatively short,
coherent and concise document is likely to create a favourable impression. As you will appreciate, the common features are:

- identify the preliminary plea;
- state what you want done with it;
- summarise briefly what the action is about;
- point to the pleadings or part of the pleadings (quote them if
  you like) which are being criticised;
- explain why there is a problem with relevancy and/or the way in
  which there is prejudice to the pursuer[54]/defender in preparing
  for proof—in this case—or entitles one or other party to a
  decree; and
- finish by confirming what is being sought in the form of further
  procedure. You may have to consider what would happen if the
  court refused to allow a debate. Does this mean that your plea
  will be repelled? If the court refused to allow a proof before
  answer, does this mean you would have to have a debate or do
  you agree to the plea being repelled?

Obtaining or avoiding a debate

6–25   The rule 22.1 note only takes you so far. At the options hearing, you
have to persuade the sheriff to allow a debate. The sheriff's overriding
duty then is to "secure the expeditious progress of the Cause".[55] After
hearing parties and considering any note lodged, the sheriff will appoint
the case to a debate if he is satisfied that there is a preliminary matter of
law which justifies a debate.[56] The rule states that the sheriff must be
satisfied "that there is a preliminary matter of law which, if established

---

[53] For an explanation, see Hennessy, *Civil Procedure and Practice*, above, 18–03 to 18–06.
[54] For example, if the defender has not answered averments on matters within their
   knowledge and the pursuer does not know if they are going to require to bring evidence to
   prove it.
[55] OCR, r.9.12(1).
[56] OCR, r.9.12(3)(c).

following debate, would lead to a decree in favour of any party or to limitation of proof to any substantial degree". It is difficult to define precisely the circumstances in which a sheriff will take that view. There is some guidance in the sheriff court cases to which reference has been made in this chapter but it should be noted that the precise terms of the rule have changed somewhat in recent years. With experience, it should be possible to obtain a good idea of what is usually regarded as sufficient for a specific sheriff.[57] Many cases do not go to debate despite the plea and often this can be traced back to an inadequate note or inadequate presentation of the submissions.

As can be seen, it is possible to appeal the decision of a sheriff at an options hearing who refuses a proof, refuses a debate, or fixes a proof before answer. There was a view at one time that such a decision about further procedure at the options hearing was a discretionary one[58] but in the recent cases of *Cyma Petroleum (UK) Ltd v Total Logistic Concepts Ltd*[59] and *IST Marine Ltd v Dillon*[60] the view was expressed that such a decision is a matter of law and can be appealed on that basis. A procedural decision of this type can be appealed but requires leave.[61]

Once a debate is fixed, it is possible to raise matters additional to those set out in the note, at the hearing of the debate itself, "on cause shown". In practice, the courts will tend to allow this in most cases without enquiring too closely about the cause. It is more likely to allow it if a supplementary note is lodged and intimated, and if this is done sufficiently far ahead of the debate to give the opponent time to prepare for the new arguments being advanced. The same effect can be achieved by advising the opponent informally in correspondence about the "new" points you intend to take. The important point is to give the other side notice and to appreciate that, if the additional matters are going to be crucial and are going to involve detailed and lengthy argument, it would be prudent to find some way of letting the court know this in advance. A failure to do this, or an attempt to argue detailed points of which notice has not been given in the note, might well lead to a discharge of the debate and an adverse finding of expenses.[62]

Preparation for the debate

Here is a checklist of points to follow which can be used in most cases. **6–26**

Form of record

Certified. The record which has been lodged in court and from which the sheriff will be working should be certified as a true copy of the pleadings as at the date stated on it. Is it?[63]

---

[57] You can always ask experienced lawyers as well.

[58] And, therefore, only appealable on a restricted basis, i.e. that the discretion was exercised unreasonably.

[59] 2004 S.L.T. (Sh. Ct) 112.

[60] Sheriff Principal Kerr, September 16, 2005, unreported.

[61] *Sharif v Singh*, 2000 S.L.T. (Sh. Ct) 188; and see Ch.12 generally.

[62] Strictly speaking, of course, the sheriff would be perfectly entitled to refuse to hear any argument not foreshadowed in the note. Paradoxically, the wider the note, the easier it is to argue that notice has been given.

[63] And are you working from the correct record? It is not unusual for there to be a number of records as a result of adjustment or amendment.

Paginated. Page numbers will be of immeasurable assistance when presenting your arguments and referring the sheriff to the pleadings.

Line numbers. Some people will jot down, on the margin of their own[64] copy of the record (every five lines or so) the number of the line. This will assist further in identifying where particular averments are located ("Your lordship will find these averments begin at page 4, near the top of the page, from line 3 down to line 15").

List of authorities

6–27 You should lodge and intimate a list of the authorities to which you intend to refer at the debate. Different courts may have slightly different practice notes regarding the time when this should be done.

What books should you use? Use the latest edition of any textbooks to which you are going to refer.[65] Make sure that you have the correct version of any statute or statutory instrument which applies to the circumstances of your case. Bring the whole statute to court with you for the debate. Copying particular sections of it is not always satisfactory. Citation of cases from *Session Cases* is recommended,[66] but it must be said that, in my experience, it will invariably suffice to work from *Scots Law Times* or any other well-known series of reports. Remember to check that the important case on which you are going to rely was not overturned on appeal. Look for recent examples rather than older ones. Printouts of cases from *Scots Law Times* on CD are convenient to obtain, but not very good to use,[67] so only use them in court if you have to. Recent or unreported decisions taken from the Scottish Courts website can be printed and supplied to the court. I have never seen this queried or criticised in the sheriff court, and it can serve as a testament to your detailed research and preparation. If the case is in point then the sheriff will usually be extremely grateful for a copy.

Any relevant practice note. Is there a practice note within the sheriffdom which contains the administrative requirements for lodging lists of authorities? These often require a list of authorities to be lodged with the court 24 or 48 hours in advance.[68] It can often be difficult to find what the "local" rule is, and it would make sense to contact the sheriff clerk and enquire about this.[69] A copy of the list should be sent to the

---

[64] But not on the certified copy of the record (although there is no reason why this could not be done).

[65] Check that it is the latest.

[66] In *McGowan v Summit Motor Policies at Lloyds*, 2002 S.L.T. 1258, the Inner House of the Court of Session gave certain directions on the proper citation of judgments to the court and the use of different law reports. See also Practice Notes No. 2 of 2004 (High Court of Justiciary) and No. 5 of 2004 (Court of Session), for citation of *Session Cases* and authorised law reports.

[67] Maybe it is just me, but these are a bit more difficult to read and assimilate and there can be problems identifying page numbers and specific parts of the text.

[68] For the very good reason that this gives the court administration the time to look out those authorities and make them available to the sheriff when he is hearing the debate.

[69] Sometimes this can appear to be a closely guarded secret.

opponent in advance if required by the rule or, indeed, even if not required. It is only fair to do so.

Photocopies. In some courts, there may not be access to all of the case reports which you are going to use, especially the more obscure reports. It would make sense to take an extra photocopy for the sheriff's use. Indeed, providing the sheriff with photocopies of all of the cases to which you are going to refer is done frequently and with approval from the Bench, by and large. It is convenient and simple to do[70] and can assist in sidestepping any rule about lodging lists of authorities in advance. Some[71] sheriffs do not like it, so again it might be as well to check the "local" practice. Do not mark anything on the sheriff's copies. If you have sent the other side a list of authorities in advance then that is all you need to do. However, some agents will bring along an extra copy of their cases for the opponent.[72]

Preparation of submissions

Preparing, noting and understanding your own argument. You can **6–28** spend minutes doing this, hours doing it, or days doing it. When starting off, you may feel that you need months to do it. Assuming it is your case, by the time you have had a debate allowed you should already have applied your mind, in some detail, to the legal issues involved. What you have to do is find a structure into which to fit your arguments. It is easy to fall into the trap of thinking that you understand the point fairly well and that will suffice. When you are starting off it will not. Some questions to ask yourself[73] are:

- Can you summarise your arguments shortly? You may have to refer to many cases to support your argument[74] but what, in simple terms, or in one sentence, are you saying or asking the sheriff to do?
- What, in simple terms, is the law on this point or the practice in relation to this pleading issue? If you are asking the sheriff to agree with a legal proposition, what is the authority (case, book, statute, etc.) which justifies this proposition? Do you know what the facts of that case were and why you are referring the sheriff to it? What if the sheriff does not agree with this point? What if the sheriff asks you if this is binding on him or suggests it can be distinguished from your case?
- What if the sheriff points out an averment which does not apparently fit with your argument?
- Should you write down what you are going to say verbatim, or just headings, or a combination of both?
- Even though it might take you 45 minutes to make all of your submissions do you understand the point(s) well enough to

---

[70] You can arrange them in order or even bind them together and index them, etc. to maximise the presentational impact.
[71] Very few.
[72] If you have not intimated a list of authorities to your opponent, that is the least you can do.
[73] And be critical about it.
[74] And it may take some time to explain what they say.

reduce it to two lines? You think you do? Well then, write out now exactly what you would say the point is in that one sentence and reread it critically.[75]

As you can appreciate, this is an essential process, and the more critical you can make yourself, the more chance you have of anticipating and dealing with counter-arguments. You will come to appreciate that you do need a defined structure on which to hang these thoughts. Clarity and precision of thought and language can be acquired but only if you work hard at it.[76] Finally, do not lose sight of the overall objective of the plea. What was it again?

6–29   **Consider your opponent's cases and try to understand[77] your opponent's argument.** If your opponent has given you a list of authorities, do take copies of them. Consider them critically. Understand what they say. Try to appreciate what point, or points, your opponent is attempting to establish with these cases. Do you know where this fits into the arguments you are advancing at debate? Do you need to look up other cases to provide you with authorities to counter these points? If you do not understand the point, phone up your opponent and ask what it is about. You may indeed find it useful to do this at an earlier stage. On the face of it, another lawyer has formed a different view to you. Give them credit for having applied their mind critically to it. What do they think? Are they right? If you think they are wrong do you know why? Can you demonstrate this by argument?[78]

Conduct of debate

Basics

6–30   The normal practice is to hear the submissions by the party who sought the debate, hear the answer to the submissions and then give the first person an opportunity to be heard in response to any specific replies which have been made. There is no obligation on the court to allow a third "speech", but that is usually done, and it is not uncommon, nor unacceptable, for matters to be focused and clarified by certain shorter submissions of the parties at the end of the hearing of the major submissions. It is really for the sheriff to direct how he wants to conduct the debate and he can invite responses or comments as he sees fit. Strictly speaking, all that is required is for the submissions to be made by one party and an answer by the other. The sheriff would be perfectly entitled to feel that, once he had heard this, there was nothing else he needed to hear before proceeding to consider his decision. The sheriff can intervene at any stage to test the arguments or clarify what is being suggested. While you are making your submissions you cannot or, at least, should not, be interrupted by the other party.[79]

---

[75] What am I really saying in that one sentence? What do I really mean?

[76] Apologies if this sounds like an advert for a new religion, but you get the point.

[77] Even, or especially, when you do not agree with them.

[78] Perhaps you do not want to rehearse the debate over the telephone, but sometimes you find that a sensible and timely telephone conversation once you have both marshalled your thoughts might avoid an unnecessary debate.

[79] The only time when that is acceptable is when they are telling you that they are throwing in the towel.

Where both parties have pleas which they are intending to argue, who goes first? If there is simply a pursuer and a defender who are each insisting on their preliminary pleas then the defender will go first. If the defender's argument for dismissal happens to be successful, then it really does not matter what argument the pursuer has against the defender's pleadings. If there is more than one defender and they are all insisting on their preliminary pleas then they would normally go in order of first defender, second defender, etc. although there is nothing to prevent the defenders agreeing that the principal argument will be presented by one of them. This presupposes that all of the defenders are taking exactly the same point, and that is not always the case. If they all have preliminary pleas against the pursuer and each one of them is taking a slightly different point then they will simply make their submissions in order, and it would probably make sense for the pursuer to reply to all of the submissions by all of the defenders once they have all concluded.

What do you actually say?

Here is an extract of submissions from an actual debate adapted to fit **6–31** Mr Hamilton's case. Do not concern yourself overmuch with the merits of the argument. Certain points have been missed out. The idea is to give you a chance to read the kind of things that would be said and the way in which they might be said. You should also consider the structure of the argument and whether it is being presented in such a way that you can follow it, and see where it is going. It is lengthy and it will be tedious if you cannot split it up into "headings" for the benefit of the sheriff and yourself, and make it sound interesting.

> *"[1] My Lord, I appear on behalf of the defenders in this case. Mr Bloggs appears on behalf of the pursuer. This is a debate in relation to the defenders' first plea in law. The defenders are seeking dismissal of the action. Has your Lordship had an opportunity to read the record?*
> *. . .*
> *[2] As your Lordship will see, this case concerns an accident allegedly sustained by the pursuer on July 23, 2004 when the pursuer says that he was walking in the Argyle Street Shopping Centre and tripped. The pursuer says the defenders are the owners of the centre and that they were negligent. He says that, as owners, they had certain duties of reasonable care to people coming onto the premises and that they were in breach of the duties of reasonable care incumbent upon them. The pursuer makes no averment of any other basis upon which he considers that the defenders are liable in damages to him other than that they were the owners at the material time. The defenders admit that they were owners but they deny that they owe any duties of reasonable care to the pursuer in the circumstances.*
> *[3] The defenders have a plea to the relevancy of the pursuer's averments which your Lordship will find on page 9 of the record and your Lordship will see that it is in a standard form. As indicated in the rule 22.1 note, the defenders' position is that the pursuer's pleadings are irrelevant, that plea in law number one for the defenders should be upheld, and that the action should be dismissed. Furthermore, as indicated in the rule 22.1 note, the defenders submit that one aspect of*

the pursuer's claim, namely the claim for loss of earnings is lacking in specification and should not be admitted to probation. As your Lordship will appreciate, this is very much a subsidiary submission and the principal thrust of my argument will be that there can be no legal liability on the defenders in the circumstances of this accident as averred by the pursuer and on the basis solely that the defenders are the owner of the centre. Any proof in this action would be bound to fail and there would be no point in hearing any evidence standing the present state of the pursuer's averments.

[4] I would propose to address your Lordship in detail as follows:

6–32

1. *I will review the relevant averments made by the pursuer regarding the circumstances of the accident and the status of the defenders.*
2. *I would propose to consider the detailed averments of fault against the defenders (which your Lordship will find in Article 3 of condescendence).*
3. *I will address your Lordship on the authorities applicable to a claim of this nature which will indicate the particular facts, and therefore, the particular averments, which would have to be present before it would be possible for the pursuer to succeed with the claim against the defenders in these circumstances.*
4. *I will then demonstrate that in the absence of these averments the pursuer's case is bound to fail.*

[5] In doing this, I am of course aware that the pursuer's averments have to be read as though they are true. I am aware that it is only in rare and exceptional cases that the court will dismiss an accident of personal injury on questions of relevancy at the stage of a debate. I accept that this is normally a formidable obstacle for a defender to overcome but it is my submission that the pursuer's pleadings plainly fail to satisfy the test of relevancy and decree of dismissal will be merited.

[6] Your Lordship will find the facts of the case as set out in condescendence 2 on pages X to Y of the record. The pursuer narrates how he had his accident and it is not necessary for me to address your Lordship in detail in these matters other than to observe that he says that he was walking in the centre and he tripped on some tiling which was located on what he describes as a 'walkway'.

[7] Can I also direct your Lordship to the averments which the pursuer makes regarding the defenders? Your Lordship will find that the only averments relating to the defenders are as follows:

> *In condescendence 1 on page X of the record the pursuer simply describes the defenders by reference to their registered office. In condescendence 2, page X, they are simply described as being the 'owners', and therefore, occupiers of the centre. Your Lordship will find this on line X of condescendence 2. Your Lordship will also see on line Y of condescendence 2 that 'it is believed and averred that the defenders have instructed the contractors to carry out work in the centre including work on the walkway averred'.*

There are also averments which could be described as purely factual averments in condescendence 3, page X, line Y at the very start of the averments in condescendence 3, the pursuer says that the accident was caused by the fault and negligence of the defenders and then he goes on to say that 'they were the owners and occupiers of the centre'. In the next sentence, they say, 'The defenders had certain responsibilities in relation to the maintenance of the centre'.

[8] *Now, my Lord, that is, so far as I can see, the full extent of the* **6–33** *pursuer's pleadings regarding the status of the defenders and their position in relation to the centre. They are said to be the owners (a matter which is not disputed) and they are also said to be the occupiers, but they are only said to be the occupiers by virtue of their ownership.*

[9] *The first legal point upon which I wish to address your Lordship at this stage is the question of whether there are any duties of care incumbent upon an owner of premises simply by virtue of the fact that such a person is the owner. Your Lordship will find the law on this matter contained in Professor Walker's book on Delict Second Edition, and in the cases of Pollok v Stead & Simpson Ltd (reference) and X v Y (reference) which, I can see, your Lordship has before him. [Or alternatively, "and I have made copies of these available to your Lordship", or "May I pass your Lordship copies of these reports?"]*

[10] *On page X of Professor Walker's book, he deals with this point under the heading of . . . and he says . . .*

[11] *Your Lordship will find that the case of Pollok v Stead & Simpson Ltd to which I have already referred your Lordship, reinforces that point. This is a case in which a woman slipped on a common staircase leading from the first floor flat of a tenement. She sued a number of people who were alleged to be the proprietors of the tenement and she said, among other things that 'by reason of their proprietorship' they were all, at the material time, in occupation and control of the close and the staircase where the accident happened. The matter was taken to debate by the second defender who said that although she might be the infeft proprietor of two of the flats in the tenement, she had actually sold the flats several years beforehand and there were missives to that effect. The pursuer denied those averments.*

[12] *The defender took the case to debate and the Lord Ordinary* **6–34** *dismissed the action. What he said, in justifying the dismissal, my Lord is (at paragraph X on page Y) . . .*

[13] *It seems to me that the crucial thing which he said was that the pursuer, in her pleadings, offers to prove that the second defender had occupation and control of the common stair 'by reason only of her infeftment in the property. She makes no other averment relative to her occupation and control . . . The pursuer must prove, if she is to succeed against the second defender, that the latter was in occupation and control of the common stair at the material time and for this purpose she must prove more than mere infeftment. She does not offer so to do and it would not be in the interests of justice to allow her to proceed in the hope that something will turn up at the proof'. That, in my submission, is precisely the position of the pursuer in this case and*

the pursuer's averments, in this case, owe more to wishful thinking that something might turn up at the proof than to a coherent statement of any legal basis for imposing liability on the defenders.

[14] Now, the pursuer may say that he avers more than just ownership. He may say that he avers certain other facts which are relevant and which would be sufficient to show that the defenders had some degree of possession and control of the premises themselves. These would be the averments which I have quoted above. . . .

[15] However, in my submission, neither of these is good enough. First, there is no specification of what they mean . . . The pursuer says that the defenders were responsible for maintenance. How were they responsible for maintenance? What were they responsible to maintain? In what sense and in what way did they actually maintain the walkway? It is not specifically averred by the pursuer but it seems reasonable to suppose that the pursuer does not take issue with the fact that the shops within the centre are all occupied by people other than the defenders. The defenders do not 'use' the centre but simply let out the shops to others who use them. So what is the legal basis for arguing that there can, in these circumstances, be any duty of reasonable care incumbent upon the defenders. I can find no authority for that proposition and it would really be a matter for my friend to address your Lordship on whether there could possibly be any circumstances in which this could arise. In any event, before the pursuer could lead evidence about any matters of fact which might have a bearing upon the question of liability of the defenders, there would need to be specific averments. The averments which the pursuer has at the moment are completely lacking in any detail and give no indication of what the pursuer thinks he can prove or intends to prove with regard to the basis for the argument that the defenders had some degree of possession and control . . .

[16] Accordingly, for all of these reasons, I submit that the pursuer's pleadings are fundamentally irrelevant: (1) because they owe no duty of care to the pursuer simply in their capacity as owners of the centre; and (2) because there are insufficient averments of any other facts which would require to be proved in order to impose a duty of care on them for some other reason. If your Lordship is with me on these submissions, then I would move your Lordship for dismissal of the whole action against the defenders. If your Lordship is not with me on this, then I would move your Lordship to allow a proof before answer on these averments. In the event that your Lordship does not dismiss the action then I should also remind your Lordship of my secondary submission in relation to lack of specification of some part of the pursuer's claim. I would move your Lordship to exclude those averments from probation, if a proof before answer is allowed. If not, of course, then the point is largely academic. My motion, therefore, is for your Lordship to sustain the first plea in law for the defenders and to grant decree of dismissal. Unless there are any other matters with which I can assist your Lordship at this stage, those are my submissions for the defenders."

6–35 By contrast, some debates can be incredibly simple, and the suggested structure would be far too sophisticated and quite inappropriate. For example:

"The pursuer has made averments of complaints having been made about the state of the flooring 'some time before the accident'. He does not say when, to whom, by whom or whether the defenders actually knew about this defect before the accident. The defenders could not possibly investigate it in preparation for the proof. Accordingly, I move your lordship to sustain the plea number one for the defenders to the extent of excluding the averments about complaints from probation."

Advocacy skills

It is not possible, in a book, to recreate the method of presentation, **6–36** outwith the words actually used, but certain points are worth highlighting. I have mentioned some of them before in other contexts but there is no harm in mentioning them again here.

Pace

The argument is developed slowly and gradually. It may be necessary **6–37** to start slowly while the sheriff familiarises himself with the details of the case. Wait until the sheriff has located the particular pleadings to which you are referring him, before you start talking about them. Assume the sheriff knows little or nothing about the law.[80] Wait until the sheriff has located the book to which you refer him and the passage on which you are going to rely heavily until he is ready to hear what you have to say about it. Pause as you go from one strand of your argument to another. Check to see if you have the sheriff's attention. Is the sheriff noting down what you are saying? Why not? Maybe the sheriff is still thinking about something you said earlier. Is the sheriff "with you" as you make your submissions? Some sheriffs will be well ahead of you, and might suggest that you move on to the point more quickly. If this means that the sheriff sees the point you are going to make, then that is good news and not necessarily a criticism of your presentational skills. You are trying to persuade the sheriff to agree with you. Some people take more persuading than others.

Voice

Do you know what your voice sounds like to other people? You are **6–38** just about to talk for a considerable time and it would do no harm if you try to make it sound interesting. A monotone is to be avoided and a degree of animation[81] would be welcomed. Speak clearly—if you are not sure of what you are saying then you will often mumble out of embarrassment. Be aware of this. Do not speak too quickly. The sheriff may be trying to note exactly what you are saying and understand it at the same time and this cannot be easy. You may be conscious that you have a lot to get through, but do not rush. Make sure that you do speak up and that you gain and maintain the ear of the sheriff.

Referring to authorities

This is a good point at which to say something about the technique of **6–39** referring to authorities. You are likely to be doing this more in debates than in other forms of procedure.

---

[80] This is not being gratuitously offensive. It is a far bigger mistake to take it for granted that the sheriff knows it intimately. If the sheriff is familiar with it, he will probably tell you.
[81] Not Mickey Mouse impressions, however.

- Explain to the court why you are referring to the case, "which contains a useful summary of" or "is the most recent authority I can trace on", etc. Do not just say, "I thought it might assist if I referred your Lordship to an interesting case which was a bit like this".
- Give the sheriff the citation of the case, and you will normally have to wait while he writes this down and then reaches across the bench to open the book.
- Tell the sheriff if, for example, it is binding, authoritative, or just an illustration of something analogous.
- Tell the sheriff briefly the facts of the case. You can just read out the rubric and/or the headnote if you want, but it is useful if you can do your own summary especially where the case has facts which are particularly similar to yours and you want to highlight this.
- It usually helps to know, and explain briefly to the sheriff, how the case got to the point when the reported decision was made. One easy way of preparing this is to jot down on a "sticky" the brief summary of the facts and the relevant procedure. This should make it concise, and if you attach it to the photocopy of the case you are using to present your argument, it is easy to locate and use it.[82]
- Next, what particular passage of the judgment(s) are you going to use. Again I find it easiest to use a photocopy for my purposes and highlight the passage(s) which I will need to read out.
- Make sure that, if you are taking an extract from a judgment by Lord X, you put the words you are quoting into context. "After dealing with the arguments addressed to him by both sides and commenting upon the unusual nature of the alternative case advanced by the pursuer, he went on to make some observations about the principles of . . . which are, in my submission, equally applicable to this case. This starts at page X paragraph Y, where he said".
- If there are parts of the judgment which are against you, or if other judges made contrary observations, then you are obliged to point that out. The best way to do so is to deal with this and explain why you still rely on what is being said in the passage you are using. Better to deal with it now than have your opponent raise it and leave the sheriff wondering if you may have misled him.[83] By the same token, and even more so, if you are aware of authorities which are against the proposition which you are advancing then you have a duty to the court to draw the court's attention to these authorities. You should deal with why they do not impact on your argument or how the

---

[82] You often find that while you are doing this the sheriff is reading ahead and scanning the case for signs of familiarity (or to check if he was counsel for the pursuer), and you should be aware of that by watching him.

[83] I am pleased to say that I have little experience of this happening, other than through genuine inadvertence.

sheriff should treat them. It can sometimes be a matter of degree and judgment whether a case is against you or not. If your opponent is going to refer to it[84] then you do not need to. What if your opponent is not going to refer to it and you know it may be on point? If it is conclusive and clear then you should not be arguing the point unless you have a good reason for distinguishing the case. If you have a reason for distinguishing it then it may be better for you to face up to this in your submissions and address the sheriff on it. "Even though this is an authoritative decision and appears to be against me may I direct your Lordship to".

- I usually try to arrange my copies in the order to which I am going to refer them to the sheriff. Then work my way methodically through them. It is the best way to keep track. You need to have prepared your line of argument, of course.
- There is no need to refer the court to every case on the point at issue. Look first for the latest binding authority which (for the sheriff court) will be the Inner House of the Court of Session or the House of Lords. Use that one. If you are satisfied that there is none, then look for any other reported case which deals with the issue and is fairly recent. If it contains a summary of the previous case law with which you would not take issue then it is sufficient to refer to this only, unless you have some particular reason for going to other cases.[85] Of course, it is rare indeed that you can find something directly and conclusively on point, so do not be surprised if you have to construct your argument and justify your position from a number of sources, authoritative and/or not.

Interventions by the sheriff

In reality, it is unlikely that your submissions will be listened to in silence by the sheriff. He will ask you questions. He will seek to clarify anything which is not obvious. He will play devil's advocate. He may test your argument.[86] He will probably focus on some of the weaker points which you hoped he would not notice. He may want to hear what you have to say about aspects of the case or the argument which you had not intended to deal with at all. He may want to hear your response to particular points before you had even got round to mentioning them. When preparing for the debate, you must try to anticipate this. You must be prepared for some exchanges between the sheriff and yourself. These will not necessarily be critical, but they will usually be to the point and may even give some idea of the way the sheriff is thinking. Sometimes the interventions will be positively helpful to you. It may show that he does understand or agree with the point(s) you are making or, conversely, that he does not follow it. This would at least give you the chance to try again. **6–40**

---

[84] Is it on your opponent's list of authorities?
[85] e.g. similarity of facts.
[86] It is, after all, the sheriff's job.

If the sheriff wants to know what you have to say about a particular matter in the course of your submissions then you must deal with this directly. It may be that the point is something you intend to deal with at a later part of your planned submissions. If you have given the sheriff an outline of your submissions at the outset then he might appreciate this. You could respond by saying that you propose to deal with that matter later, and ask if it is acceptable if you do so. If the sheriff wants you to address it now then you must. You will then find the benefit of having a clear structure to your submissions. Even though you are taken off your planned approach, if you have good notes, you should be able to find your way back to the point where you departed from them and carry on as originally intended.

There are times when a sheriff might say to you, "If I was against you on that point then does that mean that your whole argument must fail?" That is undoubtedly a useful test of the strength of your submissions. It will test if you know your case well enough. Think about the question carefully. Is that right? If so, concede the inevitable. There is nothing worse than hearing someone trying to justify the patently unjustifiable. Remember the sheriff only said "if" he was against you on the specific point.

6–41　　If it is clear from what the sheriff says or does that he has difficulty accepting that what you say makes sense or has merit then you should address this directly. "Your Lordship seems to be having some doubt as to whether this is the appropriate test for . . . Perhaps I can assist by".

Sometimes your argument could be tested by using examples, "So if what you say is correct would that mean that . . . (in another set of circumstances) . . . would have to be the position?" Again it is helpful to think about this type of response in advance of the debate. One way to counter it is to think of examples of your own which demonstrate the proposition even better. There is a skill in doing this, and a danger in picking the wrong examples. It is unhelpful if the analogy backfires.

You will, of course, have to think on your feet, but if you prepare fully and properly, and understand your submissions inside out, you may find that the required spontaneous response is the one you had made up earlier. Ask yourself constantly in your preparations "what if" the sheriff says, "How can you say that", or "What is your authority for that legal proposition?".

Response to submissions

6–42　　We are going to look briefly at how you might approach the reply to your opponent's submissions. On the face of it, your opponent may have subjected your pleadings to minute and powerful criticisms. It does not, however, follow that you have lost, or will lose. You should have seen them coming and presumably you are satisfied that you have a reasonable response, otherwise why are you attending the debate at all? You will have noted the detailed arguments against you in writing while they were being made. If they are presented in a coherent and logical way this should be easy. While noting the arguments, you may also have jotted down your response. You are going to start off by saying, "My motion is for your Lordship to repel/reserve the defender's preliminary plea and to fix a proof/proof before answer." But before you do so we had better consider whether you should seek leave to amend.

Amendment

Many debates end with a motion by one party to amend its pleadings. **6–43** Amendment is not obligatory but it gives you a chance to put things right[87] and live to fight another day. The sheriff has power "at any time before final judgment" to allow an amendment which "may be necessary for determining the real question in controversy between the parties".[88] In other words, although your pleadings might be poor, messy or insufficient to justify the remedy you are seeking, if it appears that it is possible to make some alteration to them which would cure this defect, then the court can allow you to make that alteration. If it was a small alteration, you could even make it at the Bar, during the course of the proof.[89]

Once you have heard your opponent's argument, you may think that there is merit in the criticism of your pleadings. It may also be clear to you that the sheriff thinks there is merit in it. If you lose the debate, then the whole case may be lost because of your inability to express it properly, or because there is insufficient information to enable you to express it properly, or a combination of both. You will want to avoid this if you can, so you can make a motion to the court for leave to allow you time to lodge a minute of amendment to your pleadings.[90]

How do you know if you should amend? It is entirely your decision. The sheriff will not invite you to amend, or give you an opportunity to think if you want to amend. The sheriff cannot allow you to amend your pleadings if you do not ask him to allow this.[91] You have to decide if the criticisms of the pleadings are strong enough to make it necessary for you to amend. You cannot ask the sheriff, before you respond to the debate, whether he is likely to be against you or not on some particular point.[92]

In some circumstances, it will be an easy decision to make. If you **6–44** knew beforehand what the arguments were going to be, then you should probably have given consideration to the possibility of amendment being required, so you should not really be unprepared for it. In other cases you may find yourself put on the spot unexpectedly and have to make a quick decision. The safest course, if you think that there is a prospect of the action being dismissed or some significant part of your pleadings being excluded, is to seek leave to amend. If you do not do so, and your fears are confirmed when a decision is made, you can always consider an appeal—and an amendment before the appeal—if appropriate.[93] Accordingly, without being too cavalier about it, even if you make the wrong decision, it is potentially curable.

If you do ask for leave to amend, beware of a question from the sheriff asking you what you propose to say in your amendment. Some are

---

[87] Assuming they can be put right.
[88] OCR, r.18.2.
[89] Do not forget that you can do this, although you might want to confine t2is to small and obvious amendments.
[90] The penalty for doing so is expense. Your client will almost certainly be found liable for the expense of the debate and the subsequent amendment procedure.
[91] *Lord Advocate v Johnston*, 1983 S.L.T. 290.
[92] *Gibson v SRC*, 1992 S.C.L.R. 902.
[93] Obviously, you will be penalised in expenses if you have to go to appeal before amending.

content to give you a chance to put things right, and leave it to you to do so if you can. If there are obvious technical defects in your pleadings[94] then it may be obvious that you will simply be "tidying up" your pleadings.[95] On the other hand, if there appear to be major problems in stating a relevant case on the basis of the facts averred, the sheriff may want to know how you can possibly put this in order before allowing you leave to amend. If you do not have the factual information, how can you make the additional averments required? If you need to make enquiries to enable you to find out the additional information you might need, how can you say that you will be amending? What if the additional information is not available? Do not seek leave to amend in the forlorn hope that something might turn up. If you have the information but have expressed the pleadings badly, then amendment would be appropriate. If you do not have the specific information required but you are reasonably confident that it will be available[96] then amendment would be appropriate. If you just want to amend as a knee-jerk reaction to the criticisms without having any clear idea of what you are going to be able to say in your amendment, then you can be put into a difficult position—and quite rightly so.

On a more positive note, the criticisms of your pleadings at debate may be of benefit to your case as a whole. Some agents take the view that the opponent has just told them at debate all that is wrong with the case, and they will then be given a chance to put it right. The opponent has, in effect, taken over responsibility for the other party's pleadings and, by criticising them, has suggested the cure for the defects. Better to know this before the proof, which might be too late for any amendment. The price of amendment is an adverse finding of expenses, but it may be a price you are prepared to pay.

It is beyond the scope of this chapter to review all of the considerations which apply when a party proposes a minute of amendment to rectify a flaw in the pleadings. One question which often arises in this connection is whether an amendment is too late, either in the sense of introducing averments which amount to a new case after the limitation period for the claim has expired, or in the sense of coming too late into the procedure, or too near a significant hearing or the like. Reference can be made to Macphail[97] and to recent cases which are in point.[98] Read these carefully.

Reply to submissions at debate

6–45   It is difficult to replicate a real response to submissions at debate because you have to know all the detailed submissions made and the way

---

[94] e.g. badly expressed, jumbled, irrelevant, but simply because the pleadings were confused, etc.

[95] An expression which covers a multitude of sins.

[96] If you had investigated fully and properly.

[97] *Sheriff Court Practice*, above, paras 10.01–10.59.

[98] *Urquhart v Sweeney*, 2005 S.L.T. 422; *Cork v Greater Glasgow Health Board*, 1997 S.L.T. 740; *Cameron v Lanarkshire Health Board*, 1997 S.L.T. 1040; *Edwards v Butlins Ltd*, 1996 S.L.T. 1354. See also the sheriff court cases *Reilly v Esso Petroleum Co Ltd*, Sheriff Principal Bowen, August 3, 2005, unreported; *Jaffray v Grampian Test and Certification Ltd*, Sheriff Principal Young, January 6, 2005, unreported.

in which they were received by the Bench. However, I think that there is benefit in giving a rough outline of what might be said in response. Again, I would suggest that you do not worry about the precise content, but think about the approach to the response and the way in which the submissions are made.

> *"My Lord, my motion is for your Lordship to reserve the defenders' preliminary plea and to allow a diet of proof before answer.*[99] *I have listened carefully to the submissions of my friend and, in so far as they have merit at all, it is my submission that the points would be appropriately dealt with after hearing the evidence at a proof before answer.*
>
> *In making this submission, I propose to take as my starting point what was said in the well-known case of Jamieson v Jamieson, 1952 S.C. (HL) 44, per Lord Normand at 50. The passage itself is well known and your Lordship will no doubt be familiar with it, but standing the attack on relevancy made by Mr X, it would be useful to look at exactly what it is Lord Normand said.*
>
> > *'The test of relevance is the same for all actions; there is not one standard for actions of divorce and another standard for other actions. . . . The true proposition is that an action will not be dismissed as irrelevant unless it must necessarily fail even if all the pursuer's averments are proved. The onus is on the defender who moves to have the action dismissed, and there is no onus on the pursuer to show that if he proves his averments he is bound to succeed.'*
>
> *In my submission, if one looks properly at what the pursuer says in his pleadings, then in no way can it be said that the pursuer must fail even if all his averments are proved.*
>
> **Facts**
>
> *First of all the pursuer avers that . . .*   **6–46**
>   *The pursuer is required to . . .*
> *As has been observed, it is then averred, in the third last line on page X, that . . .*
>   *The importance of that last averment as my Lord will have seen is that . . .*
>   *And it follows that . . .*
>   *Against that factual background I would like to consider the averments of duty. There are other averments of some significance in Article 2 of condescendence but I propose to return to them later.*
>
> **Duties**
>
> *The pursuer avers in terms three duties. These are set out on page X of*   **6–47**
> *the record, lines Y to Z.*

---

[99] It could, alternatively, have been to "repel the plea and allow a proof". There are numerous other alternatives depending upon the circumstances but it is important to let the court know simply at the outset what you want.

Sentence 2, duty to . . .

And I pause to observe that it is very well-established that such a duty does indeed exist in our law—certainly it was not suggested otherwise by my friend nor could it have been . . .

Sentence 3, duty to . . .

In my submission those averments alone would be sufficient to exceed the requirements of Jamieson . . .

On that basis alone, in my submission your Lordship is not entitled to hold that he must fail in this case . . .

As I understand the submission made by the defenders it is suggested that the pursuer's case should be dismissed because . . .

In my submission that is simply incorrect . . .

The approach is to see whether the defenders have been given fair notice of the facts upon which the case against them is based . . .

In my submission the defenders have ample notice . . .

After all it is the defenders' premises . . .

The defenders did this and that . . .

Lastly, I should deal with what my friend described as a subsidiary point regarding the lack of specification of . . . in Article 6 of condescendence, at page X line Y . . .

I would invite your Lordship to hold that any suggestion that the defenders are prejudiced in this respect is an entirely technical one . . .

In conclusion, I would invite your Lordship to reserve my friend's plea, and to allow a proof before answer."

Outcome of debate

6–48   The matter could be very clear and the sheriff could issue his decision there and then. Otherwise, the sheriff would normally issue a written judgment. The sheriff will, as he has no doubt been asked to do, either sustain the plea (in whole or in part), repel the plea (in whole or in part) delete certain averments from the pleadings as a consequence of deciding that they are irrelevant or not specific,[1] or reserve the plea. Certain decisions would be open to appeal. In certain circumstances a party would need to obtain leave to appeal.[2]

---

[1] Albeit allowing a proof or proof before answer on the rest of the averments

[2] For detailed discussion, see Ch.12.

CHAPTER 7

PREPARATION FOR PROOF

"I appear on behalf of the pursuer in this case, my Lord. Both parties are ready to proceed to proof."
"What is the case about?"
"It is about two days, my Lord."
"No doubt it will take longer than that if you are involved."

This chapter deals with the mechanics of preparing a case so that it is **7-01** ready for proof. In a sense, you should have been preparing for proof since you first opened the file, but as soon as a proof is allowed the preparations become much more intense and focused. I am going to consider these more intensive preparations which will commence once a date has been fixed for proof.[1] It is unlikely that the proof will be fixed sooner than two months ahead and, in some cases, it could be longer. This gives time for preparation but this time is very quickly eaten up unless you know what you are doing. The fixing of a proof concentrates the minds of agents and clients[2] alike and there is no doubt that this concentration can[3] produce the need for more work on the case.[4] It could be fine-tuning of a fully prepared case, or a major overhaul and development of a case which has some significant "gaps". At the proof diet itself, you must be in a position to present all of the evidence you want to present to the court and advance all of the arguments you want to advance, whilst countering any evidence or argument being advanced by the opponent. The court will not give you a chance to do it all again if you missed something out. It is your one and only shot. You have to get it right "on the day". You can only do this if your preparation for "the day" has been appropriate. This chapter discusses many of the practical and procedural issues involved in organising a case for proof, and some methods of dealing with cases, people, and situations which you may encounter on the way there.

By the time you have reached this stage of the action, it is quite likely that you will have amassed a large quantity of papers in your file. You will have had correspondence with the solicitors on the other side.[5] You should have a reasonably good idea what the main areas of dispute are

---

[1] For the avoidance of any doubt, this also includes proof before answer throughout this chapter.

[2] Watch out for the client/witness who then says, "But I didn't think we actually had to go to court."

[3] And in some cases, should.

[4] Of course, it should be done sooner—but that's life.

[5] Usually.

going to be.[6] You may think that there are prospects of the case settling.[7] Both sides will already have incurred quite a large amount of judicial expenses and the work involved in the preparation for the proof is going to increase those expenses substantially. From a purely practical viewpoint, before you start the detailed preparations for the proof, you should be wondering if the case is going to settle. This is not cowardice but just common sense. If it appears that there is no prospect of settlement, you should have some understanding of why the case is not going to settle. There could be a variety of reasons which could cover disagreements on crucial matters of fact, disagreements on the law applying, inability to finance a settlement, inability or unwillingness to consider a settlement from the client's viewpoint, and (frankly) the failure of one or other side to address these questions and/or to advise the client in relation to these questions. I see no weakness in enquiring if there is a prospect of settlement at this early stage.

Paradoxically, one way of making sure that the case will settle quite often is to prepare for the proof as though it is definitely going to go ahead.[8] If the other side see that you are carrying out the preparations which are required, this may well pressurise them to focus upon the forthcoming proof themselves, and they, in turn, will be obliged to focus their client on it. Remember that, if you are pursuing a claim of any kind, it is always going to be for you to prove the claim, lead the evidence, and lodge the productions. The defender can simply turn up at the proof and sit back and listen to your proof. It is a generalisation but, in a number of cases, the detailed preparation required of a defender could amount to no more than arranging for the defender themselves to turn up on time on the date of the proof and deny the allegations being made against them. The preparations required of a pursuer may often have to be more thorough and comprehensive than those of a defender.[9] The preparations I am going to suggest may seem like a counsel of perfection and incredibly detailed and complex. Some of them may seem unrealistic, or at least unachievable in a busy legal practice. They will undoubtedly involve a considerable amount of time, and it may be too much to expect this degree of preparation to take place in each and every case in which a proof has been fixed.

7–02   It is only with experience that you can learn how to "cut corners" in the preparation for a proof and, even then, that is not particularly desirable. With experience, you can often determine (regardless of what the record or your opponent says) whether a case is likely to settle or whether there are likely to be major areas of dispute in all of the matters at issue in a proof. You may be able to find formal or informal ways of narrowing this down and legitimate ways of putting some pressure on the other side. You will know the minimum that you have to do to ensure that you are ready for a proof when the time comes, and you will be acutely aware of the last date for complying with the procedural formalities for a proof rather than the first date for doing so. With

---

[6] Hopefully.
[7] Perhaps even more hopefully.
[8] Trust me, this works.
[9] But, of course, that depends on the case and the nature of the defence being advanced.

experience, you will understand exactly what the case is about and exactly what you really need to prepare fully. You can devise your own methods and time-scale for preparing for the proof. Many people do, and do so very effectively. If you have a large number of cases in which a proof is fixed, and you have proofs being fixed on a regular basis, you do learn how to cope with the preparations required without going into the details which are discussed in this chapter. The intention, however, is to highlight some of the basic practice and habits which will stand you in good stead for any cases in the future and which will enable you to develop your own style and practice in the fullness of time.

It is useful to start with the big picture. What are the big issues on which you will need to focus?

- Making sure that everyone knows that the proof is on.
- Making sure that you have satisfactory pleadings, an accurate record capable of being proved, and a clear appreciation of the matters of fact which are in dispute.
- Making sure your client and your witnesses turn up primed and ready at the proof and that you know what they are going to say.
- Making sure that you have all of the productions you might need and that they are all lodged in appropriate form.
- Having a plan for the orderly presentation of evidence at the proof.
- Knowing, at least roughly, what submissions you will make at the close of the case to justify the court granting the appropriate decree in favour of your client.

Immediate preparation

As soon as a proof has been fixed in your case, there are certain basic **7–03** things you should do immediately. If you are the pursuer:

Reserve a shorthand writer for the proof

You will need a shorthand writer for the proof "unless the parties, by **7–04** agreement and with the approval of the Sheriff, dispense with the recording of evidence".[10] One of the most embarrassing mistakes you can make when acting for a pursuer in a case is to forget to book the shorthand writer. Everyone does so once, but the experience of waking in a sweat the night before the proof and realising that you have forgotten to book the shorthand writer, makes it unlikely you will do it again. It is easy to forget, but get into the habit of doing so automatically as soon as the proof is fixed. If the case cannot proceed because the shorthand writer has not been booked, you will almost certainly have to pay the expenses of the diet of proof itself. You are going to have plenty of other things to think about in the lead up to the proof, so just book the shorthand writer early and forget about it. Remember to keep an eye open for confirmation of the reservation of the booking and make sure

---

[10] Ordinary Cause Rules (hereafter "OCR"), r.29.18. I have never actually experienced this.

that confirmation is on your file which you will have at the proof, in the rare and unlikely event that the shorthand writer does not turn up.

Put it in the court diary and your diary

7-05   Again, you might forget to do this once by mistake. That is already too often.

Write to your client

7-06   Tell them the date which has been fixed for the proof. Tell them briefly what a proof is. Tell them briefly what has to be done. Something along these lines might be useful:

> "The court has now fixed a proof before answer in your case for June 23, 2002 at 10.00 at Greenock Sheriff Court. This is the date on which the court will hear evidence from yourself and all of the witnesses regarding the case. If you have any difficulty with the date or are aware of any of your witnesses having any difficulty with the date then would you please let us know immediately?
>
> We are enclosing for your information a copy of the record in your case. You will see this is a document which sets out the written pleadings of both parties about which the court will hear the evidence. We suggest that you read it over carefully.
>
> We shall require to make detailed preparations for the proof and we will need to see you to discuss these. Please arrange an appointment".

It makes sense to tell the client the date of the proof straight away. Even if you are not ready to discuss and analyse the case with them, this makes sense for a number of reasons. In real life, you may feel that your pleadings are not as good as they might be. You may feel that the proof has been fixed before you have a full grasp of what is involved or before you have completed the investigations or researches which you wanted to do. You may feel that you would prefer to "tidy up" the case and focus your own thinking about it and what has to be done with the preparations for the case before you actually discuss it with the client. These are all legitimate thoughts and might tempt you to wait until you have addressed some of these issues before advising the client. A common problem among new solicitors is delaying advising the client of the date for the proof until the solicitor knows what to tell the client or what advice to give them. You want to sit down with the file and a bit of time and think everything through before you see the client. That is a natural human reaction, but it can mean not telling the client until very late in the day. That in itself can compound any difficulty which the solicitor might have in explaining to the client what they are going to do with the case and what evidence will be required.

7-07   I would suggest that you write this kind of letter for a number of reasons.

First, if the client knows the date of the hearing of the case and knows that the hearing is going to be of some significance[11] then the client can

---

[11] Do not take it for granted that the client realises what a "proof" is. Most members of the public have no idea. Call it a "trial" if you want the client to appreciate roughly what is involved.

be relied upon, to a certain extent, to force the pace. You might overlook a proof diet. It happens to everyone for a wide variety of reasons, good or bad. If the client is aware of the date then there is a chance they will keep you right.

Secondly, if you tell them immediately the date which has been fixed and it is unsuitable to them, or, to their knowledge, any of their witnesses, this gives you a chance to make an early motion to discharge the proof. An early motion of this type has a much better chance of being granted than such a motion made a week before the proof.

Thirdly, the letter also means that the client may well speak to the other witnesses the client will know, and you may well get feedback through the client about their willingness or reluctance to attend court as witnesses.

Fourthly, you are advising the client that work needs to be done on their case and you want to see them to discuss the preparations. You can, and should, make this a joint effort with your client. It is not like a medical operation for which the client simply has to turn up in person at the allotted time. There are practical things you need to do before the case with which they may be able to help you.[12] When you see the client at this initial meeting, you can go over the record with them,[13] you can discuss the witnesses you will need, and you can also discuss the productions you might need. It is a much more effective way of conducting the case to have your client liaising with you as quickly as possible in the preparations for the proof, rather than writing to them suddenly, three weeks before the proof, telling them that a proof has been fixed and that you need to see them urgently—because you certainly will.

Write to the witnesses

It is arguable whether you should do this immediately or should wait. **7–08** It is also arguable that as well as, or indeed instead of, writing to the witnesses you should simply send out formal witness citations. It is really a matter of opinion and preference. It is reasonable to assume that, by the time the case has been set down for a proof, you have most, if not all, of your witnesses identified. It is also reasonable to assume that you will have precognitions or, in the case of professional witnesses, reports from them. In reality, it has to be acknowledged that this is not always the case. You may well have identified the witness. You may well have spoken to the witness informally and have a basic idea of what the witness has to say but you may not have a formal precognition and indeed you may have some doubts about the willingness of the witness to attend court and give evidence on behalf of your client. If the witness is willing and has given a precognition then it is a matter of courtesy to tell the witness, as far in advance as possible, what date has been fixed for the hearing of evidence in the case. If the witness has a problem with the date then you will know at an early stage.[14] If the witness is willing, but

---

[12] For example, finding out about some matter of fact about which the client had not fully instructed you, or smoothing the path with reluctant witnesses.

[13] It does not matter if the client does not fully understand it. They will have read it and you can explain anything which they do not understand.

[14] It is always easier to deal with such matters if they arise within a short time of the proof being fixed.

you do not have a formal precognition or a reasonably full statement, you can use this letter to ask for a formal statement. If the witness is a little reluctant or evasive or at least lukewarm, you can use this letter to let the witness know that they will have to appear in court and give evidence, that it would be helpful now to have a full statement, and that it might be possible to make arrangements with the witness for the witness to attend court at a specific time or under some other specific arrangement so as to minimise any inconvenience. This again is courteous but it also means it is more likely that the reluctant or undecided witness will contact you. No witness likes the prospect of having to go to court, and you ought to appreciate this and make it as easy and painless as possible for them. In the case of professional witnesses who may well have other commitments planned months in advance, you should certainly write and advise them immediately of the proof date and that they should put this in their diary or advise you if there is a problem.[15]

On one view, you should not write to witnesses informally as suggested, but you should immediately send them out formal witness citations. This gets it out of the way and is one less thing for you to worry about in your preparations for the proof. A formal witness citation certainly makes it clear that the witness has to turn up (whether they like it or not), but it could all be a little too formal and demanding and this could, perhaps, creates a wrong impression with the witness.[16] The counter-argument is that it is more important that the witness is properly cited than that you establish a warm and caring relationship with them. It is in your interests to treat witnesses reasonably and fairly and with a degree of courtesy and understanding. Sending a formal citation to a witness you have only spoken to on the telephone, who did not think that they could help you very much, and who was not particularly keen on attending court, may make them even more reluctant and unwilling to assist your client. If you cite a witness too early, the citation could be forgotten about. The witness may ask you if the case is definitely going ahead and you will not know the answer. The witness may ask you if they will definitely be needed and you may not know the answer. The witness may ask you if they can come at a particular time of day and you may not know the answer. You could avoid all of these questions if you do not cite the witness until later.[17]

A more prudent course might be to send a formal citation straight away but also to send a separate letter by normal post advising that a citation is being sent and asking the witness to contact you[18] for various purposes. By writing to, citing, or otherwise contacting the witness at this early stage, this should establish a line of communication with the

---

[15] As a matter of practice it is desirable to know before the proof is fixed if there are dates which are unsuitable for witnesses. As a matter of practicality, it is not always possible to do this.

[16] "It says here that you are going to have me arrested if I don't turn up, is that right?"

[17] Indeed, if you wait long enough, you may not need to cite the witness at all and this would have been a complete waste of time. There is a temptation to cross your fingers and delay all of this as long as possible—but then, what if you forget that you have not cited this witness?

[18] Or to delay contacting you, or that you will contact them.

witness, and let you know if there is a problem at a time when you can try to address it.[19]

Write to the other side

You do not need to do this. You can just take the view that you will **7–09** "see them in court" at the proof diet and simply comply with the procedural requirements of intimation of witnesses and productions, dealt with below.[20] However, I would suggest there is a benefit in writing at this stage, enquiring whether there are any matters of evidence which can be agreed, and inviting them to consider a joint minute of admissions. This should, or at least could, have been done either before, or at, the options hearing. In practice, it rarely happens then, but this is a good stage at which to address it informally. There is no harm in writing a general letter to the other side at this stage and asking, very broadly, if there are matters which can be agreed.[21]

In the case of a defender, similar immediate steps can be taken.[22] There are some differences of emphasis, however. The defender would probably be less inclined to look for matters of evidence which could be agreed in advance. The defender may also be unsure about what witnesses will be required. That may well depend upon what witnesses the pursuer is going to cite. The defender may be unable to say whether and when their witnesses might be taken to give evidence. That may depend upon the extent of the pursuer's proof. There may be something to be said for delaying any formal intimation to the prospective witnesses for the defender until such time as you have seen who the pursuer's witnesses are going to be, and how many there are going to be. There are some witnesses you know you will need in any event. There may be some witnesses whose attendance might be problematic. You might simply give them informal intimation of the date and advise them that they may be required. If in doubt, send out the formal citation. If there is some doubt as to when your witnesses would actually be taken or whether they would be taken, it is useful to explain to the witness that this depends upon what the other side do. In other words, it is not your fault if the witness is going to be inconvenienced or if there is uncertainty about whether or when the witness might be taken. You can make it clear that, so far as you can control events, the evidence of the witness will be taken in such way as to minimise any inconvenience to them. As with the pursuer's witnesses, however, the bottom line is[23] that you can make them turn up on the day[24] and sit for the duration of the proof if you want.

Written pleadings and matters in dispute

The record should be accurate when proof is fixed, but it is well known **7–10** that in the run up to a proof additional information, or different

---

[19] One of the most common responses by witnesses cited to a proof seems to be, "I don't know why you want me, I don't know anything about this"—an assertion which rarely withstands enquiry.

[20] See paras 7–15 to 7–25.

[21] This also makes it clear that you are going full steam ahead to the proof-so it will settle.

[22] But the defender would never have responsibility for booking the shorthand writer for the proof.

[23] And it is not diplomatic to draw attention to this until you have to.

[24] Or days.

information, or slight changes in precognition of client or witnesses might necessitate a change in the pleadings. This may be no one's fault. Circumstances may have changed since the action was raised or your detailed preparations for the proof may throw up some inaccuracies or misunderstandings about your client's position which will have to be corrected. Additional enquiries may also have suggested themselves and you will have to take additional evidence into account. You should be alive to this, and if the alteration is significant then you may need to amend.

The need for amendment and the timing of such an amendment before a proof raises many difficult issues.[25] Some amendments may be in matters of detail, which do not materially alter the main thrust of the case or the nature and extent of the evidence to be led on either side. These may be allowed without difficulty. Some amendments can necessitate the discharge of a proof to give the other side time to answer. The court should allow any amendment necessary to ensure that the true matters in controversy are focused. If the other side is prejudiced in its conduct of the case by a late amendment then this would be a good reason for not allowing it. Alternatively, if it is allowed, then, to do justice between the parties, the court may have to discharge the proof to give the other side time to take instructions or obtain further evidence bearing upon the new point.[26]

If you need to make an amendment to enable you to prove your case, or run a full and proper defence, then make it. Make the amendment as soon as you can. If the proof is imminent then intimate to the other side as soon as you can, even if you are not going to be able to move the amendment until the proof date itself. There is nothing to prevent you making such a motion at the Bar on the first day of the proof, but if you know it is going to be opposed then it is wise to move it earlier. If it is not going to be opposed then you can move it at the Bar to avoid any unnecessary procedure, especially if it is minor, but remember that the court does have a discretion to refuse it. It is not uncommon for minor amendments to be made at the Bar before many proofs—usually they are unopposed. However, it is not a good habit to assume this will be allowed in every case.

7–11   In addition to confirming that the record remains accurate, look again critically at the pleadings to check how you are going to prove the simple facts which make up the subject matter of your dispute. For example, the defenders have not actually admitted that they did write to the pursuer or that the pursuer's invoice is accurate. Does that mean that you will have to bring evidence to prove these matters which, you had assumed at the outset of the case, may not have been disputed. There may be good reasons why they are not agreed. Where is your evidence to prove them?

On a more positive note, look at the pleadings to see if there are facts[27] which are agreed or, at least, not disputed by the other side. There may be facts which are not agreed formally but which you think the

---

[25] Each case depends upon its own circumstances, I am afraid.
[26] The court would usually find the amending party responsible for the expense of the abortive diet.
[27] And I mean facts.

other side may be willing to agree or, at least, not dispute. There may also be aspects of the case (e.g. quantum, medical reports, invoices, or descriptions of the furniture/locus of accident[28]) which you believe the opponent is not going to dispute. You will want to be sure that anything which can be agreed and which helps your case, is definitely agreed and can be presented to the court as being agreed. There are three formal ways of doing this:

Admission in the pleadings

If there is a formal admission of a fact in the pleadings then you need **7–12** no more than that. Is it a clear admission? Is it qualified in any way? Does it depend on how you read it? Every statement of fact made by one party should be answered by the other party, and if such a statement by one party is within the knowledge of the other party and not denied by them, then they shall be deemed to have admitted it.[29] Are there any such "deemed admissions"? If so, you need not prove the fact. However, can you be sure that you have what must be regarded as a "deemed admission"? I would not be inclined to rely on very much by way of admission in the pleadings unless it was clear and unequivocal. Where it appears to you to be a matter of some significance, it would be prudent to look for some confirmation before relying upon it to the exclusion of leading evidence about it.

Notice to admit

At any time after the record is closed a party may intimate to another **7–13** party a notice calling on them to admit such facts "relating to an issue averred in the pleadings as may be specified in the notice".[30] The opponent has 21 days from the date of intimation of the notice to admit to intimate a notice of non-admission specifying which fact(s) they do not admit.[31] This procedure can be used to agree evidence not admitted on record or about which there may be some dubiety. In practice, the procedure is rarely used and often any notice to admit is automatically and swiftly met by a notice of non-admission of everything.[32] However, its use should be considered in most cases. It does involve sitting down and analysing the precise details of the proof at least four weeks before it is heard, in order to allow time for the procedure.[33] I have seen it used to good effect when a pursuer in a personal injury action served a notice to admit 64 single and simple facts and only received 20 or so non-admissions.

There is no formal style for such a notice, nor indeed for a notice of non-admission. I would suggest setting it out as a part of process with the instance, dating it at the top, and saying:

---

[28] Going back to our sample cases.
[29] OCR, r.9.7.
[30] The notice can also call for an admission that documents are originals or true copies of originals.
[31] For the full rules, see OCR, r.29.14(1)–(8).
[32] There is no real practical incentive to the opponent to make such admissions and it is usually regarded as safer and simpler to bounce it.
[33] Unfortunately that may be too far ahead for many.

"X for the pursuer (defenders) calls upon the defenders (pursuer) to admit the following facts:

1. *That the defenders were, at the date of the accident, the heritable proprietors of . . .*
2. *That the pursuer attended his GP after the accident on (date)".*

There is no need to sign it, but I think it makes sense to do so and keep a record of when it was intimated. A notice of non-admission could follow the same general format. Any admission, or non-admission, can be altered[34] but this is rare, largely because the procedure itself is rare. It is difficult to know why it is poorly used. Perhaps the fact that there is no real sanction on a party who fails to respond reasonably is one explanation.

Joint minute of admissions

7–14   It is open to the parties to agree certain facts, certain issues, and certain documents prior to a proof regardless of what the pleadings actually say, and the formal way in which this is done is by the preparation and lodging of a joint minute of admissions.[35] The document advises the court that, for the purposes of the proof, various matters have been agreed. Examples might be as follows:

"X for the pursuer and Y for the defender concur in stating to the court that, for the purposes of the proof in the above action, the following matters have been agreed or are admitted:

1. *That the copy invoice (No. 5/2 of process) is to be treated as equivalent to the principal thereof.*
2. *That the pursuer lost £600 wages as a result of the accident.*
3. *That the medical report of Mr X (No. 5/4 of process) is a true and accurate report and is to be treated as equivalent to the oral evidence of the said Mr X.*
4. *That the photographs of the kitchen furniture (No. 6/1 to 6/10 of process) are true and accurate photographs of the furniture which is the subject matter of the present action and were taken by Mr James Monaghan, 23 Holden Way, Glasgow.*
5. *That, for the purposes of the present proceedings only, the defenders admits liability to make reparation to the pursuer for the loss injury and damage sustained by him in the accident stated on record, but without prejudice to the defenders' plea of contributory negligence on his part . . .*
6. *That the medical records of Aberdeen Royal infirmary (No. 5/6 of process) are true records of the hospital relating to the*

---

[34] OCR, r.29.14(7)–(8).
[35] This can also be done informally at the proof itself but that is not particularly satisfactory and a sheriff might prefer to have a formal joint minute in the process rather than recording at the start of the proof what the parties told him at the Bar had been informally agreed.

pursuer and that the medical facts and the medical opinions expressed therein are admitted".[36]

In practice, the question of a joint minute can be canvassed by either party at any time prior to the proof. It can be initiated by sending to the other side a draft of the terms of a proposed joint minute[37] and inviting them to agree it. It can be adjusted between the parties until the full extent of agreement is decided. It can often be prepared very close to the proof itself, and sheriffs are always happy to see one.[38] Care has to be taken, however, with the precise wording of the terms of the joint minute. In some circumstances this can be extremely important. What have you actually agreed? For example, the agreement in paragraph 1 above that the copy is to be the equivalent of the principal may not prove the principal. The agreement in paragraph 2 may not make it clear whether that is inclusive or exclusive of interest. The agreement in paragraph 3 might have been fairly worthless in the absence of agreement about the date on which the photographs were taken. Does the joint minute agree what you want it to agree and will it have the desired effect on the evidence you require to lead?[39]

Witnesses

List of witnesses

Within 28 days of the allowance of proof you must intimate to the **7–15** other side a list of your witnesses, and you must lodge a copy of that list in process.[40] If you want to call a witness not on that list and the other party objects to this you need the leave of the sheriff.[41] In practice, this is rarely a problem. In practice, agents and the court are usually quite lax about observance of this rule, but you really ought to get into the habit of following it—and insisting that the other side follow it too. The list should include the name, occupation (if known) and address of the witness. The purpose of doing this is to give the opponent an opportunity to precognosce the witness well in advance of the proof.

You ought to precognosce any of your opponent's witnesses whose details have been supplied to you. In practice, this does not appear to be done regularly. That is a mistake. The witness will perhaps not respond to a request for precognition. The witness might be unwilling, reluctant, or downright unpleasant about giving the precognition, but you still have a professional obligation to try to find out what they have to say in advance of the proof. You cannot insist on a witness giving you a precognition but a failure to do so could be put to them in cross-examination at the proof.[42]

---

[36] See *McHugh v Leslie*, 1961 S.L.T. (Notes) 65, for an explanation for this wording, which should be of benefit in drafting admissions generally.

[37] Open-ended, i.e. so that the opponent can add anything they want to agree.

[38] Even handwritten on the morning of the proof.

[39] A good and salutary illustration can be found in *Lenaghan v Ayrshire and Arran Health Board*, 1994 S.L.T. 765.

[40] OCR, r.9.14(1), a rule more honoured in the breach than the observance.

[41] OCR, r.9.14(2).

[42] Although, usually that cuts no ice.

It makes sense to intimate and lodge the list as soon as you can.[43] There is no reason why you could not lodge a supplementary list at a later stage, and parties will quite often exchange details of witnesses informally in correspondence without bothering with lists. The prime objective of the rule is to give the opponent an opportunity to find out about your case and it seems reasonable to say[44] that if your opponent has had the information which would have enabled them to do so prior to the proof, no matter how that has been supplied, the court is unlikely to intervene and prevent a witness giving evidence.

Finding out about witnesses

7–16   What if your client knows there are people who could be witnesses in the case and they want the witnesses to be cited to give evidence for them but they do not know the names of the witnesses, although the opponent probably does? There is a little used and not very well-known procedure for obtaining disclosure of such witnesses. Section 1(1A) of the Administration of Justice (Scotland) Act 1972 provides that the court can order any person (not necessarily a person who is a party to the action) to disclose such information as they have about the identity of any person who appear to the court to be persons who might be witnesses in the case. If you think that you may need such a person as a witness then you can lodge a motion to that effect.

Citation of witnesses

7–17   You need to make sure that the witness turns up at the proof. You do this formally by citing them as a witness. In practice, you do not need to cite the witness, if you are satisfied they will turn up. In real practice, you must always cite the witness. The citation has to be made at least seven days prior to the proof. That is not to say that you cannot send out a citation within seven days of the proof, but, if you did so, it would not be effective and the witness does not need to attend.[45] Some people would cite witnesses as early as possible, as previously discussed. Some might diary it for (say) a month before the proof. It is a matter of personal preference. If you do it earlier, then it is one less thing you have to think about and you will be able to deal with any problem with the citation, or the witness.

Witnesses have to be cited by registered post or first class recorded delivery, or alternatively by a sheriff officer. In the first instance, people will normally cite by recorded delivery. The citation has to be done in a particular form and has to be sent out in a particular envelope. The envelope contains, on the outside, a note to the effect that if the envelope cannot be delivered then it should be returned to the sheriff clerk at the court at which the proof is being heard. In practice this means that about a week[46] after a formal witness citation is sent out by first class recorded delivery it might return to you, via the sheriff clerk,

---

[43] One more procedural formality out of the way.
[44] Although I am not suggesting you ignore the rule.
[45] There may be good reason for trying this, however.
[46] But sometimes considerably longer than that.

with a note of the fact that the citation was not effective and the reason why it was not effective. If that happens, then the appropriate step to take is to cite by sheriff officer. Write to the sheriff officer and ask that the particular witness be cited. It is useful to let the sheriff officer know why the citation has "bounced". There is sometimes a benefit in asking the sheriff officer to make sure that it is delivered personally if at all possible and to ask the sheriff officer to ask the witness to contact you. In some cases, where it is expected that the witness will be difficult to cite, or is going to be reluctant or unwilling to attend, then it is prudent to cite by sheriff officer straight away. All the more so if you are citing the witness very close to the seven day deadline. That fact alone often means that there is some question mark over the witness and their attendance anyway.

It is important to remember that, once you have cited a witness either yourself or by sheriff officer, the execution of citation of the witness should be retained. Keep this on the correspondence file so that, if the witness does not turn up at the proof, you can prove to the sheriff that the witness had been formally cited.

If the witness fails to attend then the sheriff can grant a warrant for the witness to be apprehended and brought to court.[47] If it is known that the witness does not want to come to court then you can ask the court for a second diligence to compel attendance.[48] It is very rare indeed that a sheriff will grant a warrant to apprehend a witness or grant a second diligence to compel the attendance of a witness, but there are some cases in which that will have to be done. It is unlikely that the witness will be happy to be there or well disposed to the person responsible for bringing them.[49]

Organising witnesses

You will undoubtedly find in the lead up to a proof, especially if you **7–18** have a number of witnesses, that you will spend time trying to organise their attendance at court. Strictly speaking, you do not have to. You could simply advise all of the witnesses to turn up at 10.00 on the first day of the proof and leave them hanging around in the waiting room for as long as it takes until you are ready for their evidence. That may make life simpler for you, but it is not particularly courteous and it is reasonable to try and minimise the inconvenience to the witnesses. With that in mind, you may be able to make an educated guess as to when the evidence of a particular witness will be taken and you may be able to suggest to a witness not to turn up until a specific time. Alternatively, you could agree that the witness should be available at the end of a telephone throughout the day so that you can call them and they can immediately travel to the court.[50] I should stress that you have to be very

---

[47] OCR, r.29.10.
[48] OCR, r.29.9.
[49] You would only use this in extreme cases. I may have done it once. The threat of doing it (which should be used very sparingly) usually suffices.
[50] This can work well with particular witnesses (self-employed or office-based, for example). There are certain witnesses with whom I would not make such an arrangement. You have to be sure you can rely upon the witness.

careful as to how far you can go in making such arrangements. It is admirable if you try to accommodate the witness, but it can backfire. If you run out of witnesses during a proof because you have not planned it properly, then that is your fault and your problem. It is true to say that proofs rarely run to a defined timetable. They can be most unpredictable and you have to make arrangements which allow a large margin of error.[51]

Sheriffs tend to be reasonably sympathetic to any responsible and sensible attempt to try and minimise the inconvenience to witnesses. It is probably appropriate to remember, however, that the inconvenience to witnesses is as nothing compared to the inconvenience to the courts and the latter has clear priority.[52]

It is a little more difficult to organise the attendance of witnesses for the defender. There may be occasions where you think it is unlikely that the pursuer's proof will be finished during the whole time allocated for the proof. It is a matter of judgment whether the defender should bring along all of their witnesses at 10.00 on the first day. You are perfectly entitled to do this and the witnesses are perfectly entitled to charge for the expense of attending on these occasions, but with a little good will and co-operation on each side this can often be avoided. It makes sense and it is good practice for the parties to talk to each other before the proof about these arrangements, with a view to running the proof sensibly.[53]

Handling witnesses at the proof

7–19   Be aware of the fact that it is going to be a strange and daunting prospect for most individuals to give evidence in court. The witness is likely to be nervous and unsure. The witness will not be familiar with the place, the procedure, the protocol or what is expected of them. The witness will not know the people who are in the court[54] or why this particular person happens to be sitting there or that person happens to be wearing a wig. The witness will not know what has gone before their evidence or what is likely to come afterwards. Can they sit down? Should they take their notes into the witness box? Where is the witness room? Should they speak to other witnesses? It is up to you to take control of the situation and to anticipate any concerns or deal with any problems. This is your witness and your responsibility. It is helpful to take a witness into the court beforehand, if you can do so, and let them see what the court looks like, where the witness box is, where people will sit and who the people might be. If you have an anxious, unwilling, impatient, uncomprehending or irritated witness then they might be less inclined[55]

---

[51] If you run out of witnesses with court time still available that day, it would be perfectly open to the sheriff to make an award of expenses against you for the wasted time.

[52] You might find the case of *Tonner v F.T. Everard & Sons Ltd*, 1994 S.L.T. 1033, of some assistance in giving justification for attempting to accommodate your witnesses while not usurping the status of the court.

[53] If any justification is needed for this sensible and responsible practice you can refer to *Kelvin v Whyte, Thomson & Co*, 1909 1 S.L.T. 477.

[54] Apart from you. The witness should, at the very least, know who you are and who you are representing.

[55] Through choice or otherwise.

to give you the evidence you are after than one who has been looked after, treated with consideration, and had matters explained to them fully. The witness will appreciate that you are trying your best to accommodate them in what may be a rather traumatic experience, and that can do you no harm.

Productions

Documents founded upon

Any documents founded upon or adopted as incorporated in their **7–20** pleadings should be lodged by a party as a production when it is referred to in the pleadings.[56] This will normally apply to cases where the document itself is the basis of the claim or defence.

Time-scale for productions for the proof

All productions which are to be used at the proof should be lodged in **7–21** process not later than 28 days before the diet.[57] You can lodge productions later than that but they will not be allowed in without the consent of the other side, or alternatively with the leave of the sheriff.[58] Some (good) explanation will have to be given as to why these productions were late.

List of productions

This should be distinguished from an inventory of productions. Each **7–22** party is required to lodge a list of the documents which they intend to use at the proof within 14 days of the interlocutor allowing proof.[59] It is not necessary to lodge the documents themselves but simply a list of them, which should include a note of the whereabouts of the documents. The intention is to give the opponent an opportunity of seeing all documents at an early stage. This rule is rarely, in my experience, complied with, nor is the non-compliance complained about. In practical terms, if a party has a good idea that they are going to lodge the documents, sufficient to enable that party to identify them precisely, it is simpler to lodge them and intimate a copy.

Principals or copies

If you can, you would want to lodge the principal document as a **7–23** production. It is not uncommon that a party will lodge a copy. If nothing turns on the authenticity of the document and there is no issue about the accuracy of the copy[60] then lodging a copy rarely causes a problem. In formal terms, this could be dealt with by a notice to admit[61] or by a joint

---

[56] For full details see OCR, r.21.1
[57] OCR, r.29.11(1). The time limit was formerly 14 days pre-proof but this was changed with effect from August 18, 2006.
[58] OCR, r.29.11(2).
[59] OCR, r.9.13(1).
[60] As is usually the case.
[61] See para.7–13.

minute of admissions.[62] Note also the terms of s.6 of the Civil Evidence (Scotland) Act 1988, which provides that "for the purposes of any civil proceedings, a copy of a document, purporting to be authenticated by a person responsible for the making of the copy, shall, unless the court otherwise directs, be—(a) deemed a true copy; and (b) treated for evidential purposes as if it were the document itself."

Inventories of productions

7–24   Productions will be lodged in the form of inventories. It would be ideal to lodge just one inventory of productions, but normally there will be a few such inventories for each side. It can be dangerous to wait until you have all of the productions you will need for the proof and then lodge one big inventory. It is probably as well to put in an inventory of productions as and when you can. This avoids problems with lodging late productions. The actual production itself should be described in some way in the inventory and the principal production[63] should be numbered. The numbering should be sequential which means that, for example, in the first inventory of productions for the pursuer the first item in the inventory will be number 1, and the fifth item will be number 5. In the second inventory of productions for the pursuer the first item of that will actually be number 6 and so on through the third inventory, fourth inventory, etc. There is a view that there are no first, second, third, etc. inventories of productions but each inventory is just called an "inventory of productions" with the actual productions being numbered sequentially. I am not sure if this is correct nor of the extent to which this practice is followed. It is probably not very important provided that you are consistent in how you do this.

Copies of productions

7–25   You will normally want to take at least two copies of your inventory of productions along with copies of the productions themselves. One is for you; one is for the sheriff. There is no good reason not to do this. You should ensure the copies of the productions have the same numbering as the principal productions. You should send your opponent a copy of the inventory and a copy of the productions.[64] You should also lodge with the sheriff clerk an additional copy of the productions for the use of the sheriff. The Rules provide that the sheriff's copy productions should be lodged 48 hours before the proof.[65] In my experience, sheriffs are not too concerned about this provided that they have a good set of copies for the proof itself. Make sure that the copies are good copies, clearly numbered in line with the numbering of the principal productions and easy to handle, i.e. bound together or otherwise arranged in good order. This is an extremely important piece of proof preparation, which is often overlooked and can cause real problems at the proof. I find that it is

---

[62] See para.7–14.
[63] And the copies of it.
[64] There is actually no formal rule to this effect, but it is the invariable practice in my experience.
[65] OCR, r.29.12.

usually acceptable and infinitely preferable to bring along a good set of copies for the use of the sheriff at the proof to the proof diet itself, and hand them over to the sheriff then.[66] Copies lodged any earlier than this have a curious habit of going missing.

Organising your papers for the proof

It is inevitable that you will have quite a bulky client file by the time **7–26** the case is set down for proof. No matter how well, or logically the file is kept, it is likely to be awkward to extract relevant papers from it during the proof. You could of course extract the papers before the proof and find yourself with assorted sheaves of loose paper which are going to come in handy during the proof. You will, however, lose them, misplace them, drop them, staple them to the wrong things, or the like. When you are looking for something, which you need to refer to when a witness is being questioned, you will not be able to find it in the mass of papers you have in your bag. It is remarkably helpful, if not absolutely essential, to have a system for organising all of the papers you will need to conduct the proof. There is nothing clever or innovative about this. It just makes good sense.

An excellent habit,[67] is to put together a proof folder containing only the papers you need, or which you might need, to conduct the proof itself. In that folder, you should place the documents which are relevant for the proof—and only those documents—and make sure that these are securely in place and in an order with which you are familiar. You will find at least two benefits from the exercise. First, you will have to go through all of your papers once again and think about what is relevant, might be significant, or will be of use to you at the proof itself. This filtering process is a useful means of ensuring that you focus on what evidence you have as opposed to what information you have, which is not evidence. Remember that, at the proof itself, the only matters which the court can hear or see will be the evidence of witnesses and the content of documents which have been formally lodged as productions. Everything else is irrelevant and will not be needed for the actual conduct of the hearing itself. Secondly, you will now have a much reduced, and easily read, set of papers from which to work as you prepare for the proof. As you do so, you can see if there are gaps, and if you acquire additional information in the lead up to the proof you can add this to your folder (if it will be evidence). The most significant and practical benefit, however, is that when you are in court and conducting the case this folder will provide you with easy access to all relevant information. It should help you avoid embarrassing delays and searches while you try to locate things which you need to use for the proof. It will serve as your script for the proof, if you like.

Of course, you will want to have your client file, or files, with you at the proof because there may be aspects of the administration of the case to which you will have to make reference.[68] However, you want to be

---

[66] If there are a number of productions, put the sheriff's copy of all of the productions in a lever arch file, in order, and with tabs separating each inventory.

[67] Which really ought to be in a rule of court.

[68] e.g. the booking of a shorthand writer or the execution of citation of a witness.

able to discard the bulky jumble of papers comprising your correspondence file as quickly as possible and conduct the proof solely from the papers contained within your proof folder. It requires some trial and error to perfect your own system, and you need to have the confidence to discard superfluous material so as to make this work properly. The more you do it, the more you will appreciate it, and I am going to suggest how you should put this together.

Ideally, the contents of the proof folder should comprise (in order):

Up-to-date record

7–27   Since this contains the record of the pleadings about which the proof will be heard, this is all you need. You do not need a copy of the defender's second note of adjustments. Of course, you do want to be satisfied that the record is accurate and comprehensive. It would help to try and read it as if you had not read it before. I find it helpful to write out a summary of the essential averments for both sides in the record. I try to reduce the pleadings as much as possible without losing any of the crucial averments. This helps to reinforce your understanding of exactly what is said in the pleadings and to make you concentrate upon the essential parts of each party's case. I can usually reduce a 12-page record to a couple of pages and use this as an aide-memoir during the proof itself. It can sometimes make it easier for you to locate the relevant part when an issue about the content of the pleadings arises in the course of the proof. I will put this summary ahead of the record in my folder, right at the top. It gives quick easy reference to the truly essential features of the case.

A copy of the rule 22.1 note

7–28   If this is a proof before answer, and the proof before answer has been justified by a rule 22.1 note, then it is helpful to have a copy of the rule 22.1 note handy so that you are reminded what matters of law still have to be considered. If a proof before answer had been fixed after judgment at a debate you would also have the judgment following the debate at this point.

A copy of any notice to admit or joint minute of admissions.

7–29   Indeed, any formal record of what is agreed and does not need to be proved.

Pursuer's productions in order

7–30   Each party may have more than one inventory of productions. Put the pursuer's inventories in order with copies of the productions underneath each relative inventory. Make sure that the productions are in the correct order, so that you can refer to these easily. Make sure that you have the numbering of the individual productions themselves.

Defender's productions in order

7–31   The same applies as before and the benefit of doing it in this formalised way is that you will always know, in any case, where all of the productions are. The pursuer's productions come first and should be numbered sequentially. The defender's productions come next and are numbered sequentially. This should assist you in not losing bits of paper, or being unable to find the appropriate document during the proof. This can be a common, and irritating, problem.

Pursuer's list of witnesses.

Precognitions of the pursuer and any of the pursuer's witnesses

You should have precognitions. If you do not have precognitions you **7–32** should obtain them. Put them in the order that the witnesses appear on the witness list.

You will want handwritten notes for your examination and cross-examination of the witnesses. I would normally put these immediately adjacent to the precognition of the witness concerned. You cannot do an examination or cross-examination properly without preparing it. You cannot do it properly without reference to your handwritten, or typed, notes.[69]

Defender's list of witnesses

Precognitions from the defender and the defender's witnesses

You should have a precognition from the defender (if that is your own **7–33** client) and witnesses. If you do not have them you should try to obtain them. You should know who the witnesses for the other side are and you should have contacted them for precognition.

A section of notes on matters of relevance for the purposes of the proof

This might comprise any notes about the law, or about the facts, or **7–34** about possible objections to evidence. You may want to have copies of any cases or sections from textbooks which might be relevant in relation to matters of law that might arise during the proof. There is a danger of having too much in this part of the folder, but it has to be accepted that sometimes you cannot predict what will turn up at the proof. If you think that something will turn up at the proof and you need to cover it, then you should have the documents or notes in this part of the folder if need be. If you really think hard about the case and about the evidence which might, or might not, come out then you can anticipate issues arising and plan ahead by having authorities to support what you are going to lead, or the basis of an objection to that you anticipate you will take. It should not come as a surprise to you if you have prepared thoroughly.[70]

You should have an outline of what you think your submissions are going to be at the end of the proof. Of course, this is not going to be a verbatim transcript of your formal submissions, but simply a rough

---

[69] Unless you are very experienced or brilliant (or stupid).
[70] In fairness that is not really true. No matter how hard you work there will always be something you could never have thought of in advance. That is why it is such fun.

outline. You can use this and develop it once the detailed evidence has come out.

Refinements to the proof folder

7–35   It is up to you to decide when to start making up the proof folder, but it is likely that you will have to update it as and when there are further developments in the run up to the proof. Make sure that you do keep it up to date and follow the logical layout suggested. If you obtain a precognition, slot it into its allotted place. If you obtain a supplementary precognition from a witness then put it behind the first one, or, if you are now going to work from the supplementary precognition put it in front of it. If you have found an interesting case which you may be able to use at the submissions then add it to the general section, at the end. This kind of discipline will pay dividends.

If there are very bulky documents in the case, for example, medical records or a lengthy contract, then you may want to extract that from your proof folder and put it into a file of its own. The idea is to make the proof folder more manageable. It is counter-productive to clutter it up with hundreds of sheets of paper only a few of which might be relevant and referred to at the proof. Better to take out in their entirety any of the major documents in the case, which are occupying a large part of the proof folder, and keep them in a separate file. Keep the proof folder as comprehensive, concise, and manageable as possible.

It is also quite useful to have the proof folder with dividers splitting the papers into the separate sections outlined. It makes it easier to access the appropriate papers and preserves the mental discipline which keeps you organised. There are some cases where you might know there is a particular document or page(s) of a document which will be a major bone of contention. Flag this up in some way because you will constantly be referring to it, but leave it in its place in the folder.

7–36   When you are working at the proof remember to keep all of the papers in the correct place. You may find it necessary to extract a precognition or a production, in order to look at it more closely or carry it with you if you are asking a question. This is something you should probably resist, unless you are very good at doing this. Better to hold the folder with the document in it and keep it in its place rather than to start jumbling things around. If you are going to take it out, put it back where you got it from when you are finished.[71]

It will take you some time to get used to the idea, and to make up a functional folder in any case. Working in this way will help you to concentrate upon the oral and documentary evidence being led at the proof. After all is said and done, that is all the court is interested in, and that is all that counts. If the court does not hear the evidence from witnesses, or see evidence in the form of productions, then it simply cannot find facts to be proved. The proof folder contains the only things of relevance to the proof. All that you have to do after that is find the questions to make that raw material come to life.

---

[71] It is easy to overlook this—there are worse sins, but it rather defeats the purpose if you start messing it up once the proof commences.

Rough outline submissions

One of the most important features of preparing for proof is the **7–37** preparation of the submissions you will make at the end of the proof. The whole purpose of leading evidence and lodging productions is to enable you to be in a position to make the submissions which you have to make in order to argue that your case should succeed. It may take you some time to realise that the best way to approach preparation for the detailed presentation of the case is to start at the very end. What will you say when the evidence is all over? If you know what you are going to say then you will know what evidence you have to present to enable you to say it. You will have a view about what evidence and what facts are ultimately important. You will be aware when evidence is being led which might seem to be contrary to your interests whether it is really against you. You will appreciate when examining and cross-examining witnesses what evidence to explore in greater detail and what evidence to leave well alone. You will know it because you have a good idea of what you are actually going to say about it even before the evidence came out.

There is, of course, a limit to what you can anticipate but, if you think about it, you should know what your evidence is going to be, and you should know the line of defence being run. You will know what all of the productions are about. In other words, the proof should not contain too many surprises. Certainly there will be doubt about what witnesses will be accepted as credible and reliable and the court may have to make a number of decisions about what evidence to prefer, but you can deal with these matters as the proof continues. It is going to be possible to prepare a rough outline of your submissions and to have this in note form with your proof folder so that you can adapt it, and add to it, as the evidence emerges. At the very least, it will give you a good base from which to start when the time comes for you to address the court.

The making of submissions is dealt with in Chapter 11, so we will not **7–38** discuss this in detail here. However, here is the kind of broad skeleton which may stand you in good stead for many cases.

1. For the pursuer to proceed in this case they have to prove . . .
2. The following matters have been agreed or were not disputed at the proof . . .
3. The pursuer's witnesses said . . .
4. The defender's witnesses said . . .
5. Your Lordship can be satisfied that the following facts have been proved . . .
6. The law in relation to this matter is . . .
7. The authorities to justify the position are . . .
8. Applying that law to those facts, which I have asked you to hold proved, means that . . .
9. The losses sustained by the pursuer are (or, the amount of the claim is) . . .
10. The cases to justify those losses are . . .
11. The pursuer's plea in law No. X should be sustained . . .
12. The defender's plea in law No. Y should be repelled . . .
13. Decree should be granted for . . .

With your proof folder under your arm, you are going to be ready to conduct the proof and lead the evidence about the facts which you want to establish. You will do this by examination in chief and cross-examination of witnesses. These have to be focused in some way. The focus is the submission which you are going to make at the end of the proof. The most vital aspect of your preparation for the proof is the preparation—in writing or in your mind—of the submissions that you are proposing to make after the evidence has been led. You can think of the proof involving the examination and cross-examination of the witnesses as a vehicle for making the evidence come out in such a way as to fit the submissions you are going to make at the end of the case. If you conduct the case without that target to aim at you are indeed going to miss the whole point.

CHAPTER 8

EXAMINATION IN CHIEF

"Now, Mr Bloggs, we know you are a little deaf, so I am going to ask my questions loud and clear and if you cannot hear me just say so. Do you understand?"
"I am sorry sir, could you speak up. I am a little deaf."

What could be simpler than taking your client, or your witness,[1] through **8–01** their evidence in chief during the course of your proof? You have been handling the case for some time. You know it inside out. You have spent hours with the client and witnesses going over the circumstances.[2] You are going to attack your opponent's witnesses in cross-examination and expose them all to be the liars and cheats you always thought they were. You have beautifully clear and concise submissions prepared for the end of the case. You have interviewed your client more than once and you think they are an honest and straightforward person. All you have to do is invite them to tell the court, in their own words, what happened. WRONG!

It is difficult to do an examination in chief well. It is easy to do it poorly. Sometimes it will not matter too much how you do it, and, despite the shortcomings of your technique, your client's honesty and reliability will shine through. Sheriffs will usually make allowances for the fact that inexperienced agents may not be as good at this as they should be. Neither you nor your client may notice that things are not going as well as they should. There is little prospect of you receiving any feedback on what you did[3] or how you might do it better. Everyone will have an opinion about how to conduct an examination in chief, but few are likely to be able to spend time with you explaining and analysing the process. There are no real guides as to how to do it and often the technique is learned by painful trial and error. This chapter is intended to give some pointers for conducting a competent and professional examination of a witness and to remove some of the "error" during the "trial". I think it would be fair to describe the approach here as extremely basic. What I say is only an attempt to give a broad foundation, from which, with practice and experience, you can build. This chapter is based upon many years of teaching these skills to inexperienced but enthusiastic litigators almost literally starting from

---

[1] From now on I will refer only to the client (pursuer or defender) but these comments apply equally to witnesses unless otherwise noted.
[2] I am ignoring the prospect that you were handed the file last night for the first time.
[3] The client and/or the court's decision might give you a clue, but neither of these is likely to be constructive.

scratch. It is intended to assist them, but I would like to think that it will give experienced litigators some food for thought too.

Fundamentals

8–02   First, you have to think about what the aims and objectives of examination in chief in any litigation ought to be. Putting it at its simplest, you are trying to have your client tell their story to the court in their own words, in a structured and coherent way, so that the sheriff hears from your client exactly what the client[4] wants the sheriff to hear about the case. You and your client know[5] what the evidence is to be and know what the case is about. Remember that the sheriff does not. There will be facts you will take for granted as being understood about the case. There are assumptions you will consciously or subconsciously make. You must put yourself into the mind, and the ears, of the sheriff listening to the evidence in the case. Remember that the sheriff starts the case with a blank notebook. The sheriff can only fill it up with words that are actually spoken by the client in evidence. You will be asking the sheriff to find, at the end of the case, that certain facts were proved. Where facts are disputed, you must lead evidence about them. Every word spoken by the witness and heard by the sheriff is evidence. It is of no consequence that you know your client did not intend to say this or that, or that there are certain matters which you had taken for granted as being clear and indisputable. Your client's story is solely the product of their words, in court, on that day, and if the sheriff does not hear those particular words which you need him to hear then you have a problem. Your job is to assist your client to tell their story. You can do this by asking clear and sensible questions designed to elicit clear and sensible answers on all of the material facts. You are trying to present your witness as credible and reliable. You are trying to assist the client to create a favourable impression in the mind of the sheriff. You have to tune in to what the client is saying and what the sheriff is hearing. Your questions are the catalyst for that product. Do not underestimate how important that is.

     This means that you have to frame your questions in such a way as to enable your client to tell their story to the court. The words you use, the sequence in which you ask the questions, your approach to leading the evidence, and the manner in which you lead the evidence in court can all have a significant effect on the way in which the court perceives your client's evidence and your client. You want to ask your client questions which will enable them to tell their story clearly, concisely, logically, honestly, and accurately. This requires you to tailor the questions to your client's personality and ability. With some clients this can be a difficult process. Where I have a client who is not good at explaining things or where their evidence is complex, I will write out verbatim in advance for my benefit, all of the questions I will ask them or, at least, the questions in relation to particular aspects of their evidence which might take us in to areas of difficulty. If nothing else, this is a good mental exercise

---

[4] And you.
[5] Or should know.

enabling you to focus on the presentation of your client's evidence to the court. To emphasise this point for one last time, let me show you an extract from a transcript of an actual examination in chief of a pursuer in a personal injury case[6] and ask you to consider what this told the sheriff about the case and about the client. It is necessary to explain that this actually happened, and these questions were actually asked, in real life. Imagine what it sounded like.

George Hamilton (52)   **8–03**

"SOLICITOR	*Would you state your address for the record?*
WITNESS	*159 Kirkintilloch Road, Bishopbriggs.*
SOLICITOR	*What is your designation?*
WITNESS	*Pardon?*
SOLICITOR	*What is your occupation?*
WITNESS	*I am an electrician.*
SOLICITOR	*Is it correct to say that you were involved in an accident in the Argyll Street Centre, Glasgow on the afternoon of July 23, 2004?*
WITNESS	*Yes.*
OPPONENT	*My Lord, I did not object to that question but my friend should not lead the witness in relation to any of the circumstances of this accident.*
SHERIFF	*I think it is a matter of admission that the pursuer was involved in an accident at that locus on that date.*
OPPONENT	*No, it is not.*
SOLICITOR	*I will rephrase the question, my Lord.*
SOLICITOR	*Can you tell the court where you were on the July 23, 2004?*
WITNESS	*I take it you mean the day of my accident or, no, well, the time I had my accident. Well that was when I was in Glasgow going to the shops. I got to the locus about 2.30pm, where I had a fall.*
SOLICITOR	*Mr Hamilton, could I refer you to some productions which I am passing to you*
SHERIFF	*What number of process is this?*
SOLICITOR	*I think it is the third one.*
SHERIFF	*No, what number of process?*
SOLICITOR	*5/3 I think. Is that a sketch map of the locus in question?*
WITNESS	*Yes, it is the Argyll Street Shopping Centre, that is where I was that day.*
SOLICITOR	*In relation to that, can you be clear of the route you took that day?*

---

[6] I have adapted it only slightly to fit the circumstances of our personal injury case of George Hamilton—and to protect the innocent.

WITNESS	Well I came off the escalator and went down past the shops.
SHERIFF	Is that as I look at it?
WITNESS	Sorry if I am not being precise.
SOLICITOR	From the top to the bottom of the sketch you were walking down the left-hand side?
WITNESS	Yes. I got to the shrubs marked blue.
SHERIFF	There is nothing marked blue on my photocopy. What are you talking about?
WITNESS	I crossed the entrance . . .
SHERIFF	No that was not my question. What are you talking about? Can you hold it up?
WITNESS	See these two blue marks on the paper, well, that is where I was. I was just walking past there when I caught my foot and fell.
SOLICITOR	Mr Hamilton, I will look at the production in terms of the right- or left-hand side, you said that was the left-hand side.
WITNESS	Yes. This is my left side so I am coming down this way, so it is my left.
SOLICITOR	As you look at the production, is that the right?
WITNESS	Yes.
SHERIFF	Well we have dealt with that production. I think it works if you turn it upside down Mr Hamilton.
SOLICITOR	If I refer you to production 5/2 you will see that there are some shops indicated there. Is that the approximate location?
SHERIFF	Approximate location of what?
SOLICITOR	Of the place that Mr Hamilton had referred to earlier.
SHERIFF	Why don't you ask the witness to point out on the sketch plan where he says he fell?
SOLICITOR	Well perhaps you would answer that question Mr Hamilton.
WITNESS	Yes, I would say it is near enough accurate.
SHERIFF	Well what is it you are pointing to?
WITNESS	The blue marks.
SHERIFF	I do not see any blue marks on that production. Are you sure?
WITNESS	I'm sorry, they are actually marked in red on that plan there. I am getting a bit confused. It was all such a while ago.
SOLICITOR	Well, anyway, you tripped on a missing tile near there . . .

OBJECTION."

8–04 As you can see from this extract, the client has become completely confused. He has told us very little in his own words about what actually happened. He has not even been able to describe simply where his accident happened—something which should have been easy. Why has he been so poor? Because you asked him all the wrong questions.[7] I am afraid that this really happened and this was by no means the first proof the solicitor had done. I suspect that the solicitor had started with bad habits and had become rather relaxed and careless about the leading of this witness to the description of his accident. No thought or preparation had gone into this set of questions.[8] Treat this as a cautionary tale and imagine how you might have approached it.

I am now going to suggest various guidelines for a more professional and effective examination in chief of this witness. I am conscious of the fact that this means that you will be involved in a considerable amount of preparation time. This may be time which you do not have in the harsh reality of legal practice. It can, and must, be done however.[9] Some of the suggestions should eventually become second-nature to you so that you are preparing for the leading of evidence almost from day one of the case. If you want to do advocacy properly, or do it better, then you have to put this amount of work into it. You will find that it does pay dividends for you and your clients.

Preparing yourself

Do not kid yourself that all you have to do is stand your client/witness **8–05** in the witness box, let them take the oath, and ask them to talk for as long as it takes. When learning how to do this, write out in advance each and every question—using the actual words of the question—that you need to ask to enable your client to give specific answers which will build up their evidence as a whole. Do not just think that you will need to ask them to explain where they were going and why. Think about what you would actually say. Then try to hear in your mind what their answer will be. What answer could they possibly give to that question? Listen critically to the question again. If there are a range of possible answers then the question may not be good or precise enough. You should not be asking questions to which you and your client do not know the answer. How can you be sure about this? Go over it in your mind, and picture yourself asking these questions to your client in the court. For example, in George Hamilton's case you may need to establish when the accident happened.

"Do you recall what date it was?"

(Well does he?) You should know if he does or can. Most people do not remember precise dates, especially if the accident occurred some time ago.[10] What will you ask him if he does not?

It may not be disputed, in which case the question could be,

---

[7] Hardly one of those questions was appropriate.

[8] I hope.

[9] If you seriously want to do litigation then you should have been thinking about this for months anyway, and I am afraid that the night before the proof has to be a social write off.

[10] In personal injury cases the proof is often three or four years or more after the accident. Can you remember dates that long ago?

> *"It is not a matter of dispute that you had an accident on July 23 2004.*
> *Do you recall what day of the week it was?"*[11]

8–06 What if you just ask him,

> *"When did you have your accident?"*
> *or*
> *"On what day did you have your accident?"*

Would that be sufficient to enable him to give a specific answer? Maybe
not. Think about the question again. Are you asking him what day he
had his accident (Saturday) or what date he had his accident (July 23,
2004)? Think about how he would answer that question. If you can see
there might be scope for ambiguity then think about rephrasing the
question. It might not matter. Then again it might. If there is a clear way
of asking it then use that, because it will assist the client.

What if you know he does not remember the date of the accident?
The date is not conceded by the defenders, whose position will probably
be that they do not know if he had an accident.[12]

> *"Do you recall the day on which you had your accident?"*
> *"Saturday."*
> *"Do you recall the exact date of your accident?"*
> *"No."*
> *"After your accident did you have to go to hospital?"*[13]
> *"Yes."*
> *"Was that on the same day of the accident or on another day?"*
> *"It was the next day."*
> *"So if we know you were attending the hospital on July 24, 2004 from*
> *the hospital records which are agreed in the case, does it follow that*
> *your accident must have been on the July 23?"*[14]
> *"Yes, that must be right."*

8–07 What if you know he knows what date it was, because it was the day of
his wife's birthday and he was due to be going out that night and had to
cancel it.

> *"Do you recall what date it was?"*
> *"Yes, it was the July 23, 2004."*
> *"Is there any particular reason why you can remember the date, Mr*
> *Hamilton?"*

---

[11] Note that the first part is not a question but it is helpful to make it clear that the date is
not an issue and you can give him a question to which you know he knows the answer.
More people are likely to remember the day rather than the date. You should know if he
does remember it of course.

[12] After all they have no witnesses who saw it or can say it definitely happened that day as
opposed to the previous night or later that night when the pursuer fell down drunk
somewhere else.

[13] Whatever else might be disputed, we all know he did go to hospital after some kind of
accident.

[14] This is a leading question, but a legitimate leading question unless the court has some
difficulty with the fact that the 24th follows the 23rd. If so, you really do have a problem.

"Yes."

Even that might create a small problem. What if he cannot remember the year it happened? Well, does he? Again it might not be very important in the overall context of the case but you do not want him and you appearing rather foolish, floundering around with something as basic as this.

Obviously I am taking this to extremes to illustrate the point that **8–08** when you are preparing your examination in chief you have to think carefully about the precise words of the questions you will ask, rather than thinking only about the broad idea. With experience, you can reduce this somewhat, but you should be able to appreciate that if you are going in to an area of evidence which is complex or in which you have some concerns about the client's ability to express himself clearly, you have to be extremely careful about the words of the questions so that you do not make life any more difficult for him. If you have written out a full list of the actual questions in sequence, which you have thought about carefully in advance, you may find you hardly need to refer to them at all.[15] The mere process of forcing yourself to think clearly about exactly what you are going to ask may be sufficient to embed this in your mind. There is the added bonus that if you lose concentration, or lose your place, or are distracted in some way whilst doing the proof you should always have a set of questions on some aspect of his evidence which you have already thought about and which you know are sensible and pertinent.

If you do not, or cannot, write out the specific questions in advance, then at least write, in big capital letters, a note on one single piece of paper with all of the headings of the things you have to ask him, for example "ACCIDENT DATE, TIME, LOCATION, PHOTOGRAPHS, SKETCH, INJURY, HOSPITAL NOTES, TREATMENT", etc. In this way you will (you hope) not miss out anything important in the case. If you are going to refer him to productions in any part of his evidence, add to your note the production number (the process number) and check that you have it right and that you know what it shows.[16]

Preparing the client/witness for examination in chief

Even though you are inexperienced, you have been around the courts **8–09** for a little while. You may have already done a proof or two, or at least seen them done, and have some idea from your own training of what happens or is supposed to happen. Even then, you are going to be a little phased by the experience. Your client is unlikely to have had any similar experience so think how phased he might be. In advance of the proof you should prepare them for the examination in chief (and cross). I do not think you should do this too far in advance of the diet itself. Indeed, if you can do it fairly close to the diet that would be preferable.

The first thing to do is to check if the client has given evidence in court before or not. Few people have actually done so. If they have, then

---

[15] Put the list next to the witness's precognition in your proof folder and use them both.
[16] Put this note next to his precognition in your proof folder. *N.B.* Too many notes can confuse you so be careful about that too.

you can find out what they made of it. There are very few witnesses who are not daunted by the prospect of giving evidence.[17] That is understandable. You will not be looking forward to it yourself[18] and it is 10 times worse for most normal people. Imagine what it is like if it was your first proof.[19] Imagine what it is like for a lay person in that position.

So far as possible, you have to put them at their ease in advance. For witnesses, and especially for clients, it would help to explain broadly what happens in a proof sometime during the weeks before the proof. The sequence of who gives evidence first, examination in chief, cross-examination and re-examination. Who the sheriff might be. What he will say or do. What to do before and after giving evidence. Who else will be there, and so on. Car parking at the court. Time-scales. By and large, this will help.

8–10   When it comes to detailed preparation of the client for the proof we enter the slightly vexed area of whether "coaching" of a witness is permissible. The simple answer is that it is not, if "coaching" means telling a witness what to say in answer to a question, or questions. It is not your function to do this and it is quite improper. However, that does not mean there is anything objectionable in running through your examination in chief, or parts of it, with the witness to give the witness an idea of what they will be asked and to give them the opportunity of answering as if they were in court. This gives you a chance to emphasise that the client should only answer the question asked, that they should wait until you finish asking the question until they start the answer, that if you want them to explain something in more detail or justify something they are going to say that you will ask them specifically to do so.[20] What you cannot do is tell the client that one answer rather than another would be better for the case. You should not respond to any request from the client as to how they ought to answer this or that "tricky" question. The response is that it is not for you to tell them what to say. It is for them to tell the truth. They will be on oath. You have no problem assisting the client to do justice to their evidence, and to say what they truly mean to say, but the answer to any question is their responsibility. Provided that is what the client means then they can do no wrong. Do not tell the client not to say "that" as opposed to "this".

You can prepare your client for cross-examination also without doing anything improper. You can identify areas in which they may be susceptible to cross-examination. You can say they might be asked this or that. You can play devil's advocate by taking the role of the cross-examiner and actually asking the client the types of questions they might be asked. Do not also tell them the answer to these questions. You are more interested in seeing how the client would answer such questions. Is that what they meant to say? If not, what do they truly mean? This process may, apart from anything else help you to plan your examination

---

[17] In my experience, those who are looking forward to it with relish may be a cause of concern.

[18] Be honest.

[19] For readers of this book it possibly is.

[20] Be aware that he may not really take this in—you may have to repeat it while he is giving evidence.

in chief a little better to ensure the evidence comes out properly before the cross-examination. It will also give your client an opportunity to think, prior to giving evidence, about the fact that clever lawyers will be trying to trip them up and to give your client some practice at responding. There is nothing wrong with doing this. Clever lawyers with experience of court will be working hard to prepare clever questions to catch them out. It can be unfair to a witness to allow them to be led like a lamb to the slaughter.[21] The dividing line between coaching and preparing may be difficult to identify in some cases, but the simplest way to express it and to avoid crossing it is to remind the witness that it is their evidence alone that counts, it is their recollection that matters and it is their obligation to tell the truth to the best of their ability. You are asking them to do no more or less than that.

It is helpful to go through with the witness the productions which are **8–11** lodged in the case, and to which you intend to refer them. Confirm that the witness knows what they are and has had an opportunity to consider anything which might be contentious or complex in advance of the proof. It would be wrong to leave the witness in a position whereby the first time they saw or seriously thought about some documentary evidence (either yours or the other side's) was when they were in the witness box. There would be no harm in giving the witness a copy of the production(s) which might be important in their evidence, so that they can take this away and study it.[22] The only word of caution here is to warn against over-preparation of the witness whose evidence might appear to be dogmatic, stilted or not spontaneous. This can, in some circumstances, give the wrong impression and one which the witness, if unprepared, might not have conveyed. There is a balance to be struck, and it is not possible to prescribe the degree of preparation which might be helpful in any individual case. At the very least, you do not want the client in examination in chief being asked this particular question or being asked to consider that particular production for the first time ever when they are actually giving evidence. Because then, how do you know their answer?

It is not a conversation

Examination in chief is a process designed to elicit the evidence of the **8–12** witness. It is a formal process. You are assisting the client to tell the sheriff all that they have to say about the facts of their case by a series of questions and answers. You should know the questions you are going to ask and you should know[23] the answer to those questions. So you are not asking questions out of curiosity, in a casual way or as if it was a chat with the witness. "It must have come as a bit of a bummer to you when you tripped up? How come it happened? How did you feel about it? I bet you the wife wasn't too chuffed that night?"

You must use more formal and precise language. It is difficult to do this if you are not used to it. You must split the questions up into

---

[21] As I understand it, this is the primary justification for lawyers in the USA coaching—and I mean coaching—the witness. They find nothing wrong with this.

[22] You would expect that he might have them already.

[23] Or, at least, have a very good idea about.

component parts. You must use the questions to progress logically through the witness's evidence. Sloppy questions will produce sloppy, inaccurate or irrelevant answers. You have to sharpen up your use of language and bear in mind what the object of the exercise is. The object is to give the sheriff facts about how the accident happened and why it happened, to enable him to reach a conclusion in law that the accident was caused by someone's fault. What facts will your questions elicit?

Think about these questions. (1) "Were you far away from the shop front at the time?" (2) "Was it pretty dark or not around there?" (3) "Was it easy to see where you were going in the centre?" You could imagine someone asking these questions casually while chatting to Mr Hamilton after the accident. Indeed, these questions could well have been asked during the precognition taking exercise. But will they do for the proof?

8–13　　(1) What does "far away" mean? If it is just general narrative then that is unobjectionable, but it takes you nowhere. Maybe the witness will answer in feet and yards.[24] Maybe they will not. The witness might just say, "Not that far". What do you mean by the shop front? Which shop front? It runs a long way. Are you talking about the entrance to the shop, or the windows of the shop, or just the line of the shop fronts generally? What does "at the time" mean. What "time" are we talking about?

"Can you tell the court, in yards or feet, how far away from the entrance to the shop you were when you actually tripped?" As you will see, this has all of the component parts expressed more clearly[25] and gives you a much better chance of an answer which will actually mean something, and enable a sheriff to make a specific finding. Of course, the original question may just have been the first in a string of questions which would ultimately have reached that point, but it is much better to use one sharp question than 10 blunt ones.

(2) What does "pretty dark" mean? Pretty much anything. Was there artificial lighting at the point where your accident happened? Do you know what kind it was? Were you able to see clearly in front of you? Was there any reason why your view ahead was impaired? Again, these types of questions are more likely to produce answers which can be regarded as facts rather than vague impressions or personal opinions.

(3) What does this actually mean? It is not immediately obvious. Does it matter what visibility was like in the "centre"? Is it relevant for the spot where the accident occurred? The facts you might want to be establishing are whether the broken tile could have been seen by ordinary people, such as your client, or whether there was a reason why it might not have been seen. Does it matter what the lighting was generally in the centre? He had his accident at one specific point. The question might just be narrative—the lighting generally was poor—but it is not

---

[24] Metres are still a novelty for most witnesses.
[25] And yet expressed simply.

really relevant. Do you want to ask it? Does it take you anywhere? Maybe it does. The point is that if you prepare critically by asking yourself if these are the correct questions, or the correct way to ask these questions, then you will benefit and present the case better.

Use of language

You must take into account your client's character, intelligence and **8–14** speech when framing the questions you are going to ask them. You will not get the answers you want, nor the answers your client intends to give, if you ask them a question they do not understand, or you ask them to explain something which you should realise they will have difficulty explaining. It is for you to assess whether your client can understand it or can answer it clearly and coherently. You should know your client well enough to predict this. Extreme examples might be:

"How proximate were you to the central vestibule of the centre?"
"By reference to points of the compass were you walking east or west?"
"Can you explain the chronology of events after the accident occurred?"

You can well see that certain witnesses could not answer these questions whereas some might have a stab at an answer with varying degrees of accuracy or understanding. It is your fault entirely if the witness does not understand the question. Some questions are difficult to ask with precision and clarity. When running through these questions in your mind, in preparation for the proof, ask yourself if the witness will understand what they are being asked. You should also check that this question enables the witness to give the answer you expect. If not, or if you have serious doubts about it, then go back to the drawing board. I did see a case lost because the agent was unable to have his client explain to the court in examination in chief where the bus stop at the end of his road was located. The witness was not intelligent and assumed, understandably, that everyone knew what the place looked like. The sheriff eventually lost patience and made it clear that he found everything this witness said to be highly questionable and unreliable. He was the only witness to his own accident. He failed to prove it. This can happen. If, and when, it does, it will not be the witness's fault. It will be yours.

Short and simple questions

Simple questions are undoubtedly the best. That is obvious. The **8–15** witness is more likely to understand them. The answer is more likely to be clear and understandable. We probably all know this. Unfortunately we all have a tendency to over-elaborate the questions. Sometimes we want to get all sorts of questions into one, or save time by getting multiple answers to one complex question. Experience does tell you that less (words) can be more. It also tells you that more (questions) can be less.

What day was it?
Do you recall what time of day it was?
What were you intending to do?
Where had you been before you went to the centre?
Where were you going within the centre?
Were you on your own?
Who was with you?
Why did you walk that way?
How did you go from the ground floor to the first floor?
Why were you going slowly along the corridor?
Can you explain how this happened?
Do you recall where it happened?
Why were you unable to see this broken tile?

As you can appreciate, these are all extremely simple questions. They are all open[26] questions. They should be the cornerstones of your examination in chief. You will need to ask supplementary questions around these basic ones, but the best piece of advice is to concentrate on reducing the words in your question to as few as you possibly can. Start them all with who, why, where, what, how, or when. You will be surprised at how difficult it is to persuade yourself that the appropriate language to use with witnesses does not involve complex or clever legal words or ideas but simple questions asked briefly. If you cannot reduce the words of your question to about two lines (at most) then it is probably too long and the answer might be unclear. Edit your questions ruthlessly. What am I really trying to ask this witness? Can I put the question more simply? It is an excellent discipline and prevents you rambling on for minutes with a question whose beginning, middle and end seem to be entirely unrelated, and which will have everyone else in court hoping that the witness gives you the classic reply.[27]

8–16   An unclear question can leave you hoping that the witness can guess what you meant to ask.[28] You can assist the witness by focusing on what you are trying to achieve and simplifying the question by putting it into a series of simple questions which build up the evidence in a controlled way. Contrast,

> *"Where were you exactly in relation to the shop front when your accident occurred?"*

(which is, on the face of it, a simple question but its meaning is not entirely clear. It might produce the answer you hope is coming, which is that the witness went back to the locus a few days after the accident and actually measured everything out) with,

> *"Once you reached the top of the escalator, where did you walk to?*

---

[26] Not leading.
[27] Which is, "I am not sure if I understand the question. Could you possibly repeat it?"—a challenge which usually demonstrates that you did not understand it either and have already blanked it out of your mind so you are quite incapable of remembering it. The best advice in this situation is to ask to withdraw the question and try again.
[28] If you knew exactly what you intended.

How far did you walk along the corridor before you had your accident?
How far away from the shop entrance were you at the time of your fall?
Can you express that in yards and feet or in metres?
Why are you so sure about that?
When did you go back to look at the accident location and check this exactly?
Why did you do that?
How did you measure it?"

If you have planned the examination thoroughly you will know that this is a cast iron way of eliciting the answers without having to take a chance on the witness proffering the measuring exercise in answer to the first question. Again, it might not matter. You may well get there in the end but it works so much better if you lead the evidence from the witness than if you appear to be an interested bystander whose job is just to windup the witness and then let them go "blah".[29]

No leading questions

When framing questions for your examination in chief you must be **8–17** aware of the difference between leading and non-leading questions. You must not ask any questions of your own witness which are leading questions. We will go on to discuss this more generally and a little more fully in Chapter 10, but at this point we will simply look at the issue in the context of our cases.

What is a leading question? It is a question which is formulated in such a way as to suggest or even contain the answer which the questioner wishes to receive: "Were the tiles green?" "Would it be fair to say that the tiles were green?" "Would you agree with me that the tiles were green?" As opposed to a non-leading question: "What colour were the tiles?"

However, it is not quite as easy as that. Is, "Were the tiles green or blue?" a leading question? What about "Were the tiles green or not?" In a sense you are not suggesting the (one and only) answer in these questions and yet they have the flavour of leading questions.[30] The point is that the real objectionable nature of a leading question has to do with the weight which should be given to the reply and to the witness's evidence in answer to such a question. Imagine that someone conducted an examination in chief entirely in leading questions. The questioner would effectively be telling the witness what to say.

"I believe that you had an accident on July 23, 2004. Is that right?" **8–18**
"Yes."
"And this was when you tripped over a broken tile. Is that correct?"
"Yes."
"Was this tile green in colour?"
"Yes."

---

[29] There is a time to let him go "blah", but you should also control this.
[30] It is difficult to define whether these could be regarded as leading or not.

> *"Was it protruding slightly from the tile next to it and jutting up in such a way as to make it likely to catch someone's foot?"*
> *"Yes."*
> *"And is that what actually happened?"*
> *"Yes."*
> *"Would it be fair to say that if that had been visible then you would have avoided it?"*
> *"Yes."*
> *"But since you did not I assume that it must have been obscured in some way. Am I correct?"*
> *"Yes."*

Remember what the object of the examination in chief is. It is to assist the witness to tell their story. Not to have them agree to your story. The court would probably regard all of this evidence as of little value[31] and insufficient to justify making the findings in fact which a court has to make to enable the party to succeed. In other words, much as you would like the witness to agree with everything you suggest, their agreement would be virtually disregarded when weighing up any competing evidence on matters of dispute. The safest rule to apply is to ask no leading questions whatsoever. That can never be wrong. There are, however, circumstances in which it is appropriate to use leading questions in examination in chief. By and large this will be where the evidence given is purely narrative background, where it relates to the witness's own personal details, where it is non-controversial, where it is agreed, or where it is not in dispute.

> *"Is your full name George Stewart Hamilton?"*
> *"Do you reside at X?"*
> *"Are you a joiner to trade?"*
> *"Are you married?"*
> *"Is your date of birth Y, making you 45 years of age today and 43 years of age at the time of your accident?"*

8–19 I have heard agents advising the court that, with the consent of the opponent, they are going to lead the witness on certain matters which are understood not to be in dispute. I have also heard the rider that, if the agent strays into matters which are controversial, *"no doubt my friend will advise me"*. This does require a degree of sophistication and confidence. I do not recommend it for those starting off. In any event, the responsibility for asking the question in the appropriate form is with the questioner. It is worthy of note that, although opponents take objection to leading questions regularly, no objection is strictly necessary to enable you to argue that the evidence should be treated as inadmissible or should not be allowed. The point again is that the evidence is not, strictly, inadmissible, but the answer is potentially worthless, and it is the problem of the solicitor who was foolish enough to put the question in a leading way. Objection should be, and usually is, taken to such questions.

---

[31] It could be perfectly honest nonetheless.

An opponent could sit back and let you lead evidence in this way on crucial issues and then argue that it was entitled to no weight at all, especially when compared to their own witnesses on that point.

One danger when using leading questions in examination in chief is that it is all too easy to stray from the areas which can properly be explored in leading questions to those areas which are potentially controversial. It is remarkably easy to get into the habit of asking questions of a witness in a leading manner and not even notice that you are doing so. You then continue well beyond the bounds of non-controversial evidence. Leading questions should be the exception rather than the rule, and you should know when and why you can use them. Again, this is a matter you should be able to consider in the cold light of preparation for the proof. If in any doubt whether you should ask a leading question or not—do not.

Controlling the witness

When planning your examination in chief you will want to try and **8–20** assist the witness by making the questions as easy as possible and by presenting the evidence of the witness in an acceptable form to the court. There are various ways of doing this and we have already touched upon them generally above. Now we can look at more specific techniques.

Getting started

This can be extremely difficult especially when you are conscious of **8–21** the fact that you cannot ask leading questions. After you have asked the witness their personal details you should be looking at a question, or questions, which will take you right into the central issues of the case and/or explain why the witness is giving evidence. This avoids the rather fatuous,

> "*Now, Mr Hamilton, did anything interesting happen to you on July 23, 2004?*"

or

> (*in the kitchen case*) "*Mrs Gray, do you have a kitchen or not? Who supplied it to you?*"

The answer is to study the case and the pleadings carefully. See what is agreed between the parties, either by virtue of the pleadings themselves or by joint minute, or even by informal concession at the proof itself. There will always be something. Then use this to ask a leading question which is truly narrative or indisputable:

> "*Now, Mr Hamilton, it is not a matter of dispute that you had an accident in the St Enoch Centre on July 23, 2004. Can you tell the court why you happened to be there?*"

or

> *"Mrs Gray, we know that you and your husband purchased a kitchen from Parker Kitchen Design, the pursuer in this action during the spring[32] of 2004? Do you remember when you first had any discussion with that company about the kitchen?"*

Putting the witness at ease

8–22   This is difficult especially when you are starting off.[33] However, you must be aware of the fact that this is an ordeal for most people. It is a strange environment and a strange process to many members of the public. You can lead the witness on their personal details and on undisputed matters so they do not really need to answer a real question for a little time and this will give them some opportunity to get their bearings. Alternatively, I find it helpful to tell the witness beforehand that I am going to ask them their name, address, age,[34] marital status, occupation, if they have children, etc. and other "easy" questions right at the outset. This will give the witness the opportunity to become used to speaking up in court, tune in to the atmosphere and surroundings, and hopefully not get any answers wrong. You can use this for a nervous but capable witness and it does help. You can give the witness a chance to find their feet by asking these questions slowly and formally, and giving them, and everyone else, time to settle down. Alternatively, if you have a nervous and less articulate or coherent witness who is dreading the whole experience, you can lead them slowly through this part of the evidence with legitimate leading questions to which they can just agree. Try to note if the witness is speaking too quietly, eager to answer the question before you finish it, speaking too quickly and exhibiting signs which are indicative of nerves or simply an unfamiliarity with the process of taking evidence. Try to correct these gently[35] and if the witness is apprehensive you can reassure them. "I think you have never given evidence in court before. Is that correct?[36] All you have to do is allow me to finish asking the question before you answer it. Just take your time." Say this slowly and pointedly and in a reassuring way. This kind of approach might enable you to avoid problems with the delivery of the answers when the answers become much more important.

Position

8–23   One means of helping you and the witness to speak up, and helping the court to hear you both,[37] is to take up a position in the court which

---

[32] The precise date might be disputed, so you can get to the action by taking the witness to the approximate time and then going on from there.

[33] You may not be entirely at ease yourself.

[34] It is always advisable to warn witnesses that you are going to ask this (and date of birth). It is amazing how many people really need to think about it before answering. They get embarrassed and can feel foolish when they forget it. That is not helpful. Let him think about it beforehand.

[35] Do not give him a row.

[36] It had better be and you had better know it. You do not want the witness telling you that he did give evidence once before as an accused in a perjury trial in which the verdict was not proven (he thinks).

[37] Lack of audibility of a witness is probably one of the most basic and common problems in hearing a proof.

puts you some distance away from the witness and has you and the witness exchanging question and answer "across" the sheriff. In other words, the sheriff's line of hearing[38] cuts across yours. If you can hear the answers then the sheriff can. You should make it clear to the witness that you are talking at above conversational level because you have to, in order to make yourself heard by them. This should encourage the witness to reciprocate. It can be difficult to get this message across[39] and you must satisfy yourself that the sheriff and the shorthand writer can hear what the witness is saying throughout the evidence. If you start it in this way, you have a better chance of both of you keeping it up. Standing next to the witness box with the witness facing away from the sheriff and engaging in some private exchange with you is not acceptable and easily avoidable.

Setting the scene

You will remember that what you are trying to do is to allow the **8–24** witness to tell the court their story. If, in order to understand that story or explain it properly, it is necessary to know about background facts, make sure that you elicit from the witness those background facts before you invite them to explain the "meat" of their evidence.

> *"It is admitted that there was an accident in the centre that day, what happened?"*
> *"Well I was just walking along that walkway, you know, when I fell on this tile thing."*

or

> *"Can you explain to the court what problems you had with the kitchen units?"*
> *"Well it's difficult to know where to start, you know how there is a larder unit which is one of these things which slides out something like a . . . well for a start that was sticking in some way and then . . .".*

It would have been so much easier and made the evidence more understandable if you had asked Mr Hamilton first of all[40] to explain the layout of the shopping centre and to describe[41] what the location of his accident looked like before you go on to ask him about what actually happened. In Mrs Gray's case, you might have asked her all about the kitchen units, what they were, how they were supposed to work, where they were located, and so on, before asking her to say what was wrong with them. That is not to say that it is wrong to jump straight into the "action". There can be circumstances in which you might think it better to have the witness express all their crucial views in their own words in one long,[42] or short, sentence and then go back and break that down in

---

[38] If there is such a thing.
[39] No one's fault (except yours).
[40] With short simple questions.
[41] If he could coherently do so—and you will know if he can.
[42] The combination of bottling this up for 15 months during the action, and the opportunity to have his day in court can lead to an explosion of grievances. Is that good for your case?

order to put a more coherent explanation to it. I usually prefer the former. It is more effective in allowing you to control the witness and let them off the leash when you (and they) are ready and the court understands what they are talking about.

Pace

8–25 Everyone talks too quickly. Talking quickly in court is an irritating and counter-productive habit. There is no excuse for you talking too quickly. You should deliberately pace your questions in such a way as to encourage the witness to talk slowly. It is quite likely that the witness will talk too fast to start with. The witness will be anxious to get all of the evidence out as quickly as possible and end their ordeal. First of all, you might want to say to the witness that you will ask the questions by talking slowly and deliberately and that you would like them to do the same.[43] The witness will agree and then forget to do it.[44] A gentle explanation (said slowly and deliberately) that the sheriff and the shorthand writer have to note down the evidence and if the witness speaks too fast they will not be able to do so, can help, but you must pick the witness up if they stray again. In particular, you should watch to see if the sheriff and shorthand writer are struggling to keep up.[45] If you ask the questions slowly and with a brief pause in between question and answer and the next question, there is a reasonable chance[46] that the witness will take their lead from you and respond similarly.

One other aspect of this problem is the failure of the witness to let you finish your question before they start to answer and your failure[47] to let the witness finish the answer before you start asking the next question. This can lead to you both speaking at the same time, thereby compounding the problem. There should be a pause between your question and the answer and a pause between that answer and the next question. I would not prescribe the length of that pause but there has to be a natural break of some kind, otherwise the question, and more importantly, the answer, can be distorted or missed. In examination in chief there can be no benefit in quick crossfire questions and answers, so do not do it, and do not let the witness[48] do it. I have never heard a sheriff ask an agent or witness to speak more quickly.[49]

Sequence of questions

8–26 Another way of controlling the witness is to plan carefully the order in which you are going to ask the questions. Do you want to ask the witness

---

[43] Personally, I do not particularly like giving the witness a "pep talk" in court before I start asking them any questions. I usually prefer to wait and see if a problem arises during the giving of evidence and pick that up immediately. With my own witness I should have a good idea of what they will be like and can present the evidence accordingly.

[44] Once again, not his fault but yours if you let him continue in this way.

[45] In reality, the sheriff is more likely to comment before you can deal with it, but you can make it clear that you appreciate it is your responsibility to see that your witness does not speak too fast.

[46] But no guarantee.

[47] Much worse.

[48] Your witness.

[49] This section has been sponsored by Wm. Hodge and Pollok Ltd, shorthand writers.

about their injury before you ask them about the accident? Do you want to deal with the contributory negligence argument at the same time as the description of the accident or at the end? If you want to establish how long it took for the kitchen to be installed do you just ask it outright and then try to confirm it with further answers, or do you lead up to it with some preliminary questions from which the time can be deduced?

> *"Well now, Mrs Gray, how long did it take for them to install the kitchen?" "I think it must have been about four weeks."*
> *"Well is that strictly correct? Would you look at letter (No. X of process) and tell me".*

or

> *"I am interested to know how long it took for them to install the kitchen. Would you look at this letter (No. X of process) and tell me the date on it?"*
> *"Do you remember if the men came to your house to start the work on the date proposed in that letter . . ."*
> *"And look at this invoice (No. Y of process). How long after the work was completed did you receive this?"*
> *"It says on the invoice that the work was completed on Y. Do you have any reason to doubt that?"*
> *"So if we take these letters as being reliable so far as dates are concerned, the work started on X and finished on Y, so it took three weeks in total, is that correct?"*[50]
> *"Now did they tell you in advance that it would take Z weeks?"*

As you can see, by asking the questions the other way round it is possible to present the witness's evidence in a better way and avoid too many areas where the evidence may be slightly "wrong".[51]

Using documents

There is a particular skill in using documents in examination in chief **8-27** to assist the witness to tell his story.

1. You have to decide that documents will help the presentation of the case[52] and set about obtaining and lodging them. Make sure there are numbers on them.
2. You have to make sure that you have proper copies of the documents for the use of the sheriff at the proof and that they are numbered in the same way as the original productions.
3. You have to be able to prove the document either by having as a witness the person who prepared the document or by

---

[50] This is a leading question but you can lead on arithmetic unless, in some strange case, the arithmetical question is in dispute.
[51] It may not be particularly material but these things can build up into a "general unreliability" and it could easily be avoided.
[52] In a few instances, I have lodged a rough drawing by a witness which helped put across what the witness was wanting to say but might have struggled to put into words.

agreeing with the opponent[53] that it is what it says it is or some such formula. In this connection you may want to consider whether copies will do.

4. You have to be sure that the witness knows what the document says or shows and has had an opportunity to study and consider it relatively close to the proof.

5. You have to decide precisely how you intend to use it, at what point in the evidence you intend to use it and, I would suggest, exactly what questions you are going to ask about it.

In the section above we had a sequence of questions framed around some documents which were lodged as productions and which enabled the witness to be more precise about their evidence and about dates and time-scales. This is a useful example of aiding the evidence and the recollection of the witness by documentary evidence. It is possible for a witness to use a document to refresh their memory. In this case, it would be proper practice to lodge the document being used in this way so that it is available to the other side and to the sheriff.[54]

One of the most common uses of documents occurs in personal injury cases where a map, plan, or photographs of an accident location can be used to assist examination in chief and to supplement the oral evidence about the location. I am going to outline the approach to handling and using such a document (a sketch plan) in the accident case, but this can be regarded as laying down a useful template for the orderly introduction into evidence of most types of document. Before we start, however, it is important to point out that this is a plan drawn by the witness, and a different approach may be required if it was drawn by someone else. Furthermore, it is all too easy to lead when referring to a document which we all have in front of us and can understand. This should be avoided and you have to find a way of getting the witness to describe what they see in their own words.[55]

8–28   *"Mr Hamilton, you have told us that you walked from the escalator to a point on the walkway where your accident happened. You have described this to us. Could I ask you please to have before you Number 5/2 of process?" [Wait until the witness and the sheriff have it open in front of them.] "Do you see what that document is?"*
"Yes, it is a sketch plan."
"Who drew that document?"
"I did."
"When did you draw it?"
"About 10 days after the accident when my lawyer told me to go and check out the location."
"What was the purpose of drawing the plan?"

---

[53] By joint minute in advance preferably.

[54] See D. Field and F. Raitt, *Evidence* (3rd edn, W. Green, Edinburgh, 2001), pp.204–206; *McGowan v Mein*, 1976 S.L.T. (Sh. Ct) 29.

[55] In an extreme case, the use of the document itself can be leading, e.g. if the witness has an accident at a spot they cannot describe and is then shown a photograph (not taken by them) and asked to confirm this is where it happened.

"Just to make it clear where this broken tile was and that."

"Was the broken tile still there when you went to do the plan?"

"No, it was away, but you could see the gap where it was missing from."

"Were there any other tiles broken or missing at the time you went to do the plan?"

"No, just this one."

"Did you form any view from that visit as to where exactly your accident had occurred?"

"Yes, there couldn't have been anywhere else unless they had fixed it and another one had gone missing, but that was where I remember it happening anyway."

"Now, let us have a look at the plan. Would you hold it so that the number two is at the top right hand corner of the page? Have you got that? (Does your Lordship have that?)"

"Yes. Fine." [Check that we are all on the same wavelength.]

"At the top of the page we see a date which is August 8, 2004. What is that meant to indicate?"

"That is the date I went and drew it."

"At the bottom of the page we can see a couple of parallel lines with the word 'escalator' written between them and I take it this is intended to indicate where the escalator was?"

"Yes, that is the top of the escalator."

"Can you indicate on the sketch plan where you were going when you came off the escalator. Perhaps you would hold this up for his Lordship to see?"

"There. I was coming from here, and going there."

"Well now, Mr Hamilton, we can see what you mean but we have to put your evidence into words for the benefit of the shorthand notes. You are indicating that you were walking generally from the bottom of the sketch plan towards the top and walking between two other lines which are marked on the plan. What is the line on the right?"

"It is the shop front for the shop I mentioned."

"And what is the line on the left-hand side?"

"That's the row of shrubs or bushes, or whatever."

"You have marked something with an 'X' on the plan. What is that?"

"That's where I fell."

"You have put that 'X' in a small box it looks like. Why did you do that?"

"It was just to show that it was a tile."

"There are measurements around the edges of the box. What are they?"

"That's the dimensions of the tile. Well, the missing tile I mean."

"And what are those measurements?"

"Six inches by four inches."

"Now, it is not absolutely clear which measurement is which. Do you see that?"

"Well I meant to make it clear."

"It is probably my fault, Mr Hamilton, but can you just confirm what the width of the tile would have been as you walked towards it in the lead up to your accident?"

"It was six inches across, and that was the edge I caught my foot on."

"Now you have drawn a measurement from the escalator to that box, if I can put it like that. What does that measurement say and what does it signify?"
"Well it is 15 feet 9 inches and that is the distance from the top of the escalator to the edge of the box or tile as it was."
"Before we go on to look at the other details and measurements on the plan, can you tell the court how you measured these distances?"
"Well I just took my joiner's rule with me and went along with my mate who held one end while I did the measurements."

8–29 What can we take from this sequence:

- Identify the document by its number in process. Do not say "Have a look at this sketch plan here".
- Have the bar officer hand the witness the document. This is preferable to you doing so but sometimes you have to help out in identifying it for the bar officer.
- If it is obvious what the document is then just lead on that. If it is not self-evident (why should the sheriff know?) then ask the witness to tell you what it is.
- When and how was the document produced by the witness.
- Make sure everyone, or at least the sheriff and the witness, have got the document and are looking at it—the right way up—before you start asking about it.
- You can lead about the content of the document to a greater or lesser extent. Things we can obviously see and appreciate can be led. If the meaning is not self-evident then do not lead. Err on the side of caution. It should be easy to ask the witness what this mark means or what that word signifies.[56]
- Evidence which involves pointing to things or indicating spots on a map, plan, photograph, etc. is not helpful. It may be the only way the witness can do it but it is for you to convert such gestures into words. The description of what the witness is saying or showing can be difficult. You have to be very sharp and concise to enable you to give that description accurately and in such a way that a reading of the words of the evidence (which is all you will have later when the gesture is long gone and forgotten) will make it clear what the witness was talking about.[57]
- By all means clarify any ambiguity or uncertainty in the production itself. If there are mistakes in it or reasons why it might not be accurate—albeit that it was honestly prepared— try to establish this in chief with an explanation for why that should be so. If the document is largely helpful[58] an insignificant error or two in matters of detail can be forgiven.

---

[56] Especially if you have already gone through this with him.
[57] You should have anticipated this in any event and can prepare a description. Run through this type of sequence in your head very carefully so that you do not come up against dead ends in the evidence.
[58] And a good production is invariably helpful—if not absolutely essential—in most cases of this type.

- Take your time. An alternative approach to this sequence might have been, "Look at this sketch map you drew a short while after the accident. It is number 5/2 of process. Can you tell us what the measurements show?", and leave it to the witness to talk us through its contents. The witness might be able to do that without your intervention but, by now, you should appreciate the benefit of having you elicit his evidence in a coherent and controlled way. In my experience, few sheriffs would allow the witness to go very far in the explanation without having to ask him what this was or that was, and to explain other things which might mean his evidence coming out in a terrible jumble. It may not matter at the end of the day, but it is preferable to do it your way and develop this habit for every case and document. It is really your responsibility.

Hearsay, etc.

For the avoidance of any lingering doubts, you can ask any witness in **8–30** a civil case what anyone else said to them or to anyone else about any aspect of the case and that question cannot be objected to on the grounds that it is hearsay.[59] For practical purposes, it would assist you considerably if you had and kept handy for any proof a copy of the Civil Evidence (Scotland) Act 1988. Familiarise yourself with its contents. It helps if you look at some of the evidence of this (secondary) type which you think might emerge in your case, and ensure that you understand the impact of the Act in the context of your case and the evidence that might be led.[60] If part of your case is that the other party made some comment or concession which implied an acceptance of liability or some other material admission then you probably should have pleadings for this. You would presumably be intending to lead evidence about it and the only possible objection would be the lack of record for such a significant adminicle of evidence. It is beyond the scope of this book to analyse the types of statements, apart from direct testimony, which might be admissible as evidence and the circumstances in which they might be objectionable. You would have to lead evidence from your client or witness who can speak to the statement if you are going to rely on it in any way. If you do not, then you might be prevented from cross-examining on the point. A failure to lead evidence of the statement in these circumstances would undoubtedly be a matter for comment at the end of the proof because it would be unfair to put this to a witness or opponent when you had led no evidence about it. If your opponent said something which you think helps your case, make sure that you lead evidence about it.

Anticipating or spoiling cross-examination

Something you may want to consider when preparing your examina- **8–31** tion in chief is whether you want to ask questions designed to head off

[59] See Civil Evidence (Scotland) Act 1988, ss.2–3.
[60] There are numerous cases in which the Act has been referred to in relation to a wide variety of evidential problems and a search of these cases may stand you in good stead. You should be able to anticipate a possible issue on the evidence and prepare your position in advance.

cross-examination or reduce its scope or impact. I have reservations about doing this specifically. The classic type of question is usually along the lines of,

> *"It might be suggested to you that you were not really looking where you were going at the time of the accident and you just tripped over your own feet, what would you say to that?"*

or

> *"What would you say if you were asked why you had done . . . this or that?"*

I never find these questions very satisfactory. My view is that if you have asked the witness to give their evidence in chief in a controlled and coherent manner and they have done so, their answers are the best way to make cross-examination difficult for the opponent. If the evidence sounds, on the face of it, true and reliable I see no benefit in gratuitously trying to fortify it with the assertion from the witness that they would disagree with any contrary evidence. You might feel that with a vulnerable witness you could lob up the cross-examination questions in a nice easy way and allow the witness to smash them away while you are asking the questions. This might make you feel better but is it going to prevent your opponent cross-examining? I do not think so. Is it going to persuade your opponent that your witness will deal with cross easily? No. Indeed, the opponent could turn it round and suggest that the witness has got their excuses and explanations all lined up in advance even before cross-examination began. In the right hands, that could be used effectively against your client's interests. So beware.

8–32   There is perhaps a more subtle line to take. If your witness does give their evidence in a clear and apparently reliable way and you know they are going to be cross-examined about a particular matter to which they have good and effective replies, then leave these matters unexplored and unexplained in the chief. For example, if the witness knows exactly when the accident happened because it was his wife's 30th birthday and you think your opponent wants to cross-examine him about this, then let them. Do not ask the witness why he can be sure about the date. Leave it to your opponent to do this. You cannot lose. If your opponent does not cross then the evidence is undisputed. If they do, it is given a cast iron guarantee of authenticity. You have to be careful how you play this but it rarely backfires if you think it through and use it properly. It is always a little deflating to your opponent who may begin to worry what else this witness is going to say in response to cross. You can do this with some confidence when you know that you have a witness who is basically credible and reliable and who is likely to be able to handle the experience of being cross-examined.[61]

If there are allegations against your client in the pleadings, for example, that they were contributorily negligent or that they had agreed

---

[61] This is never easy to predict, however, and even experienced lawyers can be surprised at how well or badly some witnesses perform compared to how they thought they might perform.

to something or other, then you do not need to put this to your own witness because they will undoubtedly be asked it in cross.[62] On the other hand, there is nothing wrong with putting it to your witness formally by saying (where Mr Hamilton has already testified that he could not see the tile because there were so many people around in front of him), "It is said in the pleadings that this accident was your fault because you should have . . . What do you have to say about that?" or (where Mrs Gray has already testified that she only spoke on the telephone to the kitchen company once, and that was on the May 30), "It is said in the pleadings for the defender that you telephoned and agreed to this on July 12. Is that correct?" That is quite unobjectionable and it may be suggested that you cannot get your client's full story before the court without putting to them in chief all of the important features of the case both pro and con. That may be true,[63] but if you think that this will somehow fetter the cross-examination in some meaningful way I think you are destined to be disappointed. Deal with it briefly and formally and make it clear that you are doing so only for completeness.

Getting finished

How do you know when you have finished your examination in chief? **8–33** When you have stopped talking perhaps? If that is your answer then you should take another visit back to your drawing board when you were preparing the case for proof. You should have all of your questions, or at least some of them, written out. There is nothing worse than the feeling that you have forgotten to ask the witness something important but you do not know what it was. You should have headings of the areas of the case which you have to cover written out. You should know that you have followed this through logically and consistently. When you reach the end you will be reassured that you have thought about this in advance properly and you know that it is the end. There is nothing else left to cover. But, of course, it never goes as sweetly and simply as that, and you may have to deal with things which arise in the course of the examination in chief, either from the witness or otherwise, which take you off your track and which open up new areas of evidence which you have not considered fully.

If that happens, then you will have to be satisfied that you have covered everything you need to cover. It is perfectly legitimate to ask the sheriff to give you a short while to check your notes and to confirm that you have no other questions. It is professional to finish on a controlled and confident question but equally professional to take time to ensure everything has been dealt with. In extreme cases where something strange and significant has cropped up then you may need some more time, and if you need it then you must not rush it. This is easier said than done. Every second you pause will seem like a minute and every eye appears to be on you. But if you are checking your notes and plainly attempting to ensure you have dealt with everything comprehensively then do not panic. Few sheriffs would hurry you up in this situation.

---

[62] Or will they? Maybe your opponent will forget.
[63] It is a matter of opinion and circumstances—no more and no less.

Better not to be there, however, and to plan your finish on a confident note.

Do not assume that you can deal with it on re-examination. You may not be able to do so. If you have missed something out then ask leave of the sheriff to allow you to deal with an omitted matter, but subject to the right of the opponent to cross-examine on that point. It starts getting tricky when you head in this direction but, essentially, most sheriffs will allow this provided it does not prejudice a fair hearing of the case.

Objections

8–34   It is quite possible that your examination in chief will not progress as a simple question and answer session between you and the witness. Your opponent can object to questions and often does. I will deal with objections fully in Chapter 10 and, for present purposes, I simply want to remind you that objection can be taken and you must not let that put you off your stride. It has less chance of doing so if you have prepared properly. It is helpful and reassuring to know that, if you are sidetracked for five minutes or so dealing with an objection, you will always be able to return to your prepared list of questions, and (hopefully) take up where you left off.

Re-examination

8–35   It is important to appreciate that this is not an excuse for conducting more examination in chief or covering matters which ought to have been dealt with in chief but were missed out. The purpose of re-examination is to clarify or provide a fuller explanation for any matters raised in cross-examination which might reflect on the witness's credibility or reliability. Sometimes you know that the witness has an explanation for something which they were unable to give or which was misinterpreted. Sometimes there are matters which require further comment because the wrong impression has been left. Frankly, I find that there is rarely any great benefit from answers given in re-examination. If the damage has been done, it usually cannot be repaired so easily. If the cross has not really harmed the favourable overall impression the witness has given, then the particular matter which was left unclear will not count for much. In neither case is re-examination going to assist the court. The only circumstances in which I would recommend a re-examination of any length is where the witness has plainly become confused during a cross-examination, and appears to have said things, or agreed with things, which you know does not represent their position. I would also confine this to matters which are plainly important in the case. You may feel that the confusion has arisen from the nature and content of the questions rather than anything else, and it would be perfectly appropriate to take the witness back to the point and question them again.

However, you cannot ask leading questions in re-examination. In my experience, most people do. Again, it is not objectionable in the sense that such questions would be inadmissible, but the answer probably attracts even less weight than the answer to a leading question in examination in chief because it usually comprises the agent's explanation for the discrepancy in the client's evidence. This counts for little. Save that for the submissions at the end of the case. As one Q.C. put it (jokingly, of course), "That's when I get my chance to give evidence".

Practical illustrations for new lawyers

Most of the courses I have taught in recent years have been for **8–36** solicitors who are just about to start conducting proofs in real life but have not actually done so. I have listened to countless efforts at conducting examination in chief by able and willing novices and it is remarkable and informative to note that similar mistakes are made by most of them. I thought it would be helpful, and would reinforce some of the advice given in this chapter, if I were to provide some brief details of the errors which seem to be common for solicitors in that position, and some of the ways in which these errors can be avoided.

1. Asking questions too quietly and too quickly. Just about everyone does this. Many experienced solicitors do this too. You have to make a conscious effort to speak up (shout), to pace yourself properly, and to pause briefly between questions. It is easy to advise this. It is not easy to do it, but you have to try and try again.

2. Asking questions that are too long or are incoherent. The simple remedy for this is better preparation. If you have written the question out beforehand you can see if it is too long. The classic problem is starting a question which you have not fully thought through and then finding yourself talking interminably until you reach the end of your flow with what you hope is some kind of intelligible question. You can almost guarantee that it will not make sense. It requires particular skill and experience to resist this, and preparation will help you avoid the problem.

3. Noting down the answers while conducting an examination in chief. In my opinion, this simply disturbs the flow of the examination in chief. It distracts your eye and your attention from the witness. The witness is giving evidence which should not come as a surprise to you and their answers should not really need noting. Perhaps an odd word or turn of phrase might seem particularly significant to you and could be jotted down but do not conduct the examination in chief as though you were taking a precognition from the witness. It does not work. You will also have your face pressed down on your chest as you write, or put yourself into some strange contorted stance to enable you to write, as you try to look up and consult your notes at the same time. This is not a good look.

4. Are you sure that you need to ask the question. And if so, do you know why? Again this comes back to preparation.

5. Make sure that you have an extra copy of every production to which you are going to refer for the use of the sheriff. If there are a number of such productions then put these in a folder for the sheriff and mark everything clearly. This is not essential but it helps.

6. Colour photographs. If you are using photographs as productions and intend to refer to these then make sure that you have colour copies. Make sure that all photographs are numbered properly. Try and provide large prints of all photographs. You will be surprised how much easier that can make the leading of evidence about these.

7.   *Watch what a witness is doing.*   For example, if in the course of an answer the witness makes a hand gesture of some kind or other then you must be alive to the need to verbalise this. For example, "I noted that when you answered that question about . . . you used your hands to indicate something. Can you explain to us what it is you were trying to show us?"

8.   *Watch out for asking a question which is really two or three questions.*   There is a tendency to do this but if you just concentrate on asking short simple questions you should avoid it.

9.   *There is no need to introduce yourself with pleasantries to the witness.* Saying, "I have just got a few questions for you if you don't mind", or words to that effect, is unnecessary and unacceptable. I do not mean that you should be unpleasant, far from it, but sympathetic and professional is what you should aim for.

10.   *Do not repeat the answer give by the witness.*   Do not keep saying "okay" in response to each of the witness answers.[64] Do not comment on the witness's answer by saying, for example, "excellent" when they give you the answer that you are really hoping for. Ask the question, listen to the answer, and then ask the next question.

11.   *Do not interrupt the witness.*   It is your fault if the witness gives a rambling answer, because it was probably your question that gave them the scope to ramble. If the witness is completely flummoxed ask to take the question out and replace it with a different (better) one.

12.   *Try and use simple plain language.*   The number of pursuers who have been asked about "exiting the driveway" has reached mammoth proportions. It sounds easy to avoid this but it is not. There is a very real skill in asking simple, straightforward questions.

13.   *You might have a tendency to forget the essential details of the case.*   For example, the name of your client, the date of the event, the location, and so on. To avoid this, I always write on a piece of paper those very basic essential details and put it at the top of my proof folder file, so that if I have a lapse in concentration I know exactly where to turn. Forgetting your client's name or the witness's name should be avoided whenever possible.

And finally

8–37   There are many more examples I could give and many more tips that I could provide to avoid some of the common pitfalls which all solicitors

---

[64] Everyone does until you point this out to them—and they quite often continue to do so anyway. Learn to stop it.

will experience when conducting their first few proofs. I am conscious of the fact, however, that an emphasis upon all of the things that you will do wrong, must not do, or could do better, can have a negative effect. I have seen people virtually speechless with concern as to whether each and every question they are asking is too long, leading, unclear, in English, etc. This can mean that you are scared to ask any questions at all and, of course, that is not a good basis upon which to be thinking about conducting an examination in chief. Do not be discouraged by what I have said and think that it will be impossible to pick your way through the minefield of leading a witness properly. In my experience, most young lawyers who have an interest in doing court work are easily capable of applying these skills once they learn about them. The difficulty has always been that there are few ways to learn them.

My final thoughts on the process, therefore, are that you ought to be aware of the rules and conventions. You ought to be alive to the basics and aware of the more obvious errors. You should understand what the main objectives of the process are and try to act accordingly. However, do not let the rules put you off. Remember that the primary objective is to have your client tell the court their story or have the witness tell the court what they saw, or what they knew. The examination in chief which I quoted at length at the start of this chapter was a sorry affair, but eventually we all found out what we thought the pursuer was intending to say. In the real case on which it was based, the inadequacies of the examination in chief were not particularly material in the final outcome. No one can conduct the perfect examination in chief, but following the guidance in this chapter might enable you to do a competent examination in chief with the minimum of embarrassment and encourage you to keep striving to do it better.

CHAPTER 9

CROSS-EXAMINATION

"I put it to you that your evidence has been nought but a tissue of lies and half truths."
"Fair enough sir, you've got me there."

9–01 There are few greater pleasures for a court lawyer than the satisfaction of effectively cross-examining a witness and reducing their evidence to mince or worse, thereby winning the case solely by their own advocacy skills. Similar feelings are evoked by the conduct of an effective cross-examination of a witness whose evidence was apparently against your client's interests, and whose capitulation under your barrage of unanswerable questions, plainly demonstrates to the court the secret conspiracy by the opponent and all of their witnesses to defeat your client and the ends of justice. Outside of works of popular fiction, however, this rarely happens.[1] In real life, witnesses in most civil cases do not break down in tears and blurt out the words you want to hear when subjected to your withering glance and your razor-sharp intellect. Cross-examinations in civil cases are rarely spectacular events. An effective cross examination in a civil case does not need to be accompanied by fireworks, histrionics, warnings about perjury, and high drama. In this chapter I will give some basic guidance on how to conduct an effective cross-examination. It is necessary to start by dispelling some myths about the nature and purpose of cross-examination in civil cases.

Common misconceptions

9–02 *Cross-examination is about shouting at witnesses, arguing with them, and getting them to lose their temper.* No, it is not. Sometimes that does happen, and sometimes[2] you can make it happen on your terms, but a cross-examination does not have to be "cross", and will often be unsuccessful and unhelpful to your case if it is "cross".

9–03 *Cross-examination is about proving people are liars.* No, it is not. At least, in my experience, in civil cases it is more often an attack on the reliability of a witness as opposed to their credibility. This is an important and fundamental distinction which you must understand properly. Sometimes you will have to attack the credibility of a witness and even try to force a witness to admit that they are telling lies, but this is very rare indeed. Lying on oath is a criminal offence, as we all know,

---

[1] In most works of fiction it always happens, which is a bit of a pain.
[2] If you are very good.

and most witnesses are aware of this. The majority of people are more likely to give a one sided view of the "truth" than to tell an outright lie. They may want to help one side by giving evidence in as favourable a way as possible. They may omit matters in their evidence which they might perceive as unhelpful to the side which is calling them. That is human nature, and it is probably better to approach cross-examination from this starting point, than from the extreme stance that each witness against you must be telling blatant and deliberate lies and you must somehow expose that.

Cross-examination is best played "off the cuff".   No, it is not. Some **9–04** real exponents of advocacy can do so, but lesser mortals simply cannot. Remember that the real stars have been preparing for cross-examination for 20 years or more and that is an important difference. A planned approach to cross-examination[3] is infinitely more profitable. If you have not the faintest idea of how you will actually approach the cross before you start it, then you are likely to be doomed. If it is difficult to know how you might conduct it in advance, you can plan a variety of approaches and then select one depending upon the circumstances.

Cross-examination requires you to question the witness fully on every part **9–05** *of their evidence.*   No, it does not. You should challenge or test the evidence of the witness on any material issues of fact or opinion[4] which are contrary to your own position. That is all. A wider ranging cross-examination might be justified if you want to demonstrate the vagueness and unreliability of the witness generally, but that can backfire.[5] Laboriously exploring the evidence of a witness as to whether the car involved in the accident was red or burgundy (when you admit your client was driving a red car) does not help anyone, least of all you. One skill, which experience does teach you, is not to cross-examine the evidence of a witness exhaustively unless, and until, there is a very good reason for doing so.

A failure to cross-examine is fatal to your case.   No, it is not.[6] **9–06** Paradoxically, a decision not to cross-examine may be far more effective than a decision to do so out of fear that you might be regarded as conceding something, or a mistaken understanding that you are obliged to do so. Of course, this is not an easy decision to make[7] and there can be traps for the unsuspecting, such as failing to put the essence of your case to a party or witness who contradicts it.[8] You should know the case inside out and the facts which are, or are not, crucial for proof. You have to assess what impact the evidence in chief of the witness has had on the crucial facts, and on the sheriff. You can then start to appreciate the

---

[3] You can even plan how to play it off the cuff.
[4] Assuming the witness is entitled to give opinion evidence.
[5] The sheriff could become bored, or the witness could grow in confidence and certainty the more you ask. This would be a classic "own goal".
[6] For further discussion, see para.10–04.
[7] And when learning, it is prudent to err on the side of asking the question(s).
[8] For further discussion, see para.10–04

significance or otherwise of exactly what the witness actually said and/or (perhaps) the way they said it. This will enable you to concentrate your attention, time and effort on what is really important. Has the witness said anything which has an impact on what is really important, or which lends support to the credibility or reliability of other adverse witnesses? Do you have any realistic prospect of being able to undermine the evidence of the witness?[9] If the answer to one, or both, of these questions is, "No", then you may want to think very carefully about asking any questions. Cross-examining a witness who is "good" can have the effect of simply reinforcing their credibility and reliability. Sometimes it might be prudent to leave a witness alone entirely, or restrict your cross significantly.

Planning a cross-examination

Preparing questions

9–07   Planning a cross-examination and preparing it fully is essential. You can plan a cross-examination in a civil case quite thoroughly because the record will tell you the critical elements of the case and you should have precognosced all of the witnesses who are going to give evidence on both sides. At the most basic level, you might start by jotting down headings for individual witnesses, such as "Clarity of recall", "Passage of time", "See number 6/1 of process", "Contrast with letter of June 21, 2004", "Influence of alcohol", which would give you a list of areas you might want to cover in cross-examination. It might take you some time to prepare the list carefully, and you might want to break the headings down into more specific issues within the main topics for cross.

You can, however, make life extremely difficult for yourself if your preparation only goes that far. You can delude yourself into thinking that when the time comes, those headings and sub-headings will convert themselves into clear, intelligent and precise questions which focus on the points you wish to explore. Take it from me, this does not happen, especially when you are starting off as a court lawyer. This means that you have to go one, rather large, step further and try to write out the precise words of the question you want to ask in the areas you want to explore. And I mean the precise words. The planning will count for little if you cannot articulate fully and properly the question you should be asking. Do not assume that the muse will come upon you once the case is underway. Inexperience usually has the opposite effect. Much better if you have what appeared to you (in the calm of your workplace some time before the proof) to be a list of reasonably well-framed and appropriate questions. If you have a brainstorm during the proof and lose your place, or your train of thought, you will then have a number of questions in front of you which are probably relevant and sensible and may tide you over until your brain clicks back into gear.[10]

---

[9] Experience tells you how to assess this objectively, but, even with experience, you can never be sure.

[10] I am not exaggerating. This happens to us all, although in some cases it may be the result of the ageing process as opposed to inexperience.

It is correct to say that if your cross-examination consists of reading out **9–08** pre-prepared questions, it will probably appear quite stilted and you will be unable to react and respond to what the witness actually says, or how they might come across. When starting off, however, it is probably better to have the reassurance that good written questions can give, than leaving the cross largely to chance. You will have to find a balance somehow, between prepared questions and spontaneous presentation, but the written questions will give you a safety net.

When preparing your questions, consider what answer you want. Then force yourself to anticipate exactly what the answer to that precise question might be. Do not let yourself off lightly with this. Make three assumptions:

1. assume that this may be the best witness in the world;
2. assume that every possible answer to every question you could ask the witness could be the answer which does not help you at all; and, worse still,
3. assume that it will be the very answer you simply do not want to hear.

Then, start framing the questions so that the witness cannot answer them in this way or, if they do, they will come up sharply in conflict with some incontrovertible evidence which the court is likely to accept.[11] It helps if you play the question and the (likely) answer over in your mind to see how it might "work". If you are very critical of yourself, you will be amazed at how long it takes for you to find a formula of words which asks what you really want to ask and reduces the possibility of the witness coming up with plainly unhelpful answers.

The human factor

You will also have to consider the personality of the witness and take **9–09** this into account in your prepared questions. You might want to plan different approaches and questions depending upon how co-operative, aggressive, vague, dogmatic, etc. a witness might be. This means that you may have to take on the role of an amateur psychologist in assessing the witness while they give evidence in chief. I do not want to overstate this, but it helps if you are alive to the particular personality of the witness based on your knowledge of human nature, your knowledge of the witness pre-proof (which may be limited), and your perception of them during the examination in chief. This will involve listening closely to precisely what the witness says, watching them and observing how they say it. You might want to assess very roughly what kind of person the witness is and what kind of impression they are making on the court. It can influence your approach and your use of the pre-planned questions. I remember an expert witness who was (unconsciously to him) rather patronising to everyone in court as he explained his specialist subject to

---

[11] This is not always easy to identify in advance but in a case where there are documents or clear pleadings or plainly credible witnesses, you can see there would be opportunities to put their evidence into conflict with these to good effect.

us philistines. He was quite oblivious to the irritation this was generating, not least from the Bench. This dictated an approach to cross-examination which was almost bound to reap some rewards. It helps if you can tune into this type of feature and have some idea of how you might deal with different character traits or responses from a witness. I will mention some more obvious approaches to different types of witness.

1. A witness (as opposed to a pursuer or defender) may not have much of an idea of what significance one particular piece of their evidence might have in the overall context of the case and you can use this to your advantage. A casual question to the witness asking if it was raining at the time may be met with a clear denial of what appears to the witness to be an incidental feature of the case. However, you may be able to use this as a clear contrast to the evidence of the pursuer that, for example, they could not see the barrier they tripped on because they had their umbrella up.

2. On the other hand, some witnesses may demonstrate a heightened appreciation of just how important their evidence is and will stick to their guns with an emphatic certainty about events, or matters of detail, that no one could possibly recall. These witnesses can be challenged not by calling them liars, but by asking innocent[12] questions designed to emphasise the absurdity of their recall (they will not notice)—"And did he land on the third or fourth tile from the escalator?"—and by encouraging them to take an even more extreme stance (which, again, they are unlikely to notice). This can then be contrasted with all of the other evidence in the case in the submissions at the end of the case.

9–10   3. Most, or at least many, witnesses will be expecting your cross-examination to attack them and their evidence vigorously, shout at them and aggressively, "Put it to them". That is what they see on television and that is what they assume lawyers do in court. This can make them defensive and suspicious of every word of every question you ask. You can turn this to advantage by asking innocent, simple questions, the answers to which are obvious and not controversial. The unco-operative witness might do their best to avoid giving you the obvious answer. The aggressive witness will go out of their way to disagree with everything you say, because they think that you are the enemy. A failure by a witness to accept reasonable propositions can impact upon the impression they give and upon the view the court might take of their evidence on other matters.

4. You can be pleasant and reasonable to a witness and give the witness options to allow them to explain their way out of a hole they have dug in their testimony—"You did not seem too sure about the colour of the car when you were asked about it. Was it rather dark at the time or did you perhaps not see it for too long?" You can "suggest" things to a witness helpfully—"Do you think she might have said something about lights being on?"—and a reasonable witness facing such a question, reasonably put, might be compelled or persuaded to agree. Contrast this with, "I put it to you that she said the lights were definitely on?" Which question stands a better chance of being answered to your

---

[12] As opposed to sarcastic or incredulous.

advantage? If you think that the witness can be persuaded to agree with reasonable propositions then this might also affect your approach to the type of question you put.

5. Finally, you may have the liar. By this I mean someone who is deliberately and consciously telling lies on oath. This cannot be treated lightly. You may have a good idea prior to the proof that some witnesses are going to come to court and tell lies. It may be the only logical conclusion you can draw from a clear divergence of evidence on a critical fact. The witness may make it clear that they are going to support the opposing case come what may. It is prudent not to jump to that conclusion too readily. It may be that people are mistaken. If there is a clear conflict and no apparent reason why a witness should lie about it then you have to consider the possibility of a genuine mistake or misapprehension. The possibility of a poor recollection of events, or some other genuine and innocent distortion of the truth (at least so far as your client's case is concerned) should also be considered. If and when you reach the conclusion that this is just a deliberate lie, then you have to confront it in cross-examination and your approach to cross-examination has to reflect this. You cannot suggest in submissions at the conclusion of a case that a witness is lying without putting it to the witness that this is the case. It may not be necessary to accompany this with a caution about perjury and the consequences of perjury. It would be appropriate to remind the witness that they are on oath and that they must tell the truth so far as they are able. On a crucial point you would want to be sure that the question you asked was clear and unambiguous before using the answer as a foundation for an accusation of lying.

You may be fortunate and find that the sheriff is ahead of you, and **9–11** has already formed a view about the nature of the evidence or the character of the witness. That certainly helps, but if you sense that the sheriff is not with you, or adopts a neutral stance, then you should hesitate even further in taking the point. However, once you decide you must do it then you must confront the (alleged) liar. "I put it to you that you are lying about" always sounds rather false and theatrical to me, although there is nothing wrong with this. "That simply is not true, is it?" works just as well. In any event, it may be slightly academic because, unlike the quote at the head of this chapter, it is rare indeed for the witness to agree with you or break down in tears. Having said that, it may well have the effect of reining in a witness who thinks they can simply say what they please without any thought for its truth. I do recall one (genuine) witness who was plainly not telling the truth. She gave evidence about something she had not seen, but she belatedly explained that she thought she had to answer something to all of the questions she was asked and she was simply testifying to what she had heard about the circumstances from others.

I should say finally, under this section, that these observations are not intended as suggesting "tricks" or ways of distorting the evidence the witness gives. Witnesses usually give evidence in words. Some express themselves more clearly and accurately than others. Some have preconceptions and biases. Some want to help everyone. Some are reluctant to say anything. Most are giving evidence after a passage of time, which would test the recall of most people to breaking point, and yet witnesses can say the most precise things about events which took place many years ago and were over in a split second. In their various ways, these features can be seen as leading to distortions of the truth. Often unwittingly, witnesses are not going to give the objective truth. One of the functions of cross-examination is to test that objectivity, accuracy and reliability. It is your function, and one of the functions of the cross-examination, to test the words that people use to express the substance of what they have to say. If nothing else you are entitled to be satisfied that the witness means what they say and says what they mean. To do so, you must try to reach a view about the character and demeanour of the witness before you can choose your best line of cross-examination, and you must be equipped with questioning techniques which will test the evidence fairly and rigorously.

Types of questions in cross-examination

9–12   For the avoidance of any doubt, you can ask as many leading questions as you like in cross-examination. There is nothing objectionable about this. Indeed, the NITA technique[13] for cross-examination involves only asking leading questions in cross-examination. I could not possibly do justice to the NITA approach in this book, but reference can be made to the textbook mentioned below which is well worth reading if you have an interest in court room advocacy. Even though it is founded on US experience, practice and procedures, there is a vast amount of guidance which can be adapted to our system. Many advocates in this country use the techniques to very good effect. The staple questions in cross-examination might be, "She never called you, did she?" or "You have no record of that order, do you?"

To give you a flavour (and no more) of the NITA technique, you might ask a series of questions in cross-examination thus:

> *"There was a tree between you and the pursuer, wasn't there?"*
> *"It was at least 30 feet high and in full leaf at the time, wasn't it?"*
> *"You were at least 40 metres away from the pursuer, weren't you?"*
> *"You said in your examination in chief that you were paying no particular attention to what was going on around you, didn't you?"*

These are termed "closed questions". The answer to all of these would be, "Yes". The witness would have said most or all of these things in examination in chief anyway. This evidence would then be used to make submissions at the end of the proof that the witness could not possibly have seen the accident. The essence of the approach is that you do not ask the witness, "How could you possibly have seen the accident then?" at the end of that sequence of questions. You do not want to invite an explanation for a state of affairs which seems, on the face of it, to imply

---

[13] The National Institute for Trial Advocacy, based in the USA, advocates a very rigid and structured approach to cross-examination in which the cross-examiner controls the witness closely. There are many supporters and promoters of the technique which can be very successful in the right hands and in the right circumstances. See S. Lubet, *Modern Trial Advocacy: Analysis and Practice* (NITA), for more details and an insight into what many regard as the "modern" approach to cross-examination. In my view, a careful combination of this and more "traditional" advocacy works best in Scotland.

that the witness must have had some difficulty with visibility. Asking the final question suggested above might allow the witness to explain what appears to be inexplicable. For example, "The bottom branches of the tree had been cut away to a height of about six feet and I happened to be looking for the entrance to the shop which was just behind him."

As you will observe from the above, some of these questions could be asked in the form of statements which simply invite the witness to agree with a proposition, rather than being framed as questions. You might want to note that if you do it this way, some sheriffs might query whether you are, in fact, asking a question.

An "open question" gives the witness the opportunity to say whatever **9–13** they want in answer to your cross-examination question.

> *"Do you really expect us to believe that you could actually see what happened?"*
> *"Well, I did."*
> *"Well could you just explain to us how you could have done so then?"*

or

> *"We have heard evidence that no one ever keeps a copy of draft invoices but you said that sometimes they do. Can you tell us in what circumstances, according to you, that might be done?"*

As you can appreciate, those types of question give the witness the opportunity to say just about anything in their answer. You may not know what they are going to say and hence you might be entering into completely uncharted, and unprepared, waters. However, I think that this is not necessarily a bad approach in cross-examination. If you know the case and all of the evidence, there is a chance that you can get the witness to give their explanation or comment in their own words, clarify exactly what they are saying and what their justification might be, and then demonstrate that they could not be right or that they must be mistaken. Watching and listening to a witness wriggling around trying to justify something they said, in their own words, can help to create a poor impression of the witness in the eyes of the court. If it is not done unfairly, then it can have a significant impact.

You can use leading questions to control the nature and extent of the evidence that the witness can give in cross-examination, and prevent them wandering off into detailed explanations, or volunteering additional adverse information. To do so effectively, you have to know your case intimately and prepare the questions with great care. It is beyond the scope of this book to explore the merits of these different techniques any further, but it is important that you understand basically when and how such techniques could be used.

Specific questions in a cross-examination

As part of your preparation for cross-examination, you will have to **9–14** consider the precise words of your questions. You must satisfy yourself that you know exactly what you are asking, have expressed the question clearly and accurately, and are inviting a response which is clear and understandable. Bear these points in mind:

Plain language

9–15   *"Were you under any pressure with regard to time in complying with the arrangements to meet that you had previously made with your spouse?"*

I usually hear this type of question from novice litigators who initially feel obliged to talk in "legal" language and use complex terms, presumably because they are now in court, and that is what you are supposed to do. In fact, you should try to do the exact opposite for various reasons, not least of which is that it will give you a much crisper and more focused cross-examination—"Were you late for meeting your wife?"

Simple/short questions

9–16   *"While you have said that you were walking in a carefree manner, some people might think that this would mean they were not paying very much immediate attention to their surroundings and certainly not looking closely at their feet or the ground, wouldn't they?"*

You know what you mean to ask, but the point is obscured by the unnecessary complexity of the question—"While walking along the walkway, were you looking at anything in particular?"[14] or "While walking along the walkway, you would not have been studying the exact placement of your feet, would you?"[15]

Comprehensible questions

9–17   *"So when you were proceeding in a careful manner, and watching where you were going, with your friend on the left hand side of you and the sun streaming through the skylights above, were you aware of what exactly was ahead of you or was your vision obscured even if only to some extent by the shine of the sun on the tiles or by any other feature on the walkway or at the side of it?"*

I doubt if any comment on this is necessary, but it is remarkable how often questioners[16] can come up with this kind of rambling question which may have made sense for a short while as it was being processed through the brain, but has acquired a hieroglyphic quality by the time it emerged from the mouth. Train yourself to spot these aberrations. The appropriate method of dealing with it is to ask the court to allow you to take the question out and rephrase it. Better this than have the sheriff and/or your opponent pour scorn and objections on it. This could easily have been split into four or five short simple questions with a bit of thought. If this type of question is asked often, it is usually a sign of woefully inadequate preparation.

Double/Treble questions

9–18   *"Are you clear about where it was or were you standing to one side of the shrubbery?"* or *"What speed were you doing, were you exceeding*

---

[14] An open question: Where will it lead?
[15] A closed question: Might this work better? Where will the answer lead?
[16] I wish I could exclude myself from this, but I am not entirely free from guilt.

the speed limit, or at least were you going faster than the other cars on the road?"

Again, it is not uncommon to get carried away in the heat of the moment and start asking multiple questions in one because you cannot wait for the witness to give their erroneous answers, or because[17] you did not properly think about the question you really wanted to ask before you opened your mouth. Just think short, simple, controlled, deliberate and precise.

Questions about what the witness said in chief

It is worth mentioning here a problem which I have observed often in cross-examinations and which should be avoided. Often, it is necessary and appropriate to question a witness about exactly what they said in an answer to a question posed in examination in chief, by referring the witness directly to the words of their answer—"When my friend asked you how many paces you had taken from the escalator to the point where you had your accident you said it was about four, is that right?" There can often be an argument about whether a witness did actually say those words or not. That can frustrate and interrupt a cross-examination, and cause you to miss the point you were hoping to make. Make sure that if you are going to put this to a witness that you have a clear note and an accurate record of what the witness actually did say. If a witness says something specific which I want to use against them in cross-examination I usually try to note it within quotation marks, so as to signify to me that I am absolutely clear about the words used. In the final analysis, it is the record kept by the court (usually the shorthand writer) which rules in the event of any dispute or misunderstanding, but it is extremely helpful to develop a reliable practice of note-taking upon which you can depend if you need to refer to it. In the same context, it is unfair and improper to quote a witness inaccurately or to omit any qualification or modification of their evidence in chief on a particular point when cross-examining them about it. Misleading or misquoting a witness in this way is quite unacceptable and should be avoided at all costs. There can be genuine misunderstandings, of course, and in that case you can deal with a conflict by simply asking the witness, in an open question, to restate their position on the point at issue and taking it from there. **9–19**

Credibility generally

While you must direct your questions primarily to the critical points at issue in the case, as demonstrated in the record, you are entitled to question a witness on any matters which may have a bearing on their honesty and credibility. Questions can go outwith the facts of the case and suggest that the witness has an interest in assisting the party calling them, or a motive for giving evidence in a particular way or not being entirely objective. You can cross-examine a witness about their charac- **9–20**

---

[17] I apologise for repeating this.

ter. This would usually be directed at their honesty and might involve questions about convictions for crimes of dishonesty. It would be foolish to ask questions of that type with no way of establishing the contrary. It would not be proper to put specific allegations, for example, about criminal convictions, without having satisfied yourself that there is prima facie evidence of that fact which you would be in a position to lead, if the conduct was denied. As previously noted, it is necessary to be extremely careful about your reasons and grounds for cross-examining a party or a witness on their credibility or character.

Putting to a witness a prior inconsistent written statement

9–21   It is not uncommon for you to cross-examine a witness about something they wrote at some time prior to the proof, where the evidence they give during the proof contradicts it. This is all the more significant if the witness does not know there is such a contradiction. You could just crash straight into this by asking, for example, "You said in a letter earlier that the tile was missing for a few hours, but now you say it was missing for three days, can you explain that?" That is unlikely to work well. This type of evidence can be a very powerful line of cross-examination and you want to try and maximise its impact.

It is perfectly acceptable to put to a witness a document written by them to test their credibility without lodging it as a production.[18] This is one of the few instances when you can keep something up your sleeve until the proof, and do a "Perry Mason" for dramatic effect. It is important that you lay the foundation for this properly. The first thing is to establish exactly what the witness is now saying. Then you can ask the witness if they have ever thought or said anything different to this in the past. Take your time with this and be fair and clear with your questions so as to avoid any accusation of misquoting the witness. Then, establish, first, what the prior statement, or writing, is, or was, that it was made by the witness, and the circumstances in which it was made. Then ask the witness if they agree that there is an inconsistency. Then invite the witness to explain, or not.[19]

Where a witness is completely unaware that something like this is going to be cast up to them during the proof they are likely to be wary and suspicious of this line of questions and may twig sooner or later that a trap is being set. The witness may well wriggle around a bit trying to avoid being boxed into a corner, but you may have to do this patiently before hitting the witness with the unqualified contradiction of their own evidence in their own words.

9–22   I have envisaged a cross-examination of a wary and unco-operative witness to whom you are going to put this type of document. While reading it, think about some of the tips already given about framing questions, and bear in mind that the witness may well be hostile and is likely to do their best to find an excuse for the discrepancy. That is just human nature and you have to try and "head off" any plausible

---

[18] See *Paterson & Sons (Camp Coffee) v Kit Coffee Co Ltd* (1908) 16 S.L.T. 180: followed in *Robertson v Anderson*, Lord Carloway, May 15, 2001, unreported.

[19] Depending upon whether you are adopting a NITA or non-NITA approach.

explanation by framing your questions carefully and simply. It might go something like this:

> "Mr X, when my friend asked you how long the tile was missing you said that you thought it was at least three days, is that correct?"
> "Yes."
> "So do I understand you to mean that it may have been even more than three days, but it could not possibly have been less than that?"
> "Yes."
> "I am sorry if that sounds rather obvious, but I just want to be absolutely clear that I understand what you are saying about this."
> "Fine, you have understood it properly as far as I am concerned."
> "Has that always been your recollection of events?"
> "What do you mean?"
> "I am sorry if that was not clear, but what I mean is has there ever been a time when you had a different recall of the length of time the tile had been missing to what you have said about it today?"
> "No, not as far as I am aware."
> "And you would be aware if there had been such a difference, wouldn't you?"
> "I suppose so."
> "Well don't suppose anything, Mr X, just tell us from your own recollection if you ever had a different memory of this?"
> "No."
> "Do you remember being asked by my firm to complete a brief statement in your own words about the circumstances of this accident?"
> "Maybe."
> "And do you recall that you did not complete the statement but you wrote a letter instead?"
> "I am not sure, I didn't keep a copy of the letter."
> "Well we will come to that in a minute, but I take it you do at least remember that you wrote something back to us?"
> "Yes."
> "And this related to the circumstances of the accident, didn't it?"
> "Yes."
> "You would have tried your best to write it out accurately and honestly, wouldn't you?"
> "Of course."
> "Do you remember how long you spent on it?"
> "Not really."
> "But I take it you didn't just scribble down the first thing that came into your head?"
> "No, I wouldn't have done that."
> "So, as a responsible person, you presumably gave it some thought, spent a bit of time on it, and tried to write it out accurately?"
> "Yes, I suppose so."
> "So, if the letter is dated February 20, 2005, we should be able to take it that this was your considered recall of events at that date?"
> "Yes."
> "That was, of course, not too long after the accident, and at least 18 months before today, wasn't it."

"Yes."

"Would you agree with me that one's recollection tends to diminish with the passage of time?"

"Probably, yes."

"So, in general if someone is recalling events shortly after they happen this is likely to be somewhat more accurate than if they were describing them some years later?"

"Yes."

"Now I am going to hand you a letter which I am going to ask you to read. Before I do so, I have a copy for your Lordship and for my friend."

[Take time to ensure that everyone has this—and also to see if there is going to be an objection from the opponent. it might be prudent not to let the witness see the letter until you have dealt with any objection which might be taken to its production.]

"Can you confirm that this is a letter written by you on . . . to . . .?"

"Yes, that is my handwriting."

"And could you read out the second paragraph of that letter please?"

9–23 This can perhaps be seen as providing the witness with the minimum opportunity to explain it away (as they are likely to want to do). Before the witness realises fully what is happening and before they are reminded of what they said, you have shut all of the escape doors through which they might have found an explanation. You have the witness's own evidence that the information in a letter like this may well be more accurate than their own oral testimony. This is preferable to just handing the witness the letter and saying, "So, what have you got to say about that then?"

Answers

9–24   The whole purpose of asking good questions is to obtain answers from the witness which are clear, will carry some evidential weight, and will bear upon significant features of the case and the credibility and reliability of the witness and other witnesses. The terms of the questions will usually dictate the quality, clarity and significance of the answer.

Make sure you get the answer

9–25   The fundamental aim is to get an answer from the witness to the question you have asked. You do not want an answer to the question the witness thought you had asked, or hoped you had asked, or would have preferred you to ask. You would be surprised at how carefully you have to consider the answer sometimes before you realise that it was not an answer to your question. If you ask a complex, confused, or imprecise question the answer will be of little weight. If you ask a clear and simple question you are entitled to a clear and simple answer, and it will be easier to see if you did not receive one. In my experience, it is often the case that when witnesses start not answering such questions, you may have stumbled upon an area of evidence in which they are "uncomfortable". That, of course, is good news.

If a witness does not answer the question, you might want to clarify with the witness that they understand the question first of all. If there is no apparent problem with this, then one way to respond to an evasive or inappropriate answer is to ignore the answer given, tell the witness that is not an answer to your question, and then repeat the question. Take your time with this. This is all the more effective if the question is simple and straightforward. If you do not get an answer the second time then you can, and should, persist until you do. Different circumstances will suggest different approaches thereafter. I recall one exchange in these terms:

> *"I have asked you that [simple] question now three times and you have not answered it yet. Is there any particular reason why you do not want to answer it?"*
> *"No." [Well, he could hardly answer, Yes.]*
> *"Well, in that case, can I take it that you cannot answer it without saying something which might not support your [the pursuer's] case?"*

You can imagine the discomfort being experienced by the witness at this stage as the small hole that he might have been digging, by trying to be evasive, has now been enlarged by a JCB of his own making, and his evidence generally may be regarded as suspect from now on.

That is one way of turning the circumstances to your advantage, but it would be unrealistic to suggest that it will always come out like that and you have to make a judgment at the time as to what you want to make of this and how far you can take it. It is always handy to check if the sheriff is "with you".[20]

Answer "Yes" or "No"

I have heard this a few times, and I have some reservations about its **9–26** usefulness. An illustration might be:

> *"You should have seen that missing tile Mr Hamilton, shouldn't you?"*
> *"Well, it was only a very small gap."*
> *"You should have seen it, yes or no?"*
> *"I was being as careful as possible."*
> *"You should have seen it, yes or no"*
> *"No."*

If you want to take a contentious approach to the witness then this would be one way of doing so. Be aware, however, that there are only certain questions to which the answer can properly be given as a yes or no. You might find yourself arguing with the witness, your opponent, and the sheriff as to whether this is one of them. There is a danger in trying to use this approach inappropriately. If the witness is prevaricating[21] it may be the only way to tie him down. I think it is of limited value in civil cases. It may sound like the stuff of masterly cross-examination, putting the witness in their place and even intimidating them to some extent. In reality, it is not often used, and it almost inevitably leads to the witness giving the answer you do not want.[22]

---

[20] Or thinks that you are a pompous, irritating know-all.
[21] In this context, I would define this as "deliberately and knowingly being evasive".
[22] It is used, and works, in some situations in criminal cases, but there are particular reasons why that may be so.

When the answer is a question

9–27   Sometimes the witness might respond by asking you a question. If the purpose of the question is to ask you what your question meant or the like, then you should apologise for not making it clear,[23] and repeat or rephrase the question so that it is understandable. If it is something like, "So what do you think I should have done then?" or "Who told you that is what I said?", do not respond to this. The cross-examination is not a dialogue involving an exchange of views and opinions. Your job is to ask questions. The witness has to answer them. If the witness does not understand the question and asks for clarification or explanation then you can deal with that. If the witness asks you a question in response to your question, then you should say something like, "My function in this is to ask you questions, and not to answer questions from you. Would you now answer the question that I asked?" Do not engage in a debate about this. Keep control of your cross-examination and make it clear to the witness, politely, that you are in charge of what is asked.

Do not interrupt the answer

9–28   There may be slightly different views about this, but I would suggest that it is only in the most extreme circumstances that you should interrupt the answer which the witness is giving. If it is clear that the witness has misunderstood your question and is in the middle of a long explanation which is of no benefit to anyone, then an interruption may be a relief to all. On the other hand, if the witness answers your question and then goes on to give an explanation of why they can say what they say, I do not think it would be proper to cut the witness off there and say that if you wanted an explanation you would have asked for it. The witness could, of course, volunteer gratuitously, in the course of an answer about X, a whole catalogue of prejudicial evidence about Y and Z which had never been raised before. This can be difficult to deal with. The point is that you probably should not have asked that question in the first place.[24] Whether an interruption is necessary, appropriate, or improper does depend upon the precise circumstances, but I would suggest that it should normally be avoided.

Listen to the answer

9–29   This is extremely important and may seem very obvious, but it is a skill which you have to develop. If you have prepared your questions for cross, there is a risk that you will have a sequence of questions you intend to follow, and a line of questioning which takes you from one to the next. This would be particularly so in a set of closed questions. In these circumstances, you might not pay as close attention as you should to what the witness actually says in their answer. You must tune in to this with some concentration. The car driver who says that they "would

---

[23] It is your fault if they do not understand it, even though they might be the only person in the court who does not.

[24] This is another justification for only asking closed questions in cross-examination. The witness is given no opportunity to elaborate in an answer to a closed question. The same effect can be achieved by properly focused open questions, if you are careful about this.

have been doing about 30 mph" might be saying something different from the driver who "was doing 30 mph". It may just be a matter of terminology, but it may be much more than that. The witness who says, "so I believe" may be talking about something they saw, something they deduced, something they were told, or something about which they cannot be absolutely certain but about which they are reasonably sure. You have to listen carefully to words and phrases like this to understand the evidence. Furthermore, a witness can answer a question and make a supplementary comment about something else which was important but might be missed, if you are not expecting to hear it. I am fairly sure that the level of concentration required to do this is one of the main reasons why new litigators usually find a proof very tiring.[25]

Cross-examination: An illustration

Most books on advocacy give examples of dramatic interrogations **9–30** which led to a case being won or a murderer being acquitted. These are fascinating and worth reading, but can often seem far removed from the reality of the daily litigations in which we lesser mortals are involved. The principles are of universal application nonetheless. I would like to stimulate some detailed appreciation of the basic skills required which might enable the reader to apply them in practical ways. I will give an illustration of the thought process which could go into the preparation of a particular cross, the planning of it, and the presentation of it. The case itself and the evidence of the witness concerned is, in many ways, quite mundane, but the intention is to give some guidance on how to approach a cross-examination in the routine real life cases which many of the readers will have to conduct.

I am going to look at the evidence of Mrs Stewart in the case of *Parker Kitchen Designs v Gray*. This is not a spectacular piece of evidence, nor particularly exciting, but her evidence is important. (Otherwise why is she giving evidence at all?) We shall assume that you are representing the defenders. You ought to have precognosced her. It is reasonable to assume that she was not particularly helpful, nor co-operative at precognition. She gave it over the telephone. You did not want to ask her too many detailed questions, because there were some specific points you wanted to put to her in court, and you felt that if you did so beforehand this might "tip her off" as to what you were going to ask her,[26] and she would have had time to think up suitable responses.[27] So you know beforehand what she does, you know roughly what she will probably say (based on the precognition and the pleadings for the pursuer) and you know roughly what sort of person she is.[28] She could be mild and inoffensive, vague and unsure, businesslike and "nippy", or reasonable and articulate, or, of course, any combination of these.

The first points you may want to consider (and note) are: **9–31**

---

[25] Frankly, if you do not find it extremely tiring, you have not done it properly.

[26] A legitimate concern, and a matter for your judgment when taking the precognition.

[27] And, by that, I do not mean "lies", but simply a more considered and consistent explanation for certain things.

[28] For the purposes of this illustration I have included a precognition (brief) from Mrs Stewart as Appendix 3 and some of the relevant paperwork as Appendices 4 and 5.

- What bearing does her evidence have on the case as a whole?
- What particular matters of fact will she be speaking to?
- In what particular respects is her anticipated evidence of the facts going to be in conflict with your case?
- What needs to be challenged in her evidence?
- What is your objective in your cross-examination of her?
- What would you like to have achieved by the time she finishes her evidence?

You may also want to go on to consider: How do you approach this type of person? Will she easily make concessions? Will she be dogmatic? Is she unsure about dates, times, and so on? Are there any clear areas of conflict in her evidence where you will have to suggest to her that she is simply not telling the truth? In reality, of course, she may not have given you that precognition. You may not know exactly what she will say or how, even though you have read the pleadings and understand the pursuer's position on record (which, of course, she will have to stick to[29]).

It is important to start your cross-examination well. What does that mean? You want to sound prepared and "primed". You want to go on the offensive, but not be offensive, early. You want the witness to be on the back-foot. You want the sheriff[30] to be able to see, fairly quickly, what your cross-examination strategy is, and what the purpose of your questions might be. Where are you going with this? What is your point? You might have some options already prepared or might pick up on something the witness said which sounded odd, or untrue, or unlikely, in her examination in chief.

9–32   Are you going to suggest that the witness is mistaken, unclear, or vague? Are you going to suggest that she is simply not telling the truth? Are you going to suggest that she is unclear about everything she says, or just one or two matters of detail? Are you going to suggest that she is of dishonest character generally, or that she is being untruthful about one or two specific points in the case? It may be that, in your preparations for the proof, you do not know exactly what the approach is going to be. You may have to give the witness the benefit of the doubt and start with questions directed at her reliability, but eventually you may find that you have little option but to attack credibility. It would be prudent not to expect all opposing witnesses in all of your cases to be dedicated liars, nor to see conspiracies in every word of evidence given. Sometimes witnesses are just "wrong", and there are various ways of trying to demonstrate that by suitable questions, short of accusing them of making it up.

What are your objectives in your cross-examination? I have seen it suggested that you can probably only make a few "hits" with cross-examination, and therefore you should not set your sights too high. Is the witness ever likely to agree with you when you suggest the very opposite of her evidence in chief is true? You might aim to demonstrate her unreliability on a particular piece of evidence, her inability to

---

[29] You assume, and about which you will cross-examine her if she does not.
[30] But not the witness.

comment directly on some other piece of evidence, and her unreliability in her evidence generally. You might even be able to get her to say something which is not particularly crucial to her evidence but is going to be contradictory of what you think other witnesses for the pursuer are going to say. There is a real skill in thinking through all of the evidence in the case and finding connections between the evidence of all of the anticipated witnesses which enable you to place one against another, even if they do not see this coming.

"Are there any circumstances in which you have authority to bind the firm?" asked of her, might just produce a different answer when asked of the proprietor, or of other employees, and contradictory answers to that question from the witnesses on one side might damage the weight and quality of their evidence generally.

You can prepare good questions in detail by using the record, **9–33** productions and any other evidence which is agreed or is not likely to be disputed. You can use this as a means of demonstrating a witness is not credible, or reliable. If something is admitted on record, or appears clear from the content of productions, you might want to target this for a question or two. It may not be crucial in itself but a witness might not see it coming, might not think it is of any significance, and might contradict the incontrovertible. This may impact on her credibility and reliability without the witness having any idea that she has given the "wrong" answer. Asking the question casually or incidentally and not reacting to the "good" answer,[31] might work very well in these circumstances and enable you to go on with similar questions without the witness realising what is happening. An individual "good" answer from the witness may not be significant on its own, but you may be able to build up a succession of such points (which you have carefully targeted) in order to argue that her credibility and reliability have been undermined—"If she is obviously wrong about these simple points, how reliable is she on the more important issue of". I do not want to overemphasise this, however, because, in reality, this might be regarded by the sheriff as truly incidental and of no practical significance. The emphasis, rather, is on approaching cross by trying to identify "targets" for cross-examination, rather than conducting a cross-examination which could be summarised thus:

> *"Right, Mrs Stewart, you are just going to have to stand in the witness box for another hour while we go for a ramble through your evidence in chief once again and hope that you contradict yourself and make a couple of mistakes on the way"*.

I am only going to look in detail at a small part of her cross-examination. **9–34** Say you have decided to cross-examine her on the details of her recollection of the discussions with your client pre-contract, where you know there is a conflict. You could, of course, just ask her if she is mistaken or "put it to her" that she is making this up. A more subtle approach, designed to get her to agree with you or, at least, concede

---

[31] High-fives with your client would not be appropriate.

there is some uncertainty, might be highly desirable. Attacking her head-on might be pointless and quite ineffective. In your preparation, you could try out opening questions like this:

> *"Mrs Stewart, you knew that my clients could not afford the kitchen at the price you originally quoted and you had to give them a discount to persuade them to go ahead, is that not right?"*

[This is combative, direct, and unlikely to succeed. Do you really think she is going to say, "Yes"? She might say:

> *"No, it's not a question of persuading anybody. We are a very busy company and we do not need to persuade people to buy kitchens from us. It is entirely up to them if they want to proceed or not. They are under no obligation to accept our quote."*

Apart from the approach, there were too many problems with that first question. It was too wide. The witness could answer any part of it she chose. The word "persuade" causes a problem too, and enables her to answer it as a semantic point. You are going nowhere with this.]

9–35   Try again:

> *"Mrs Stewart, you would agree with me that people usually want to pay as little as possible for their kitchen, wouldn't you?"*

[That might get a yes, but then again she is suspicious of any questions you are going to ask and might find a way of avoiding a direct answer. You might get a:

> *"Well actually, we have a number of customers who are not too concerned about the price and prefer to have high quality, so that's not always the case."*]

9–36   Try again:

> *"Mrs Stewart, You did the design for my client's kitchen?"*
> *[Short, clear, indisputable.]*
> *"Yes."*
> *"People can be very particular about what they want in their kitchens, can't they?"*
> *"Of course."*
> *"And I am sure that your company would always want them to be satisfied about the kitchen they are going to live with for the next several years?"*
> *"Yes, well, that stands to reason."*
> *"I take it that, in your experience, most customers would take a very keen interest in the proposals for the design of their kitchen?"*
> *"Certainly they do, although usually its the female who takes the lead as you would expect."*
> *"In this case, it was Mrs Gray who took the lead?"*
> *"Yes, indeed."*

"The customers were very happy with the design and they asked you to send out a quote?"
"Yes, that is right."

[Everything is leading so far. It sounds businesslike and efficient. The court will be interested because it sounds as though you are going somewhere with this. The witness, rather than being abused as a liar from the outset, which might have been an alternative approach, can hardly fail to agree with all of this.]

"You knew [there was a delay in them accepting that quote][32] *[the quote was not accepted straight away]?"*
"Yes, it was not accepted by return if you like."
"In fact, there was no acceptance until the letter of May 30, 2001 from Mr Gray; that is the document that you have already spoken about, Number 6/1 of process?"
"Yes, that would allow us to go ahead once the deposit was paid."
"You would agree with me that this letter was sent after a telephone conversation between Mrs Gray and yourself?"

[By now you have got her agreeing with all of the reasonable and non-controversial points you have put. You are not shouting at her. She is still a bit suspicious of you. What are you up to? She decides to be a bit careful about these apparently innocuous questions.]   **9–37**

"Well, I can't actually be sure about that because I can't remember every call I had, you know."

[That was a mistake. She does not want to be tied down to something about which she cannot be sure on detail. She could have answered in a number of different ways. You could have prepared for her giving an answer like this to your question. But, what can you do with this answer?]

"That is perfectly understandable, Mrs Stewart. After all, this was just one of a number of kitchens you would have been involved with at the time, isn't that right?"

[Or alternatively, "So, if we hear from Mrs Gray that she spoke to you on the telephone and you agreed a discount, you would not be in a position to contradict this?" She might agree, but the question is risky and imprecise. Why do you not establish, first of all, that there may well have been a conversation (not too difficult for the witness to concede) before going on to more detail?]

"Yes, well we were quite busy then."
"You would no doubt receive numerous calls from customers during a busy day?"

---

[32] Does that form of words lead to potential confusion about what "delay" means? Is the alternative better?

> *"Yes, well, you can do."*
> *"I mean, if it was the only kitchen you had ever dealt with, you would probably have remembered it rather well?"*
> *"Yes, I imagine that I would."*
> *"The more things you have on your plate, the more difficult it is to recall the details of each individual discussion (isn't it?)."*

9–38 [Round about now (or perhaps not) the witness might see where you are going with this. But she might be stuck. The proposition that you have put to her could easily be regarded as a matter of pure common sense based on universal experience. How can she disagree with it without sounding foolish?]

> *"So that a person who had just one kitchen to concern herself with, might be in a better position to recall the details of her dealings than someone who had numerous kitchens to look after?"*
> *[How can she answer this question other than to say,]*
> *"Yes."*[33]

[She might see where you are taking her now and she is on guard. She wants to start disagreeing with you if she can. But you want to keep her off guard, so you go slightly off track.]

> *"In any event, Mrs Stewart, the letter refers to a telephone conversation and I don't imagine that you intend to suggest that the reference in the letter, number 6/1 of process, to a telephone call was some kind of fabrication on the part of the customer do you?"*

9–39 [She is under a bit of pressure now. She could say something stupid. She wants to disagree with you about something. If she does fall for it and suggest your client is making up a story then she may have a major problem. Your client may have misunderstood the position and the content of the conversation with her, but it is highly unlikely that a court would think she was engaged in a scam and fabricating evidence to help her save money. Is Mrs Stewart really going to suggest she is a fraudster?]

> *"Well, No, I can't say that."*
> *"So we can take it that Mrs Gray did speak to you and can we also take it you have no detailed recall of what was said in that conversation?"*

[She already told us that a short while ago. Can she deny it now? In these circumstances "Yes" or "No" is an equally helpful answer.]

---

[33] If she answered "No" you open the door for all sorts of questions to illustrate that she is simply defending her position. If she says, "I do not know about that" then you simply persist and remind her that she has agreed that customers take a keen interest in this kind of thing and that it is a big event for them although not so for her. Failure to make the concession makes her seem unreasonable and plainly partial. We have not even got to the point yet and already she is trying to weasel out of it. If she tries to avoid answering it then you ignore her irrelevant response and go back (pleasantly) to repeat the question.

"Look, I know I never said anything about a discount, if that is what you mean?"

[That is not what you asked. Your question was simple and easily **9–40** understood, so she has jumped ahead of herself and is now worried about what you might be getting her to say. She knows this is all about the discount—she is "clear" about that. She is anxious to tell the court about this—and not about "conversations".]

"That is not what I asked you, Mrs Stewart, I simply want to know if you agree that you have no recollection of what was actually said."

[Keep control. Note the answer is not appropriate. Get the answer.]

"Well it would have been about the kitchen, I know that, and sometimes we would telephone up people who had received quotes if we hadn't heard from them, but I cannot say for sure."
"But you have no specific recall of the conversation itself, isn't that true?"

[Get the answer. You do not need to be aggressive about this, but you can if you want, and perhaps all that is required is a certain firmness in your voice and manner which makes it clear that she has to concede the inevitable now.]

"Yes, that's right."

[Got it. It may not escape the notice of the court that it was reluctantly **9–41** given. Do not forget that this evasiveness might have an impact on her other evidence, even in areas about which she should be more comfortable.]

"So if we heard about the content of that conversation from Mrs Gray, you would not be in a position to contradict her from your own memory of events?"
"I can't remember, I have told you."

[This drives it home. It may have been unnecessary to do so. It may even have been imprudent if it opens the door for the witness to make some other qualifying comment about this point, for example, "Well, there are certain things that I know we did not discuss." That is down to your judgment, and your skill.]

"Did you discuss with her any amendment of any kind to the quote?"
"No, it would just have been a courtesy call to the customer to see how they were getting on."
"Did you discuss any amendment of the quote with her?"
"Why would I have?"
"Well it is not for you to ask me questions, Mrs Stewart, that is my function here. Can I ask you once again, do you have any recollection of discussing any [emphasise this with your voice] amendment whatsoever in the course of that conversation?"

"If there had been any alteration we would have put it in writing."
"And we know that you did not put anything in writing did you?"
"No."
"Can I take it then that you are saying that you did not discuss any change in the original quote and the reason you can say that is because you did not put anything in writing afterwards?"
"No."

9–42 [Note that this question is bad and the answer is ambiguous. The answer could mean: "No, that is not the reason I can say that"; "No, I did discuss a change"; or "No, I did not discuss any change". A different formulation of question would have made this clearer.]

"So, on your evidence, there would have been no reason, for anyone to think that, as a result of that conversation with you, any amendment was required to the original quote?"
"No, definitely not. It would be wrong to think that."
"And yet, Mrs Stewart, there was an amendment made in one particular respect. In the course of that conversation you offered her a discount of 10 per cent on the price if the quote was accepted by the end of the month, isn't that right?"

[This is infinitely better than "I put it to you that", and much more effective.]

"No, I did not. I couldn't give people discounts."
"Well, we will look at that in a moment."

9–43 Of course, this is entirely fictional and you might ask why should we assume that any of these questions would be answered in the way I have predicted? The answer is that no one knows for sure how a question would be answered. That is not the point, however. Properly prepared questions maximise the chance of the answers coming out "right" for you. This sequence will hopefully illustrate that your choice of words, use of language, structure of approach and clarity of purpose in your precise questions can influence the way in which the evidence can be allowed to come out in cross-examination. The ideal is to find the question(s) which cannot be answered "properly", i.e. without making some concession or admission against the interest of the witness and the party relying on their evidence. This is easier said than done, and you should be willing to prepare by playing around with questions like this to see if you can come up with a crisp, clear approach for putting the witness on the spot, or persuading them to accept something which is detrimental to the opposing case or helpful to yours.

The impression you might have gained from the brief extract quoted above is of a questioner in control of their questions. They have an agenda. They have certain objectives. Maybe they are being a bit slow and pedantic. Maybe that was necessary. The questioner is challenging the critical parts of the evidence of the witness on the specific matters of importance but they are using the answers by the witness to introduce some doubt about her reliability and impartiality. She has reason to be biased (she could, in theory lose her job for exceeding her authority) and this could be put to her directly and forcibly at some stage, or rather more gently. Indeed, the approach to that issue might well be dictated by your impression of how she is dealing with the initial questions you have been asking her. I am, of course, being terribly unfair to Mrs Stewart who may actually be a decent, honest, hard-working woman who is doing her best to recall events and will reasonably concede so much, but not the critical points you are after. That takes me back to the initial important guidance given at the start of this chapter about the assumptions to be made when preparing your cross. If you assume the worst (from your perspective) then the reality might be a pleasant surprise, with a witness scoring own goals all over the place.

Practical illustrations

I will finish with a reinforcement of some of the advice given in this **9–44** chapter by noting some errors in cross-examination which seem to be common for novice litigators, and some of the ways in which these errors can be avoided.

1. Establish an appropriate relationship with the witness. "Good afternoon, Mrs Stewart. How are you today? I just have a couple of questions for you. I will not keep you very long", is not how to start your cross-examination—especially if the sheriff then restricts you to the "couple" of questions you were only going to ask. There is no reason to be unpleasant, but a courteous businesslike approach is to be preferred. A good start to the cross which demonstrates to the court quickly where and how you are going to challenge the evidence of the witness can be extremely important. Otherwise, the court may lose interest quickly and fail to pay any real attention to your clever questioning.
2. Sharpen up your thoughts, language and oral presentation. Every word and nuance of meaning might count. Make sure that you know what you mean, say what you mean, and everyone can hear what you say. There is nothing worse than an incoherent, unintelligible cross-examination. Even if you do not feel like it, you must try to give the impression that you are in control—of the witness, the facts of the case, and yourself.
3. Use plain language. When starting off many litigators seem to be under the impression that questions have to be couched in legal language. I have absolutely no doubt that the best questions are those which feature in normal daily conversation. Try and convert your questions to simple language that can be understood by the court and the witness you are cross-examining.
4. Try not to interrupt the flow of your cross-examination. This **9–45** means that you should have any documents you are going to use for cross-examination readily to hand (and properly numbered) and ensure that the witness has them too. If you want to refer a witness to a part of a report, for example, make sure that you have the process number of the document, and the

page or section number of the passage concerned, in your notes for cross-examination. Time can be wasted, and concentration and attention lost, if you are all wandering around the papers to find the highly-crucial section which was so important that you cannot find it now.

5. Establish a practice of noting the evidence during cross-examination which suits you and is effective. Noting evidence during your examination in chief should be unnecessary, for the reasons already explained. Answers during cross are far more unpredictable and you may well want a record of them. Some people may note every answer as they go on to the next question, but that seems to me to be quite intrusive and not at all conducive to a good cross. You want to keep watching the witness and assessing what they say as you go along, and you really cannot do this if you are busy scribbling down the answers. Some people make a play of rather theatrically and pointedly writing down a word or phrase that the witness has just said as if to demonstrate that this was very important (and usually a mistake on the part of the witness). If the evidence of the witness on cross is lengthy and contains "new" information, there may be no option but to keep some written note of what they say, but I would try to keep that to a minimum. In most cases, I find the best method for me[34] is to take the briefest note of anything particularly significant and immediately expand upon it in my notebook as soon as I have finished the cross, and while it is still fresh in my mind. It is generally true that there are not likely to be too many big "hits" during any cross-examination, so a brief note may well suffice. If you have prepared, you will, in any event, know the crucial evidence you are after (and whether you realised this during cross).

6. Try not to repeat the answer given, say "Okay" in response, or otherwise comment on the answer, or the witness, without asking a question. We are all guilty of this to some extent, but it can be quite irritating and incur judicial wrath if it is repeated frequently.

9–46

7. Do not allow the witness to interrupt your question. This is one way of emphasising who is "in charge" of the cross-examination, but it is also essential for the proper leading of evidence in any case. If the witness starts to answer before you have finished the question then you should immediately ask them to let you finish the question. Ignore their putative answer, and ask the full question again. If necessary, you can explain to the witness that the question has to be noted and the answer has to be noted, and this cannot be done if they cut across each other. In any event, the witness would undoubtedly want to ensure that they heard the question fully in case their answer was misinterpreted. Some witnesses do have great difficulty in waiting for the question to be asked in cross-examination, because they feel under pressure and are anxious.

---

[34] And this is entirely personal.

You can also point out to such a witness (the serial interrupter) that they really ought to think about the question before they answer it, and that they might want to pause after the question has been asked to give time for consideration, otherwise it might be thought that the witness is just saying the first thing that is coming into their head.[35]

8. Do not be rude or sarcastic to any witness. There may be a temptation to question a witness in this way, especially if their demeanour towards you is challenging. Do not do it under any circumstances. First, it is not professional. Secondly, and more pragmatically, it does not work. I have never heard a worthwhile reply from a witness to a rude or sarcastic question. The asking of it simply reflects adversely on the questioner, so it is a "lose-lose" strategy, in my experience.

9. Sometimes, as well as answering in words, a witness may respond in gestures, facial expressions, hesitation, etc. You may want to consider whether, for the purposes of the shorthand notes, these features should be made part of the written record. I will give two examples where it might be appropriate. In a case where a witness was asked to read something from a document which contradicted their evidence, they paused for about one minute before they did so, when they realised that it was against them and they searched other parts of the document as well for an explanation of the note. In the shorthand notes, the question appears, followed by the witness's reading of the section. There was, of course, no record of what was a significant delay. A question, "I notice that it took you about a minute to read that out, Mr X, can you explain why that was so?" would put the delay on record. In another case, where the words of the answer were clear, but the demeanour of the witness was not, "You seemed a little confused while answering that question, Mr X, and you hesitated quite obviously, are you entirely clear about that?" would again put the answer into context.

10. Listen to the answer. This is worth emphasising. Sometimes you **9–47** may be so glad that you are actually asking half-decent questions that the answers become largely incidental. Yet, if you do listen, and if you are concentrating, you can come across some pearls which are well worth the effort. I will close with one of my favourite examples from a recent course in which the skills of listening to an answer, in combination with sharp advocacy, might well have deflated an impressive witness.

The witness was a car driver who had allegedly caused an accident. She was a middle-aged woman who was quite clear, indignant, and dogmatic about her lack of responsibility for the crash. There was evidence to suggest that she had been confused about her destination shortly before the accident, and this was a line of cross-examination for the opponents. The

---

[35] If it becomes particularly annoying, your tone of voice might indicate what you really think.

question was, "You were lost, weren't you?" The answer was imperiously and disdainfully given as, "No. I knew exactly where I was going, I just did not know how to get there." The questioner seemed to find that a suitable, if unhelpful response and abandoned any further questions on this line. In the right hands, that answer would have been a god-send.

If you think about it, the answer is, in fact, a concession that she was lost. That is what her words actually mean. The questioner did not really listen to what she was saying. A sharp cross-examiner could have made capital of this by pointing this out to the witness, and developing further questions to demonstrate how unreasonable, partial and foolish she actually was. This could be used to reflect adversely on all of her evidence— "She wasn't even prepared to concede she was lost when that was exactly what she said she was. She was determined to say anything to support her own innocence, including denying the undeniable."

On their own, examples like these might seem of no more than passing significance, and unlikely to have any real effect on the outcome of the case. However, you are testing her evidence of facts and her ability and willingness to explain the "true" facts of what happened. You may be able to undermine her reliability and objectivity in the eyes of the court. This might reflect generally on her other evidence, and an accumulation of small "victories" in cross-examination of her might be sufficient for the court to find her evidence unacceptable. This finding may be far more capable of being achieved in this way, than by aiming for a confession of dishonesty and culpability on her part. A good cross-examiner would appreciate that this may not be a realistic objective with a witness like this and set their sights somewhat lower. There is a good chance that the witness might not notice the small wounds being inflicted upon her, because she is too busy watching for the atomic bomb she expects to be dropped on her. There are many ways to conduct a cross-examination and it is hoped that this outline will give you some of the basic tools with which to do so.

CHAPTER 10

COMMON ISSUES DURING PROOF

This chapter deals with miscellaneous issues which can arise during **10–01** proof and require more detailed consideration. In some instances, I am simply elaborating upon points which have been explained briefly earlier. In other cases, I am dealing with much broader issues than how to ask questions and the wording of questions. They might be termed strategic issues involving choices as to how one might conduct the proof. They all tend to arise with reasonable frequency in a variety of proofs and I thought it would be helpful to give a more detailed explanation and discussion of them. The particular issues are:

- Whether to cross-examine a witness.
- Leading questions.
- Objections to questions.
- Amendment during proof.
- The best evidence "rule".

Whether to cross-examine

After hearing the evidence of an opposing witness in examination in **10–02** chief, the first decision that a prospective cross-examiner has to make is whether to cross-examine the witness at all. Generalising about this is unhelpful, but a practical tip for the inexperienced is that, unless you are absolutely clear that the evidence of the witness has done your case no harm then you should cross-examine. If you have any doubts about it, then you should cross-examine. If the witness's evidence in its entirety does your case no harm, or even if it does your case some good, it may well be the most prudent course to leave it unqualified and unaltered by anything else the witness might say in answer to your questions. It is a matter of judgment and it is a judgment which has to be made fairly quickly, but prior to the proof you should know, at least roughly, what the witness is likely to say. You should be aware of the areas of the witness's evidence in which they might come into conflict with your case. You should know what facts are truly material and what are not. Do not be embarrassed or reticent in asking the court to adjourn for five minutes after an examination in chief to enable you to consider the effect of the evidence of a witness and to decide on whether you want to cross-examine. There can be something quite satisfying in indicating to the court that you have no questions. Implicit in this is your view that the witness has been of no real consequence, or indeed positively helpful to you. The court and your opponent will know that is your view.[1]

---

[1] You have to have the courage of your convictions and some confidence that the court will share that view.

A less extreme variation of this dilemma is where a part of the evidence of the witness is favourable to your case, or causes no harm to your case. Again, it is essential that you understand exactly what the significance of this might be in the context of the overall proof. Depending upon your view, you could decide not to ask the witness any questions at all on this aspect of the case, and rely upon what they said in chief. As the witness can only be re-examined on matters raised in cross-examination, your opponent would not be able to salvage the position in re-examination, unless your questioning strays into that particular area. Be careful that it does not do so during the course of your cross-examination on other matters.

Finally, you might find that the evidence of the witness in chief is so favourable to you, that you are encouraged to seek even more useful evidence on cross. This can be rare and any attempt to do this should be exercised with caution. You may not have a great deal to gain by doing so, and indeed you may have more to lose.

10–03   The basic principle is that it is not essential to cross-examine every witness in a civil case. If the pursuer in the personal injury case does not give evidence in chief that he fell as a result of a missing tile but actually slipped on a sweetie wrapper,[2] why cross-examine him? The case is entirely dependent upon him proving that his accident was caused by the fault of the defenders in relation to a broken or missing tile. You will be quite happy to accept his evidence. You do not want to cross-examine him and ask him: "So you are sure that you slipped on a sweetie wrapper and not on a broken tile?" or even, "So there is no question of your accident having anything to do with a broken tile?" You might just receive the answer: "Yes, the sweetie wrapper was lying inside the hole left by the broken tile. Did I not mention that?" So you must listen carefully to what the witness says and be clear in your own mind—and have a good record of it—what his exact words were. Your justification for not cross-examining is dependent upon that.

The same observation applies, for example, to the corroborating witness who describes the pursuer slipping on a sweetie wrapper after the pursuer has blamed a missing tile. The temptation to ask: "So he could not possibly have lost his footing on a broken tile then?" could be met by, "Well you see I think he slipped a wee bit on the sweetie wrapper but he would have been okay if he hadn't then caught his slipping foot on the uneven surface. It could have been a broken tile for all I know. I didn't really look at the time." If he did not mention this in his evidence in chief then you do not want to give him a chance to mention it in cross. It is a serious mistake to ask a party or a witness in cross-examination simply to repeat a reply favourable to your case which they had given in chief. The evidence does not increase in quality because they say it twice. Provided the sheriff heard it—and you should know if he did—the one answer is more than sufficient. The danger is that the witness will qualify or retract it.

Failure to cross-examine

10–04   What are the evidential consequences of failing to cross-examine on all or part of the evidence of a witness? The concern might be that if you

---

[2] I have had this one!

do not cross-examine the witness, either on anything or on some particular part of their evidence (for reasons you may consider to be perfectly justifiable), you might be taken as agreeing the witness's evidence in its entirety, or accepting the witness's evidence on that particular point. If the sheriff and your opponent do not agree with your approach to the witness's evidence, then does this automatically mean that you are to be treated as admitting it?

The answer is that you are not, but the precise effect is not easy to explain in principle. Guidance can be found in the textbooks noted[3] and the cases to which we shall refer. The cases have to be read carefully so that the decision is understood in the context of the very particular facts of each case.[4]

A failure to cross-examine might be commented upon.[5] It does not mean that the evidence must therefore be accepted by the opposing party as true.[6] It may preclude the cross-examiner from leading evidence subsequently to contradict the witness.[7] "If it is intended later to contradict a witness upon a specific and important issue, or to prove some critical fact to which that witness ought to have the chance of tendering an explanation or denial, the point ought normally to be put to the witness in cross-examination".[8] This passage took, as its foundation, the "most obvious principles of fair play" and that is the basic principle which underlies all of the decisions on this.

However, the failure to cross-examine is not absolutely fatal.

"There is nothing in any of these cases to suggest that where one **10–05** party has failed to lay a foundation in cross-examination for evidence which he is subsequently to lead, and proceeds to lead that evidence without objection, the court is bound to disregard it. In a number of cases it has been emphasised that the principles of fair play make it necessary to give a witness who is to be contradicted an opportunity of commenting upon the evidence which is to be given to a contrary effect."[9]

To put this into a practical context, if you know that you were going to be leading evidence that the pursuer had been staggering up the

---

[3] A.G. Walker and N.M.L. Walker, *The Law of Evidence in Scotland* (2nd edn, T. & T. Clarke, Edinburgh, 1983), pp.192–193; D. Field and F. Raitt, *Evidence* (3rd edn, W. Green, Edinburgh, 2001), pp.215–217; I.D. Macphail, *Sheriff Court Practice* (3rd edn, W. Green/Scottish Universities Law Institute, Edinburgh, 2006), para.16.76; I.D. Macphail, *Evidence* (Butterworths/Law Society of Scotland, Edinburgh, 1987), paras 8.28–8.30; W.G. Dickson, *The Law of Evidence in Scotland* (3rd edn, 1887).
[4] See *Stewart v Glasgow Corp*, 1958 S.L.T. 137; *Bishop v Bryce*, 1910 S.C. 426; 1910 1 S.L.T. 196; *Wilson v Thomas Usher & Son Ltd*, 1934 S.C. 332; 1934 S.L.T. 307; *McKenzie v McKenzie*, 1943 S.C. 108; 1943 S.L.T. 169; *Jordan v Court Line Ltd*, 1947 S.C. 29; 1947 S.L.T. 134; *Dawson v Dawson*, 1956 S.L.T. (Notes) 58; *McGlone v British Railways Board*, 1966 S.C. (HL) 1; 1966 S.L.T. 2; *Lee v HM Advocate*, 1968 S.L.T. 155.
[5] *Stewart v Glasgow Corp*, 1958 S.L.T. 137.
[6] *Walker v McGruther & Marshall Ltd*, 1982 S.L.T. 345.
[7] In this situation, questions to that witness may be met by the objection that the point had not been put to the earlier witness, or witnesses, who could have commented upon it.
[8] *McKenzie v McKenzie*, 1943 S.L.T. 169, *per* L.J.C. Cooper.
[9] *Bryce v British Railway Board*, 1996 S.L.T. 1378.

escalator and across the floor of the centre apparently under the influence of drink then it is only fair that you should put this to him. You cannot simply suggest he is not telling the truth about his accident and then lead your own evidence of what was seen to have happened without having put that version to him.

Of course, in the case quoted above, it can be noted that the evidence was led without objection being taken to this. Objection could, and perhaps should, have been taken. What would have happened if that had been done? It appears that if the failure to put this in cross-examination might cause prejudice to the party, then the court could do a number of things:

1. allow the evidence but allow the pursuer to recall the witness for cross-examination;
2. allow the pursuer a proof in replication (this means a proof of the facts necessary to answer the defender's reply to the pursuer's claim)[10]; or
3. allow the evidence but subject to comment.[11]

Technically it might be inadmissible for you to lead this evidence, but the accepted view seems to be that the contradictory evidence can be led but will be subject to comment.

10–06   An issue might arise as to how far it is necessary for you to go in cross-examination. For example, if your defence includes the proposition that the pursuer had been drinking in the local public house before the accident and had been seen to take four whiskies and some beers before leaving in an inebriated state, do you need to put these specifics to him before you can properly lead evidence of that detail? Or would it be enough for you to say to him, "Were you drinking that day?" to which he replies, "I did not touch a drop that day", and then you move on, without saying, "Did you not have four whiskies in the local pub between 12 noon and 2pm that day?"

In reality, you might want to put these questions to him anyway if you know that you have a witness who saw it and will give evidence to that effect but, once you have his blanket denial, it may not be necessary to put all of the gory details to him before you lead the contrary evidence.

"I should be slow to affirm that, where, as here, a defence is explicitly set forth on record, there is in general any duty on a cross-examining counsel who has already received a negative answer, and one which necessarily excludes an affirmative reply to further

---

[10] "It is no doubt true that ordinarily a pursuer leads his proof in replication along with his initial proof, and by anticipation negatives the case of which he has notice in the pleadings. But while this is the familiar and almost invariable practice, it is always open to a pursuer to move the court for leave to recall his witnesses or to lead additional evidence in any case where it can be said that prejudice might result to the pursuer through the basis of the defender's case not having been properly put in cross-examination": *Wilson v Thomas Usher & Son Ltd*, above.

[11] It may make the court less inclined to disbelieve the witness who gave the contrary version which was not put: see *Dollar Air Services Ltd v Highland Council*, 1997 G.W.D. 28–1435.

questions, to put further questions which can only be similarly answered in the negative."[12]

A good recent example of the significance or otherwise of a failure to cross-examine and the effect this can have upon the accepted evidence can be found in *Currie v Clamp's Exrs*[13]:

"The fact that the pursuer was not cross examined on this matter [who was driving a vehicle], in my opinion, was significant. I accept that the effect of a failure to cross examine a witness on a matter does not mean that the evidence, for which no foundation has been laid in cross examination, but which has been led without objection, falls necessarily to be disregarded. Nevertheless it is for the court hearing the evidence to pay particular regard to the way in which the evidence emerged in judging of the weight, if any, to be given to it. Considerations of prejudice also arise in such a situation It seems to me that I should not readily accept the evidence of X [witness], on this matter, when the pursuer was not given a chance to contradict it, or even to explain why it could not be true. The principles of fair play, in my judgment, mean that this should have been done and, in this case, the failure to observe fair play by seeing that this was done, can be said to be prejudicial to the pursuer".

Leading questions

Lawyers frequently ask leading questions in court. It is important to **10–07** understand when and why that might be objectionable. In the conduct of an examination in chief and re-examination of your own party or witness, you should not ask leading questions except in the limited circumstances described here. The opponent can object to them. The sheriff may also admonish you for asking them, and that will help neither you nor your witness. The court and your opponent will usually prevent you from asking a leading question, but, if they do not do so, that does not mean that you have triumphed. The evidential consequence of a leading question is that the court may attach little or no weight to the answer given. At its most extreme, the answer is worthless. So, technically, you can ask inappropriate leading questions if you wish. The problem is that they do not elicit what would be regarded as "evidence" from the witness.

A good (if somewhat extreme) illustration is *McKenzie v McKenzie*[14] in which,

"the only contributions made by some witnesses for the pursuer when speaking to important branches of the case consist of mono-syllabic assents to extracts read from precognitions. The leading question has its place in dealing with introductory narrative, non-controversial matter, and the like, but its habitual and persistent use

---

[12] *Wilson v Thomas Usher & Son Ltd*, 1934 S.L.T. 307.
[13] 2002 S.L.T. 196.
[14] 1943 S.L.T. 169; see also *Bishop v Bryce*, 1910 S.C. 426; 1910 1 S.L.T. 196.

when examining in chief witnesses on central issues of disputed fact will not only displace entirely the confidence we ought to put in the deposition of a witness . . . but may make the answer as it is given a 'worthless answer'."

You can, by contrast, ask as many leading questions as you like in cross-examination. Indeed, the NITA technique recommends that only leading questions be asked in cross-examination as part of a very structured and controlled method of conducting a cross-examination.[15] I am not convinced that this works well in Scotland, but a careful combination of leading and non-leading questions in cross-examination can be useful. A good answer to a non-leading question in cross-examination can be worth much more than a good answer to a leading one, but the important point to emphasise is that there can be no objection to any leading questions in cross-examination.

Leading questions in re-examination are subject to the same constraints as in examination in chief.[16] That is not to say that leading questions are not asked in re-examination.[17] In very limited circumstances, answers to such questions may carry some weight but I would positively discourage any reliance on this speciality.[18]

What is a leading question?[19]

10–08   This is a question which, by its form or terms, suggests the answer desired by the questioner—"Did you notice that the car was going too fast?" It can also be described as a question which actually contains the answer—"Would I be right in thinking it was doing more than 60 mph?" It can also include a question the words of which assume something (in this example the speed) which has not yet been established in evidence—"As the car was travelling at 60 mph, did you have much time to notice it?"

The meaning and significance of leading questions is explained and discussed in the undernoted books.[20] The issue of whether a leading question is unfair and objectionable or not, will depend upon the context, upon the circumstances of the case, upon the kind of witness

---

[15] You have to be particularly skilled to use this technique effectively. See S. Lubet, *Modern Trial Advocacy* (NITA).

[16] See Macphail, *Sheriff Court Practice*, above, para.16.78.

[17] See, e.g. *Rehman v Ahmad*, 1993 S.L.T. 741: "The matter was taken up again in re-examination. On this occasion the form of questioning was such as to deprive the answers of any value."; and *Inglis v London Scottish and Midland Rly*, 1941 S.L.T. 408: "[I]t is usually perilous to rely on a witness's assent to leading questions in re-examination." See also *Mclelland v Greater Glasgow Health Board*, 2001 S.L.T. 446.

[18] "However, less than satisfactory as it was, this testimony was the closest the evidence in the case came to what has turned out to be the decisive factual issue. That testimony was unchallenged. It was also uncontradicted.": *Ritchie v Lloyds*, 2005 S.L.T. 64.

[19] Well this is not one, for example.

[20] J.M. Lees, *A Handbook of Written and Oral Pleading in the Sheriff Court: And notes on the structure of interlocutors in the sheriff court*, p.104; Walker and Walker, above, pp.181–182; Field and Raitt, above, pp.206–207; Macphail, *Sheriff Court Practice*, above, paras 16.69 *et seq.*; J. Munkman, *The Technique of Advocacy* (4th edn, LexisNexis Butterworths, London, 2003), p.39; A. Boon, *Advocacy* (2nd edn, Cavendish, London, 1999), pp.89–91.

who is under consideration, and upon how the case has actually been conducted beforehand. It will also depend upon the precise words of the question.[21]

The opposite of a leading question is an "open" question. This can often be so deceptively simple and straightforward that the questioner may wonder in retrospect why he did not ask it in the first place—"What speed was the car travelling at?"[22]

It can be difficult to decide whether some questions are leading or not. There is scope for a difference of opinion. Asking questions in a certain way might be seen as influencing the answer but there can be very subtle nuances at play here which defy easy analysis.[23] I have heard many discussions between experienced court lawyers and sheriffs as to whether a question was leading or not, so do not be surprised if there is some uncertainty in your mind on this. It is usually quite easy to spot the important leading questions.

Why do you not want to ask leading questions?

They are not the best way of eliciting and demonstrating the truth of **10–09** the witness's evidence. If you have an untruthful or unreliable witness, then you can mask this by asking such a question. If you have a truthful and independent witness they may be inclined, unconsciously, to give their evidence as favourably as they can to the party calling them. The witness may readily adopt, without much thought, a word or phrase or a description put to them which does not accurately express their views. People may agree with you for an easy life, and often a witness in court is delighted to accept the questioner's hint or turn of phrase without thinking too deeply about it. However, the result is that it is not their evidence, it is yours—and yours does not count.

It can be argued that this is not absolutely fatal to a fair trial. It can always be cleared up in cross-examination. The problem is that once the idea is out and spoken to by the witness,[24] it is difficult to remove it from the mind of the witness and it can distort the proof. The proper course is to object to it,[25] especially when it is put to an impressionable witness. Some lawyers might take the view that they do not need to object because the answer to a leading question is completely worthless—in extreme cases that may well be so, but an objection should be taken to every such question in relation to material and disputed facts.[26]

---

[21] For example, look at the first "speeding" question above. Would it have been leading if you had substituted "if" for "that"? I do not think so, and yet that one word might not have made much difference to the witness's interpretation of the question.

[22] Again, I appreciate that this might seem so obvious as to be unworthy of comment, but experience has taught me never to underestimate the capacity of some court lawyers to over-complicate the process.

[23] For example, asking a witness, "How far away was the car when it braked?" might suggest or assume that it was "far away". Compare that with, "How near was the car when it braked?" To what extent might this question influence the answer? Better to ask, "What distance away was the car?"—but are the first two questions unfair?

[24] And often elaborated upon once it is established.

[25] Immediately the question is asked—and before it is answered.

[26] Apart from anything else it may well expose an ill-prepared opponent who does not know what you are on about, and might have a problem asking a non-leading question. I have heard this more than once.

When can you lead?

10–10   Leading questions are objectionable only when they are "unfair". It would normally not be unfair to ask leading questions in examination in chief in relation to matters such as:

1. personal details of the witness;
2. narrative or non-material (background) evidence;
3. matters which are plainly not in dispute, even if not formally admitted;
4. matters agreed or admitted on record or in a joint minute of admissions;
5. matters on which the opponent agrees in the course of the proof that you can lead[27]; and
6. sometimes, in the course of a proof, you can see that the opponent is not challenging evidence of one fact or another when it has come from previous witnesses even though there is no formal admission or concession of that fact. If you are clear about this, then it would not be unreasonable to lead a subsequent witness, or witnesses, on that fact.[28]

For example, take the personal injury case of Mr Hamilton. If you were leading evidence from him in chief you could probably lead him on:

1. his name, address, age, occupation and marital status;
2. the fact that he had some kind of accident on that specific date at that shopping centre;
3. how he came to be in the shopping centre and who he was with[29];
4. the location—but not the cause—of his accident; and
5. the fact that he sustained some kind of injury, was taken to hospital, and was told that he had broken his ankle.

Although, depending upon the very precise circumstances of the case, and the line(s) of defence being advanced, even some of these issues may be unsuitable for leading questions.

You can, and should, plan this by studying the record and noting carefully what matters are admitted and the extent to which they are admitted.[30] You may also note the matters which are not positively disputed and assess if it would be worth clarifying with your opponent whether the witness might be led on these.

How to avoid leading

10–11   One familiar problem you can encounter is that once you start leading your witness you can get into the habit very easily and you just keep

---

[27] You can ask him if he objects to you leading on X or Y, and it would be as well to let the sheriff know that this has been agreed between you.
[28] But only on that.
[29] Although you might not want to lead him on drink as that might be material.
[30] You must be very careful about this.

doing it. Do not worry, everyone does. It is extremely difficult to get out of the habit, especially when neither your opponent nor the sheriff seem to notice, or care. The best advice is not to start it unless you have prepared your questions thoroughly. Look at the matters which are clearly not in dispute on the pleadings, or otherwise. Prepare those questions as leading questions. For everything else, use questions beginning with who, why, where, what, when, how, what happened after/ next, can you describe, could you estimate, and so on.

I know this might seem remarkably simple and almost unworthy of stating, but it works. You will find it is virtually impossible to ask a leading question if you start with those words and phrases.[31] It is a good discipline and, indeed, once you get into the habit you will find that it works extremely well. There is a skill in asking open questions only in a sequence of a logically progressive examination as a means of fairly and accurately eliciting the whole evidence of a witness in court.

Practical example

Let us look at another practical illustration. In the kitchen case, once **10–12** you have established that Mrs Gray did talk to Mrs Stewart after the quote had been given, asking Mrs Gray:

1. "Did you have any discussion with Mrs Stewart regarding the price they had quoted?" would not be a leading question.
2. "Did Mrs Stewart offer you a discount?" is probably not a leading question, because she could answer, "Yes" or "No." However, from the pleadings in the case itself, you know this is a major bone of contention and there is a "leading flavour" to it. It would be preferable to ask it another way, although strictly speaking it is not objectionable.
3. "And did she tell you there was a discount of 10 per cent available if you ordered before the end of the month?" would certainly be leading.
4. "When you spoke to her about this on the telephone did she . . ." could also be leading if it was disputed that a discussion had taken place at a certain time and in a certain way and if you had not yet established that the "discussion" was actually on the telephone.

A non-leading sequence of questions to elicit this evidence might have been: "Did you discuss the price thereafter with anyone?", "Who was that?", "How did that discussion take place?", "When did that discussion take place?", "What did you discuss?", and so on.

Language to avoid

There are certain words and phrases which can creep into your **10–13** vocabulary and which can immediately create the foundations for a

---

[31] I am almost tempted to offer a prize for anyone who can actually do this.

leading question. If you really prepare properly you will be able to spot them while writing them out, and avoid them. If you just prepare to the extent of deciding that you will ask "about speed", then you can find yourself struggling to overcome the casual and colloquial language which usually suffices for everyday usage. When you are inexperienced and make up the words of the question while on your feet, things can go wrong. Phrases to watch out for and to prevent creeping in to your examination in chief are: "Would it be fair to assume that", "Would I be right in thinking that", "Did it seem to you that", "Did he then", "Would you say it was rather", "Can I take it that", and so on. If you hear yourself start off in this vein, then you are just about to ask a leading question.[32]

Taking objections in the course of proof

10–14   Most lawyers appearing in court, no matter how inexperienced, will have a general appreciation that it is open to a solicitor to take objection to questions being asked by an opponent in the course of a proof. This section gives some guidance on why you might take an objection, when you would take an objection, how you would take an objection, how an objection would be adjudicated upon, and some of the more common grounds for taking objection.

Remember that the proof is an exercise in putting before the sheriff all of the relevant facts with the ultimate objective of having the sheriff make findings in fact based upon the evidence from witnesses which he is legitimately allowed to hear. The proof is not a free for all in which any witnesses can stand up in court and have their say. It is a regulated and structured hearing in which evidence is put before the court in a formal way. The right to take objection gives both parties the opportunity to restrict or control the evidence being led by the opponent that can legitimately be heard by the court. It should, of course, be noted that the primary mechanism for controlling the evidence that can be heard at any proof is the record. This should outline clearly what the parties have come to court to prove by means of admissible evidence.

I shall explain some basic practical guidelines about taking objections:

10–15   1. You can only take objection to a question. You cannot object to an answer.[33] You are objecting to the fact that your opponent has asked a question which you consider is not proper or acceptable. This means that you have to listen to the words of the question carefully and take steps to prevent the witness answering the question.

---

[32] But do not despair, they were asking them a hundred years ago, so you will not be the first. Look at this from *Bishop v Bryce*, 1910 S.C. 426; 1910 1 S.L.T. 196: "And then, instead of being asked, 'What did Mr Bryce say to you?' which, of course, was a proper question, he was asked: 'Did Mr Bryce say to you that if you took £300 worth of shares he would be responsible?' That is, of course, absolutely putting the words into the man's mouth, and the result of that is that the answer, as he made it, is a worthless answer."

[33] It may be that if a witness answers a question in a way which introduces evidence which might be inadmissible, the admission of that answer itself could be objected to. However, I cannot recall ever having seen that done.

2. In objecting to one question you can also indicate that you are objecting not just to the precise terms of that question but to any similar question which attempts to explore a particular fact, or set of facts. Objecting to the "line of questions" or objection to "questions on that line of evidence" means that you are not just complaining about the precise choice of words used in the particular question but that any further questions, however framed, on that same topic are going to be unacceptable to you. It is usually apparent at an early stage whether an objectionable question is a one off, or is the precursor to a line of questions on and around the same topic. An objection to a line of questions would make it unnecessary to wait for each individual question to be asked and then objected to individually.[34]

3. You must take the objection at the right time. The right time can often be the brief millisecond between the questioner completing the question and the witness beginning the answer. As you will appreciate, this may require some physical and mental agility on your part. You might think that the question is going to be objectionable, but if you object before it is completed, you may be faced with the argument that it is not possible to rule upon whether the question is objectionable or not until the whole question has been completed. On the other hand, if you wait until the full question has been asked and the import of the question has sunk in, you may find that the witness has started answering, and perhaps even finished answering, the question. Since the whole object of the exercise is to prevent the answer being made, then taking an objection after the answer has been given may be quite ineffectual. Such an answer would normally be recorded for consideration as part of the whole evidence in the case. The prime purpose of an objection is to prevent the answer being evidence at all.

4. To take an objection effectively you have to be on your toes **10–16** mentally, on your feet physically, and speaking clearly as soon as you think that the opponent has asked, or is about to ask, an objectionable question. Sometimes you can see it coming. Sometimes it may be signalled by a hesitant question. An experienced questioner may, however, ask a potentially objectionable question rather quickly and, of course, is perfectly entitled to do so.

Once you have made the necessarily rapid decision to object you should stand up immediately and address the court. It is a matter of preference, and might sometimes depend upon the circumstances, but the first thing you may want to do is to address the witness and say quite clearly and pointedly to the witness "Do not answer that question [until his Lordship rules on the matter]." You should then advise the sheriff clearly, "I

---

[34] A good modern example which is well worth reading is *Hislop v Lynx Express Parcels*, 2003 S.L.T. 785 in which an objection to the leading of evidence on matters not in the pleadings was made at an early stage and was considered by the appeal court (but not by sheriff at first instance) to cover all subsequent questions directed to the same matters.

object to that question." You can achieve the same effect by simply standing up immediately on conclusion of the question and advising the sheriff loudly "I object", or "Objection", in a manner which will attract everyone's attention.

The sheriff may well have seen this coming and he may have anticipated your objection. You may indeed have started to rise to your feet as the question was being asked, so by that the time it is finished you have reached your full height and are ready to say the appropriate words. The point is that you want to make it clear to the witness, the sheriff, and your opponent (probably in that order) that the question must not be answered before the witness even has a chance to draw breath to start their answer.

A timid, hesitant or apologetic objection can be ignored or overlooked. Indeed, if it sounds half-hearted this might well suggest you have little confidence in its merit.

5. It can be difficult for people to object confidently and comfortably when they are just starting to appear in court. You are making a fuss. You are making a noise and interrupting the flow of the proof. Perhaps you should not be doing so. You might decide against taking objection in the hope that the sheriff might spot the objectionable question and prevent it being answered. Alternatively, you might take the view that the sheriff will treat an answer to a plainly objectionable question to be insignificant and inadmissible. In some cases, the sheriff will point out that he considers the question to be objectionable and that might take the responsibility from you. However, the primary obligation is yours. One of the most common reasons for not taking a legitimate objection is that the lawyer is not absolutely clear whether they should, or should not, do so. Not only that, the lawyer may not be absolutely clear what the reason for their objection is. The lawyer may have a clear impression that the question is not right in some way, but may not be able to characterise immediately why that should be so. Experience will help with this but, while gaining that experience, it is probably as well to trust your instincts and make the objection even though you might not be able to explain with clarity and precision exactly why you are doing it. You might find that the sheriff will agree the question is objectionable and you may not need to justify your objection. Even if you do not have that bonus, you will have a little bit of time between saying the words of objection and explaining the reason for the objection to enable you to marshal your thoughts and justify it.

10–17
6. Once you have said the magic words, it is likely that the sheriff will ask you what the basis of your objection is. It might be obvious, but you will normally need to tell the sheriff why the objection is being taken. In these circumstances, it is sometimes prudent and occasionally necessary to ask that the witness to leave the court while you advance your arguments in support of the objection. This can be all the more so in a situation where you are objecting to a line of questions. It is difficult to generalise about this, but with some thought you may be able to

appreciate the circumstances in which it would be prudent to ask for the witness to leave the court. You may have to explain the reason for your objection by discussing, for example, what the pleadings say, or what a previous witness has said, or how significant this particular point might be and why, in the context of the case as a whole. Any witness who is allowed to remain in court at that time, and listen to a discussion of that kind, could quite easily be influenced by the argument on the objection. The witness could, indeed, be encouraged to provide the telling answer to that question (if the sheriff ultimately allows it to be asked) or indeed to any later question, which might give them the opportunity to say the very words they think you are desperate to prevent them saying.

7. In many cases, the sheriff would ask the objector to justify or explain the objection. The objector would then have to do so, and the justification might be quite brief at that point. It might be that no detailed explanation would be given until the witness was taken out of court. Thereafter, normally the sheriff would ask the questioner to respond to the objection and to justify the question if there was any dispute about it. It would not be unusual for a sheriff to anticipate the basis of the objection and require little explanation. Nor would it be unusual for a sheriff to form a view fairly easily that there was no good basis for the objection and require little, if any, response from the questioner. In some circumstances, the point at issue may be extremely critical and the objection may be highly arguable. It might even give rise to the necessity for both parties to make legal submission, with reference to authority, and engage in detailed legal argument before the sheriff was prepared to make a decision on the question. In practice, this would be relatively unusual for reasons which I will explain shortly.

If the questioner accepted that there was justification for the objection then they would normally volunteer that the question be taken out (i.e. not recorded in the notes of evidence) and that they be permitted to reframe the question in an unobjectionable form. If the objection was more than a complaint about the choice of words used, then the questioner might accept the criticism, withdraw the question and try to deal with it by asking different questions or staying away from the area of evidence to which objection had been taken. If the sheriff considers that, on the face of it, the objection is justifiable, and if the questioner disagrees, then the sheriff will have to rule on the objection. The sheriff can sustain the objection and not permit the question or the line of questions to be asked. The sheriff can repel the objection as having no real justification and allow the question to be asked. In that case, the questioner should simply repeat the question verbatim. If it is a lengthy or complex question then the questioner could ask the shorthand writer to repeat the question for the sake of accuracy.

8. The final, and relatively common, method of dealing with an **10–18** objection is for the sheriff to allow the question to be asked "reserving all questions of competency and relevancy" or

"subject to all questions of relevancy and competency". This means that the sheriff may not be in a position to decide whether the evidence is admissible, or not, until he has heard all of the evidence in the case and is able to put this particular matter in context. Objections taken to the particular words used in the framing of a question can usually be dealt with there and then. However, objections taken as to whether evidence of a particular type would be admissible to support the cases that either party is presenting to the court would be more likely to lead to the sheriff reserving his decision on whether the question—and, more importantly, the answer, or answers, which it might elicited—should be allowed. The sheriff would simply allow the question to be asked and allow the witness to answer the question. It would be noted that the question (and answer) were allowed subject to that condition. It would then be left for the parties to address the sheriff in the course of their submissions at the end of the proof on the question of whether the evidence (as per the question and answer) should be admitted. At that stage, it should have become clear exactly what is in dispute and exactly whether that evidence is likely to be significant, or even critical, for adjudicating upon the issues between the parties. It is not unusual for an objection which is forcibly taken, and forcibly argued, and upon which the sheriff has reserved his decision, to be abandoned in the course of submissions. The objector may take the view that, in reality, the evidence is not particularly important. If the objector does not make submissions in support of the objection which they had taken earlier with a view to having that evidence excluded, then the sheriff can take it that the objection is not being insisted upon. If the objection is insisted upon, and the sheriff then decides the question of the admissibility of that evidence in favour of the objector, then the evidence will be excluded from consideration and cannot form the basis of any finding in fact in the decision of the sheriff.

10–19 9. It is virtually impossible to cover the whole range of reasons for objecting to questions, but here is a brief checklist of some of the more common grounds of objection:

(a) *The question is leading.* We have already dealt with what this means in paragraph 10–08. You can object to a leading question in examination and re-examination, but a leading question is perfectly justifiable in cross-examination.

(b) *There are no averments in the record in relation to the facts about which the witness is being asked.* For example, if a party or a witness is asked about complaints which might have been made, and there are no averments of any complaints being made, then that might well be objectionable, especially if this might form a crucial part of the case.

(c) *That prior evidence (by the witness or by other witnesses) has been put to the witness inaccurately.* For example, saying to a witness, "We have heard earlier that it was raining all that day" when, in fact, an earlier witness had said that it had just rained for an hour would be objectionable. A particular example of such an objection might arise in a cross-examination where it is put to a witness that they had said something specific in their examination in chief when the witness had not actually done so. In these circumstances, such a question would be quite unfair to the witness and the objector is entitled to ensure the proof is conducted fairly.

(d) *That the question is irrelevant.* In other words, that it has no apparent connection with the pleadings nor, indeed, with any aspect of the case upon which the court will be required to adjudicate.

(e) *That the question asks for an opinion from a witness who is not qualified to give an opinion.* Sometimes witnesses will be asked to express opinions when answering a question. There are obvious examples of witnesses who are called as expert witnesses and who can be expected to be asked questions of opinion. However, other witnesses may be asked for their opinion of various matters as well. It would be open to a party to object to a question which is designed to elicit opinion evidence unless this is something upon which the witness is qualified to have an opinion, and that qualification is obvious or has been demonstrated to the court.

(f) *That the question is designed to elicit evidence which is not "the best evidence".* This can cover a variety of circumstances and it is difficult to generalise.

(g) *That the question has already been asked and has already been answered.* It is not unusual for the same or similar questions to be asked and answered by a witness more than once, and while this might be irritating and unnecessary it would not necessarily merit an objection. However, in the context of a cross-examination where the same point has been put in cross-examination to a witness repeatedly, and has been answered repeatedly, it may be quite legitimate to object.

(h) *That the question is a "bad" question.* This might cover a multitude of sins. The question might be unclear, in which case the witness may not know how to answer, and the answer might be capable of being misinterpreted. The question might be too long so it is difficult to understand and answer properly. The "question" might actually be two or three questions and this again leads to the risk of the answer being confused and confusing. The question might be misleading with a risk that the answer might be misleading too. The question might be rude, abusive, or argumentative.

While in limited circumstances that might be necessary or even appropriate, it may be regarded as quite unfair to the witness to subject them to this unless they are patently setting out to lie or prevaricate. The question might not be a question at all. Inexperienced, and even experienced, solicitors can often be found making a speech or a statement to a witness which simply does not call for an answer.

10–20   10. Of necessity, the above is not an exhaustive list. Different cases and circumstances, and indeed different solicitors, can produce a wide variety of potentially objectionable questions. The principal purposes of taking an objection are to try and ensure that the rules of evidence are complied with, and that the answer given by the witness to a question is a true and fair reflection of what the witness intends to say and what they mean. Bear in mind, however, that one of the skills of cross-examination is to force or to encourage the witness to say something which they might not necessarily have volunteered, and which might reflect upon their credibility and reliability as a witness. It is not a legitimate ground of objection to say that the question should not be allowed because it might tend to undermine the credibility and the reliability of the witness, or that the questioner is trying to be clever and trap the witness into saying something they do not mean. If the question is admissible and cannot be objected to on the types of ground explained above, then you cannot take objection to it, even if you can see that the answer might well harm the witness.

11. Finally, I should mention a rather vexed and sensitive issue as to whether you can object to a question, or questions, asked by the sheriff which might, if asked by your opponent, have been objectionable. This is a difficult point in theory, and even more difficult in practice. There is authority for the proposition that objection can be taken to the sheriff asking a question which would otherwise have been objectionable.[35] However, when the point was considered in *Hislop v Lynx Express Parcels*,[36] the court reserved its opinion on the general issue of objecting to questions asked by the court. The prudent and diplomatic course to take may be that, if the sheriff asks a question which you consider objectionable on the grounds mentioned above, you could indicate respectfully that you are not sure if it is open to you to take objection to the question but, if it had been asked by your opponent you would have done so. That may require an element of courage, confidence or foolhardiness depending upon the circumstances.

Amendment during proof

10–21   No matter how carefully you may have investigated the case, precognosced the witnesses, and drafted your pleadings, evidence may come

---

[35] *McCallum v Paterson*, 1969 S.C. 89.
[36] 2004 S.L.T. 785.

out at the proof which is different from the facts as you had understood these to be—and, most importantly, from the averments, you have made about those facts. It is not unusual for this to happen. It is most commonly seen in the evidence of a pursuer who might come up with something new and unexpected, but the same considerations apply if such evidence emerges from a witness or from the defender. This can create real difficulties for the solicitor who is hoping to rely upon that evidence to prove the case, or the defence.

Various consequences can flow from this. For present purposes, it is necessary to generalise. In practice, when a witness or party gives evidence which may not fit your record it is necessary to consider very carefully the precise pleadings, the precise evidence, and the extent to which it is crucial to the case or to the defence. This will often require an instantaneous analysis of how critical the discrepancy might be and since the evidence usually emerges unexpectedly, it is difficult to prepare for this eventuality. It will be helpful, however, to provide some general guidance upon how this might be dealt with in the course of a proof. For present purposes, I will discuss this on the basis that it is the evidence of the pursuer which has emerged differently from their averments, but the same observations would apply in relation to the evidence of a witness or of a defender and their witnesses.

The starting point for considering this is the assumption that, in the course of examination in chief, the pursuer, or witness, has responded to a straight forward question with an answer which was not expected and which demonstrates that they are adopting a position which is not the same as the averments on record. You can only lead evidence about matters which have been outlined in the pleadings. Sometimes the outline that you have given in your pleadings would be broad enough for you to say that any divergence from the pleadings is simply a variation, modification, or development, of what has actually been said on record. In other words, the exact words of the pleadings and the exact meaning of the pleadings may not be so clear and restrictive as to make it plain that the pursuer's case was founded upon completely different facts. The first matter to be analysed, therefore, is whether, upon detailed consideration of exactly what the pleadings say (and in these circumstances these would probably be interpreted quite liberally) and exactly what the witness was asked and answered, there is a material difference between the two. It is quite likely that the solicitors for both parties will have different interpretations of this. Both solicitors have to decide on how they should deal with that "divergence".

In this situation, the opposing party might well adopt one of two **10–22** responses:

1. If we assume that the question to which the "rogue" answer was given was a fair and reasonable one then the opposing solicitor could do nothing to prevent the answer being given by taking objection to it. Of course, if the question was clearly intended to elicit something from the witness which was not part of the case on record then it would, and should, have been objected to. In any event, assuming that the answer is out, the solicitor for the opposing party would have to be alert to ensure that no further questions directed at this piece of evidence

(which was not foreshadowed in the pleadings) was led from this witness. A failure to object to such questions could reasonably be interpreted by the court as an acceptance that this was no more than a legitimate variation or extension of the pursuer's case.

2. The opposing party could simply allow the pursuer to continue giving evidence entirely contrary to the record, or different to the record. This would be on the reasoning that the purpose of the proof is to prove the averments on record. If a witness gives evidence on crucial matters which are not in the record then this is of no consequence. The sheriff cannot make findings in fact of crucial matters which are not foreshadowed in the pleadings. If the pleadings say X and the witness says Y, then the sheriff cannot find that Y has been proved unless Y could be regarded as a variation, modification or development of X.

The opponent can indeed turn this piece of evidence (and indeed any evidence from follow up questions if they decide not to object to them) to some advantage in cross-examination, although it is a matter of opinion and circumstance as to whether this is the most effective approach. It might be useful to illustrate the types of questions which could be asked in cross-examination in order to have the maximum impact in the circumstances. It is very important to set this up properly:

> *"You told us in your evidence, Mr X, that . . . Is that correct?"*
> *"Yes."*
> *"Are you clear about that?"*
> *"Yes."*
> *"Has there ever been an occasion when you thought differently about that?"*
> *"No."*
> *"So I take it you would never have told anyone anything different from that?"*
> *"No."*
> *"Now, in this case, are you aware that both sides are required to set out their position in writing before anyone gives evidence?"*
> *"Yes/No."*
> *[If no:] "Well would you take it from me that this is what both parties are under an obligation to do?"*
> *"Okay."*
> *"Have you seen the written pleadings in your case before today?"*
> *"Yes/No."*
> *"Well let me [tell you/remind you] of what is said on your behalf in the pleadings in this case. [Reads pleadings.] Would you agree with me that this says something quite different from what you have told us today?"*
> *"Yes/No."*
> *"Indeed, what I have read out to you from the pleadings has never been your position has it?"*

10–23 If you think about this carefully you will see that the penultimate question is the crucial one. The witness could say that they do not see much of a difference between the pleadings and their evidence. The opposing solicitor could object by saying that they do not think there is much of a difference either. The opposing solicitor could also object by saying that there are other parts of the pleadings which ought to be read out to the witness because they elaborate or qualify averments that you have read out. The cross-examination can be rendered ineffectual if you do not demonstrate clearly and fairly what the witness said and what the pleadings say, and the divergence between the pleadings and the evidence. However, if you do draw out that distinction then this can be a very powerful piece of cross-examination affecting the credibility and/or reliability of the witness. In this context, it should be remembered that this will usually be the pursuer and, in personal injury cases, the credibility and reliability of the pursuer is often paramount.

Having considered the possible reaction or response from the opposing party to evidence which emerges contrary to record, I now want to consider the appropriate response from the questioner when this situation arises. When the evidence comes out in this way—and it will usually come as a surprise—the questioner has to make a fairly quick decision as to how to deal with it. I am assuming that the answer was given in response to a legitimate question to which no objection could have been taken. You might decide that the answer can be left, but if it is critical or crucial (and it is impossible to generalise about this) you will probably want to follow it up. Indeed, there might be an obligation on you to follow it up. If you do so by asking follow up questions then you might expect an objection from the opposing party as previously indicated. In that case, you simply have to deal with the objection.

If no objection is taken to any follow up questions and further development of the evidence on a matter which is not on record then you can continue to ask those questions and elicit that evidence. In both situations, however, you will also have a decision to make as to whether you ought to be amending your pleadings to take into account the evidence which has emerged, or might be emerging.

If objection is taken to you exploring this evidence any further your response might well be that the evidence is no more than a variation or modification of the case on record. You may think that the evidence itself is not crucial or critical. Although it may not be specifically stated in your pleadings, it may not necessarily be excluded by your pleadings. It may be a matter of opinion and argument as to whether what the witness is saying could be regarded as a legitimate interpretation of what your pleadings say. This is the very situation in which it may be likely that the court would allow the evidence to be heard, subject to competency and relevancy, and then hear arguments upon that evidence when the time comes for submissions.

However, if the divergence is clear and you consider that the evidence **10–24** from the witness is critical and important you may need to consider moving the court to allow an amendment to your pleadings. It may be that you yourself have made a mistake or had, until the proof, misinterpreted or misunderstood what the witness was saying. It may be necessary for you to correct the pleadings. If you are going to correct them, it is as well to do so at the earliest opportunity. This might mean that you would have to move the court to allow an amendment to your pleadings there and then. You would have to indicate what that amendment would be and the opponent would have an opportunity to object to it. The sheriff would have to rule on it.

(Alternatively, you could wait until the proof had finished and then make a motion at the time when submissions are being made for the court to allow your pleadings to be amended in line with the evidence. If the point is truly critical, this might not be wise. Again, it is difficult to generalise but let me try to illustrate this with a practical example.

Assume that in the kitchen case Mrs Gray gave evidence about a telephone call between herself and Mr Parker which formed a part of the discussions and negotiations regarding the contract for the supply of the kitchen. She had either not mentioned this to you, or you had not appreciated the significance of it until she was being asked in detail about it at the proof. It may seem to you that you required to elicit more detailed evidence from her about this because it might well have an impact upon the precise terms of the contract agreed between the parties, which is one of the critical issues in the case. You would take the view that it would be important for you to have this evidence recognised in some way as a finding in fact at the conclusion of the case. Since you do not have any averments about it, it could not be a finding in fact unless you moved to have an amendment allowed. You would move the court for leave to allow you to amend, and you would have to advise the court what the terms of your amendment might be. Bear in mind that, by that time, there may already have been a considerable amount of evidence led from other witnesses, including examination and cross-examination of Mr Parker to whom this purported telephone conversation had not been put.

10–25   In that context, you can easily see that the opponent could object to any further questions about this point. The opponent could decide not to object, and if you did not amend they would simply argue that the evidence could not justify any finding in fact at the conclusion of the proof (although they would probably not want to take that chance). The opponent could simply file this away for cross-examination of Mrs Gray on the basis that we have outlined above.

If you sought leave to amend immediately after the evidence came out, you could address all of these issues at once. The problem you might have, however, is that if you ask for leave to amend, the motion would be argued. The motion might be refused. A refusal would cut off any other evidence of this and might serve to highlight (if it needed highlighting) the difficulty which existed in your case, and which has not been remedied. On the other hand, if you do not ask for leave to amend then you run the risk of being unable to prove that part of the case which, on this assumption, you have considered to be critical.

Rule 18.2 of the Ordinary Cause Rules 1993 provides that the sheriff may "at any time before final judgment, allow an amendment". By rule 18.2.(2)(c) the court may allow any amendment of "[p]leadings which may be necessary for determining the real question in controversy between the parties". Accordingly, it can be seen that the court has power to allow amendment during the proof or at submissions at the conclusion of the proof, and even (although I have no experience of this) after the submissions have been concluded but before final judgment has been issued. It is a discretionary decision. The matter is dealt with in

Macphail,[37] and the considerations which the sheriff may take into account are discussed there. In the example which I have given, a sheriff might be disinclined to allow the amendment for various reasons, for example, that it might be necessary to recall witnesses who had already given evidence, or to permit the pursuer time to answer the amendment and make further enquiry.

As will be appreciated, amendment during the course of a proof is **10–26** something that you would want to avoid if at all possible, but remember that if there is a flaw or omission in your pleadings (for whatever reason) which prevents your client putting forward the case, or the defence, which they want to put forward (even though the true story only emerges at the proof diet itself) then there is an argument that the interests of justice demand that amendments should be allowed because that is the only way in which the "real question in controversy" can be adjudicated upon.

As a final illustration from my own practical experience, I can recall a case in which the pursuer said that he had slipped on the internal stairs of a building frequently used by the public and which were wet. In his evidence, the pursuer volunteered that he had actually slipped on a crisp packet which was lying on the stairs and he was really complaining that the stairs were not cleaned often enough. Various thoughts may occur to you as to how that could possibly have come about, but I will leave you to ponder what you could/would/should have done as the pursuer's solicitor when hit by that bombshell.

It is when this particular problem emerges and you realise the difficulty you are in that you begin to understand the importance of pleading your case fully and properly. This is the real reason why accurate and considered pleadings are so vital in our civil procedures.

Best evidence

There can sometimes be arguments about whether the evidence being **10–27** led by a party is the "best evidence" and whether it is admissible or otherwise on that basis. This is an extremely complex area and it is difficult to explain or analyse this in detail in this section. The reader is referred to the opinion of Lord Macphail in the case of *Haddow v Glasgow City Council*[38] in which his Lordship discussed the matter, referred to the relevant authorities and expressed his views about the true nature and effect of the "best evidence rule". Particular reference can be made to paragraphs [12] to [16] of his opinion and the authorities cited there.

---

[37] *Sheriff Court Practice*, above, paras 10.7 *et seq.*
[38] [2005] CSOH 157.

CHAPTER 11

SUBMISSIONS ON EVIDENCE

"Your Lordship has heard all of the evidence. There is nothing I can usefully add. It is all a matter of credibility."

11–01 Once both parties have completed the process of examination and cross-examination of all of the witnesses they would then make submissions on the evidence. The general idea is to summarise and analyse the evidence which has been led and to demonstrate how it can be seen as proving your case and disproving your opponent's case. The party who led at the proof makes submissions first. The other party replies with their submissions. If that reply raises matters which were not dealt with in the opening speech, then the sheriff will invite the first speaker to respond on these matters. Indeed the sheriff might well ask both parties to make further submissions about any issues which he considers appropriate or necessary to assist him in making his decision.

Aim of submissions

11–02 It is difficult to find any guidance on how you should make submissions.[1] Each case is, of course, different, but it is possible to identify a structure for doing submissions which will work in most cases. There is no benefit in doing a "quality of mercy is not strained" speech or the civil equivalent of a plea in mitigation. "My Lord, I implore you to decide this case in favour of my client. The pursuer was an ordinary working man who found himself in a shopping centre in Glasgow with some time on his hands and not a care in the world. His whole life was subsequently shattered by the events of the next 20 minutes, the effects of which will remain with him for the rest of his days". Submissions are usually much more dispassionate and analytical than that. In very simple cases, there might well be a temptation to address the sheriff briefly at the conclusion of the evidence in the words quoted in the heading at the start of this chapter. However, if there is a conflict in the evidence, you really have to say considerably more about it. It is necessary to invite the sheriff to resolve any such conflict in your client's favour for some good reason and with some detailed justification. The general aim of submissions after proof is to: draw the sheriff's attention to the critical features of the case or the defence; detail and discuss the evidence bearing upon

---

[1] As ever, assistance can be derived from Macphail, *Sheriff Court Practice* (3rd edn, W. Green/Scottish Universities Law Institute, Edinburgh, 2006), paras 16.98–16.102, 17.02–17.08. In some reported cases judges will detail the submissions made by the parties and this might give you an idea about how this might be done.

those critical features; and persuade the sheriff that he can find sufficient facts to be proved from the evidence competently before him that would justify the legal remedy being sought or the defence being advanced.

It would not be unusual for submissions to last for an hour or two and there are cases in which they could last for a whole day. The general aims and objectives of your submissions will always be the same, although the detailed presentation will inevitably be different depending upon many circumstances. I will illustrate this later in the chapter.

When are submissions normally made?

This can vary depending upon the type of case, the length and **11–03** complexity of the case, and the preference of the sheriff. The possibilities are:

1. Submissions can be made immediately after the last witness has finished their evidence.
2. Sometimes a sheriff will allow a solicitor a short adjournment to permit them to prepare their submissions,[2] albeit the sheriff may want to hear the submissions that same day.
3. It is more common nowadays for the sheriff to fix a hearing on evidence to take place at some later date. The main reason why that would be done is that the sheriff (and indeed the parties) might consider it preferable to have the shorthand notes of all of the evidence available before submissions were made. As it usually takes some weeks for the notes to be extended and issued, a significant delay is inevitable. Such a hearing may be fixed where evidence in the case might have been spread over a number of different days, or where the evidence was particularly contentious or complex, or where the application of the law in the case might involve very careful consideration of the facts and detailed legal argument.
4. A hearing on evidence could also be fixed for some later date if the sheriff wanted submissions made in writing by both parties.[3] This itself would usually involve a request by the sheriff for extension of the shorthand notes but, even if that was not going to be required, additional time might reasonably be needed for the parties to prepare the written submissions.

In many ways, a separate hearing on evidence is not ideal.[4] The case should be dealt with expeditiously, and should not be unduly delayed. On the other hand, where the evidence is lengthy, potentially confusing, and raises issues of real complexity it may be in the interests of justice that any submissions are made with everyone having the benefit of the shorthand notes. These will contain a comprehensive and accurate

---

[2] Indeed, most sheriffs would be amenable to such a motion especially if the proof has raised difficult or complex issues.

[3] This is becoming more popular now especially for complex cases.

[4] With a little experience you may see the benefit of finishing the whole proof at once— and not coming back to a case some months later when the details might have become a little blurred.

record of precisely what everyone said in evidence. Giving parties the time and opportunity to reflect on the exact evidence and its significance might enable the submissions to be better focused and may well assist the sheriff in the task of making his decision.

In the final analysis it is for the court to decide whether the notes should be extended and/or whether there should be a separate hearing on evidence. It is often possible to find out during the proof if the sheriff is likely to want the notes extended and whether he is likely to want a separate hearing on evidence.[5] If the sheriff indicates that he is not intending to reach any decision in the case without having first read the shorthand notes, it would be sensible to defer your submissions until you have seen these. Otherwise, you might make submissions on the basis of your own (inaccurate or incomplete) notes of the evidence. When the sheriff comes to consider the case and the submissions he will have the luxury of reading the accurate version of the evidence which may conflict with your notes of the evidence. This may include evidence of crucial significance in his mind on which you may not have addressed him fully or properly because your notes were wrong or incomplete. Delaying your submissions until both you and the sheriff have the shorthand notes in front of you and can read exactly what the evidence was makes more sense.

Preparation of submissions

11–04   The submissions come at the end of the proof. The preparation of them should have been done before it began. The secret is to have prepared your submissions, or a very good outline of them, well in advance of the proof. They should be in a relatively final state and should only need limited amendment. It is worth explaining why that should be so, how you can do it, and the benefits to be gained from adopting this approach.

You should not be leading evidence or cross-examining at the proof to find out things about the case of which you did not have a good idea in the first place. You should have conducted the proof to prove, or disprove, various facts of which you should have been well aware. The record should have identified the agreed facts and the areas of dispute. Proper preparation should have enabled you to anticipate the areas of conflict. If there is evidence in the case which might come as a surprise to you, this should be minimal. You should intend to lead evidence to establish your version of the facts. If you prepare your submissions in advance of the proof on the assumption that you can establish those facts, you can make the evidence fit the submissions rather than making the submissions fit the evidence. Indeed, if you understand this connection between the submissions and the evidence, it will give you a focus for conducting the whole case effectively. You will see the importance (or otherwise) of particular pieces of evidence, the need for objection to some evidence, the need to challenge (or not) some evidence in cross-examination, the relationship and significance of the evidence of dif-

---

[5] I see no harm in enquiring at some later stage of the proof whether the sheriff intends to have the notes extended.

ferent witnesses on particular areas of fact. You will have planned the ending before anyone has even begun the beginning. You will know the "big picture" and how to ensure that the evidence will help you paint it. You will also know the areas of evidence in the case which are not so important, because you will know in advance what evidence is likely to emerge, how you are going to analyse and explain it and what you are going to say in your submissions about it. The process will make you focus on the evidence which is truly critical to your case.

Submissions after proof/proof before answer

Submissions at the end of a proof would have a different structure to **11–05** submissions at the end of a proof before answer. In a proof, neither party would have preliminary pleas. No questions of law would have to be considered at the conclusion of the proof. In essence, it is likely that there would be two different stories (or one story and a denial). The purpose of the proof would be for the pursuer to satisfy the sheriff on the balance of probabilities that they had established the facts necessary to prove their story and therefore prove their case against the defender. The defender might argue that the evidence was such that the pursuer had failed to prove the essential facts, or the defender might seek to establish by positive evidence that some other facts had been proved.

In a proof before answer, at least one party would have at least one preliminary plea. That plea would have been reserved on the basis that a question of law arising in the case probably could not be resolved until evidence had been led. The purpose of a proof before answer would be first, to establish by evidence that a particular state of facts did exist, and, secondly, to demonstrate by legal argument that the particular facts which had been established gave rise to a legal obligation on the part of the defender. The existence or otherwise of that legal obligation, and its precise nature and extent, may not be capable of being determined until the court heard evidence and decided on the balance of probabilities the precise facts which might or might not give rise to that obligation.

In a proof, the submissions would concentrate on the facts alone. In a proof before answer the submissions would normally deal with the facts and the law. In a proof before answer the facts may emerge in such a way that the legal obligation is obvious or not disputed.[6] Otherwise, when making submissions in a proof before answer, it would be necessary to make additional submissions designed to identify what the law is, explain in principle what facts would have to be established before any legal remedy could arise, and argue that the pursuer had proved (or not proved) those facts in that particular case.

Findings in fact

The whole purpose of leading evidence in any case is to enable you to **11–06** ask the court to make findings in fact.[7] It is extremely important that you understand what this means and its full significance. The sheriff is required by the Ordinary Cause Rules 1993,[8] to make findings in fact

---

[6] This can often happen.
[7] Though you may not realise it fully until you have a little experience.
[8] (Hereafter "OCR"), r.12.2(3).

and law after a proof in the type of cases we are considering. The sheriff has to issue an interlocutor following the proof which must start with findings in fact and law and he must append to the interlocutor a note with the reasons for his decision. The interlocutor (which includes the findings in fact and law) is what is called the operative part of the judgment of the sheriff, and it is critical to the success of your claim or defence that the sheriff makes findings in fact in your favour. The findings in fact of the sheriff is the detailed list of particular facts which the sheriff has decided have been proved after consideration of all of the evidence led before him. It will assist you enormously, in your proof and in your submissions, if you focus on the task of persuading the sheriff to make specific findings in fact that justify your case.[9]

Outline structure

11–07   I am now going to suggest an outline structure for submissions. I have in mind a proof before answer in our personal injury action for George Hamilton. Each case will vary. Some of these points will be unnecessary or inappropriate depending upon circumstances. It should be fairly obvious in any individual case what you might need to include and what can be omitted. When starting off it would be prudent to prepare to include everything.

1. Provide the sheriff with a list of authorities[10] (if any) to which you propose to refer him.[11]
2. Deal briefly with the onus and standard of proof.[12]
3. Address the sheriff on the findings in fact which you wish him to make in relation to the question of liability. Start with the areas of evidence which are non-contentious. These can usually be found in: admissions on record; a joint minute of admissions; concessions during the proof; and evidence which was not disputed/cross-examined in the proof.
4. Address the sheriff on the findings in fact which you want him to make in relation to the parts of the case in which the evidence was disputed or conflicted. Explain what you think you have proved, and exactly what finding(s) in fact you want him to make, before going on to discuss and analyse the evidence on these matters in detail.
5. Address the sheriff on any pieces of evidence to which objection was taken[13] and in which he reserved all questions of competency and relevancy.[14]
6. In relation to conflicts of evidence or sufficiency of evidence, address the sheriff on all of the evidence led about the

---

[9] For further discussion, see Macphail, *Sheriff Court Practice*, above, 17.04–17.07; see also *Sutherland v Glasgow Corp*, 1951 S.L.T. 185.

[10] And a photocopy of the authorities.

[11] You might need authorities on the question of liability and on legal issues relating to evidence, e.g. admissibility, weight, sufficiency, etc. This may or may not be necessary. You would almost certainly want to have authorities on the quantification of the claim.

[12] These issues rarely cause too much of a problem in the routine personal injury case.

[13] See para.10–19.

[14] This would be on the assumption that the objection was still being insisted upon by that stage.

important findings in fact that you wish him to make and persuade him to accept your evidence as sufficient, credible and reliable.

7. This may lead to, or be combined with, a detailed analysis of **11–08** the evidence given by all of the individual witnesses and detailed assessment of their credibility and reliability. It may also involve discussion and argument regarding the weight to be attached to different pieces of evidence.

8. Identify what you consider to be the crucial fact(s) relating to liability, concentrate on these and the evidence about these. If you want the sheriff to make a finding in fact about which no direct evidence was led but which is based upon an inference from other findings in fact, then explain this.

9. Once you have exhausted the facts you wish the sheriff to find proved, you could then go on to consider what the law is and whether the facts are sufficient to demonstrate, as a matter of law, that there has been negligence or a breach of statutory duty on the part of the defender.

10. An alternative approach might be to start with the law, identify what facts need to be proved to establish liability, and then proceed to consider if those particular facts have been proved, by analysing the evidence. It will depend upon the precise circumstances which order might work better in any individual case.

11. If there is a plea of contributory negligence, address the sheriff on the evidence relating to this, although it is sometimes appropriate to defer detailed submissions on this point until the defender has made their submissions.[15]

12. Having dealt with the facts and law relating to liability, go on to deal with the evidence about the quantification of the claim. This will involve a similar analysis of the individual witnesses and their evidence as above. It is helpful to have prepared a schedule of damages showing the heads of claim you are seeking, although that information should be in the pleadings. The schedule could outline the essential facts relating to each individual head of claim and could contain details of any authorities justifying particular awards. Evidence in support of these facts would have to be identified and any shortcomings or conflicts in evidence addressed.

13. Address the sheriff on interest on the damages sought in relation to each separate head of claim.

14. Conclude your submissions by directing the sheriff to the pleas in law for the parties. Each case will be different but generally you would move the sheriff to sustain one or more of your pleas in law as appropriate, and repel those of the defender as appropriate. You would then ask the court to grant decree in favour of your client for the sum of £X as set out in your submissions or your schedule.

---

[15] It may not be clear at this stage to what extent, and in what respect, the defender is going to argue contributory negligence.

Expenses

11–09   Practice differs, and there is no right or wrong way of doing it, but you should also deal with the issue of expenses at some stage of your submissions. You can do it as the final part of the above speech or later, after the opponent's speech, once the merits of the action have been fully canvassed. In some courts, and in some cases, the practice might be to reserve any question of expenses until the sheriff has issued his decision on the merits. A separate hearing on expenses would then be assigned in the interlocutor which contains the decision of the sheriff. If you want expenses—and you will always want expenses—you have to make a motion for expenses. I do not intend to dwell upon expenses unduly here but, suffice it to say that, the normal rule is that expenses would follow success. If you were making a motion for expenses before the decision on the merits, you might be able to indicate to the court that there were no specialities about expenses which would obviously prevent the operation of the normal rule. This might enable the sheriff to deal with expenses without a further hearing after his decision has been made. Some issues about expenses which might have to be borne in mind include: whether a party is legally aided; whether a tender had been made; certification of experts; certification of the cause as suitable for counsel; or the possibility of an additional fee. The sheriff will not know, and may not want to know, about some of these matters at the conclusion of the proof. The decision of the sheriff on the merits may make some of the issues redundant or unnecessary. For these reasons, it is usually preferred that all questions of expenses be reserved. In practical terms, of course, this means the additional delay and expense of another hearing. It can be avoided in a clear case where parties are aware that there are no reasons to depart from the normal rule and that expenses will not be contentious, and can advise the sheriff accordingly.

Example

11–10   I will now proceed to give you an outline of the "script" for the submissions in the case. I hope that you can see how it fits into the structure outlined above, and I hope you can appreciate how that structure might be capable of being transferred to other types of case and other circumstances. A little imagination is needed to deduce what might have happened in the proof which preceded these submissions.

Submissions

11–11   *"My Lord, I have passed to your Lordship's clerk a list of the authorities to which I propose to refer in the course of these submissions and copies of those authorities.*[16]

For the pursuer to succeed on liability in this case, it is necessary for the pursuer to establish, to the satisfaction of the court,[17] that his crucial averments about the circumstances and cause of the accident are true, that the defenders were [at fault/in breach of statute], and that the accident was caused by their fault.

---

[16] Or not.
[17] Civil Evidence (Scotland) Act 1988, s.1.

The onus is on the pursuer and the pursuer has to satisfy the court that, on the balance of probabilities, he has proved the essential elements of his case.[18]

The pursuer must establish the basic facts of the accident which he has averred. If the evidence heard and accepted does not satisfy the court of facts from which negligence can be demonstrated or from which an inference of negligence can be drawn, or if the evidence simply establishes facts which are equally consistent with negligence as with no negligence, then the pursuer has not proved his case.

I propose to address your Lordship first in relation to the facts which   **11–12**
do not seem to me to be disputed and I would invite your lordship to make findings in fact along these lines[19]*:*

1. *The pursuer is a 35-year-old heating engineer and resides at the address stated in the instance. [Not disputed.]*
2. *The defenders were the owners and occupiers of the Argyll Street Shopping Centre Glasgow on Saturday, July 23, 2004. [Admitted on record.]*
3. *The pursuer was in the centre, accompanied by John Wallace at around 14.15 on the above date. [Not disputed.]*
4. *Workmen from a company called MD Construction had been employed by the defenders to carry out refurbishment work. They had been working there for approximately three days prior to July 23, 2004. [Defenders' pleadings—Not disputed.]*
5. *The work primarily involved repairs to the roof and the company only worked between 19.00 and 06.00 so as not to interfere with the passage of shoppers during opening hours. [Not disputed]*
6. *To carry out repairs the company used, among other equipment, mobile scaffolding units on wheels. The scaffolding units would be placed on the surface of the walkway on the first floor level of the Centre. [Evidence of site agent of defender—Not disputed.]*
7. *The pursuer took the escalator to the first floor of the centre and started to walk along the walkway towards the shop known as Fine Gowns [Not disputed.]*
8. *The walkway and the shop are shown in the photographs (No. 5/2 of process, Nos. 1 to 8). [Admitted in joint minute.]*
9. *The floor of the walkway was made up of concrete tiles approximately 30 centimetres square. [Partially admitted and partially conceded at proof.]*
10. *At a point approximately 10 metres from the main entrance to the shop mentioned above, the pursuer fell and sustained an injury to his ankle [Not disputed that he fell somehow and he had an injury of some kind.]*

---

[18] *Hendry v Clan Line Steamers Ltd*, 1949 S.L.T. 280. Authorities for these basic propositions may be regarded as trite and unnecessary, but I recommend that you have them and know them anyway, especially when you are starting off.

[19] Actually handing up to the sheriff a written or typed list of these findings would be helpful but may not be practicable—although if you have prepared properly beforehand it should be manageable.

11–13   *It appears to me, my Lord, that the principal areas of dispute about the facts in this case relate to:*

1. *the precise mechanism of the pursuer's accident. In other words, did it have anything to do with the state of the flooring;*
2. *whether there was any defect in the flooring at the time of the accident;*
3. *what the nature of that defect was;*
4. *how it might have been caused;*
5. *when it might have been caused;*
6. *whether the defenders knew or should have known about it; and*
7. *when the defenders knew or should have known about it.[20]*

11–14   *Now, in relation to the mechanism of the pursuer's accident, we have the evidence of the pursuer himself. He is supported by his friend John Wallace. The pursuer was cross-examined by my friend as to whether he was telling the truth about the cause of his fall. He led evidence from the casualty doctor who dealt with the pursuer when he attended the Western Infirmary the next day and who had noted the pursuer saying 'I just went over on my ankle.' Your Lordship will find this in the records of the Western Infirmary which were lodged as productions by my friend (No. 6/4 of process, page 6). I will comment on that evidence shortly but, in the first instance, I ask your Lordship to accept the evidence of the pursuer and his witness as entirely credible and reliable in all material respects. Your Lordship had the opportunity of hearing the pursuer give evidence for some time and he was cross-examined very closely by my friend on this matter and indeed on many other aspects of the case. In my submission his evidence was given well and truthfully. He was measured in his responses. He did not try to exaggerate any matters or indulge in speculation to assist his position. Where he was unclear or undecided about matters of detail relating to . . . he said so, and although my friend might argue that this makes his evidence unreliable to some extent, in my submission this would actually give it some credence. It is some time since the accident and it is not the type of detail that one could reasonably be expected to remember.*

The pursuer's friend could be regarded as biased to some extent by virtue of that friendship but again I would submit there was nothing in his evidence or his demeanour which would indicate that this was a man coming into court to tell lies or tailor his evidence to suit his friend. He was frank about the fact he was not paying a great deal of attention but one very telling piece of real evidence is his recollection that he saw a piece of the tile lying at the side of the pursuer and out of its proper place after his fall. That is not the kind of thing someone can be mistaken about. Either he is telling the truth or telling a lie about this. In my submission he is plainly not lying. He was unable to say that he saw the precise mechanism of the pursuer's fall and if he was

---

[20] It is good advocacy to list, and to number, these points rather than just wandering your way through them, prefacing each point with, "And another matter which is important is".

intending to assist the pursuer's case he might have been expected to assist him more on this. My point is that if part of a tile was indeed out of place at the very moment of the accident this makes it more likely on the balance of probabilities that the accident involved some contact between the pursuer's foot and the tile . . .

Turning to the evidence from the casualty doctor, Mr X, of course he **11–15** *was, not surprisingly, unable to recall the details of Mr Hamilton's attendance at the hospital on the next day after the accident. He sees hundreds of patients and there was by his own admission nothing special about this case. It would have been a matter of routine for him and he agreed with my suggestion that the precise mechanism of the accident would not have been of any significance from a medical point of view. A fracture is a fracture and would be dealt with accordingly. He also agreed that the type of fracture involved in this case was not inconsistent with the mechanism described by the pursuer. He accepted that he may have noted the history wrongly or imprecisely and indeed if one looks at the exact words used, one can suggest that 'I just went over on my ankle' does not exclude the explanation of the pursuer catching his foot on the defective flooring and then 'just going over' on his ankle. Indeed, the pursuer himself described the accident in rather imprecise, everyday, terms in his evidence in chief and was only persuaded to be more precise about it on cross-examination by my friend. Even if he did say to the doctor (although he doubts it) that he had gone over on his ankle he was not doing so as a precise analysis of the injury but as a casual and colloquial term which would have been more than adequate for the purpose at the time.*

Accordingly, I would ask your Lordship to hold that it has been proved to your satisfaction that the pursuer's fall occurred because he had tripped on . . . and to make a finding in fact to that effect.

With regard to the second contentious issue identified above . . . [Deal with the other contentious issues in the same way.]

Accordingly, I would invite your Lordship to make findings in fact to **11–16** *the effect that:*

- *The pursuer tripped on the defective flooring.*
- *The flooring was defective on the day of the accident because it had . . .*
- *The defect was a result of the activities of the workmen employed by the contractors to repair the roof.*
- *The likeliest cause was the pressure of one of the wheels of the scaffolding directly onto the tile.*
- *This was caused at least eight hours before the accident.*
- *The defenders employ staff to inspect, inter alia, the state of the flooring on that walkway at regular intervals of every four hours.*
- *The employees of the defenders inspected (or should have inspected) the flooring at about 09.00 that morning and again at about 13.00.*
- *They did not inspect (or, having inspected, did not note the defect in) the flooring which caused the pursuer's accident.*

In my submission, and on the basis of the above findings in fact, the **11–17** *accident was caused by the fault of the defenders. It is a matter of admission that they were the occupiers of the premises on the material* *date and it is clear from the evidence that they employed staff to see that members of the public had a safe passage through the premises. There is a duty on occupiers of premises, such as the defenders, to take reasonable care for members of the public such as the pursuer using the premises. I would refer your Lordship to [legal authorities to support your legal propositions, including, if possible a similar case].*[21]

It is part of the defence that the accident was caused or materially contributed to by the fault of the pursuer. It is said that the pursuer had a duty to take reasonable care for his own safety and had a duty to keep a proper look out. I accept that these general duties would apply to the pursuer in the circumstances (or not) but in my submission he did comply with them. He told us that . . . [review the evidence on this]. In any event, even if the pursuer had done . . . In my submission that would not have prevented the accident happening [explain why] and accordingly I would ask your Lordship to make no finding of contributory negligence at all. If your Lordship is against me on that and considers it appropriate to make some finding, in my submission the degree of contributory negligence should be no greater than 25 per cent [explain why, with authority if suitable].

I now propose to go on and address your Lordship in relation to the quantification of this claim. I have prepared and now submit to your Lordship, with a copy to my friend,[22] *a schedule of the damages sought by the pursuer . . ."*

Here is a simple schedule. The use of such a document itself is by no means obligatory but you can convert its contents into oral submissions quite easily.

11–18

SCHEDULE OF DAMAGES

GEORGE HAMILTON

AGAINST

ARGYLL PROPERTIES PLC

INJURIES

Pain, suffering, and loss of faculties.
Shock—initial accident—pain.
Bruising to face, burst lip, teeth.
Extensive grazing to legs, face and arm.

---

[21] In the imaginary circumstances the law is quite clear and not complex. If you can establish these facts, there is unlikely to be any real dispute about the legal consequences. In many cases, the arguments about legal liability (whatever the facts) could occupy the major part of the submissions, but, for the sake of brevity I will not illustrate this here. Reference can be made to Ch.6 because this part of the submissions could, in effect, be a debate.

[22] Although there may be no reason why you should not have given your opponent a copy before the proof—after all, he might have been able to consider it and agree it or some of it. Reducing areas of contention is always worth exploring.

Fractured ankle.
Attendance at hospital.
Disturbance of sleep.
Off work nine months.
Continuing pain discomfort and loss of function.
Continued problems.
Possibility of further operation.
Risk of developing osteoarthritis.

Fractured ankle
X v Y, 1998 S.L.T. 000 (£9,750)—with inflation now £10,005)
A v B Ltd, 1995 S.L.T. 000 (£10,700)—now £X
I v C, 1994 S.L.T. 000 (£3,000—soft tissue only)—now £X

Judicial Studies Board Guidelines—Seventh Edition
Chapter X

SOLATIUM   £C
Interest on past solatium (£X) @ 4 per cent
From April 26, 2004 to 2006 (2 years
11 months) =   £X

PAST LOSS OF EARNINGS
Off work nine months.
Average net earnings pre accident £A per week
Less paid by employers—£Z   £Z
Interest on past loss of earnings from A to B
@ 4 per cent   £A

FUTURE LOSS OF EARNINGS
Disadvantage on the labour market (?)   £M
A v B, 1999 S.L.T. 000

SERVICES
Inclusive of interest   £N

TOTAL   £D[23]

"So, to conclude, my Lord, I am moving your Lordship to sustain the pleas in law for the pursuer numbers 1, 2, and 4, which your Lordship will find on page 12 of the record. I am asking your Lordship to repel the pleas in law for the defenders numbers 1, 2, 3, and 4, on page 13. I move your Lordship for decree in favour of the pursuer for the sum of £X, as brought out in my schedule [or otherwise]. Unless there are any other matters on which I can assist your Lordship, those are my submissions for the pursuer."

---

[23] *N.B.* There may well be significant areas of contention in the schedule both in relation to the precise facts that you have established relating to the losses and also to the proper legal basis upon which any of the heads of claim should be calculated. While that may be so, many sheriffs, quite understandably like these matters to be agreed where possible and would be particularly grateful if you do the arithmetic for them.

Devil's advocate

11–19   It should be possible to adapt this outline submission for a defender in a similar case because the defender would be obliged to cover the same areas with the important difference that the defender usually does not have to prove anything. In such a case, the defender's submissions will often concentrate upon what the pursuer has not proved but the same structure and analysis could be followed for that purpose. By the time the defender comes to respond, the sheriff may have already given various clues[24] as to what he is thinking, what he considers important, or what he thinks of various witnesses. That might assist you to focus upon what the sheriff is finding to be critical and it might cause you to change your script and adapt your submissions. That is, of course, easier to do if you have a script to change. If you think the sheriff has reached a provisional view which is adverse to you, about a matter which you consider important then you will really have to work hard to persuade him otherwise. Do remember, however, that it is perfectly possible that the sheriff will play devil's advocate with both sides and emphasise the weaknesses or problems in both of their submissions in order to test the arguments they are advancing. I can recall the first time I was aware of this technique when I sat smugly listening to my opponent being slated to the extent that I was not sure if it was going to be necessary for me to say anything. When it came to my turn, the sheriff took me completely by surprise by being just as critical of our case. I hasten to say that this was done with complete fairness and courtesy to both sides, but it certainly teaches you to remain on your toes until the very end and to think very carefully about every word you say in the course of your submissions. Any careless or illogical submission could be turned around by an inquisitive sheriff to demonstrate the weakness of your argument rather than its strength. One way to head this off is to play devil's advocate with yourself and subject your own submissions to a critical analysis before you say a word. Bear in mind that, even if you disagree with your opponent's argument, plainly your opponent thinks it has some merit. Can you see why? Can you understand how they might think so? Can you see how they might criticise your case? If you are unable and unwilling to contemplate any contrary argument you may put yourself at a disadvantage when being required to justify your position. If you prepare properly, you will already know your opponent's possible strengths and your possible weaknesses.

Concise submissions

11–20   Many people might regard the script above as a rather elaborate and unnecessarily complex method of doing submissions, but the intention is to give an idea of all of the elements of a structure which can be adapted as suitable to individual cases. As a brief illustration of how you may be able to cut through some of the detail, consider the kitchen case and submissions for the defenders after that proof. By the time the defenders are about to make their speech, the pursuer has already made submis-

---

[24] Subtly or otherwise.

sions at length. You may see how their arguments were received. It might be advisable and effective just to jump straight in.

Submissions

> *"My Lord, it is fairly clear from the evidence we have heard and from* **11–21**
> *my friend's submissions, that there are only two significant areas of*
> *dispute, namely what was the contract price and whether the purser*
> *was in material breach of contract. I simply propose to confine my*
> *address to your Lordship to these issues.*
>
> *First, we have to look at the evidence of how the contract was*
> *constituted. We can see from the pleadings that the pursuer is relying*
> *upon the terms of . . . That was the evidence too. So they say that this*
> *is what the parties had agreed and this is the only evidence of the*
> *precise terms of the contract.*
>
> *We say in the pleadings that the parties actually agreed that there*
> *should be a discount and that there was a discount. That is what Mrs*
> *Gray said in evidence. This simply comes down to a conflict of*
> *evidence between (say) Mrs Gray and Mrs Stewart about . . . I am*
> *going to ask your Lordship to prefer Mrs Gray's evidence on this point*
> *for three reasons which I shall set out shortly, and if your Lordship is*
> *with me on this, then that will take care of the first point . . . [Discuss*
> *and analyse their evidence.]".*

That might be perfectly sufficient for the purposes of that case. It may have become apparent to everyone that it was (or at least that point was) all down to one word against another. There might be a benefit in going straight in to address that point because there are no subtleties or complexities of evidence, fact or law, which have to be taken into account. It is fair to say, however, that you may have to be particularly confident, experienced, or lucky to launch right into this without any preamble and know that you have hit the right nail on the head. Like many other advocacy skills, you can always take a short cut, but if you only know how to take short cuts you can run the risk of misunderstanding the terrain, confusing the sheriff, and finding yourself lost. It is better to have studied and understood the full topography first.

Written submissions

It is likely that requests from the Bench for written submissions will **11–22** increase, and the practice of providing them will extend over the next few years. Such submissions are generally very helpful to everyone involved in the case.[25] There is nothing to prevent you volunteering written submissions even if not asked and I am sure that such submissions would never be refused. Everyone has a different way of doing written submissions after a proof and it is difficult to determine what works best. Perhaps one of the benefits of the structured approach discussed above is that it would provide a good framework for written submissions. The preparation of written submissions does take quite

---

[25] Apart from the apocryphal advocate who could not do them because "I have absolutely no idea of what I am going to say before I stand up"—a skill indeed.

some time and considerable thought.[26] Drawbacks are that you do not know in advance what your opponent is going to say, nor what the sheriff really wants to hear about, so written submissions may have to deal with everything which might conceivably be important. It can also be disconcerting to think that you might omit completely from your submissions a point which the sheriff thinks is important and in your favour.[27] Perhaps the fact that you did not bother to mention it might give the sheriff second thoughts about its significance.

One way to avoid this might be to do the written submissions as no more than a broad outline, with headings only, of issues you are going to elaborate upon in your oral submissions. You can use the outline to sketch out the framework—as discussed here—and you can use it to list matters (for example non-contentious findings in fact) which do not need to be discussed. You can also use it in a case in which the shorthand notes have been extended to direct the sheriff to particular passages of evidence by page number. If you list the headings clearly it can ease note-taking for the sheriff.

11–23   You might want to think first about how you want to present the oral argument to the sheriff. Think about keeping it concise and following a structure. Do headings for the structure and do the submissions in a shortened or note form, so that you can elaborate on particular matters if you wish or if required by the sheriff. Remember that the sheriff may still want, or need, to take notes of what you are saying so the written submissions do not need to be comprehensive. In this connection, one good tip I received recently was to leave plenty of space between the written text of your submissions so that the sheriff can note directly onto them and add, at the appropriate place, any observation or comment that he wishes to make as a result of your oral submissions on the point. It can be confusing and unhelpful for the sheriff to be unsure as to whether he needs to note what you are saying or can rely upon the terms of your written note alone. The sheriff can then find himself with your submissions and his notes of what you said with some inexplicable lack of connection between the two. As the whole object of the submissions, however presented, is to make the sheriff's life easier and persuade him to find in your favour, anything that might confuse him should be avoided. Anything which will make his task easier is to be commended. There is no reason to prevent you doing written submissions on one part of the case only—for good reason. Presenting the sheriff with proposed findings in fact (and nothing else in writing) can be very useful. In my experience, this is being done much more frequently now, and often to good effect.

---

[26] Not that oral submissions do not, but you do not have the flexibility which oral advocacy allows.

[27] In oral advocacy you could have said, "Exactly my Lord, I was just coming to that".

CHAPTER 12

APPEALS

"Old lawyers never die, they simply lose their appeal."

Occasionally you may find that despite following the guidance in this **12–01** book and despite your best efforts, you will lose a case, lose an argument or have a motion refused. There is a temptation, to think, on these occasions, that life is terribly unfair, followed by a concern that this simply demonstrates that you are a useless lawyer whose abilities and powers of persuasion are simply not up to the task. There can be few more depressing feelings than those you experience when a judgment lands on your desk and you find that you have lost. Of course, there are some cases you might suspect that you have lost, for good reason or bad, but in other cases an adverse outcome can be quite deflating. It is difficult to resist the temptation that you must immediately appeal against such an aberration and put matters right. However, the first thing you really ought to do is sit down and read the judgment carefully and objectively more than once. You must take some time to consider an adverse finding against your client before turning your mind to the question of an appeal.

Appeals can be taken against a number of different types of decision. The presentation of appeals can vary quite considerably depending upon the type of decision under attack and the circumstances of each case. I am going to concentrate on appeals to the sheriff principal against decisions by a sheriff and I am going to discuss in detail the practice and procedure for appeals in an ordinary action only. I will suggest a basic structure for presentation of an appeal which can be adapted and developed in particular circumstances. I will be looking at the presentation of an appeal primarily from the appellant's perspective but I think it should be fairly easy to see how the presentational aspects of the appeal can be adapted to fit the respondent's perspective. I will deal briefly with the procedure for appeals in a summary cause action at the end of the chapter. Similar principles apply to the presentation of such appeals, although they are confined to questions of law only.

This chapter will deal specifically with whether you ought to appeal, whether you can appeal, when you should appeal, how you should prepare for an appeal and how you would present an appeal.

Should your client appeal?

You cannot appeal simply because you do not like the sheriff's **12–02** decision and you would like another judge to look at the whole case again. This is trite but it is worth saying. When the adverse judgment comes in you will have to send it out to the client. You will have to advise the client either in a letter or at a meeting what rights of appeal exist, and whether you have any views or advice about the prospects of an appeal. Most clients will not appreciate that you cannot just appeal because you are unhappy with the result. Many of them will be under the impression than an appeal is some kind of rehearing of the whole case by a different judge. It is not the client's fault if they are under that misapprehension but it is important to make it clear to your client exactly what an appeal entails.

For reasons which will be explained, you may not have a great deal of time in which to take instructions regarding an appeal. A decision may have to be taken fairly quickly. It is prudent to advise the client about time-scales so that there is no delay in the client giving instructions and they are under no illusions about the cut-off date for appealing. In a case where a judgment has been issued after proof you would want to check particularly if the interlocutor deals with the question of expenses. If it does, then it is likely to be a final judgment, and you have 14 days from the date of the interlocutor to mark an appeal. In practice, there can be delays in receipt of the interlocutor, and delays in reading and assimilating the interlocutor which can mean that by the time you are writing to the client about it you may have very little time left to mark an appeal. If there is any doubt on the part of the client as to whether an appeal should be marked, or if you are unable to obtain clear instructions in time, then the prudent course would be to mark an appeal.[1] If, on the other hand, the interlocutor does not deal with expenses and fixes a date for a hearing on expenses (which is often the case) the 14-day period will not run until that date at the earliest. In practice, this is likely to give you a few weeks to consider the position before any decision has to be taken as to whether to appeal or not.

Can you competently appeal?

12–03   This is a question which, in my experience, can often cause difficulty. Although I am not aware of any statistics on the point, I suspect that a significant number of appeals are dismissed on grounds of incompetency. The relevant provisions applicable to ordinary actions are contained in s.27 of the Sheriff Courts (Scotland) Act 1907, and it is worth repeating them here. An appeal to the sheriff principal shall be competent against "all final Judgements of the Sheriff".[2] An appeal is also competent against interlocutors:

> "(a) granting or refusing interdict interim or final;
> (b) granting interim decree for payment of money other than a decree for expenses, or making an order *ad factum praestandum*;
> (c) sisting an action;
> (d) allowing or refusing or limiting the mode of proof;

---

[1] Assuming that there is at least some ground for doing so.
[2] Whether something is a final judgment or not has to be considered carefully. For details reference should be made to Macphail, *Sheriff Court Practice* (3rd edn, W. Green/Scottish Universities Law Institute, 2006), paras 18.33–18.35.

(e) refusing a reponing note; or
(f) against which the Sheriff . . . either *ex proprio motu* or on the motion of any party grants leave to appeal."[3]

It is worth reflecting carefully on each of these individual headings and on the nature of the interlocutor under consideration for the very good practical reason that, if the interlocutor is not a final judgment and if it is not one which would be covered by paragraphs (a) to (e) above, it will be necessary to obtain leave to appeal before any appeal would be competent.

Leave to appeal

If leave to appeal is necessary then this must be obtained from the **12–04** sheriff who made the decision within seven days of the date of the interlocutor against which leave is sought.[4] The types of decision against which leave might be required usually relate to the grant or refusal of some incidental procedural motion. It is open to the aggrieved party to seek leave to appeal in court at the Bar immediately after such a decision has been made. In some circumstances there could be doubt as to whether leave is required. It is preferable to check in advance whether leave might be required in the event of an adverse decision but, if in doubt, there is little harm in seeking leave to appeal at that stage. You may have to be prepared to justify to the sheriff the possibility, at least, that leave is needed. If leave is not sought at the time of the decision itself, then it is open to the aggrieved party to lodge a written motion for leave to appeal. As long as the motion is lodged within seven days of the interlocutor appealed against, it does not matter if the hearing on, and decision about, the motion for leave to appeal occurs outwith the seven days.

If the aggrieved party wants to apply for leave to appeal outwith the seven-day period, a written motion for leave should also contain a motion for relief in terms of rule 2.1 of the Ordinary Cause Rules 1993.[5] It will be appreciated, therefore, that at any hearing of the motion the party will first of all have to justify the delay in lodging the motion in accordance with rule 2.1. The party will then have to go on and argue that leave should be granted. This can present quite formidable obstacles and it is preferable, for a variety of reasons, for a motion for leave to appeal to be made immediately after the decision is given.

If you are making such a motion, it is helpful to indicate what the grounds of the proposed appeal might be, although that might be fairly obvious from the submissions that you have previously made on the matter. The granting or refusing of leave is a discretionary decision of the sheriff and the principles upon which leave might be granted or refused are discussed fully in Macphail.[6] It has been argued that it is a breach of human rights for a sheriff who refused a motion to be the

---

[3] Sheriff Courts (Scotland) Act 1907, s.27.
[4] Ordinary Cause Rules 1993, r.31.2.(1).
[5] Hereafter "OCR".
[6] *Sheriff Court Practice*, above, paras 18.50–18.52.

same sheriff who decides whether a party should be given leave to appeal against that refusal.[7] Having said that, you may find it somewhat uncomfortable to be asking for leave to appeal immediately after the sheriff's decision. In some circumstances, it might appear as little more than a knee-jerk reaction to a decision which has gone against you, as opposed to a careful conclusion reached about the prospects of a successful appeal. It might be prudent to take some time for consideration before seeking leave, but on the other hand, lodging a written motion later will lead to some delay and expense which would have been avoided if the motion had simply been made at the Bar. If leave is granted then it is important to bear in mind that any appeal must be marked within seven days after the date when leave was granted.[8] If that is not done, then the appeal is incompetent even though leave had been granted.[9]

Time-limits for appeal

12–05   Any interlocutor which may be appealed against should be appealed within 14 days after it is dated. It is worth emphasising that it is the interlocutor that is appealed against. It is important to appreciate that it is the interlocutor (as opposed to the note, or comments or observations made by the sheriff during the hearing of the case which gave rise to the proposed appeal) which is the prime target for the appeal. It is obvious, therefore, that, especially in decisions about procedural matters, you must satisfy yourself about exactly what the interlocutor says. You do need to consider carefully what the note says, but it is the interlocutor which you are seeking to change in the appeal. In cases where there is a "final Judgment" as mentioned above, the 14 days runs from the date when the whole action was disposed of. This usually means the date of the interlocutor dealing with expenses. It is possible to appeal out of time, although obviously not recommended. At the same time as the appeal is marked, the party should lodge a written motion applying to the sheriff principal for leave to appeal out of time and for relief in terms of rule 2.1. It should be noted that such a motion is made to the sheriff principal and not to the sheriff who made the decision appealed against. There would have to be a hearing on that motion before the appeal could be allowed to proceed. The failure to comply with the time-limit would have to be justified on the well-known grounds contained within rule 2.1. If there was some doubt or uncertainty as to whether the client wanted to appeal, it would be prudent and preferable to mark the appeal in time and then abandon it if necessary rather than delay the marking of an appeal. A delay in these circumstances may not be regarded as justifying the provision of relief.

Appeals to the Court of Session

12–06   Although I do not intend to deal with this here, I think it is desirable to point out at this stage that there are quite significant differences of

---

[7] It has been authoritatively held that there was no breach of the Convention by the same judge deciding both the substantive issue and the issue of permission to appeal: *Umair v Umair*, 2002 S.L.T. 172 . Indeed, it could be suggested that no other judge would be in a better position to decide the question of leave to appeal than the judge who has just heard the arguments in the substantive issue.

[8] OCR, r.33.2.(2).

[9] Although you can mark the appeal out of time and seek relief for this failure.

procedure and practice in relation to appeals direct from the sheriff to the Court of Session. The rules governing these appeals and the procedure and practice in these appeals can be rather complex and confusing. I think it is sensible to make clear that none of what has been said above regarding competency, leave to appeal, and time-limits should be assumed to apply for a proposed appeal to the Court of Session. You are warned.

Marking an appeal

The provisions about marking an appeal to the sheriff principal are **12–07** contained in rule 31.4 of the OCR. The appellant lodges a note of appeal in Form A1. Reference should be made to that form, the outline of which is very basic indeed. A copy of the note of appeal should be sent to every other party. It is important to appreciate that, where the sheriff has not provided a note along with the interlocutor appealed against, then the appellant should request that the sheriff write a note setting out the reasons for his decision. Obviously, this would not be required for an appeal against a judgment following a proof but it may well be required in appeals against judgment dealing with procedural issues and the like. Sometimes, the terms of the note will influence the insistence upon the appeal or lead to the fairly prompt abandonment of it. The form of note of appeal should be dated, but the operative date for deciding whether it complies with time-limits is the date when it is lodged with the sheriff clerk. This means that it is not particularly advisable to post it, especially where time is running out. It has been · observed that the form does not require the appellant to state the date of any interlocutor, or interlocutors, appealed against although this is something which could prudently be dealt with in a brief preamble to the grounds of appeal in the note of appeal.

Grounds of appeal

The Ordinary Cause Rules 1993 require that the grounds of appeal **12–08** shall consist of "brief, specific, numbered propositions stating the grounds on which it is proposed to submit that the Appeal should be allowed". Essentially, what you are obliged to do in the grounds of appeal is to give an outline of the argument, or arguments, which you are proposing to advance at the appeal. There is little guidance available to illustrate the wording of grounds of appeal,[10] but considerable assistance can be obtained from considering decided cases.[11] Although the cases referred to all relate to appeals to the Court of Session, the general approach to the content of grounds of appeal would apply to the sheriff court.

"[T]he preparation of the grounds of appeal, which require to be lodged as a step in process, should never be regarded as a mere

---

[10] But see *Greens Litigation Styles*, para.F04–01.
[11] *McAdam v Shell UK Ltd*, 1991 S.L.T. 881; *City of Glasgow DC v Secretary of State for Scotland (No. 1)*, 1993 S.L.T. 198; *Clark v Chief Constable of Lothian and Borders, 1993 G.W.D. 11-759; Eurocopy Rentals Ltd v Tayside Health Board*, 1996 S.L.T. 1322; *Ferguson v Whitbread & Co Plc*, 1996 S.L.T. 659.

formality. The purpose of the rule, which is a simple example of case management, is to give notice to the parties and to the court of the points which are to be argued. Specification of the grounds enables the parties to direct their argument, and their preparation for it, to the points which are truly at issue."[12]

The Rules provide that the grounds of appeal should be numbered, so that if you have more than one argument in support of your appeal you will number the arguments separately. The interpretation of "brief" and "specific" is perhaps no more than a matter of opinion but it is obviously worth reflecting on the fact that the grounds of appeal are intended to give the sheriff principal a reasonable indication and outline of the matters to which the appeal is going to be directed. This means that, by the time of marking of the appeal, you will have to have given reasonably detailed consideration to what you would be proposing to say at the appeal. Although the Rules provide that the grounds of appeal can be amended up to 14 days before the hearing of the appeal,[13] it is advisable to start with good grounds of appeal.[14]

12–09   The exercise of drafting grounds of appeal is not easy but it can make life easier for you in the long run. Let me just start with a broad outline. You might want to consider, first, whether you think the sheriff has made a mistake in law or whether he has made a mistake in fact, or indeed whether there is a combination of errors of fact and law. In an appeal from any interlocutor which does not follow a proof then your argument must be that the sheriff has erred in law, or that he has erred in the exercise of his discretion. This would apply, for example, to an appeal against the dismissal of an action following upon a debate. It would also apply, for example, to a refusal to allow a minute of amendment.[15] You should bear in mind that in appeals against procedural interlocutors, and indeed in some other interlocutors, the sheriff may be exercising a discretion in reaching a decision and you may have to think about grounds upon which an appeal court would be entitled to interfere with the exercise of such a discretion.

In some cases a decree may have been granted as a result of some procedural default, for example, a failure to lodge defences on time. The sheriff has a discretion to grant decree by default. An appeal against that would have to recognise the difficulty that an appellant has placed themselves in by being in default in the first place. In those circumstances, the grounds of appeal would almost certainly have to be accompanied by the lodging of the defences together with the lodging of a motion seeking relief under rule 2.1 of the OCR and a prorogation of the time for lodging of defences.

Grounds of appeal after proof

12–10   In an appeal against an interlocutor following proof attention should be directed first to the findings in fact in the interlocutor itself. What are

---

[12] *Ferguson*, above.

[13] And even within 14 days of the hearing if the sheriff principal allows it: OCR, r.31.4.(5) and (7).

[14] See *Smith v International Development Co (Aberdeen) Ltd*, Sheriff Principal Sir Stephen Young, May 26, 2006, unreported, in which he expressed the view that the party litigant had not actually set out any grounds of appeal and dismissed the appeal.

[15] For which leave to appeal would have been required.

the critical findings in fact with which you disagree (if any)? Why do you think the sheriff should not have made those findings in fact? Alternatively, or additionally, why should the sheriff have made a different finding in fact, or indeed no finding in fact, on a particular topic? This will lead you on to consider questions relating to the sufficiency of evidence and will also involve consideration of the law regarding the extent to which an appeal court can interfere with findings in fact made by a judge at first instance.

Appealing against findings in fact

It is beyond the scope of this book to analyse the relevant legal **12–11** principles in detail, but it is essential for anyone dealing with an appeal following proof and wishing to attack findings in fact to read and understand the undernoted cases.[16] It is not easy to understand the subtle distinctions which can be drawn in different cases between the circumstances which would entitle an appeal court to interfere with such findings and those which would not. Each case has to be looked at in detail. Although the general principles upon which the court is required to consider such matters are well accepted, it can be seen in recent cases that there have been quite stark differences between the Inner House of the Court of Session and the House of Lords on the application of these principles to the facts of individual cases, which only serves to underline the care which has to be taken in trying to prepare an appeal against the findings in fact of a sheriff.

As an illustration of some of the arguments which can be made **12–12** regarding appeals against findings in fact and the approach of appeal courts to these points, I think it is helpful to give a small selection of extracts from some of the relevant decisions:

Hamilton v Allied Domecq

"This court was entitled to interfere with that finding only if it were **12–13** demonstrated that the Lord Ordinary had, in his assessment and evaluation and in the context of the manner in which the proof had been conducted, plainly gone wrong . . .

In approaching the task before this court I am acutely conscious of the constraints to which, on matters of fact, it is, as an appellate court, subject. These constraints are well known and have recently been re-emphasised in a number of judgments of the House of Lords. But the existence of these constraints does not absolve this court from its obligation as a court of appeal on matters of fact to reconsider the evidence led before the Lord Ordinary and to determine upon such reconsideration whether critical findings of fact, both primary and secondary, made by the Lord Ordinary were justified. In undertaking that reconsideration it is always necessary

---

[16] *Thomas v Thomas*, 1947 S.C. (HL) 45; 1948 S.L.T. 2; *Caledonia North Sea Ltd v London Bridge Engineering Ltd*, 2000 S.L.T. 1123; *Piglowska v Piglowski* [1999] 1 W.L.R. 1360; [1999] 3 All E.R. 632; *Simmons v British Steel Plc* [2004] UKHL 20; 2004 S.C. (HL) 94; 2004 S.L.T. 595; *Thomson v Kvaerner Govan Ltd* [2003] UKHL 45; 2004 S.C. (HL) 1; 2004 S.L.T. 24; *Hamilton v Allied Domecq*, 2005 S.L.T. 1151; *T v T*, 2000 S.L.T. 1442.

for the appellate court to bear in mind the advantages, identified in the authorities, which a judge of first instance enjoys and which an appellate court does not. These include the opportunity to form, from the manner in which a witness gives his or her evidence before that judge, an impression as to the reliability or otherwise of the evidence given by the witness. That impression is likely also to be informed by the manner in which other witnesses, whether contradictory or confirmatory, give their evidence on the same or related matters. The personality of a witness may also have a bearing on the credibility or reliability of his or her testimony on particular matters; that cannot be assessed from the printed page. The way in which the case is conducted by legal representatives in the court of first instance (including the absence of challenge to the admission of particular evidence or to its truth or accuracy) may also legitimately affect the approach adopted by the court to the assessment of evidence. Moreover, in so far as concerns the evaluative exercise of drawing, or declining to draw, factual inferences from primary facts, an appellate court should exercise due caution before reversing such an evaluation . . .

On the other hand, when, on examination by the appellate court of the printed evidence, it is plain that it could not constitute a proper basis for some primary finding of fact made by the judge of first instance, the appellate court has a power and a duty to reverse that finding. If findings of fact are unsupported by the evidence and are critical to the decision of the case, it may be incumbent on the appellate court to reverse the decision made at first instance."

T v T

12–14   "The sheriff misdirected himself in a fundamental fashion by approaching the evidence on the basis that it would not be surprising if . . .

This serious flaw affects the whole of the judgment and is the background against which the other criticisms must be considered. Very importantly, the sheriff failed to assess the credibility and reliability of any of the witnesses in the case, except Mr S . . . In particular he made no assessment of the credibility and reliability of the pursuer, his mother and the defender. By inference the sheriff rejected the pursuer as a liar and also rejected his mother's considered evidence, without giving any indication of why he did so. He wrongly thought that the pursuer's expert witness, Dr L . . . had prepared a report and then discounted that non-existent report. In doing so, he preferred the evidence of the defender's expert, Dr B . . . without explaining why he did so or how he resolved the points upon which the two experts had joined issue in the evidence."

Lamarra v Capital Bank Plc[17]

12–15   "The function of an appellate court will usually be to scrutinise the approach of the court below to determine whether the law has been

---

[17] 2005 S.L.T. (Sh. Ct) 21.

interpreted and applied correctly. If it has, the appellate court will be unlikely to interfere with the decision of the court below in so far as it reached its decision on the facts. The exercise of that court's discretion will be interfered with if it was plainly wrong or unjust, if material considerations have been overlooked or irrelevant considerations taken into account or if the evidence has been misunderstood. The reason for the reluctance of appeal courts to interfere in other circumstances is that the judge at first instance has had the advantage of seeing and hearing the witnesses. That judge is best able to assess which evidence to prefer on contentious issues and what weight to attach to different factors when balancing the matters relevant to the decisions which that court is required to take. No amount of reading a transcript of the evidence can put an appeal court in the same position."

One final point to note, in the context of appealing against findings in fact is that even if you argue successfully that a sheriff has misdirected himself in making a factual finding or findings, that does not automatically mean that the appeal must be allowed. If you can satisfy a court that the sheriff has misdirected himself thus, that simply means that it is open to the appeal court to consider all of the evidence in the case afresh and reach its own view on the evidence as a whole. Accordingly, the appeal court could criticise the approach of the sheriff to the evidence but still reach the same decision on the merits of the case. When thinking about your grounds of appeal, it is necessary to bear this in mind.

Reverting back to the general considerations you should have before you when thinking about grounds of appeal, you may consider that, in conjunction with an error or errors in findings in fact, the sheriff has erred in law. It may be your position that if the findings in fact were different, or even slightly different, this would have an effect upon the law which would be applicable to the case.

Finally, you might take the view that you have no complaints about **12–16** the findings in fact made by the sheriff and your appeal is simply confined to a question, or questions, of law as to whether the sheriff was entitled, as a matter of law, to reach his decision on the basis of those undisputed facts. Even if you are challenging the findings in fact you may consider that if that challenge is unsuccessful, you would still have an argument on the law to be applied to the existing facts. Ideally, your grounds of appeal should incorporate any and all of these propositions which might arise in your case.

This is intended as no more than a rough generalisation as to how you might approach the drafting of grounds of appeal in a variety of circumstances. The detail into which you may go in drafting the written grounds of appeal is a matter for you, but remember that if you have not given notice in your grounds of appeal of all of the propositions which you are intending to argue at the appeal then additional arguments may not be allowed. The grounds of appeal are, if you like, your record for the appeal and the court and your opponent could legitimately confine you to that record. You can, of course, amend your grounds of appeal as has been noted above. If additional matters occur to you after the original grounds of appeal are lodged then it is prudent to intimate these as quickly as possible. You have until 14 days before the hearing to amend your grounds of appeal and it is not unreasonable to suppose that, by that time, you will have reached a final decision as to what arguments you will run or not. In the event that the imminence of the appeal focuses your mind even further and you do not wish to insist upon certain grounds of appeal you should make that clear to the sheriff principal, at the very latest, in your submissions at the outset of the appeal.

With the qualification that this is not intended as a style, here is an example of a note of appeal following proof:

> "*The defender appeals to the sheriff principal on the following grounds:*
>
> *By interlocutor of January 23, 2006 the learned sheriff granted decree against the defender to make a payment of damages of £10,000 together with expenses to the pursuer. This interlocutor is appealed on the basis that:*
>
> 1. *The learned sheriff has erred in fact by:*
>
>   (a) *Giving no reasons for preferring the evidence of X to the evidence of Y in relation to the critical question of Z.*
>
>   (b) *By expressing no view on the credibility and reliability of the evidence of the pursuer and his witnesses and the evidence of the defender's witnesses.*
>
>   (c) *By failing to take into account and attach proper weight to the inconsistency in the evidence of the pursuer and his witnesses in relation to Z . . .*
>
>   (d) *By failing to deal satisfactorily with the evidence of the engineers for the pursuer and the defender, giving no satisfactory reasons for preferring the evidence of the pursuer's engineer to the evidence of the defender's engineer and by failing to appreciate the significance of the evidence of the engineers in relation to his assessment of the critical facts.*
>
>   *And consequently ought not to have found it proved on balance of probabilities that . . .*
>
> 2. *The sheriff has erred in law in holding that, on the facts which he found to be proved the defender owed any duty of reasonable care to the pursuer and, separately, were in breach of any duty of care which they might have owed to the pursuer*".

12–17　As I have said, this is not intended as a style and I would repeat that it is a matter of opinion as to whether that is sufficiently brief and specific as required by the rule. It may, however, be regarded as giving sufficient notice to the sheriff principal of the areas of attack. There would be nothing to prevent the appellant from adding more grounds, or making more specific the grounds which have already been set out. The appellant could, for example, explain in a little more detail the "critical facts" referred to in the grounds of appeal. The appellant could also elaborate upon the issue of law to some extent, by outlining the legal proposition to be argued.

In practise, an appellant might well make written submissions[18] which expand upon the grounds of appeal. If these were forwarded to the sheriff principal prior to the appeal, with a copy to the other side, then that might be regarded as a satisfactory means of giving fair notice to everyone of the precise arguments which are to be advanced, in the event that there was any dispute as to whether your specific argument at the appeal had been foreshadowed in the grounds of appeal. The exercise of preparing written submissions would be likely to highlight in advance of the appeal any arguments which had simply not been dealt with at all in the grounds of appeal. However, if you think that there is a significant alteration in your grounds as stated in such written submissions then it would be prudent to seek to amend them formally.

Abandoning, withdrawing, agreeing an appeal

A party may wish to abandon or withdraw an appeal. That may be **12–18** done where, for example, the appeal has been marked in order to preserve the client's position but after further consideration they decide they do not want to proceed. This would usually allow the appeal to be disposed of administratively and there are some practical considerations to bear in mind. Rule 31.11 of the OCR provides that an appellant will not be entitled to abandon the appeal unless with the consent of the other parties or with the leave of the sheriff principal. It is suggested that a motion to that effect should be lodged and the question of expenses should be dealt with in that motion. Abandonment of the appeal does not mean abandonment of a cross-appeal if one has been taken, and that is something to be borne in mind.

If the parties agree, after the appeal has been marked, as to how it should be disposed of then they can prepare a joint minute setting out the terms of the agreement. The joint minute should include a note of the terms of the interlocutor which they want the sheriff principal to pronounce and it should deal with the expenses of the appeal. It would be advisable and may be necessary also to prepare and lodge a joint motion to interpone authority to the joint minute. In this way, the matter can usually be disposed of without the necessity for the appeal to call and without the necessity of any hearing before the sheriff principal.

It is important that both parties consider the full implications of whatever they might have agreed in relation to the appeal and are able to explain this in the joint minute and to justify whatever interlocutor they have agreed the sheriff principal ought to pronounce. This situation might arise most frequently in relation to appeals where there had been a default on the part of the appellant and the parties subsequently agree that a decree should be recalled on certain conditions as to further procedure and as to expenses.

Administration and procedure prior to appeal

Although there is a considerable degree of uniformity in the different **12–19** sheriff court districts, sheriffdoms may have slightly different practices

---

[18] For which there are no rules or formal requirements.

regarding administration and procedure after an appeal has been marked. There is no great benefit in discussing this in any detail in the present context. Most (if not all) sheriffs principal have a secretary/clerk who will invariably be efficient and helpful. It is well worth making a telephone call to that individual if you have any doubts about practice and procedure before that particular sheriff principal. In addition, there are practice notes in most (if not all) sheriffdoms relating to appeals which set out the administrative arrangements for appeals. The practice notes should be available on the Scottish Court website[19] or in *Parliament House Book*.[20] If you have any difficulty locating these the secretary/clerk to the sheriff principal would no doubt be able to assist. It is worth having a look at a recent practice note for the Sheriffdom of Lothian and Borders. Practice Note Number 1 of 2005 is a comprehensive note relating solely to appeals to the sheriff principal of that sheriffdom which gives directions as to how their appeal proceedings are to run, with additional comments and observations upon various procedural and other issues. These directions are not necessarily followed in other sheriffdoms, but it is a very useful guide to many practical issues which are likely to emerge in the course of any appeal. One such issue relates to the preparation and lodging of a note of your authorities for the appeal, an important step which must not be overlooked.

Preparation for appeal

12–20   It is axiomatic that you must prepare thoroughly for an appeal. Although you should spend a considerable amount of time in preparation, that does not mean that you will inevitably or necessarily have a considerable number of things to say in the appeal. It is arguable that most of the time you spend should be "thinking time", and in your preparations for the appeal you should concentrate on expressing concisely what you wish to say. I am going to discuss the preparation of an appeal from an interlocutor following proof and the structure of your submissions for that type of appeal. I have already mentioned the benefit of written submissions, and, even if your preparations do not produce written submissions which you can hand up to the sheriff, these should produce a very good framework for your oral submissions. I have no privileged information on the point, but it is almost certain that, prior to hearing an appeal of this kind, the sheriff principal would have read the record, the judgment and note prepared by the sheriff, the grounds of appeal, and any productions which are obviously important. The sheriff principal may also have checked the interlocutor sheets in the process to gain some idea of the history of the case, although in some appeals, the detailed history will not be particularly relevant. With this in mind, you can appreciate that there may be certain things upon which you do not need to dwell unduly, and I will suggest a basic formula for getting to the heart of the appeal quickly and efficiently. That is not to be misinterpreted as suggesting that you should race through your oral submissions until you get to the main point of your appeal. The sheriff principal

---

[19] See *www.scottishcourts.gov.uk*.
[20] W. Green, Edinburgh, looseleaf.

will have a basic familiarity with the case based upon his reading of the papers but it is good advocacy to start your submissions in a measured way, if for no other reason than to give the sheriff principal time to reassure himself that his broad appreciation of the position is correct.

You should also bear in mind that the sheriff principal will require to take notes of your argument. In all but the simplest of appeals the argument might well involve detailed consideration of extensive facts and law. In these circumstances, it would be helpful to provide the sheriff principal with a "road map" at an early stage of your submissions so that he can see where you are going with your argument. This might be apparent in written submissions, although you may want to ensure that you construct these in such a way that the various steps in your argument are emphasised. If you are preparing oral submissions only, then giving the sheriff principal lists and numbers[21] helps to make the argument easier to note and to follow.

This is what you might want to consider as components of the **12–21** structure for the presentation of an appeal:

1. *A brief introduction to the nature of the case.*
2. *A brief history of the case so far as relevant to the appeal.*
3. *Identification of the decision appealed against.* This should be obvious in the circumstances envisaged, although even then it is possible that the appeal could be limited to the merits, or to contributory negligence or to quantum. In other appeals, it might not be so obvious, so it is sensible to identify the decision which you are attacking.
4. *Reference should then be made to the grounds of appeal.* You may or may not want to refer to these in detail at this stage. It is a matter for you. As you are still really at the preamble to your submissions, you might refer to these simply in general terms and explain that you are going to address the sheriff principal in detail about these later.
5. *Advise the sheriff principal at this stage what you are going to ask him to do at the conclusion of the appeal.* By now, you will have explained why you are there and it is important to explain what you want the sheriff principal to do if he is with you in your appeal. Again, in the type of appeal under consideration, that may be fairly evident but it may be less so in other appeals. This also gives the sheriff principal an opportunity to consider what your aim is, and to consider, if only in a preliminary way, whether he can competently and possibly do what you are asking. If you are going to ask the sheriff principal to do something inappropriate or unusual this gives him an opportunity to stop you there, or even just look quizzically at you and indicate that he is not entirely convinced that he can give you what you want. Of course, it may be open to you to advise the sheriff principal that you have an alternative, or alternatives, to suggest depending upon the view he takes of the appeal but

---

[21] Headlines, headings, bullet points, etc.

again it would be helpful to set this out broadly now so that the sheriff knows where you are intending to go with your arguments.

12–22

6. *Provide a "road map" of your submissions.* I apologise for using the jargon, but it makes sense next to advise the sheriff principal in outline how you are proposing to present your argument to support the order which you wish him to make at the conclusion of the appeal. This may be the point at which to make reference to the grounds of appeal in somewhat more detail and to make reference to your written submissions (if any) or provide the sheriff principal orally with an outline of what you are proposing to say. If you can number this or break it down into propositions or a list that would be very useful. You may also want to indicate at this stage whether consideration of your submissions will involve the sheriff principal looking at shorthand notes of evidence in detail or particular productions so that he can have them readily to hand.

7. *Suggest proposed alterations, variations, recall, or additions to findings in fact.* If your appeal includes an appeal on questions of fact it might be appropriate at this stage to indicate to the sheriff principal the findings in fact to which you take exception or, more broadly, the alterations to the findings in fact which you will be asking him to make. It is undoubtedly preferable to have a typed list of these alterations (especially if they are lengthy). It will make it easier for the sheriff to note what you want. It will save time. It will ensure accuracy and, incidentally, will prove that you have prepared matters thoroughly, right or wrong. In relation to suggested alterations to findings in fact, you may also find it helpful to make reference to the undernoted cases.[22]

8. *Analyse the relevant evidence (if appropriate to your appeal).* If you are going to take the sheriff principal to the shorthand notes in the appeal (and you are bound to do so if you are appealing on a question of fact) then you will have to refer him to the shorthand notes of evidence. It is unlikely that the sheriff principal will have read these before the appeal, and there is really no reason why he should. Accordingly it might be helpful, as a preamble to any reference to specific pieces of evidence, to give the sheriff principal a brief summary of the witnesses who actually gave evidence in the case and, very broadly, what part they had to play. That should enable the sheriff principal to put the particular passages of evidence to which you wish to refer into some kind of context. It does not make sense to ramble in detail through 25 pages of shorthand notes of evidence of one witness to come to the two answers which are really at the crux of the appeal. Of course, that may be necessary in certain circumstances, for example where you are attacking the credibility or reliability of a witness on the basis of their evidence as

---

[22] *Martinez v Grampian Health Board*, 1996 S.L.T. 69; *Laing v Scottish Grain Distillers Ltd*, 1992 S.L.T. 435; *Marshall v William Sharp & Sons Ltd*, 1991 S.L.T. 114.

a whole and arguing that the sheriff should not have found them credible or reliable.

In this context, questions of sufficiency of evidence, questions of credibility and reliability of witnesses, and issues about the weight of evidence may all come into play. It may be necessary to refer at length to authorities on the proper approach of an appeal court, to questions of evidence, sufficiency, weight, etc. The object of the exercise here might be to demonstrate that the sheriff has not understood or appreciated the evidence of witnesses properly, either individually or collectively, or that the sheriff has relied upon evidence upon which he should not have relied for various reasons which can be gleaned from the reported cases. We have already dealt with the authorities which can come into play on this point. You can guarantee that the sheriff principal will be familiar with these cases but, nonetheless, it is necessary to take him to the cases, discuss the principles with him, and, most importantly, apply these principles to the facts and circumstances of your own case.

9. *Address the sheriff principal on the matters of law (if any) which may be the subject of the appeal.* This would involve full reference to authority and it would assist if you advised the sheriff principal what you consider the sheriff to have decided the law to be and what you suggest the law actually is. It would be helpful in advance if you set that out in a proposition, or series of propositions, that you can dictate to the sheriff principal, or provide him with a written note of any proposition, or propositions, which you can then go through in detail, justifying these.

10. *Where the appeal involves mixed questions of fact and law you* **12–23** *must then consider the alternatives.* You may need to have alternative or subsidiary propositions depending upon whether the sheriff principal is prepared to interfere with the findings in fact wholly, or partially, as advanced by you. What is your position if the sheriff principal accepts all of your proposed alterations? What is your position if the sheriff principal accepts none of them? What is your position if the sheriff principal accepts some of them? As can be appreciated, this can take you into areas of great complexity and it is particularly in relation to this that you might find written submissions and/or a good outline to be very helpful for you and the sheriff principal.

11. *Advise the sheriff principal exactly what interlocutor you wish him to pronounce.* Having presented the substance of your arguments in the appeal you must then repeat what you want the sheriff principal to do. There are a variety of orders which the sheriff principal can make. The sheriff principal can refuse the appeal and adhere to the original decision. The sheriff principal can grant the appeal, recall the interlocutor in its entirety, and substitute a new interlocutor. The sheriff principal can grant the appeal to the extent of adhering in part but not in another part and he can make an order following upon that. The sheriff principal can grant the appeal and vary the interlocutor with an order consistent with that. The sheriff principal can remit the

case back to the sheriff for some specified reason. There are other options open to him. For example, in the case we have been considering above you could ask the sheriff principal at the conclusion of the proof to,

"grant the appeal, vary the interlocutor dated . . . to the extent of altering the findings of fact [in accordance with your proposal]; alter the findings in law to the extent of finding that the accident was not caused by the fault of the defender, and grant decree of absolvitor in favour of the defender in accordance with their plea in law number one and quoad ultra repel all of the other pleas in law".

12. *Expenses.* Either at the end of your submissions or at the conclusion of both parties' submissions on the appeal you would deal with expenses. The sheriff principal would normally invite parties to make submissions regarding the expenses of the appeal and also the expenses of the action leading up to that point. The norm is for expenses to follow success. There may be certain specialities which make it desirable that a separate hearing on expenses should be fixed. One such speciality might be if there was divided success at an appeal. Obviously, it would be impossible to hear submissions about expenses in this situation where the sheriff principal's decision was not yet known, and could encompass a wide variety of possible findings.

Submissions at appeal

12–24 I am now going to set out a brief script for what might be said at an appeal, following so far as appropriate the structure which I have outlined above. In this example, I have in mind the contractual dispute (Case Study 1) and I would like you to assume that the sheriff decided, after hearing proof, that there was no agreement between the parties that there was to be any discount on the purchase price and that the contract for the supply of the kitchen was constituted by the letters and other documents passing between the parties and nothing else. Leaving aside other issues in the case, assume that the appeal is going to be directed simply to that. Assume also that the sheriff made findings in fact in relation to this matter as follows:

"Finding in fact 4. On April 3, 2004 the pursuer sent a quotation to the defenders for the supply and fitting of a fitted kitchen at a total price of £12,337.50 including VAT. Number 5/4 of process is a copy of that quotation.

Finding in fact 5. The quotation offered a discount of 10 per cent on the price provided that the order to purchase the kitchen was placed with the pursuer by May 31, 2004. The order had to be accompanied by a payment of £5,000 before that date for the discount to be given.

Finding in fact 6. Mrs Gray spoke to an employee of the pursuer by telephone on May 30 to say that they would almost certainly go ahead with the purchase of the kitchen.

Finding in Fact 7. The pursuer received a cheque for the deposit of £5,000 from the defenders on June 2, 2004."

Assume also that decree has been granted in favour of the pursuer for £6,000 on the basis of the agreed price (as the sheriff has found) of X pounds with a set off of Y pounds for the cost of replacing units which were not conform to contract. Assume the decision was made on April 14, 2006 and that the interlocutor containing the decision also dealt with question of expenses and was, in other words, a final judgement.

You would have sent a copy of the decision to the clients. You would have given them written advice about the prospect of an appeal, or alternatively you would have met with them to discuss the prospects of an appeal. You have had to reach a decision as to whether you are appealing on facts or law, or both. Given the date of the interlocutor you must mark an appeal by April 28, 2006. You have done so and lodged grounds of appeal on April 23. You have intimated these grounds of appeal to the other side. You have asked the shorthand writers to extend the shorthand notes in connection with the appeal because you are going to need to refer to them when presenting the appeal. You have amended your grounds of appeal on further reflection and consideration. You have looked at the authorities. You have provided a list of authorities in accordance with the administrative requirements of this particular sheriffdom. You have annotated, for your own benefit, the shorthand notes of evidence and you have prepared your submissions.

You have identified the findings in fact which you want to challenge and you have noted the alternative or extra findings in fact which you want the sheriff to make. You have prepared these in writing to hand up to the sheriff principal. You have also prepared an outline of your argument although, for the purposes of this illustration, you have not supplied any written submissions. Your submissions would proceed along these general lines.

Submissions

"My Lord, I appear on behalf of the defenders and appellants, Mr and **12–25**
Mrs Gray. My friend, Mr X, appears on behalf of the pursuer and respondent. This is an appeal against the interlocutor of Sheriff Y pronounced after proof in the present action.

This is an action of payment for the supply and fitting of a kitchen at the defenders' house. There were two principle lines of defence, first, that the parties had agreed a discount on the price, and secondly that the pursuer was in material breach of its contract by failing to carry out the fitting properly. This appeal relates to the decision of the learned sheriff on the first of these defences, namely on the question of whether the parties had agreed a discount on the price.

The action was raised in March 2005 and after sundry procedure a proof before answer was assigned for November 12 and 13, 2005. The matter proceeded to proof on those dates and the evidence was completed then. The learned sheriff then assigned a date for hearing of submissions on January 6, 2006. After hearing submissions on that day the sheriff made avizandum. He then issued his judgement on April 14, 2006, in which he found in favour of the pursuer and granted decree for £6,000 together with expenses. Appeal was marked by the defenders on April 23, and today's diet was assigned thereafter.

My Lord, the appeal is confined to the findings of the learned sheriff on the question of the contractually agreed price for the kitchen. At the proof there was a considerable amount of contradictory evidence from the parties as to whether the fitting of the kitchen had been carried out properly. The sheriff made findings about this and although the original note of appeal lodged in this case included grounds of appeal directed towards those findings, the appellants indicated shortly thereafter that they did not intend to insist upon their appeal on those grounds and amended grounds of appeal were lodged on May 11, 2006.

12–26   *At this stage, my Lord, I should simply outline the contents of the grounds of appeal now before your Lordship, and, as your Lordship will see, there are three specific grounds. First, that the sheriff misdirected himself on a matter of fact by deciding that the contract between the parties was constituted by the documents to which he has referred in his judgment. Secondly, by failing to make a finding that the contractual relationship between the parties did not include the terms agreed by the defenders in two conversations between the parties to which I shall refer in due course. And thirdly, that the sheriff erred in law in that, even if the sheriff was entitled to make the factual findings that he did, on a proper interpretation of the letters passing between the parties, the price agreed between the parties was as contended for by the appellants.*

My Lord, I propose to ask your Lordship at the conclusion of my submissions to vary the interlocutor dated April 14, 2006, by deleting the findings in fact to which I shall draw your Lordship's attention and substituting therefore the findings in fact which I intend to put before your Lordship, by altering the findings in law to which I shall refer, and by substituting therefor . . . and to grant decree in favour of the pursuer for the reduced sum of £X.[23]

My Lord, I would intend to start my submissions on the merits by advising your Lordship of how I intend to present this argument. Your Lordship will no doubt appreciate that I will be confining my submissions to what might be seen as a relatively narrow and self-contained aspect of the case and I shall be focusing entirely upon the argument that the decision of the sheriff on the agreed price for the kitchen was not justified as a matter of fact nor as a matter of law.

12–27   *First, I intend to review the precise pleadings of the parties in relation to the crucial aspect of the price for the contract. Secondly, I intend to review, with your Lordship, the documentation lodged as productions in the case which has a bearing on this point. Thirdly, I have prepared a note of the suggested findings in fact which I will be asking your Lordship to make and will pass these to your Lordship. Fourthly, I propose to address your Lordship on the evidence given by the witnesses who spoke to the negotiations and discussions between the parties at the time the contract was concluded. This will involve consideration of certain limited parts of the shorthand notes of the evidence given by the witnesses X, Y and Z. I will submit that the evidence justifies the proposed findings in fact which I am putting*

---

[23] In case this seems a little strange, bear in mind that the defenders may well have lodged a tender the benefit of which may depend upon how successful this argument is going to be.

forward. Fifthly, I intend to address your Lordship on the legal principles applying to the constitution of contracts such as this and to the construction and interpretation of the terms of the parties' agreement.

I will be arguing that the relevant law on this can be summarised as follows:

1. . . .
2. . . .
3. . . .

and that, on a proper understanding and appreciation of the evidence which was properly and competently before the sheriff, and the legal principles applying to the facts, he misdirected himself in holding that the contract was for a price of . . .

[After dealing with parts of the above outline.]

My Lord, I turn now to a consideration of the evidence led in the case on this critical issue. I appreciate that there are only limited circumstances in which an appeal court can interfere with findings in fact by a judge at first instance but, in my submission, the grounds on which this can legitimately be done are present here. These grounds were set out in the well-known case of Thomas v Thomas . . . and I wish to direct your Lordship specifically to what Lord . . . said at page . . . [Reads] The same issue was considered very recently and approved by the House of Lords in the case of . . . [Reads] . . . And it is with those strictures in mind that I approach the question of the evidence given in this case.

My primary submission is that your Lordship will see that there is a very sharp contradiction between the evidence of X and Y on . . . and the learned sheriff has not expressed any intelligible reason for preferring the evidence of Y to X. Indeed, it respectfully seems to me that he has left out of account the evidence of the document . . . and of the witness Z which have a significant bearing on the truth or otherwise of this point and indeed upon the credibility and reliability of Y generally. May I direct your Lordship to what Y said on this issue? Would your Lordship turn to page 45 of the first volume of the shorthand notes. This is the examination in chief of Y and, after giving evidence about . . . the questioner then begins to ask him about . . . on page 45, letter E . . . [Reads]

Now, if we then look to see what . . . says . . .

[Further submissions directed to evidence.]

In my submission, taking all of these matters into account, the **12–28** *sheriff plainly failed to appreciate the significance of the other evidence in the case and the impact which this should have had upon his assessment of the reliability of Y on this point. This goes to the heart of the case and I would respectfully submit that the learned sheriff is 'plainly wrong' on this point and that it is open to your Lordship to consider the matter afresh . . .*

Accordingly, my Lord, I move your Lordship to allow the appeal, vary the interlocutor of April 14, 2006 to the extent of substituting for findings in fact 6 and 7 the findings in fact referred to in my note. I would then move your Lordship to find in law that . . . to sustain the defenders' plea in law to the extent that . . . to repel the pursuer's plea in law . . . and to grant decree against the defender for . . . (£3,500).

> *Finally, in relation to expenses, I would respectfully submit that it might be more appropriate to defer any decision on expenses in this case until your Lordship has decided the appeal, and I would invite your Lordship to continue consideration of any question of expenses to a separate hearing on expenses. Unless I can assist your Lordship further then those are my submissions for the appellants."*

As will be appreciated, the presentation of an appeal tends to be slightly more formal and considered than presentation of other legal arguments. It does not need to be that way. It may be that, by the time the case has reached the appeal stage, the point(s) at issue are focused very sharply and are obvious. Some sheriffs might prefer a shorter and less wordy submission, highlighting the precise point, or points, for consideration in the appeal at an early stage and indicating very clearly exactly what you are intending to say. Be prepared to be put on the spot in this way, so that, although you may have this more lengthy submission on paper, you might have to pare it down to the essentials and to demonstrate clearly that there is substance to the point you are taking before you are allowed to develop it. In appeals, you are much more likely to be asked, "What exactly are you saying?" or "Can you just explain to me what you say the law is on this point?" than in some other hearings. There is a danger that over-elaboration of the submissions might be counter-productive. On the other hand, if there are complexities or subtleties in the case which really have to be understood before the force of your argument can be seen, you do have to take this more slowly. It does help if you can find a way of illustrating the core of your argument at an early stage, and being aware of exactly what that is in words of one syllable and expressed in one or two short sentences. You might be asked to explain it in this way. It is as well to anticipate this. As with other forms of hearing, however, the preparation of a structured submission and the knowledge of what you must cover should give you confidence and the ability to adapt to the requirements of the particular hearing. If you really do not know why you are there, and you are hoping that something might turn up or you will suddenly be struck by some hitherto unnoticed inspiration, an appeal is the one hearing in which you are almost certainly going to be found out.

PRECOGNITION 1
OF
KEVIN MURDOCH
residing at
The Steading, Fairview, Cambuslang

STATES:

I am 52 years of age. I am married. I reside at the above address.

I am the owner of "Fine Gowns" store which is located in the Argyle Street Centre in Glasgow. I am the sole proprietor and it is my business.

I am asked about a case where a man called George Hamilton is supposed to have had an accident outside the shop in the Argyle Street Centre a couple of years ago. I work in the shop regularly. I am told that this accident happened on a Saturday. I am always in the shop all day on a Saturday. On Saturdays I have usually got three or sometimes four assistants who help out. Sometimes, my wife will come in and help out as well.

I have no memory of any individual having an accident outside the shop. I remember once there was a woman who fell and cut her hand in the passageway outside. We took her in and into the back shop. It was really quite a bad cut and we ran cold water over her hand for a while and then tried to bandage it up as best as we could. One of the staff eventually drove her down to the Royal. That is the only accident of note that I can remember.

If someone did have an accident outside the shop there is a fairly good chance we would have recorded it in the accident book. This is kept in the back shop as well. I have had a look at the accident book and there is nothing in it.

I am afraid I can't help you any further.

PRECOGNITION 2
OF
KEVIN MURDOCH
residing at
The Steading, Fairview, Cambuslang

STATES:

I am 53 years of age. I am married. I reside at the above address. I am the proprietor of Fine Gowns which is a clothing business. We have a shop in the Argyle Street Centre. We have had the shop since the centre opened about five years ago.

The shop consists of a large sales area with clothes racks on all of the walls and racks of clothing located around the shop floor as well. We tend to specialise in eveningwear for the mature female. We sell a large number of evening gowns and we even hire out evening gowns as well. I have quite a number of regular customers.

The shop till and serving counter are at the end of the shop farthest away from the door. The fitting rooms and the back shop are at that end as well.

I usually employ about three assistants in the shop. On Saturdays, my wife will come in to help me or I might have someone in part-time because it can get quite busy.

I am asked if I know anything about an accident to a Mr George Hamilton which is supposed to have taken place on July 23, 2004 outside the shop. I do not remember any such accident. I can't remember anyone coming into the shop and saying that they had an accident outside it.

I am told that he says he was attended to by the manager of the shop. He certainly was not attended to by me. I would have remembered that. If he had been attended to by anyone else in the shop then I think I would have remembered it. Of course, that is assuming I was there at the time. I am told that the accident happened just after lunchtime. I suppose it is possible I could have been away from the shop for a while during the course of the day although that does not happen often on Saturdays. If my wife was in helping out that day then I might have gone for a quick lunch with her but otherwise I would just normally have a couple of sandwiches in the back shop. I think the date of the accident might have been during the Glasgow Fair. If that was so, then the shop might not have been so busy and I might have taken the opportunity to go and do something myself at the time. I can't really be sure about this.

If I had been out of the shop and something like this had happened then I think that one of the other staff might have told me. I have quite a high turnover of staff and I am not absolutely sure who would have been working for me at the time. I can try to check my records but it is going to be a little difficult.

We keep an accident book. If there was ever an accident in the shop or sometimes even if there was an accident close to the shop then this is something which would go in the accident book. I remember a lady cut her hand very badly and we looked after her in the back shop before one of the staff drove her up to the Royal. I have been asked to check if that is in the accident book and I have noted, to my surprise, that we don't seem to have a record of it. I do remember it quite well. I would have thought that one of the staff would have filled it in but obviously I am wrong about that.

I certainly have no recollection of this man or an accident of the kind that you are interested in.

I am asked about the condition of the walkway outside the centre. As far as I know it is fine. I can't really remember what it was like at the time of this man's accident. I do recall that the owners of the centre did up the walkways during that summer. In fact, I think they did it during the Glasgow Fair because they thought it would be quieter and there would be less disruption.

We leased the shop from the owners. It is part of our lease that we are responsible for the maintenance of the common parts of the centre. We had an argument with the owners when they were talking about doing up the walkways. We did not think this was really part of maintenance and we (that is all of the leaseholders) objected to the work being done. In fact we weren't so much objecting to the work being done as the fact that we were going to be asked to pay for it. We also were concerned about the disruption to the centre. Eventually we reached an agreement with the owners that they could have the work carried out at their expense and by their contractors on the understanding that we would have no responsibilities and they would keep the disruption of the centre to a minimum so that we could carry on trading.

I do remember that the work involve replacement of the flooring. New tiles were laid. I think there were one or two problems with the tiles initially. I seem to recall that the workmen were using quite heavy machines and they were storing materials on the walkways. The walkways aren't really supposed to be for this. The story was that they had to re-lay quite a number of tiles because they were damaged or easily damaged but I can't say that I ever saw any of this myself.

I don't know if there ever was a broken tile outside the shop. I don't remember it. I am fairly sure the workmen were working there around the time of the accident although again, if it was a Saturday, I don't think they ever worked on a Saturday afternoon.

If they were working on a particular part of the walkway then they would cordon it off so that the public couldn't have access to it. They would try to do it so that they would not obstruct access to your own shop and sometimes they had to do it at night. If a problem arose whilst they were working there then they were actually quite good at sorting it and they had obviously been told to bend over backwards to help us out. I remember that the owner had an architect or an engineer or a site agent, or at least someone like that who kept a close eye on the work that was being carried out. He used to come into the shop every now and then and ask how things were going and if we had any problems. I remember seeing him talking to the workmen and there were times that he would get them to move materials or put up barriers because I think he was concerned about the safety of the public. I can't remember his name.

PRECOGNITION
OF
MRS ANNE STEWART
residing at
103 Ardmore Road, Chryston

STATES:

I work for Parker Kitchen Design as a Kitchen Design Consultant. I have been working there for eight years.

I remember the job involving Mr and Mrs Gray. I did the design for their kitchen and after that was done, we sent out a quote. The quote was not accepted straight away. I did speak to Mrs Gray on the phone in the middle of May sometime because we had a problem with the types of units she wanted. She was quite happy to go ahead with a different type of unit and once the quote was accepted and the deposit paid we just went ahead with the job.

It was just a normal job. There was a wee bit of a delay in starting it but as far as I am concerned, the job went as planned and an invoice was sent out at the end of it.

I was amazed to hear that the customer has made complaints about the job because they never made any complaints to me until about two months after it had been completed. I think they found that they couldn't really afford the job and that is when they came up with these complaints because I don't think they really have any cause for complaint at all.

I am told they say that I offered them a 10 per cent discount on the price after the quote was sent out. There is no way that I would have done that. They are really telling lies about this. I did have a phone conversation with Mrs Gray before the quotation was accepted. I never agreed a discount. There is no way you could agree it verbally.

I think that they found they could not afford the job and that is why they are raising all these matters now because they are just trying to pay as little as possible. I am happy to go a witness in the case and I just think this has all been made up.

LETTER 1
FROM JOHN GRAY

33 Fordham Place
GLASGOW

30th May 2004

Parker Kitchen Design Limited
Unit 12
Cart Industrial Estate
PAISLEY

Dear Sirs

Following my wife's telephone conversation with Mrs Stewart last week, I am writing to confirm that we want to proceed with the job now and would like you to make arrangements for the job to be scheduled as quickly as possible.

Are you going to send us an amended quotation or will this letter be sufficient for the time being? Will you let me know and I will send you a cheque for the deposit thereafter?

Yours faithfully

LETTER 2
FROM JOHN GRAY

33 Fordham Place
GLASGOW

5th June 2004

Parker Kitchen Design Limited
Unit 12
Cart Industrial Estate
PAISLEY

Dear Sirs

I understand there is no need for you to send out an amended quotation and I am quite happy with this. I am enclosing cheque for £5,000 in payment of the deposit. Presumably the price alteration will be reflected in the final invoice.

Yours faithfully

INDEX